LETTER TO BEAUMONT,
LETTERS WRITTEN FROM THE MOUNTAIN,
AND RELATED WRITINGS

JEAN-JACQUES ROUSSEAU

LETTER TO BEAUMONT, LETTERS WRITTEN FROM THE MOUNTAIN, and RELATED WRITINGS

THE COLLECTED WRITINGS OF ROUSSEAU
Vol. 9

EDITED BY CHRISTOPHER KELLY AND EVE GRACE

TRANSLATED BY
CHRISTOPHER KELLY AND JUDITH R. BUSH

ROGER D. MASTERS AND CHRISTOPHER KELLY,
SERIES EDITORS

DARTMOUTH COLLEGE PRESS
Hanover, New Hampshire

DARTMOUTH COLLEGE PRESS
An imprint of University Press of New England
www.upne.com
© 2001 Trustees of Dartmouth College
All rights reserved
First Dartmouth College Press paperback edition 2012
Manufactured in the United States of America
Designed by Katherine B. Kimball
Typeset in Galliard by Passumpsic Publishing
ISBN for the paperback edition: 978-1-61168-287-8

For permission to reproduce any of the material in this book, contact Permissions, University Press of New England, One Court Street, Suite 250, Lebanon, NH 03766; or visit www.upne.com

This project has received support from the French Ministry of Culture — Direction du Livre et de la Lecture, the Florence gould Foundation, and Pro Helvetia.

Cet ouvrage, publié dans le cadre d'un programme d'aide à la publication, bénéficie du soutien du Ministère des Affaires Etrangères et du Service Culturel de l'Ambassade de France aux Etats-Unis.

This work, published as part of a program of aid for publication, received support from the French Ministry of Foreign Affairs and the Cultural Services of the French Embassy in the United States.

Library of Congress Cataloging-in-Publication data

Rousseau, Jean-Jacques, 1712–1778
[Selections. English. 2002. University Press of New England]
Letter to Beaumont, letters written from the mountain, and related writings / edited by Christopher Kelly and Eve Grace.
p. cm. — (The collected writings of Rousseau ; vol. 9)
Includes bibliographical references and index.
ISBN 1-58465-164-4 (alk. paper)
1. Rousseau, Jean-Jacques, 1712–1778 — Censorship.
2. Church and state. I. Grace, Eve. II. Title.
PQ2034 .A3 1990 vol. 9
[B2132.E5]
848'.509 s—dc21
[848/.509   2001005385

Contents

Preface vii

Chronology of Works in Volume 9 ix

Note on the Text xi

Introduction xiii

Pastoral Letter of His Grace the Archbishop of Paris 1
Translated by Christopher Kelly

Letter to Beaumont 17
Translated by Judith R. Bush and Christopher Kelly

Fragments of the *Letter to Christophe de Beaumont* 84
Translated by Christopher Kelly

History of the Government of Geneva 102
Translated by Christopher Kelly

Letters Written from the Mountain 131
Translated by Judith R. Bush and Christopher Kelly

FIRST PART

First Letter 134
State of the question in relation to the Author. Whether it is within the competence of the civil Tribunals. Unjust manner of resolving it.

Second Letter 153
On the Religion of Geneva. Principles of the Reformation. The Author opens the discussion of miracles.

Third Letter 169
Continuation of the same Subject. Short examination of some other accusations.

Fourth Letter   188
The Author assumes himself to be guilty; he compares the proceedings to the Law.

Fifth Letter   200
Continuation of the same Subject. Jurisprudence drawn from proceedings done in similar cases. Goal of the Author in publishing the profession of faith.

Sixth Letter   229
Whether it is true that the Author attacks Governments. Short analysis of his Book. The proceeding done in Geneva is without precedent, and has not been followed in any country.

SECOND PART

Seventh Letter   237
Present State of the Government of Geneva, settled by the Edict of the Mediation.

Eighth Letter   256
Spirit of that Edict. Counterweight that it gives to the Aristocratic Power. Undertaking of the small Council to annihilate this counterweight by means of deeds. Conclusion.

Ninth Letter   283
Manner of reasoning of the Author of the Letters Written from the Country. His true goal in this Writing. Choice of these examples. Character of the Bourgeoisie of Geneva. Proof by facts. Conclusion.

The Vision of Pierre of the Mountain, Called the Seer   307

Translated by Christopher Kelly

Notes   315

Index   331

Preface

Although Jean-Jacques Rousseau is a significant figure in the Western tradition, there is no standard edition of his major writings available in English. Moreover, unlike those of other thinkers of comparable stature, many of Rousseau's important works have never been translated or have become unavailable. The present edition of the *Collected Writings of Rousseau* is intended to meet this need.

Our goal is to produce a series that can provide a standard reference for scholarship that is accessible to all those wishing to read broadly in the corpus of Rousseau's work. To this end, the translations seek to combine care and faithfulness to the original French text with readability in English. Although, as every translator knows, there are often passages where it is impossible to meet this criterion, readers of a thinker and writer of Rousseau's stature deserve texts that have not been deformed by the interpretive bias of the translators or editors.

Wherever possible, existing translations of high quality have been used, although in some cases the editors have felt that minor revisions were necessary to maintain the accuracy and consistency of the English versions. Where there was no English translation (or none of sufficient quality), a new translation has been prepared.

Each text is supplemented by editorial notes that clarify Rousseau's references and citations or passages otherwise not intelligible. Although these notes do not provide as much detail as is found in the critical apparatus of the Pléiade edition of the *Oeuvres complètes*, the English-speaking reader should nevertheless have in hand the basis for a more careful and comprehensive understanding of Rousseau than has hitherto been possible.

Volume 9 focuses on the last of Rousseau's writings intended for publication in his lifetime, supplemented by his "History of the Government of Geneva," which provides the groundwork for his analysis in the *Letters Written from the Mountain*. These works are united both chronologically and thematically. They were written in response to the uproar that broke out throughout Europe in response to the publication of *Emile* and the *Social Contract*. Rousseau's answers to his critics provide important clarifications of the understanding of religion and politics presented in these major theoretical works. In addition they present his most developed accounts of his understanding of the public responsibility of authors and of the proper limits of freedom of speech.

Of the works contained in this volume, "The History of the Government of Geneva," *The Vision of Pierre of the Mountain, Called the Seer*, the fragments to the *Letter to Beaumont*, and the *Pastoral Letter of His Grace the Archbishop of Paris* are being presented in English translation for the first time. The *Letter to Beaumont* and the *Letters Written from the Mountain* appeared in imperfect translations in *The Miscellaneous Works of Mr. J. J. Rousseau*, published in 1767. We would like to thank M. Robert Thierry, Conservateur of the Musée Jean-Jacques Rousseau at Montmorency, France for supplying us with the image of Rousseau used as the frontispiece of this volume, and Stephen Lange for his help in preparing the manuscript. We would like to thank Alison Lawlor and Glen Feder for their work on the index.

Chronology of Works in Volume 9

1712
June 28: Jean-Jacques Rousseau born in Geneva.

1749
October: The Academy of Dijon proposes the topic, "Has the restoration of the sciences and arts tended to purify morals?" for its prize competition. Rousseau reads the announcement in the *Mercury of France* while walking to Vincennes to visit Diderot, who has been imprisoned there. His response to the question becomes the *First Discourse*.

1755
Publication of the *Discourse on the Origins of Inequality* and "Political Economy."

1761
January: Publication and immediate success of *Julie, or the New Heloise*.

1762
April: Publication of the *Social Contract*.
May: Publication of *Emile*.
Night of June 8–9: Rousseau learns of the certainty of legal action against him resulting from the condemnation of *Emile* by the Parlement of Paris. He flees France on the same day that the warrant is issued for his arrest.
June 19: *Emile* and the *Social Contract* are burned at Geneva and a warrant is issued for Rousseau's arrest.
July: Rousseau arrives at Môtiers and requests permission from Frederick the Great to reside there.
August 28: Publication of Archbishop de Beaumont's Pastoral Letter condemning *Emile*.
November 18: Rousseau dates his *Letter to Christophe de Beaumont*.

1763
March: Publication of the *Letter to Beaumont*.
May 12: Rousseau renounces his Genevan citizenship.
September–October: Publication in Geneva of the *Letters Written from the Country* by Procurator General Tronchin. These letters condemn the *Social Contract* and *Emile*.

1764
December: Publication of the *Letters Written from the Mountain*.

December 27: Publication in Geneva of the *Sentiment des citoyens* (almost certainly written by Voltaire). This work attacks Rousseau and reveals his abandonment of his children.

1765

Letters Written from the Mountain burned in numerous European cities.

Summer: Populace stirred up against Rousseau by Pierre Boy de la Tour among others.

August 31: Rousseau sends the manuscript of the *Vision of Pierre of the Mountain* to Du Peyrou.

September 6: Rousseau's house stoned following sermons directed against him by the Pastor Montmollin.

September 15: Du Peyrou sends Rousseau the first printed copies of the *Vision*.

1766

January 13: Rousseau arrives in London accompanied by David Hume.

1767

May 21: Rousseau leaves England to return to France.

1778

July 2: Rousseau dies at Ermenonville.

Note on the Text

The Pléiade edition of Rousseau's *Oeuvres complètes* was used as the basic text for the translations of the *Letters Written from the Mountain*, *Letter to Beaumont*, "Fragments from the *Letter to Beaumont*," and "History of the Government of Geneva." These works can be found in Volumes III, IV, and V respectively. The "Fragments" represent the major fragments from drafts of the *Letter*. Other fragments, along with manuscript variants of the *Letters Written from the Mountain*, can be found in Pléiade. *The Vision of Pierre of the Mountain* can be found in Volume II of Pléiade, but we have relied on the more recent version to be found in *"Des Pierres dans mon jardin": Les années neuchâtelois de J.-J. Rousseau et la crise de 1765* by Frédéric Eigeldinger (Paris-Geneva: Champion-Slatkine, 1992). Beaumont's "Pastoral Letter" can be found in Rousseau, *Oeuvres complètes*, Volume 3 (Paris: Editions du Seuil, 1971), which is cited as "Launay."

Introduction

In a sense the works contained in this volume, all of which were written between the end of 1762 and the middle of 1765, represent the conclusion of Rousseau's career as an author. Although he went on to write his three great autobiographical works (the *Confessions*, *Dialogues*, and *Reveries*) as well as the important *Considerations on the Government of Poland*, none of these was, or was intended to be, published during his lifetime. The only work Rousseau published through his own initiative after 1765 was his *Dictionary of Music* (1767), which he had substantially completed five years earlier.[1]

In fact, in the *Confessions*, Rousseau says that by 1759 he "had been forming the plan of leaving literature altogether and above all the trade of Author."[2] He had just published the *Letter to d'Alembert*, and *Julie* was in press. Moreover, he was nearly finished writing *Emile*, his "last and best work,"[3] and had decided to extract the *Social Contract* from an unfinished larger work, the *Political Institutions*. The money he expected from these last books was to finance his life of retirement. Thus, when they finally appeared in 1762, Rousseau "had given up literature completely" and "no longer thought of anything but leading a tranquil and sweet life as far as it depended on me."[4] As it happened, this possibility no longer depended on him. The storm that broke out after the publication of *Emile* and the *Social Contract* deprived Rousseau of tranquillity and ultimately caused him to resume "the trade of author" for several more years. Each of the works written during this period was a response to a specific attack on either his character or his recent publications.

Rousseau had fled France in June of 1762 to avoid arrest after the condemnation of *Emile* by the Parlement of Paris. Shortly thereafter both *Emile* and the *Social Contract* were burned in his native Geneva, and a warrant was issued for his arrest. As a result, he settled at Môtiers, near Neuchâtel, which was under the control of Frederick the Great of Prussia. In August *Emile* was attacked in a pastoral letter by the Archbishop of Paris, Christophe de Beaumont. Believing that he owed it to himself to reply, Rousseau responded with the *Letter to Beaumont*, dated November 18, 1762, and published the following March. Two months later he renounced his Genevan citizenship because of the failure of the government to reverse the warrant it had issued against him. This dramatic gesture led to a wave of controversy in Geneva, including a pamphlet war in which the partisans of the government were represented by the Procurator General Tronchin's anonymously published *Letters Written from the Country*, a work that Rousseau undertook to refute with his *Letters Written from the Mountain*, composed in secrecy during 1764. It was published at the end of the year and quickly burned in numerous cities, although in Geneva itself it was declared to be "unworthy of being burned by the Hangman."[5] In addition to the furor it caused throughout Europe, the work had consequences for Rousseau's effort to live his tranquil and sweet life at Môtiers. The local minister, Montmollin, who had been praised in the *Letters*, began proceedings to excommunicate Rousseau and stirred up the populace against him with sermons comparing him to the Antichrist. This culminated with the stoning of Rousseau's house in September of 1765. In the midst of these events, which forced him to leave Môtiers, Rousseau wrote the *Vision of Pierre of the Mountain, Called the Seer* to poke fun at one of his local enemies, Pierre Boy de la Tour, a relative of his landlady who apparently had urged her to evict Rousseau on the basis of a revelation he said he had received from God.[6]

The circumstances of the composition of these works give a clear indication of their themes. They are defenses of both Rousseau's character and the substance of *Emile* and the *Social Contract*. They use the occasion of very specific attacks to present his thoughts on the general issues of censorship, religion, and politics, issues that had always been at the center of his concern. Although Rousseau's focus on these issues was continuous from the beginning of his literary career, it is important to keep in mind the polemical context of his treatment of them here. Evaluating the relation between the positions he takes in these works and those he takes in earlier ones is complicated by this polemical context. He is addressing the general public, but also has specific interlocutors ranging from the Catholic Archbishop of Paris who was also a peer of France, to a Protestant official of the Genevan republic, to a local drunkard of no repute.

Even the participation in polemical controversy over his works is something of a reversal for Rousseau. After the publication of the work that made him famous, the *Discourse on the Sciences and the Arts*, he had taken it upon himself to respond to several of the innumerable attacks made on this work.[7] This period of controversy took up two years. Throughout the series of exchanges, first for comic effect and then more seriously, Rousseau remarked on his distaste for such polemics.[8] At its conclusion he resolved to engage in such controversies no longer. Subsequently, he did write replies to several criticisms of the *Second Discourse*, but he did not publish these replies. In sum, he sustained his policy of public silence toward critics for ten years of active publication until he decided to respond to Beaumont's pastoral letter.

Both the *Letter to Beaumont* and the *Letters Written from the Mountain* begin with expressions of distaste for the polemical genre.[9] The reasons Rousseau gives for departing from his resolution to avoid such disputes point in two different directions. First, he emphasizes, as he had in his polemics of 1751–1752, the personal nature of the attacks against him. While the arguments of his books can stand without further support from him, he is required to defend his character against claims that he is impious, reckless, and seditious. Moreover, as he insists in his later autobiographical writings, these attacks threaten to prejudice readers against him, thereby keeping the arguments of his books from receiving a fair hearing. Second, he argues that even more is at stake in the disputes over *Emile* and the *Social Contract* than his reputation or the fate of his books. In the *Letters Written from the Mountain*, he argues that his renunciation of citizenship has eliminated his personal stake in the situation in Geneva, but that the constitutional crisis caused by a governmental usurpation of power remains. Even more emphatically, in both this work and the *Letter to Beaumont*, he argues that his presentation of the relation between religion and politics represents the only satisfactory alternative to an unceasing battle between dogmatic intolerance and equally dogmatic disbelief.

The essence of Rousseau's project of resolving the theological-political problem is shown by his description of the "religious condition of Europe" at the time of the publication of *Emile*. In the *Letters Written from the Mountain* he describes this condition: "Religion, discredited everywhere by philosophy, had lost its ascendancy even over the people. The Clergy, obstinate about propping it up on its weak side, had let all the rest be undermined, and, being out of plumb, the entire edifice was ready to collapse. Controversies had stopped because they no longer interested anyone, and peace reigned among the different parties, because none cared about his own anymore. In order to remove the bad branches, they had cut down the tree; in order to replant it, it was necessary to leave nothing but the trunk."[10] The disputes between Rousseau and the religious authorities who attacked him concern the nature of the "trunk" or heart of religion and whether this heart is compatible with "philosophic liberty."

Letter to Beaumont

The boldness of Rousseau's exchange with the Archbishop of Paris is underscored by the power of his interlocutor and the continued threat of persecution. The Archbishop's Pastoral Letter banned Rousseau's *Emile* as an "erroneous, impious, blasphemous, and heretical" work containing "an abominable doctrine, suited to overturning natural Law and to destroying the foundations of the Christian Religion."[11] The Archbishop accused Rousseau of being an agitator for atheism who takes "pleasure in poisoning the sources of public felicity."[12] Rousseau countered that not he but the dominant orthodoxies have "cruelly wounded humanity" by propping up with their authority the truly "abominable doctrines" that, unlike the "simple and pure" religion of the Savoyard Vicar, "inundate French fields" with "rivers of blood."[13] The issues between them involve nothing less than the foundation and consequences of traditional natural law doctrines and of Christianity itself.

Rousseau pointedly suggests that the "interest of Beaumont's belief" can be seen at work in the *Pastoral Letter*—if only because the partisan passions unleashed in response to the publication of *Emile* make it necessary for the Catholic prelate to "howl with the wolves."[14] Against accusations that he himself is a hypocrite and an atheist, Rousseau defends not only his teaching but also his character by asserting the sincerity with which he writes. He argues that he has always written with the same principles, that it is not easy to understand why he would have disguised himself, and that he has never been heard to say or do anything that contradicts his writings. He repeatedly points out that, in fact, he would have fared better had he "openly declared himself in favor of atheism," in part because he would have been aided by the party of the philosophers. What conviction does Rousseau champion alone against the two parties, the Christians and the philosophers, arrayed against him? His "sentiment in matters of religion," which he states with "his usual frankness," is that "the essential truths of Christianity . . . serve as the foundation of all good morality" and that Jesus Christ "ordered belief only in what was necessary to be good."[15] All the diseased branches from this fundamentally healthy trunk have to be cut off in order to save the tree. This position offends the philosophers because it favors religion too much, and the Christians because it is not pious enough.[16]

The philosophical novel *Emile*, the target of the Archbishop's Pastoral Letter, investigates nature and the possibility of an education according to nature that would produce a human being who would be not only "good for others" but "good for himself."[17] The centerpiece of Rousseau's attempt to reconcile human being and society is the *Profession of Faith of the Savoyard Vicar*, which he thought "may one day make a revolution among men."[18] In the *Profession*, the character called the "Savoyard Vicar" preaches a faith according to nature or reason grounded in the inner "revelation" of sentiment. The *Profession* is "an example of the way one can reason with one's pupil" so that he might find his "true interest in being good, in doing good far from the sight of men and without being forced by the laws . . . in fulfilling his duty, even at the expense of his life, and in carrying virtue in his heart."[19]

In the *Letter to Beaumont*, Rousseau argues that we must examine the possible differences between religion considered from the point of view of its temporal or moral effects, and considered as truth. He insists that doing so is not a lapse in piety. He immediately concedes, however, that to suggest the possibility of a disparity between these two considerations raises doubts about the goodness of God, for since He made man for society, then "the truest Religion is also the most social, for God does not contradict himself."[20] Yet countless hecatombs have been the principal harvest the human race has reaped from the religions that have insisted on being considered true. In the context of this examination, Rousseau tells us that we must read his later works in light of the former, the *Letter to Beaumont* in light of the *Second Discourse*. He thus reminds us that whether social religion and the true religion coincide in his view depends upon whether *Emile* and the *Second Discourse*, works in which Rousseau reveals his principles "boldly," teach that it is the finger of God upon the axis of the world, rather than accident, that impelled man out of the prehuman state of nature and into society, and that society and morality fulfill, rather than corrupt, nature.[21] The issue turns on the question of how Rousseau's "great discovery" regarding the natural goodness of man is understood by him to provide decisive guidance for human life.

The "human and social religion" begins from the principle that the religion that is useful for the human race, that conduces to peace and prosperity, is the one that should be considered true. For "it can be presumed that what is most useful to his creatures is what is most pleasing to the Creator." We, however, can know nothing else of what is "pleasing to God."[22] The fallibility of reason and the equivocation of language, Rousseau argues, make it impossible for human beings ever to agree on what is the true revelation or what it might demand of us. Thus societies must take their bearings not from revelation but from what all men might hypothetically agree upon, that is, from the handful of essential tenets historically accepted by all the different religious parties or major faiths. These should be considered the essential religion and the "fundamental laws" of each society. The civil core of this faith is that "he who disobeys the Laws disobeys God."[23] Moreover, any part of each particular religious doctrine that extends further than these essential tenets should be understood by its adherents as being only the content of their own "national religion." In any society, anyone who dogmatizes against the simplified or universal religion can be justifiably banished, because the conduct of men "in this life is dependent on their ideas about the life to come."[24] All shall believe that any decent man who sincerely follows his own religion shall be saved, and that it is impious to subject anyone to an accusation of insincerity on account of "opinions that are not connected to morality."[25] Rousseau argues for "theological tolerance" as the only means of finally obtaining peace. Because he conceives there to be an essential relation between the health of societies and a common civil religion, however, he also argues for "civil intolerance": while any legitimate, established religion within a country shall be left alone for the sake of public tranquillity, the sovereign should protect the established national forms of religion and can justly prevent the introduction of a new cult as being against the laws.[26] Further, it is the sovereign that regulates the forms of worship in each society. Theological tolerance and civil intolerance mean public indifference on all points of doctrine save the core of the "essential religion" that is required for the maintenance of public morality, and public authority over the practice of the national religion. The "social and human religion" aims at producing peace and both political and individual freedom by bringing human beings closer to their duties, removing the weapons from intolerance and fanaticism, and eliminating the authority of priests and theologians.

The Archbishop judges that Rousseau's universal or essential religion based on utility "sets all the facts aside."[27] Rousseau must therefore show that his reduction of the Christian revelation to these essentials is in perfect accord with that revelation and leaves out nothing essential to it. Rousseau's point of departure is the Archbishop's own statement that reason and revelation necessarily coincide: "if reason and revelation were opposed it is certain God would be in contradiction with Himself." Rousseau notes that this "is an important admission you make there, for it is certain that God does not contradict Himself."[28] The Archbishop insists that any individual's reason, if it is not deficient and if his heart is open to the truth, is always able to come to knowledge of God by attending to "the impressions of nature."[29] Rousseau argues that perhaps not one in a million human beings outside of Christian society can come to know the existence of the Christian God through their own unaided reason, and thus are in a position of "invincible ignorance," which differs from perversity of will. The difficulties of attaining a true or rational religion are such that, whatever may be the case of the pagan philosophers to whom the Archbishop points, the people are no more capable of theology or of understanding "the order of the universe" as proof of the divine existence than are children. Indeed, even with assistance, most Christians only succeed in attaining an anthropomorphic conception of God. Most human beings, then, are in a condition of "invincible ignorance" when left to the devices of their own reason. Now, we must think that a God who has made it so difficult for us to obtain knowledge of him, and so also to judge among the various revelations, would be unreasonably cruel to condemn human beings who err. Rousseau raises with increasing persistence the question whether we can be punished for the conclusions of our reason, whatever they might be, for God cannot blame us for the failings of the reason he gave us. One is in good faith when one reasons as sincerely as possible; one cannot help but will what one's judgment leads us to conclude is good.[30] Thus sincerity is all that God can demand of us. We see that among those of good faith there is a great variety of opinions regarding God and what he demands of us. Many then would seem to be sincere if belief is a hostage to a limited reason: the Christian as much as the Turk.

The human limits of reason affect not only our capacity to come to knowledge of the divine unaided, but also our capacity to submit to revelation. For the authority of revelation, in Rousseau's view, necessarily depends upon the authority of those who attest to the event. One would thus be obliged "on pain of damnation" to believe the word of human beings whom we know are all too often limited, credulous, and even liars. Thus, Rousseau's famous question: is it "simple, is it natural, that God should have sought out Moses in order to speak to Jean-Jacques Rousseau?"[31] We therefore "need reasons to submit our reason"; the authority of revelation as transmitted to us must ultimately be established on the basis of "moral proofs," that is, on the basis of our own experience and judgment of what is credible.[32] Nor do miracles constitute convincing proof of the authority of doctrine, because, since they can be counterfeited, they must in turn be authenticated by doctrine. Thus "proof" from miracles is nothing but a vicious circle, and we are constrained to abandon them and "[r]eturn to reasoning."[33] While Rousseau agrees with the Archbishop that it is not easy for materialists to prove that "the Dogmas we consider to be revealed combat the eternal truths," it is also impossible for reason to testify for mysteries such as that of transubstantiation.[34] Rousseau's character, the Savoyard Vicar in *Emile*, thus adopts an attitude of "respectful doubt" toward revelation, because while the Gospel bears certain "hallmarks of truth," it is also "full of unbelievable things, of things which are repugnant to reason and impossible for any sensible man to conceive or to accept."[35] To insist that belief in them is essential for salvation is to do nothing but incite men to parrot words and even to be willing to kill their neighbor simply because he does not mouth them as they do.

Yet Rousseau insists that to see "insoluble difficulties" in a doctrine is not to reject it, so there is a category of things "beyond reason" essentially different from the category of things that are clearly "contrary to reason." The Archbishop condemns Rousseau for holding, through "the character who serves him as mouthpiece"—that is, the Savoyard Vicar—that the question of "the creation and unity of God" is an "idle question" and "beyond his reason."[36] According to Rousseau, though the human mind cannot decisively comprehend the "origin of things," we have two fundamental ways of conceiving of it. The principle of "the eternal and necessary existence of matter" has a great number of difficulties; but, of all the ideas we can have of the origin of beings, the idea of creation *ex nihilo* is the "least comprehensible" to reason. Thus the philosophers "have all unanimously rejected the possibility of creation" except for a small number the sincerity of whose motives can be doubted.[37] Rousseau insists that reason's preference is not incompatible with revelation on this point, since the eternity of matter was an idea accepted by the Church fathers, and the word "created" in the Bible has an ambiguous meaning.[38] Reason tends to the view that the "coexistence of two principles," matter and will, "seems to explain the constitution of the universe better" and that it "remove[s] difficulties which are hard to resolve without it, such as among others the origin of evil."[39]

Nevertheless, Rousseau agrees with the Archbishop that the question of the unity of the creator God is not an "idle question," and even claims in the *Profession* that unity is "established and sustained by reasoning."[40] The Vicar, however, "[s]topped on both sides by these difficulties . . . does not torture himself with a purely speculative doubt that does not influence in any manner his duties in this world." What does the origin of beings matter, as long as we know "how they subsist, what place [we] have to fill among them, and in virtue of what this obligation [to perform duties toward others] is imposed on [us]?"[41] The Vicar's "involuntary skepticism" does not extend to the doctrine of the Gospel regarding those things "every reasonable Christian of good faith . . . wants to know about Heaven," namely, "those that are of importance to his conduct." A "superior proof" of the "true certitude of Christian revelation is the "purity and sanctity" of its moral teaching and the "wholly divine sublimity" of Jesus Christ, or of "the person who was its author."[42] About conduct the Gospel is clear—but apparently no clearer than reason alone. For, as Rousseau indicates, philosophy is sufficient to teach us how to control the passions, how to prevent vice from arising, or even why the necessity of moral conduct leads to that of belief in divine sanction.

The Archbishop belittles the Vicar's position that, despite his ignorance regarding our origins, reason allows him to determine God's attributes as "necessary consequences" of his being. One of God's central attributes according to the Vicar is that "his will constitutes his power," and from this power flows God's goodness and his justice: "goodness is the necessary effect of a power without limit and of the self-love essential to every being aware of itself," while God's justice "is a consequence of his goodness."[43] But God's justice is an attribute ultimately no more comprehensible to the Vicar than creation through will: he admits that "I affirm them without understanding them, and at bottom that is to affirm nothing."[44] The question persists, therefore, whether to live in the light of what is beyond reason is contrary to reason, because the Vicar is "forced" to reason about the nature of God in the light of "the sentiment of his relations with me": so, for example, he is compelled to argue that "the triumph of the wicked and the oppression of the just in this world" alone prevents him from doubting the existence of providence, because God cannot justly disappoint the hope implanted in us that, if we are just, we will be happy.[45] The only final defense of revelation, in the Vicar's account, lies in our moral sentiment. Metaphysics no longer supports morality but is supported by it, or rather, at most, they prop up one another.[46] Rousseau's "unanswerable" reply to the Archbishop is the Vicar's statement that the "worthiest use of my reason is for it to annihilate itself before [God] . . . it is the charm of my weakness to feel myself overwhelmed by [God's] greatness."[47] This reply would seem to leave intact the question in dispute: whether a fundamentally moral as opposed to a metaphysical conception of religion is "reasonable" and sufficient.

Beaumont is vehement that the principal fruit of the Vicar's teaching on sincerity is that it is "sufficient to persuade oneself that one possesses the truth," even if one "[adopts] the very errors of Atheism."[48] This assessment would seem to follow from the view that the *Profession* teaches that the truth, as opposed to any sincerely held opinion, about God has become irrelevant for salvation, since God is just and cannot blame us for sincerely choosing the moral opinions we deem to be true. Since God cannot punish us for error, and therefore even for atheism, the believer need only concern himself with whether the "consolations" furnished by his reason are in the end only "chimeras."[49] That is, he need now fear only a mistaken belief in God altogether. Rousseau dismisses this characterization of the Vicar's teaching. Rousseau could finally resolve the believer's concern if he showed that following one's conscience is the fulfillment of self-love on this earth, that an Emile could find the true reason for doing his duties "far from the sight of men" without being taught a version of the *Profession*.

In his other writings as well as elsewhere in *Emile*, Rousseau gives a different account of human nature than that which informs the *Profession of Faith* and the *Letter*. Rousseau sets down as "an incontestable maxim that the first movements of nature are always right. There is no original perversity in the human heart."[50] He shows how "[a]ny man who only wanted to live would live happily."[51] The Archbishop views human nature as a violent torrent that constantly overflows the "powerful dikes" we must build in order to direct it toward salvation.[52] Since Rousseau's educational philosophy entails a denial of original sin, it corrupts the young because it does not teach them to steel themselves against the "fatal inclination" of their corrupt natures. The Archbishop therefore rejects it as "not even suited to making Citizens or Men."[53] He insists that Rousseau does not account, as Christianity does, for "the "striking mixture" of nobility and baseness, virtue and vice that is to be found within human beings, nor does it provide a sufficient account of human evil.[54] Rousseau asserts that this is what the Vicar himself has "explained best."[55] The Vicar attempts to explain evil by embracing a dualistic account of the soul in which an active will, guided by a love of order, engages in a battle against self-love. This battle is the necessary price of the exercise of the freedom of will granted to us so that we may possess the "morality that ennobles" human life. The Vicar's moral profession of faith stresses self-reliance and the free exercise of each individual's will, and thus seems to reduce our dependency upon God's intervention: God made us so that we can be good should we choose to be; and God made moral goodness akin to happiness such that it is almost, but not quite, its own reward. Thus we do not need to pray for God's grace to escape from evil in ourselves, but can in principle prevent it from arising in us by our own efforts. This consoling teaching can be understood as a dualistic version of Rousseau's own more radical account of natural goodness. Whether moral goodness has a foundation in nature in Rousseau's thought depends upon a final understanding of what he means by the "active principle" and "conscience," and how he responds to the Archbishop's—and the Vicar's—challenging claim that the development of moral goodness from a single source in self-love cannot be accounted for.

In the *Letter*, as in the *Profession*, Rousseau analyzes "difficulties about a sentiment" as geometers might determine that certain consequences are falsely derived from fundamental premises.[56] At the same time, he clarifies the moral premises of religious thought, and attempts to build a human religion fully consequent to these, while seeking to persuade human beings to adopt a theology founded upon morality as a doctrine salutary to public felicity. Rather than destroying religion and virtue in his works, as the Archbishop alleges, Rousseau paints them in more natural forms while exposing their foundation in the human heart

Letters Written from the Mountain

While the *Letter to Beaumont* addresses Christianity as represented by a Roman Catholic Bishop, the *Letters Written from the Mountain* addresses Christianity as represented by the Protestant Reformation. In the former work Rousseau emphasizes his disagreements with Beaumont. In the latter he takes as a given the legitimacy of the Reformation as the established religion of Geneva. Because in this work he treats religion in the context of the political question of his citizenship, Rousseau confronts it somewhat less radically than he does in the *Letter to Beaumont*. Moreover, since his treatment of Protestantism stresses liberty of interpretation of Biblical texts, he avoids the issue of religious authority posed so strongly in the dispute with Beaumont.

In order to defend himself against the claim that his books undermine the established religion, Rousseau presents an interpretation of the Reformation. He insists that the Reformation is based on two fundamental principles: first, "to acknowledge the Bible as the rule of one's belief" and, second, "not to admit any other interpreter of the meaning of the Bible than oneself."[57] Protestantism shares the first of these principles with Catholicism and has the second as its distinctive position.

To begin with, Rousseau focuses on this second principle, arguing that the essence of the Reformation consisted of a dispute over authoritative interpretation of the Bible. Disagreeing with the established interpretation on a variety of issues and unable to perform miracles to establish themselves as prophets, the reformers could appeal to nothing but the authority of their own reason. To the extent that a reformed church then presents a new interpretation as authoritative (as opposed to merely "probable" or the sign of a consensus) over the individual reason of its members, it undermines the basis of the Reformation itself. As Rousseau says, "Let someone prove to me today that in matters of faith I am obliged to submit to someone else's decisions, beginning tomorrow I will become Catholic, and every consistent and true man will act as I do."[58]

Having shown the implications of the second principle of the Reformation, Rousseau turns to the first. Does he accept the Bible as the rule of his belief? In other words, does he accept the revealed character of the Bible? This issue turns on the status of miracles, which Rousseau concedes that he has called into question. In fact, in the *Vision of Pierre of the Mountain*, Rousseau very boldly attributes to himself simple disbelief in miracles.[59] Within the *Letters Written from the Mountain*, however, he does not go that far; rather, he insists only on the impossibility of knowing whether a particular fact is a miracle. "Since a miracle is an exception to the Law of nature, to judge one it is necessary to know these Laws, and to judge one reliably, it is necessary to know them all."⁶⁰ Even the wisest of humans, however, lacks such comprehensive knowledge. As Rousseau makes perfectly clear, this argument establishes, at most, the unknowability of miracles. It is no refutation of their possibility. He concludes, "*That cannot be*, is a phrase that rarely comes from the lips of wise men. They more often say, *I do not know*."⁶¹ The question remains whether belief in these uncertain miracles is demanded by the Bible.

Rousseau answers this question in the negative. Considered as proof of the doctrine taught in the Bible, miracles are superfluous for those, like Rousseau, who accept that doctrine based on their understanding of "its utility, its beauty, its sanctity, its truth, its depth."⁶² He argues further that many passages of the Gospel deny that miracles should be considered as inseparable from the teaching.⁶³ In short, he argues that, acknowledging the Bible as the rule of one's belief means accepting a non-miraculous moral doctrine taught by the Bible. This doctrine, severed from miracles and not imposed by the government or any other authority, is the "trunk" of Christianity, which Rousseau intends to preserve against the attacks of the Enlightenment.

Rousseau attempts to establish this understanding of Christianity through argument based on scripture, but he knows that argument has an effect on few people. In his discussion of the basis of belief he suggests that "good and upright people" (as distinguished from both the wise and those who are simply "incapable of coherent reason") base their belief on the character of those who announce a doctrine rather than on the character of the doctrine itself.⁶⁴ Later, in the Fifth Letter, Rousseau tacitly applies this account to himself. Contrasting himself to Voltaire and other authors who published anonymously in order to avoid persecution, Rousseau insists that his own frankness in publicly acknowledging his books is evidence in favor of the content of his books. In other words, his evident good faith is evidence for the truth of his position, and the evident bad faith of writers like Voltaire is evidence of the falseness of theirs.

The transition from the first to the second part of the *Letters Written from the Mountain* is made in the Sixth Letter, in which Rousseau turns his attention from religion to politics. In this letter he defends the *Social Contract* against the charge that it tends to destroy all governments. By presenting an analytic summary of the argument of the *Social Contract* he lays the foundation for the second part of the *Letters*, in which he gives an account of the present state of the Genevan republic. In short, he summarizes the principles that he then applies to the Genevan situation.

The analytic summary of the *Social Contract* does, indeed, show that

Rousseau does not reject any form of government. While he expresses a preference for elective aristocracy in principle, he also argues that each of the other forms might be best in particular circumstances. Thus, far from arguing for the destruction of governments, Rousseau can present himself as a defender of all of them. To defend all forms of government, however, is not to defend all existing governments. The dynamite hidden in Rousseau's willingness to defend all forms of government can be seen from his novel account of the difference between sovereignty and government and the novel account of chronic political problems that follows from it.

Sovereignty, which is identical to the legislative power, can legitimately reside only in the community as a whole. Government (except in a direct democracy) is a smaller body that executes the laws. Although the sovereign is the supreme power, it "always tends toward relaxation," while the government (which must always be active in its execution of the laws) "tends to become stronger."[65] Rousseau has little confidence in the ability of institutions to check this tendency in the government. Moreover, he insists that admirable qualities such as loyalty and a sense of responsibility are likely to foster a corporate spirit in the government. In the end, in every community that has an effective government, the government will usurp the sovereign's power and become oppressive. In sum, while every form of government is potentially legitimate, every existing government is a present or future oppressor.

The two sides of Rousseau's position show themselves clearly when he turns to the Genevan situation.[66] Confronting the controversy over whether the city is free or enslaved, he says, "Nothing is more free than your legitimate state; nothing is more servile than your actual state."[67] Genevans are particularly confused between the legitimate and actual state for two reasons. First, as a democracy, Geneva is the sort of state that is least well understood. "The democratic Constitution is certainly the Masterpiece of the political art: but the more admirable its contrivance is, the less it belongs to all eyes to penetrate it."[68] Second, because of the turbulence of Genevan history, the precise location of sovereignty has been constantly contested.

One might think that the obscurity is removed once and for all, not only for Genevans and democracy but also for all communities, by Rousseau's insistence that the only legitimate locus for sovereignty is in the people as a whole. The logical consequence of this insistence would be the right of the sovereign to dismiss the government whenever the latter begins to usurp power. In short, Rousseau's account of sovereignty seems to lead to a demand for radically new beginnings when inevitable corruption occurs. Rousseau, however, presents his doctrine as requiring the attempt to resist, rather than to initiate, innovation. This presentation, in turn, leads him to attempt to demonstrate the "original" state of the government that is to be preserved.

This demonstration is undertaken in the *Letters Written from the Mountain* and the unfinished "History of the Government of Geneva," which was written as preparation for the larger work. In the "History" Rousseau argues that confusion about the underlying principles of politics is the hallmark of all modern governments, which were "built up successively out of pieces related less in accordance with the public needs than in accordance with private aims."[69] The search for the historical origins of political authority in a community that has no reliable history of its beginnings can only be fruitless. Instead Rousseau looks for a hypothesis that can explain the genesis of the existing government. He finds this hypothesis in the claim that, after the dissolution of the Roman Empire, sovereignty was in the hands of the Bishops of Geneva. Far from looking for evidence of a time when the Genevans themselves exercised legitimate sovereignty, Rousseau is content to focus on actual sovereignty.

One of the distinctive parts of Rousseau's account is the positive role played by the Bishops, who were normally cast as the archenemies of Geneva. Rousseau reverses the view that political freedom came as a consequence of the Protestant Reformation. Rather than making religious reform the basis of political reform, he argues that the reformation could not have happened without the prior establishment of political freedom, and that the reformation only affirmed the liberty that had been essentially acquired beforehand. He argues that the entire history of the government of Geneva can be shown to flow from the facts that its sovereignty was held by an ecclesiastical power and that its size made it vulnerable to its neighbors. Because the spiritual authority of the Bishops limited their temporal power, they were obliged to make concessions alternately to the Counts of the Genevese or to the Genevan people. Later the neighboring Dukes of Savoy took on the pretensions of the Counts. It was the efforts of the Bishops to resist this usurpation of their own authority that led them to strengthen the city enough to assert its independence. Having thwarted the pretensions of Savoy, the Genevans unwittingly found themselves with the fundamentals of a republican government, which came to completion with the expulsion of the Bishops during the Reformation.

These fundamentals consisted of a democratic general Council that ruled largely by delegating power to four Syndics who further delegated functions to advisors who came to make up the small Council. The history of the Genevan republic, traced in the second part of the *Letters Written from the Mountain*, is the history of the usurpation of sovereign authority by the small Council. This history frequently led Geneva to the point of civil war and ultimately to intervention of neighboring powers who imposed on the Genevan parties the Edict of Settlement. Rousseau both defends the Settlement as the salvation of the republic and attacks it as unwittingly providing cover for further usurpation. First, because the mediating powers misunderstood the democratic nature of sovereignty, they did not explicitly identify the general Council as sovereign.[70] Second, they enumerated, and thereby limited, the powers of the general Council, leaving the impression that all other conceivable powers belonged to the small Council.

These misunderstandings have opened the door to the continuation of attempts at "innovation" by the small Council.[71] The practical question facing the Genevans is how to prevent these innovations. In the *Social Contract* Rousseau had argued that the fundamental way to prevent usurpations by the government is to provide for periodic assemblies of the sovereign.[72] In Geneva, however, these assemblies were suspended except for the purpose of electing new Syndics, who are nominated by the usurping small Council. The question, then, is how to draw the abuses of the government to the attention of the unassembled sovereign.

The answer to this question is found in the right of remonstrance, or complaint against the government. Rousseau argues that, while the sovereign can issue new laws only in the general Council, "outside the general Council it is not annihilated; its members are scattered, but they are not dead; they cannot speak by means of Laws, but they can always keep watch over the administration of the Laws."[73] A remonstrance against the government, then, is not a vote against the government, it is a statement of an opinion by a member of the sovereign that the government is usurping. The government can respond by satisfying the complaint, although it is more likely to answer the charge by branding as troublemakers those who raise it. This situation requires a judge to decide between the remonstrators and the government. One might think that an appeal is being made to the sovereign, but this cannot be the case because the sovereign can make pronouncements only in the form of general laws, it cannot judge individual cases. Consequently, Rousseau argues that the situation requires an assembly "that by a very important distinction will not have the authority of the Sovereign but of the supreme Magistrate."[74] In effect, a provisional government must be formed.

In Geneva, however, the existing government has refused to act in any way upon the remonstrances that have been made on behalf of Rousseau and his writings. Rousseau concludes the *Letters* by stopping just short of urging a revolution or an appeal to the intervention of foreign mediators.

He says, "After having shown you the condition in which you are, I will not undertake to trace out for you the route that you must follow in order to leave it. If there is one, being on the very spot, you and your Fellow Citizens should be able to see it better than I can; when one knows where one is and where one should go, one can direct oneself without effort."[75] This caution is the result of the hope that the unity of the remonstrators may yet influence the government, but it is also the result of Rousseau's view that—whatever might happen in the short run—either the present or a new government will continue to tend to usurpation.

Conclusion

The fact that the works contained in this volume were written in polemical contexts means that Rousseau's expression in them is influenced by his need to defend himself and his books. The fact that he is responding to specific charges means that these works are sometimes narrowly focused on those charges. Nevertheless, the essential charges against Rousseau—that his works undermine religion and government—are fundamental enough to draw responses that enter very deeply into his thought. Moreover, the fact that the context in which these writings occur involves warrants issued against him, burnings of his books, and civil unrest compels Rousseau to address in a quite comprehensive manner the significance of his project as a writer.

Christopher Kelly and Eve Grace

PASTORAL LETTER OF HIS GRACE THE ARCHBISHOP OF PARIS

Pastoral Letter
of his Grace the Archbishop of Paris
Declaring the Condemnation of a Book That Has as its Title *Emile, or On Education* by Jean-Jacques Rousseau, Citizen of Geneva

Christophe de Beaumont, by Divine Mercy and by the grace of the Holy Apostolic See, Archbishop of Paris, Duke of Saint-Cloud, Peer of France, Commander of the Order of the Holy Spirit, Patron of the Sorbonne, etc; to all the Faithful of our Diocese, salutation and blessing.

I. Saint Paul predicted, My Very Dear Brethren, that *perilous days* would come *when there would be people, lovers of themselves, proud, haughty, blasphemous, impious, slanderers, bloated with pride, lovers of sensual pleasures rather than God; men of corrupt spirit and perverted Faith.*[1] And in what unfortunate times has this prediction come to pass more literally than in ours! Disbelief, emboldened by all the passions, presents itself in every form, so as to adapt itself in some manner to all ages, to all characters, to all stations. Sometimes, in order to insinuate itself into minds that it finds already *bewitched by trifles*,[2] it assumes a light, pleasant, and frivolous style: from this so many Novels, equally obscene and impious, whose goal is to amuse the imagination in order to seduce the mind and corrupt the heart. Sometimes, feigning an air of profundity and sublimity in its intentions, it pretends to go back to the first principles of our knowledge and claims to found its authority on them in order to shake off a yoke that, according to it, dishonors humanity, even the Divinity. Sometimes it declaims like someone enraged against Religion's zeal, and heatedly preaches universal tolerance. Sometimes, finally, uniting all these diverse languages, it mixes the serious with playfulness, pure maxims with obscenities, great truths with great errors, Faith with blasphemy; it undertakes, in a word, to harmonize light with shadows, Jesus Christ with Belial. And such is especially, My Very Dear Brethren, the object that appears to have been proposed in a recent Work, which has as its title *Emile, or on Education*. From the bosom of error, there arose a man full of the language of Philosophy without being a genuine Philosopher; a mind endowed with a multitude of knowledge that did not enlighten him, and that spread darkness in other minds; a character given to paradoxes of opinions and conduct, alloying simplicity of morals with ostentation of thoughts, zeal for ancient maxims with the rage for establishing novelties, the obscurity of retreat with the desire to be known by everyone. He has been seen to rail at the sciences he was cultivating, extol the excellence of the Gospel whose dogmas he was destroying, depict the beauty of virtues he was extinguishing in the soul of his Readers.[3] He made himself the Preceptor of the human race in order to deceive it, the public Monitor in order to lead everyone astray, the oracle of the century in order to complete its destruction. In a Work on the inequality of conditions, he lowered man to the level of the beasts;[4] in another, more recent production, he had introduced the poison of sensual pleasure while appearing to proscribe it.[5] In this work, he seizes upon man's first moments in order to establish the domain of irreligion.

II. What an enterprise, My Very Dear Brethren! The education of youth is one of the most important objects of the solicitude and zeal of Pastors. We know that, in order to reform the world, as much as the weakness and corruption of our nature permits, it would be enough to observe, under the direction and impression of grace, the first gleams of human reason, to grasp them carefully, and to direct them toward the path that leads to the truth. In that way those minds, still exempt from prejudices, would always be on guard against error; those hearts, still exempt from the great passions, would acquire impressions of all the virtues. But to whom is it better suited than to us, and to those who Cooperate with us in the holy Ministry, to keep watch in this way over the first moments of Christian youth; to dispense to it the spiritual milk of Religion, *so that it might grow for salvation*[6]; to prepare in good time, by salutary lessons, sincere Adorers of the true God, faithful Subjects of the Sovereign, Men worthy of being the support and ornament of the Fatherland?

III. Now, My Very Dear Brethren, the author of *Emile* proposes a plan of education that, far from agreeing with Christianity, is not even suited to making Citizens or Men. Under the vain pretext of restoring man to himself and of making his student into nature's student, he sets up as a principle an Assertion denied, not only by Religion, but also by the experience of all Peoples and of all ages. *Let us set down*, he says, *as an incontestable maxim that the first movements of nature are always right. There is no original perversity in the human heart.*[7] From this language one does not at all recognize the doctrine of the Holy Scriptures and of the Church touching the revolution that has happened in our nature: one loses sight of the ray of light that lets us know the mystery of our own heart. Yes, My Very Dear Brethren, there is to be found within us a striking mixture of greatness and baseness, of zeal for truth and taste for error, of inclination to virtue and penchant to vice. Astonishing contrast, which, disconcerting Pagan Philosophy, leaves it to wander in vain speculations! a contrast whose source revelation uncovers for us in the deplorable fall of our first Father! Man feels himself drawn by a fatal inclination, and how would he resist it if his childhood were not directed by Teachers full of virtue, wisdom, vigilance, and if—during the entire course of his life—he himself, under the protection and with the grace of his God, did not make powerful and continual efforts? Alas, My Very Dear Brethren, despite the healthiest and most virtuous principles of education, despite the most magnificent promises of Religion and the most terrible threats, the follies of youth are still only too frequent, too manifold. Left to itself, into what errors, what excesses would youth not throw itself? It is a torrent that overflows despite the powerful dikes built to contain it. What would happen, then, if no obstacle stopped its flow and broke its force?

IV. The author of *Emile*, who recognizes no Religion, nevertheless indicates, without thinking about it, the way that leads infallibly to the true Religion: "We," he says, "who want to grant nothing to authority, we who want to teach nothing to our Emile which he could not learn by himself in every country, in what Religion shall we raise him? To what Sect shall we join the Student of nature? We shall join him to neither this one nor that one, but we shall put him in a position to choose the one to which the best use of his reason ought to lead him."[8] I wish to God, My very Dear Brethren, that this object had been well accomplished! If the author had really *put his Student in a position to choose among all the Religions the one where the best use of reason ought to lead*, he would infallibly have prepared him for the lessons of Christianity. For, My Very Dear Brethren, the natural light leads to the evangelical light; and the Christian worship is essentially *a reasonable worship*.[9] In fact, *if the best use of our reason* did not lead us to Christian revelation, our Faith would be vain, our hopes would be chimerical. But how does this *best use* of reason lead us to the inestimable good of Faith, and from that to the precious end of salvation? It is to reason itself that we appeal. As soon as one acknowledges one God, it is no longer a question of anything but knowing whether he has deigned to speak to men other than by the impressions of nature. Thus one must examine whether the facts that verify revelation are not superior to all the efforts of the most cunning quibbling. A hundred times disbelief has attempted to destroy these facts, or at least to weaken their proofs, and a hundred times its criticism has been convicted of impotence. By means of revelation God has testified for himself and this testimony is evidently *very worthy of faith*.[10] What is left then for the man who makes the *best use of his reason*, but to acquiesce to this testimony? It is thy grace, oh my

God! that consummates this work of light; it is what determines the will, which forms the Christian soul: but the development of the proofs and the force of the motives have previously occupied and purified reason; and it is in this labor, as noble as it is indispensable, that this *best use of reason* consists, about which the author of *Emile* undertakes to speak without having a settled and genuine notion of it.

V. In order to find young people more docile for the lessons he prepares for them, this Author wants them to be devoid of any principle of Religion. And that is why, according to him, *To know good and bad, to sense the reason for man's duties, is not a child's affair.* . . . *I would like as little*, he adds, *to insist that a ten-year-old be five feet tall as that he possess judgment.*

VI. Doubtless, My Very Dear Brethren, human judgment has its progression, and forms itself only by degrees: but does it follow from this that at age ten a child does not know the difference between good and evil at all, that he confuses wisdom with folly, goodness with barbarity, virtue with vice? What! at that age he will not feel that obeying his father is a good, and that disobeying him is an evil! To claim that, My Very Dear Brethren, is to slander human nature, by ascribing to it stupidity it does not have.

VII. "Every child who believes in God," says this author again, "is an idolater or an anthropomorphite."[11] But, if he is an Idolater, he believes then in several Gods; he attributes, then, divine nature to insensate simulacra? If he is only an Anthropomorphite, while acknowledging the true God he gives him a body. Now, neither one nor the other can be assumed in a child who has received a Christian education. If the education has been faulty in that regard, it is supremely unjust to impute to Religion what is only the fault of those who teach it badly. Moreover, the age of ten is not at all the age of a Philosopher. A child, although well instructed, can express himself badly; but by inculcating in him that the Divinity is nothing perceived or that can be perceived by the senses, that it is an infinite intelligence that, endowed with a supreme Power, performs all that pleases it, one gives him a notion of God suited to the reach of his judgment. It is not doubtful that an Atheist, by means of his Sophisms, will easily succeed in troubling the ideas of this young believer; but all the skill of the Sophist will certainly not make this child, when he believes in God, be *an Idolater* or *Anthropomorphite*, that is to say, believe only in the existence of a chimera.

VIII. The Author goes farther, My Very Dear Brethren, he *does not even grant that a young man of fifteen has the capacity to believe in God*. Man will not know, then, even at that age, whether there is a God or whether there is not one; no matter how much all of nature announces the glory of its

Creator, he will understand nothing of its language! He will exist without knowing to what he owes his existence! And it will be healthy reason itself that will plunge him into this darkness! This is how, My Very Dear Brethren, blind impiety would like to be able to obscure with its black haze the flame that Religion presents to all the ages of human life. Saint Augustine reasoned well based on different principles when he said, in speaking about the first years of his youth: "I fell, from that time onwards, Lord, into the hands of some of those who are careful to invoke you; and I understood from what they told me about you, and in accordance with the ideas that I was able to form about it at that age, that you were something great, and that although you might be invisible and beyond the grasp of our senses, you could hear our prayers and help us. Therefore I began from my childhood to pray to you and regard you as my refuge and my support; and to the extent that my tongue became loosened, I used its first movements to invoke you."[12]

IX. Let us continue, My Very Dear Brethren, to call attention to the strange paradoxes of the author of *Emile*. After having reduced young people to such a profound ignorance relative to the attributes and the rights of the Divinity, will he at least grant them the advantage of becoming acquainted with themselves? Will they know whether their soul is a substance absolutely distinguished from matter? or will they regard themselves as purely material beings, and submitted only to the laws of Mechanism! The author of *Emile* doubts that at eighteen it is yet time for his student to learn whether he has a soul: he thinks that *if he learns it sooner, he runs the risk of never knowing it*.[13] Doesn't he at least want young people to be susceptible to the knowledge of their duties? No: to take his word for it, *only physical objects can interest children, especially those whose vanity has not been awakened, and who have not been corrupted ahead of time by the poison of opinion*[14]: consequently he wants all the cares of the first education to be applied to what is material and earthly in man: *Exercise*, he says, *his body, his organs, his senses, his strength, but keep his soul idle for as long as possible.*[15] This is because this leisure appeared necessary to him to dispose the soul to the errors that he proposed to inculcate into it. But, isn't wanting to teach man wisdom only at the time when he is dominated by the fire of the nascent passions to present it to him with the design that he will reject it?

X. How much is such an education, My Very Dear Brethren, opposed to the one prescribed together by the true Religion and sound reason! Both of them want a wise and vigilant Teacher to spy out in some way in his Student the first gleams of intelligence in order to occupy it with the attractions of the truth, the first movements of the heart, in order to arrest it by the charms of virtue. In fact, how much more advantageous is it to avoid obstacles than to have to surmount them? How much is it not to be feared that if the impressions of vice precede the lessons of virtue, man, having reached a certain age, will lack the courage or the will to resist vice? Doesn't happy experience prove every day that after the disorderliness of an imprudent and quick-tempered youth, one finally returns to the good principles that one received during childhood?

XI. Moreover, My Very Dear Brethren, let us not be surprised that the Author of *Emile* postpones the knowledge of God's existence to such a distant time. He does not believe it is necessary for salvation. "It is clear," he says through the organ of a chimerical character, "it is clear that a man who has come to old age without believing in God, will not for that be deprived of his presence in the other, if his blindness was not voluntary, and I say that it is not always voluntary."[16] Note, My Very Dear Brethren, that the issue here is not a man who would be deprived of the use of his reason, but solely of someone whose reason would not be aided by instruction. Such a claim is supremely absurd, especially within the system of an Author who maintains that reason is absolutely sound. Saint Paul guarantees that, among the pagan Philosophers, several arrived at knowledge of the true God through the strength of reason alone. "What may be known of God," says that Apostle, "has been manifested to them; for God having made it known to them. For the consideration of things that have been made since the creation of the world having made visible what is invisible in God, even his eternal power and his divinity; so that they are without excuse. Because, having known God, they have not glorified him as God and have not given him thanks, but are lost in the vanity of their reasoning, and their foolish mind has become darkened. Calling themselves wise, they have become mad."[17]

XII. Now, if such has been the crime of these men, who, although subjected by the prejudices of their education to the worship of Idols, did not fail to attain knowledge of God, how would those who have not had similar obstacles to overcome be innocent and just to the point of deserving to enjoy the presence of God in the other life? How would they be excusable (with a sound reason such as the Author assumes) for having enjoyed during this life the great spectacle of nature, and for having nevertheless refused to recognize the one who created it, who preserves and governs it?

XIII. The same Writer, My Very Dear Brethren, openly embraces Skepticism relative to the creation and the unity of God. "I know," he makes the assumed character who serves him as mouthpiece say, "I know that the world is governed by a powerful and wise will. I see it, or rather, I sense it; and that is something important for me to know. But is this same world eternal or created? Is there a single principle of things? Or, are there two, or many of them, and what is their nature? I know nothing about all this, and what does it matter to me. I renounce idle questions which may agitate my amour-propre but are useless for my conduct and are beyond my reason."[18] What does this reckless Author want to say then? He believes that the world is governed by a powerful and wise will; he admits that that is something important for him to know and nevertheless *he does not know*, he says, *whether there is a single principle of things* or if there are many, and he claims that it doesn't matter to him very much to know. If there is a powerful and wise will that governs the world, is it conceivable that it not be the only principle of things? and can it be more important to know the one than the other? What contradictory language! He does not know *what the nature* of God is, and shortly thereafter he acknowledges that this supreme Being is endowed with intelligence, power, will, and goodness. Isn't that having an idea of the divine nature? The unity of God appears to him an idle question and beyond his reason, as though the multiplicity of Gods were not the greatest of absurdities. *The plurality of Gods*, Tertullian states forcefully, *is a nullifying of God*[19]; to acknowledge a God is to acknowledge a supreme and independent Being, to which all other Beings are subordinate. He implies then that there are several Gods.

XIV. It is not surprising, My Very Dear Brethren, that a man who has a taste for such errors touching the Divinity protests against the Religion It has revealed to us. To hear him speak, all revelations in general *have only the effect of degrading God by giving Him human passions. I see that particular dogmas, far from clarifying the notions of the great Being,* he continues, *confuse them; that far from ennobling them, they debase them; that to the inconceivable mysteries surrounding them they add absurd contradictions.*[20] This author is very much more the one, My Very Dear Brethren, who can be reproached with inconsistency and absurdity. It is he, mind you, who degrades God, who confuses and debases the notions of the great Being, since he attacks its essence directly by calling into question its Unity.

XV. He has felt that the truth of Christian Revelation was proven by the facts; but since miracles form one of the principal proofs of this revelation, and since these miracles have been transmitted to us by means of testimony, he cries out: *What! Always human testimony? Always men who report to me what other men have reported! So many men between God and me!*[21] For this complaint to make sense, My Very Dear Brethren, it would be necessary to be able to conclude that Revelation is false as long as it has not been made to each man individually. It would be necessary to be able to say: God cannot require me to believe what I am assured he said, unless he has addressed his word directly to me. But aren't there an infinite number of facts, even prior to that of Christian Revelation, that it would be absurd to doubt? By what means other than human testimony, then, has the Author himself come to know this Sparta, this Athens, this Rome whose laws, morals, and heroes he praises so often and with so much certainty? How many men there are between him and the events that concern the origins and fortune of these ancient Republics! How many men between him and the Historians who have preserved the memory of these events! His skepticism is based here, then, only on the interest of his unbelief.

XVI. "Let a man," he adds later, "come and use this language with us: 'Mortals, I announce the will of the Most High to you. Recognize in my voice Him who sends me. I order the Sun to change its course, the Stars to form another arrangement, the Mountains to become level, the Waters to rise up, the Earth to change its aspect.' At these marvels who will not instantly recognize the Master of nature?"[22] Who would not believe, My Very Dear Brethren, that someone who expresses himself like that wants only to see miracles to become Christian? Listen, however, to what he adds. He says, "the most important examination of the proclaimed Doctrine remains. . . . After the Doctrine has been proved by the miracle, the miracle has to be proved by the doctrine. What can be done in such a case? One thing only. Return to reasoning and leave aside the miracles. It would have been better not to have had recourse to them."[23] That is to say: show me miracles and I will believe. Show me miracles, and I will still refuse to believe. What inconsistency, what absurdity! But learn then once and for all, My Very Dear Brethren, that in the question of Miracles the Sophism reproached by the author of the book *On Education* is not allowed at all. When a Doctrine is recognized to be true, divine, and based on sure Revelation, it is used to judge miracles, that is to say to reject the alleged marvels with which Impostors would want to oppose this Doctrine. When it is a matter of a new Doctrine announced as emanating from God's bosom, miracles are produced as proofs. That is, the person who takes on the role of Envoy of the Most High confirms his mission and his preaching by miracles, which are the very testimony of the Divinity. Thus doctrine and miracles are arguments used respectively according to the differing points of view adopted in the study and teaching of Religion. There is in this neither abuse of reason, nor ridiculous sophism, nor vicious circle. This has been demonstrated a hundred times; and it is probable that the author of *Emile* is not at all unaware of these demonstrations: but, in the plan he has made for himself of enveloping every revealed Religion, every supernatural operation, in clouds, he cunningly imputes to us dealings that dishonor reason; he represents us as Enthusiasts, whom a false zeal blinds to the point of proving each of two principles by the other without diversity of objects or of methods. Where then, My Very Dear Brethren, is the philosophic good faith this Writer parades?

XVII. One would believe that after the greatest efforts to discredit the human testimony attesting to Christian Revelation, the same Author nonetheless defers to it in the most positive, most solemn manner. To convince you of this, My Very Dear Brethren, and at the same time to edify you, this part of his Work must be put before your eyes. "I admit that the majesty of the Holy Scripture amazes me, and the holiness of the Holy Scripture speaks to my heart. Look at the books of the Philosophers with all their pomp. How petty they are next to this one! Can it be that a book at the same time so sublime and so simple is the work of men? Can it be that he whose history it presents is only a man himself? Is his the tone of an enthusiast or an ambitious Sectarian? What gentleness, what purity in his morals! What touching grace in his teachings! What elevation in his maxims! What profound wisdom in his speeches! What presence of mind, what finesse, and what exactness in his responses! What a dominion over his passions! Where is the man, where is the sage who knows how to act, to suffer, and to die without weakness and without ostentation. . . . Yes if the life and death of Socrates are those of a wise man, the life and death of Jesus are those of a God. Shall we say that the story of the Gospel was wantonly contrived? . . . It is not thus that one contrives; the facts about Socrates, which no one doubts, are less well attested than those about Jesus Christ. . . . It would be more inconceivable that many men in agreement had fabricated this Book than that a single one provided its subject. Never would Jewish Authors have found either this tone or this morality; and the Gospel has characteristics of truth that are so great, so striking, so perfectly inimitable that its contriver would be more amazing than its Hero."[24] It would be difficult, My Very Dear Brethren, to pay a more beautiful homage to the authenticity of the Gospel. However, the Author believes this only as a result of human testimonies. It is always men who report to him what other men have reported. How many men are there between God and himself! Behold him, then, manifestly contradicting himself. Behold him, confounded by his own admissions. What strange blindness, then, enabled him to add, "With all that, this same Gospel is full of unbelievable things, of things repugnant to reason and impossible for any sensible man to conceive or to accept. What is to be done amidst all these contradictions? One ought always to be modest and circumspect . . . to respect in silence what one can neither reject nor understand, and to humble oneself before the great Being who alone knows the truth. This is the involuntary Skepticism in which I have remained."[25] But can Skepticism, My Very Dear Brethren, be involuntary then, when one refuses to submit to the Doctrine of a Book that cannot have been invented by men? When this Book bears such large, striking, perfectly inimitable hallmarks of truth that the book's inventor would be more astounding than its Hero? Surely here we may say that iniquity has given itself the lie.[26]

XVIII. It seems, My Very Dear Brethren, that this author has rejected Revelation only in order to limit himself to natural religion: "What God wants a man to do," he says, "He does not have told to him by another man. He tells it to him Himself, He writes it in the depths of his heart."[27] What! Hasn't God written in the depth of our hearts the obligation to submit to him as soon as we are sure that it is he who has spoken? Now, what certainty do we not have about his divine word? The facts about Socrates about which no one doubts are, by the very admission of the author of *Emile*, less attested than those about Jesus Christ. Natural Religion thus leads itself to revealed Religion. But is it very certain that he acknowledges even natural Religion, or that at least he recognizes its necessity? No, My Very Dear Brethren: "If I am mistaken, it is in good faith. That is enough for my error not to be imputed to a crime. If you were to be similarly mistaken, there would be little evil in that."[28] Which is to say that according to him it is sufficient to be persuaded that one possesses the truth; that this persuasion, even if it were accompanied by the most enormous errors, can never be a subject of reproach. That one must always consider as a wise and religious man a person who, adopting the very errors of Atheism, will say he is of good faith. Now, isn't that opening the door to all superstitions, to all fanatical systems, to all the deliriums of the human mind? Doesn't that allow there to be as many religions, forms of divine worship, in the world as there are Inhabitants? Ah! My Very Dear Brethren, do not be led astray on this point. Good faith is worthy of esteem only when it is enlightened and docile. We are ordered to study our Religion, and to believe with simplicity. We have the authority of the Church as guarantee for promises. Let us learn to know it well, and afterward to cast ourselves into its bosom. Then we will be able to count on our good faith, to live in peace, and to reach without perturbation the moment of eternal light.

XIX. What glaring bad faith does not burst forth again in the manner in which the Disbeliever, whom we are refuting, makes the Christian and the Catholic reason! What speeches full of absurdities does he not give to both to make them despicable! He imagines a Dialogue between a Christian, whom he calls *the Inspired man*, and the Disbeliever, whom he qualifies as *Reasoner*; and this is how he makes the first talk: "Reason teaches you that the whole is greater than its part, but I teach you on behalf of God that it is the part which is greater than the whole." To which the

Disbeliever answers: "And who are you to dare tell me that God contradicts Himself, and whom would I prefer to believe—Him who teaches me eternal truths by reason, or you who proclaim an absurdity on His behalf?"[29]

XX. But with what effrontery, My Very Dear Brethren, does one dare to make the Christian speak such language? The God of Reason, we say, is also the God of Revelation. Reason and Revelation are the two organs by which it pleased Him to make Himself understood by men, either to teach them about the truth, or to intimate His orders to them. If one of these two organs were opposed to the other it is certain that God would be in contradiction with himself. But does God contradict himself because he commands belief in incomprehensible truths? You say, oh Impious people, that the Dogmas we consider to be revealed combat the eternal truths; but saying that is not sufficient. If it were possible for you to prove it, you would have done so long ago, and you would have uttered shouts of victory.

XXI. The bad faith of the Author of *Emile* is no less revolting in the language he puts into the mouth of a supposed Catholic: "Our Catholics," he has him say, "make a great to-do about the authority of the Church; but what do they gain by that, if they need as great an apparatus of proofs to establish this authority as other Sects need to establish their doctrine directly? The Church decides that the Church has the right to decide. Is that not an authority based on good proofs?"[30] Hearing this Imposter, who would not believe, My Very Dear Brethren, that the authority of the church is proved only by its own decisions, and that it goes about it in this way: "I decide that I am infallible; therefore I am." A slanderous imputation, My Very Dear Brethren. The constitution of Christianity, the Spirit of the Gospel, even the errors and the weakness of the human mind lead to the demonstration that the Church established by Jesus Christ is an infallible Church. We affirm that since this divine Legislator has always taught the truth, his Church also teaches it always. Thus we prove the authority of the Church, not by the authority of the Church, but by that of Jesus Christ; a method no less precise than the one for which we are reproached is ridiculous and senseless.

XXII. My Very Dear Brethren, the spirit of irreligion did not begin today to be a spirit of independence and of revolt. And how in effect could these audacious men, who refuse to submit to the authority of God himself, respect that of Kings who are the images of God, or that of the Magistrates, who are the images of Kings? "Be aware," says the author of *Emile* to his student, "that it (the human species) is composed essentially of a collection of peoples; that if all the Kings ... were taken away, their absence would hardly be noticeable; and that things would not be any the worse." He says later, "The multitude will always be sacrificed to the few, and the public interest to particular interest. Those specious names, justice and order, will always serve as instruments of violence and as arms of iniquity. From this it follows," he continues, "that the distinguished orders who claim they are useful to the others are actually useful only to themselves at the expense of their subordinates; it is on this basis that one ought to judge the consideration which is due them according to justice and reason."[31] Thus, then, My Very Dear Brethren, impiety dares to criticize the intentions of the one *through whom Kings reign*[32]; thus it takes pleasure in poisoning the sources of public felicity, by inspiring maxims that tend only to produce anarchy and all the calamities that follow from it. But what does Religion say to you? *Fear God, respect the King . . .*[33] *Let every man submit to superior Powers: for there is no Power that does not come from God: and it is He who has established all those that are in the world. Whoever, then, resists the Powers resists the order of God, and those who resist it draw damnation upon themselves.*[34]

XXIII. Yes, My Very Dear Brethren, in everything that belongs to the civil order you must obey the Prince and those who exercise his authority, as God himself. Only the interests of the supreme Being can set limits to your submission; and if someone wished to punish you for your fidelity to his orders, you should still suffer with patience and without murmur. The Neros, the Domitians themselves, who preferred to be the scourges of the Earth rather than fathers of their peoples, were accountable only to God for the abuse of their power. *Christians*, says Saint Augustine, *obeyed them within time because of the God of Eternity.*[35]

XXIV. We have exposed before you, My Very Dear Brethren, only a portion of the impieties contained in this Treatise *On Education*, a Work equally worthy of the Anathemas of the Church and of the severity of the Laws. And what more is needed to inspire in you a just horror for it? Woe to you, woe to society, if your children were brought up in accordance with the principles of the Author of *Emile*! Just as there is nothing but Religion that has taught us to know man, his greatness, his misery, his future destiny, it also belongs to it alone to form his reason, to perfect his morals, to procure for him a solid happiness in this life and in the other. We know, My Very Dear Brethren, how delicate and laborious a truly Christian education is: how much enlightenment and prudence does it not demand! What an admirable mixture of gentleness and firmness! What sagacity in order to proportion itself to the difference of conditions, ages, temperaments, and characters without ever deviating in anything from the rules of duty! What zeal and what patience in order to make the precious seed of innocence bear fruit in young hearts, in order to uproot from it, as much as it is possible, those vicious inclinations that are the sad effects of our hereditary corruption! in a word, in order to teach them, following the Morality of Saint Paul, *to live in this world with temperance, according to justice and with piety, while waiting for the beatitude for which we hope!*[36] We say then to all those who are charged with the care, equally arduous and honorable, of bringing up the youth: Plant and water, in the firm hope that the Lord—seconding your labor—will grant growth; *insist seasonably and unseasonably,* according to the advice of the same Apostle, *employ reproof, exhortation, severe words, without losing patience and without ceasing to teach.*[37] Above all, join example to instruction: instruction without example is a disgrace for the one who gives it and a subject of scandal for the one who receives it. Let the pious and charitable Tobias be your model: *Carefully recommend to your children to perform acts of justice and charity, to be mindful of God, and to bless him at all times in truth and with all their strength,*[38] and your posterity, like that of this holy Patriarch, *will be beloved of God and of men.*[39]

XXV. But at what age should education begin? With the first gleams of intelligence: and these gleams are sometimes premature. *Form the child at the beginning of his way,* says the wise man; *even in his old age he will not swerve from it.*[40] Such is in fact the ordinary course of human life: in the midst of the delirium of the passions and in the bosom of libertinism, the principles of a Christian education are a light that flares up by intervals, in order to uncover for the sinner all the horror of the abyss into which he has plunged, and to show him the exits from it. How many, once again, who, after the lapses of a licentious youth, have returned, from the impression of that light, to the paths of wisdom, and have honored, by means of belated but sincere virtues, humanity, the Fatherland, and Religion.

XXVI. In concluding, it remains for us, My Very Dear Brethren, to entreat you, in the name of the bowels of the mercy of God, to fasten yourselves inviolably to this holy Religion in which you have the happiness of being brought up; to sustain yourselves against the dissolution of an insane Philosophy, which proposes nothing less for itself than to overrun the legacy of Jesus Christ; to render his promises vain, and to put him in the rank of those Founders of Religion whose frivolous or pernicious doctrine has proven their imposture. Faith is not despised, abandoned, insulted except by those who do not know it, or whose disorders it impedes. But the gates of Hell will never prevail against it. The Christian and Catholic Church is the beginning of the eternal Empire of Jesus Christ. *Nothing is stronger than she is,* cries out Saint John Damascene; *she is a rock which floods do not overturn; she is a mountain which nothing can destroy.*[41]

XXVII. For these causes, considering the Book that has as its title, *Emile or On Education, by J.-J. Rousseau, citizen of Geneva, at Amsterdam, from Jean Néaulme, Publisher, 1762*; after having sought the advice of a number of people distinguished by their piety and by their knowledge, the holy Name of God invoked, We condemn the said Book as containing an abominable doctrine, suited to overturning natural Law and to destroying the foundations of the Christian Religion; establishing maxims contrary to Evangelical Morality; tending to disturb the peace of States, to stir up Subjects against the authority of their Sovereign; as containing a very great number of propositions respectively false, scandalous, full of hatred against the Church and its Ministers, departing from the respect due to Sacred Scripture and the Tradition of the Church, erroneous, impious, blasphemous, and heretical. In consequence We very expressly forbid all people of our Diocese to read or possess said Book, under penalty of law. And our present Pastoral Letter will be read at the Sermon of the Parish Masses of the Churches of the City, outskirts and Diocese of Paris; published and posted everywhere there will be need.

Given at Paris, in our Archepiscopal Palace, the twentieth day of August one thousand seven hundred and sixty-two.

Signed: *CHRISTOPHE*
Archbishop of Paris,
By Monseigneur,
De la Touche

LETTER TO BEAUMONT

JEAN-JACQUES ROUSSEAU

Citizen of Geneva

To

Christophe de Beaumont

Archbishop of Paris,

Duke of St. Cloud,

Peer of France,

Commander of the Order of the Holy Spirit

Patron of the Sorbonne, etc.

Da veniam si quid liberius dixi, non ad contumeliam tuam, sed ad defensionem meam. Praesumsi enim de gravitate et prudentiâ tua, quia potes considerare quantam mihi respondendi necessitatem imposueris.
Aug. Epis. 238 ad Pascent.[1]

At Amsterdam

By Marc Michel Rey

1763

Why must I have something to say to you, your Grace? What common language can we speak, how can we understand one another, and what is there between you and me?

Yet I must reply to you. You force me to do so yourself. If you had attacked only my Book, I would have let it pass, but you also attack me personally. And the more authority you have among men, the less I am permitted to remain silent when you want to dishonor me.

As I begin this Letter, I cannot help but reflect on the peculiarities of my destiny. Some of them have happened only to me.

I was born with some talent. Such was the judgment of the public. Yet I spent my youth in happy obscurity, from which I did not seek to emerge. If I had tried, it would have been peculiar in itself that during all the ardor of the first age, I could not succeed, and that I succeeded only too well after that, when this fire was beginning to diminish. I was approaching my fortieth year, and, rather than a fortune, which I always scorned, and a name, for which I have been made to pay so dearly, I had peace and friends, the only two goods for which my heart hungered. A wretched Academic question, which troubled my mind in spite of myself thrust me into a profession for which I was not made.[2] Unexpected success showed me attractions that seduced me. Throngs of adversaries attacked me without understanding me, with a stupidity that made me ill-tempered, and with a pride that perhaps inspired some in me. I defended myself, and from one dispute to the next, I felt myself engaged in a career almost without giving it any thought. I found I had become an Author, so to speak, at an age when one ceases being one, and a man of Letters out of my very disdain for that estate. From then on I was something in the public realm, but repose and friends disappeared as well. What ills did I not suffer before finding a more stable position and happier attachments! I had to swallow my sorrows. A little renown had to take the place of everything else for me. While that may be a compensation for those who are always far from themselves, it never was one for me.

If I had counted on such a frivolous good for even a moment, how quickly I would have been disabused! What perpetual inconsistency was I not subjected to in the public's judgments about me! I was too remote from them. Judging me only by the caprice or interest of those who lead them, they hardly saw me in the same way on two consecutive days. One moment I was a blackguard, the next an angel of light. In the same year I saw myself praised, feted, sought after even at Court; then insulted, threatened, detested, cursed. In the evenings, they waited to murder me in the street; in the mornings, they informed me about a *lettre de cachet*.[3] Good and evil flowed from approximately the same source. Nonsense prompted all of it.

I have written on various subjects, but always with the same principles: always the same morality, the same belief, the same maxims, and if you will the same opinions. Yet contradictory judgments about my books, or rather about the Author of my books, have been made, because I have been judged by the subjects I have treated much more than by my sentiments. After my first *Discourse*, I was a man of paradoxes, who made a game of proving what he did not think.[4] After my *Letter on French Music*, I was the avowed enemy of the nation. Little more was needed for me to be called a conspirator. One might have concluded that the fate of the Monarchy was linked to the glory of the Opera. After my *Discourse on Inequality*, I was an atheist and a misanthrope. After the *Letter to d'Alembert*, I was the defender of Christian morality. After *Heloise* I was tender and mawkish. Now I am impious. Soon perhaps I will be devout.

Thus the foolish public vacillates about me, knowing as little why it detests me as why it liked me before. As for myself, I have always remained the same: more ardent than enlightened in my quests, but sincere in everything, even against myself; simple and good, but sensitive and weak, often doing evil and always loving the good; bound by friendship, never by things, and clinging more to my sentiments than to my interests; demanding nothing of men and not wishing to depend on them, yielding no more to their prejudices[5] than to their wills, and keeping my own as free as my reason; fearing God without being afraid of hell, reasoning about Religion without libertinism, liking neither impiety nor fanaticism; but hating intolerant people even more than freethinkers; wanting to hide my ways of thinking from no one, without pretense, without artifice in all things, telling my faults to my friends, my sentiments to all the world, and, to the public, the truths that concern it without flattery and without rancor, and caring as little about angering as about pleasing it. Such are my crimes, and such are my virtues.

At last, weary of an intoxicating vapor that inflates without satisfying, worn out by the annoyances of idle people burdened with too much of their own time and prodigal with mine, sighing for the repose so dear to my heart and so necessary for my ills, I had joyfully put down my pen. Satisfied to have taken it up only for the good of my fellows, as a reward for my zeal I asked them only to let me die in peace in my retreat, and to do me no harm there. I was mistaken. Some bailiffs came to inform me of it, and it is at that period, when I hoped that my life's troubles were about to end, that my greatest misfortunes began.[6] There are already some peculiarities in all that. It is only the beginning. I ask your forgiveness, your Grace, for taxing your patience. But before beginning the discussions I have to have with you, I must talk about my current situation and the causes that reduced me to it.

A Genevan has a Book printed in Holland, and by decree of the Parlement of Paris this Book is burned without regard for the Sovereign whose authorization it bears.[7] A Protestant poses objections to the Roman Church in a Protestant country, and a warrant is issued against him by the Parlement of Paris. A Republican states objections against the monarchic State in a Republic, and a warrant is issued against him by the Parlement of Paris. The Parlement of Paris must have strange ideas about its dominion, and believe itself the legitimate judge of the human race.

This same Parlement that is always so careful about the order of procedures in dealing with the French neglects them all as soon as a poor Foreigner is involved. Without knowing whether this Foreigner is indeed the Author of the Book bearing his name, whether he acknowledges it as his own, whether it is he who had it printed; without regard for his sorry state, without pity for the ills he suffers, they begin by issuing a warrant for his arrest. They would have torn him from his bed to drag him into the same prisons where scoundrels rot. They would have burned him at the stake, perhaps even without a hearing, for who knows whether they would have followed more normal procedures after such violent beginnings, of which there is scarcely another example to be found, even in the countries of the Inquisition? Thus it is for me alone that such a wise tribunal forgets its wisdom. It is against me alone, who believed it loved me, that this people who boasts of its gentleness arms itself with the strangest barbarity. This is how it justifies the preference I gave it over so many other sanctuaries I could have chosen for the same reward! I do not know how this fits with international law,[8] but I know very well that, with such procedures, every man's freedom and perhaps his life is at the mercy of the first Printer.[9]

The Citizen of Geneva owes nothing to unjust and incompetent Magistrates who, on the basis of a slanderous indictment, do not summon him, but issue a warrant against him. Not being summoned to appear, he is under no obligation to do so. Only force is used against him, and he evades it. He shakes the dust off his shoes and leaves this hospitable land where they hasten to oppress the weak and where they put the foreigner in irons before they give him a hearing, before they know whether the act of which they accuse him is punishable, before they know whether he committed it.

He abandons his beloved solitude with a sigh. He has only one possession, but it is a precious one: friends. He flees them. Weak as he is, he endures a long trip. He arrives and believes he draws breath in a land of freedom. He draws near his Fatherland, the Fatherland about which he has boasted so much, which he has cherished and honored. The hope of being welcomed there consoles him for his disgrace. . . . What am I about to say? My heart sinks, my hand trembles, my pen falls. I must be silent and not imitate Ham's crime. Why can I not swallow in secret the most bitter of my sorrows?[10]

And why did all that happen? I do not say for what reason, but on what pretext? They dare accuse me of impiety without thinking that the Book where it is sought is in everyone's hands! What would they not give to be able to suppress this justificatory document and to say that it contains everything they have claimed to find in it! But it will remain, whatever they do. And looking in it for the crimes for which the Author is reproached, posterity will find even in his errors only the wrongs of a friend of virtue.

I will avoid talking about my contemporaries. I do not want to harm anyone. But the Atheist Spinoza peacefully taught his doctrine. His books were published without obstacle; they were retailed publicly. He came to France and was well received. All states were open to him; everywhere he found protection or at least safety. Princes honored him and offered him professorships. He lived and died in tranquillity, and even well respected.[11] Today in the very celebrated century of philosophy, reason, and humanity, for having proposed with circumspection, even with respect and for love of the human race, some doubts founded on the very glory of the supreme Being, the defender of God's cause—dishonored, banished, pursued from State to State, from sanctuary to sanctuary, without regard for his indigence, without pity for his infirmities, with an animosity that no malefactor ever experienced and that would be barbarous even toward a healthy man—is forbidden fire and water almost throughout Europe. He is chased from the heart of forests. It requires all the firmness of an illustrious Protector and all the goodness of an enlightened Prince to leave him in peace in the bosom of the mountains.[12] He would have spent the remainder of his unhappy days in chains, he would perhaps have died by torture if, during the first vertigo that took hold of Governments, he had found himself at the mercy of those who persecuted him.

Having escaped the executioners, he falls into the hands of the Priests.[13] That is not what I affirm to be astounding. But a virtuous man, whose soul is as noble as his birth, an illustrious Archbishop, who ought to reprove their cowardice, authorizes it. He who ought to pity the oppressed is not ashamed to overwhelm one of them at the height of his disgrace. He, a Catholic prelate, issues a Pastoral Letter against a Protestant Author. He climbs into his Pulpit to examine as Judge the particular doctrine of a heretic. And although he indiscriminately condemns anyone who is not of his Church, without allowing the accused person to err in his own way, in a sense he prescribes for him the path he must take to Hell. Immediately, the remainder of his Clergy hurries, strives, relentlessly pursues an enemy it believes is crushed. Small and great, all join in. The most insignificant Prig[14] sets himself up as competent; there is not a fool in a little collar, not a puny, unbeneficed Parish priest who—joyfully affronting the person against whom their Senate and their Bishop are united—does not want the glory of delivering the final kick.

All that, your Grace, constitutes a combination of which I am the only instance, and that is not all. . . . Here, perhaps, is one of the most difficult situations of my life, one in which vengeance and amour-propre are most easily satisfied and least permit a just man to be moderate. Only ten lines and I cover my persecutors with indelible ridicule. If only the public knew two anecdotes without my saying them![15] If only it was acquainted with those who have planned my ruin and what they did to achieve it! By what contemptible insects, by what shadowy means it would see the Powerful being alarmed! What leavening it would see heating up by their rot and putting the Parlement into ferment! For what a laughable cause it would see the States of Europe form a league against the son of a watchmaker! What pleasure I would take in its surprise if I could avoid being the instrument of it!

Until now, my pen—bold in stating the truth, but untarnished by any satire—has never compromised anyone; it has always respected the honor of others, even when defending my own. In setting it down, would I sully it with slander and tinge it with the baseness of my enemies? No, let me leave to them the advantage of delivering their blows in the darkness. For my part, I want to defend myself only openly, and I even want only to defend myself. What the public knows or can know without offending anyone is sufficient for that.

One amazing thing of this type, and one that I can state, is to see the intrepid Christophe de Beaumont—who does not know how to bend to any power nor to make any peace with the Jansenists—without knowing it become their satellite and the instrument of their animosity; to see their most unreconcilable enemy raging against me for having refused to embrace their faction, for not having wanted to take up the pen against the Jesuits, whom I do not like but who have not given me cause for complaint and whom I see oppressed.[16] Deign, your Grace, to glance at the sixth Volume of the first edition of the *New Heloise*. In the note on page 138*[17] you will find the true source of all my misfortunes. I predicted in that note (for I dabble in predictions, too, sometimes) that as soon as the

---

* Page 282 of the new edition constituting Volume VI of the *Works*; note of the Book dealer.

Jansenists were the masters, they would be more intolerant and harsh than their enemies. I did not know that my own story would verify my prediction so well. The thread of this scheme would not be hard to follow for anyone who knows how my Book was denounced.[18] I cannot say more without saying too much, but I could at least inform you by what people you have been led without your suspecting it.[19]

Will people believe that, if my Book had not been denounced in Parlement, you would nonetheless have attacked it? Others could believe or say it, but you whose conscience is incapable of tolerating a lie, you will not say it. My *Discourse on Inequality* circulated throughout your Diocese, and you did not issue a Pastoral Letter. My *Letter to d'Alembert* circulated throughout your diocese and you did not write a Pastoral Letter. The *New Heloise* circulated throughout your diocese and you did not write a Pastoral Letter. Yet all these Books, which you have read, since you judge them, are imbued with the same maxims. The same modes of thought are not more disguised in them. If the subject was not suited to developing them to the same extent, they gain in force what they lose in extent, and the Author's profession of faith is found expressed there with less reserve than that of the Savoyard Vicar. Why then did you say nothing at that time? Was your flock less dear to you, your Grace? Did they read me less? Did they enjoy my books less? Were they less exposed to error? No, but there were no Jesuits to condemn then. Traitors had not yet entangled me in their snares. The fatal note was not known at all, and when it became known the public had already given its approval to the Book; it was too late to raise an uproar. It was preferable to delay, await the right occasion, watch for it, seize it, take advantage of it with the usual rage of the devout. People talked only of chains and the stake. My Book was the Tocsin of Anarchy and the Trumpet of Atheism. The Author was a monster to be stifled; there was astonishment that he had been allowed to live for so long. In that universal rage, you were ashamed to remain silent. You preferred committing an act of cruelty to being accused of lacking zeal, and serving your enemies to enduring their reproaches. That, your Grace, you must acknowledge is the true motive of your Pastoral Letter. And that, it seems to me, is a convergence of facts peculiar enough to call my fate bizarre.

Proprieties of state have long since been substituted for justice. I know there are unfortunate circumstances that force a public man to deal harshly with a good Citizen in spite of himself. Whoever would be moderate among the enraged exposes himself to their rage, and I understand that in an outburst like the one of which I am the victim, it is necessary to howl with the wolves or risk being devoured by them. I do not complain therefore, because you wrote a Pastoral Letter against my Book, but I do complain that you wrote it against my person, with as little decency as truth. I complain that, authorizing with your own language the language you reproach me for having placed in the mouth of the inspired man,[20] you heap insults on me that—without harming my cause—attack my honor, or rather yours. I complain that lightheartedly, without reason, without necessity, without respect at least for my misfortunes, you insult me in a tone so unworthy of your character. And what had I done to you, then, I who always spoke of you with so much esteem; I who admired your unshakable firmness so many times, while deploring, it is true, the use your prejudices had you make of it; I who always honored your morals, who always respected your virtues, and who still respect them today though you have defamed me?

This is how one gets out of difficulties when one wants to quarrel and one is in the wrong. Unable to resolve my objections, you have treated them as crimes. You believed you degraded me by mistreating me, and you were mistaken. Without weakening my reasons, you have interested generous hearts in my misfortunes. You have made sensible people believe that one might not be judging the book well when one judged the Author so poorly.[21]

Your Grace, you have been neither humane nor generous toward me. And not only could you have been so without sparing me any of the things you said against my work, but they would have become more effective in that way. I also admit that I had no right to require these virtues of you, nor any reason to expect them of a Clergyman. Let us see if you were equitable and just at least, for that is a strict duty imposed on all men, and even saints are not excused from it.

You have two aims in your Pastoral Letter: one to censure my Book, the other to discredit my person. I will believe I have answered you well if I prove that everywhere you refuted me you reasoned badly, and that everywhere you insulted me you slandered me. But when one proceeds only with one's proof in hand, when the importance of the subject and the quality of the adversary force one to plod along and to follow all his censures step by step, pages are needed for each word. And whereas a short satire is amusing, a long defense is boring. Yet I must defend myself or remain charged by you with the falsest imputations. I will defend myself, then, but I will defend my honor rather than my book. I am examining not the profession of faith of the Savoyard Vicar, but the Pastoral Letter of the Archbishop of Paris, and it is only the bad things he says about the Editor[22] that force me to talk about the work. I will give what I owe myself because I owe it, but I am not unaware that it is a sorry situation to have to complain about a man more powerful than oneself, and that the justification of an innocent person is very dull reading.

The fundamental principle of all morality about which I have reasoned in all my Writings and developed in this last one with all the clarity of which I was capable, is that man is a naturally good being, loving justice and order; that there is no original perversity in the human heart, and that the first movements of nature are always right. I have shown that the only passion born with man, namely love of self,[23] is a passion in itself indifferent to good and evil; that it becomes good or bad only by accident and depending on the circumstances in which it develops. I have shown that all the vices imputed to the human heart are not natural to it; I have stated the manner in which they are born. I have followed their genealogy, so to speak, and I have shown how, through continuous deterioration of their original goodness, men finally become what they are.

I have also explained what I meant by that original goodness, which does not appear to be deduced from indifference to good and evil, natural to the love of self. Man is not a simple being. He is composed of two substances. While everyone does not agree on that, you and I do, and I have tried to prove it to the others. Once that is proved, the love of self is no longer a simple passion. But it has two principles, namely the intelligent being and the sensitive being, the well-being of which is not the same. The appetite of the senses conduces to the well-being of the body, and the love of order to that of the soul. The latter love, developed and made active, bears the name of conscience. But conscience develops and acts only with man's understanding. It is only through this understanding that he attains a knowledge of order, and it is only when he knows order that his conscience brings him to love it. Conscience is therefore null in the man who has compared nothing and who has not seen his relationships. In that state, man knows only himself. He does not see his well-being as opposed to or consistent with that of anyone. He neither hates nor loves anything. Restricted to physical instinct alone, he is null, he is stupid. That is what I have shown in my *Discourse on Inequality*.

When, by a development whose progress I have shown, men begin to cast their eyes upon their fellows, they also begin to see their relations and the relations between things; to adopt notions of propriety, justice, and order. Moral beauty begins to become palpable to them, and conscience acts. Then they have virtues, and if they also have vices, it is because their interests conflict and their ambition is aroused as their understanding is extended. But as long as there is less opposition of interests than convergence of understanding, men are essentially good. That is the second state.

When all the agitated particular interests finally collide, when love of self put into fermentation changes into amour-propre, when opinion, making the whole universe necessary to each man, makes them all each other's born enemies and determines that none finds his own good except in someone else's ill, then conscience, weaker than the excited passions, is stifled by them, and is no longer in men's mouths except as a word made to deceive each other. Each one then pretends to wish to sacrifice his interests to those of the public, and they are all lying. No one wants the public good except when it agrees with his own. Thus this agreement is the object of the true political thinker[24] who seeks to make people happy and good. But here I am beginning to speak a strange language, as little known to Readers as to you.

That, your Grace, is the third and last stage, beyond which nothing remains to be done; and that is how, man being good, men become wicked. I dedicated my Book to seeking how to go about preventing them from becoming so. I did not affirm that this was absolutely possible in the present order. But I certainly affirmed and still do that there are no other means to succeed to this end than those I have proposed.

Whereupon you say that my plan of education,* *far from agreeing with Christianity, is not even suited to making Citizens or men.* And your sole proof is to oppose me with original sin. Your Grace, there is no other way to be absolved of original sin and its effects than by baptism. From which it would follow, according to you, that only Christians had ever been Citizens or men. Either deny this consequence or agree that you have proved too much.

You draw your proofs from so far back that you force me to seek my replies from afar also. First, it is not at all certain, in my view, that this doctrine of original sin, subject as it is to such terrible difficulties, is contained in the Scriptures either as clearly or as harshly as it has pleased the Rhetorician Augustine[25] and our Theologians to construct it. Is it conceivable that God creates so many innocent and pure souls purposely to join them to guilty bodies, to make them contract moral corruption thereby, and to condemn them all to hell for no other crime than this union that is his work? I will not say whether you clarify (as you boast of doing) the mystery of our heart with this system, but I see that you greatly obscure the justice and the goodness of the supreme Being. If you eliminate one objection, it is to substitute others that are a hundred times stronger.

But at bottom what is this doctrine to the author of *Emile*? Although he believed his book to be useful to the human race, he destined it for Christians, for men cleansed of original sin and its effects, at least with respect to

---

* *Pastoral Letter*, in quarto, page 5; in duodecimo, page x [4 above].

the soul, by the Sacrament established for that. According to this same doctrine, we all recovered the primitive innocence in our infancy, we all emerged from baptism as sound of heart as Adam emerged from the hand of God. We have contracted new impurities you will say. But since we started out by being delivered from them, how did we contract them again? Isn't the blood of Christ powerful enough yet to erase the stain completely, or is it rather an effect of the natural corruption of our flesh, as if God—even independently of original sin—had quite deliberately created us corrupt in order to have the pleasure of punishing us? You attribute to original sin the vices of peoples you admit have been delivered from original sin. Then you blame me for having given another origin to those vices. Is it just to make it a crime for me not to have reasoned as badly as you do?

One might, it is true, tell me that those effects I attribute to baptism* do not appear through any external sign; that Christians are not seen to be any less inclined to evil than infidels. Whereas, according to me, the inborn maliciousness of sin ought to be marked in the latter by palpable differences. With the help of evangelical morality in addition to baptism, all Christians, the argument would continue, ought to be Angels; and the infidels, in addition to their original corruption, yielding to their erroneous forms of worship, ought to be Demons. I conceive that, if pursued, this difficulty could become awkward. For what reply can be given to those who would have me see that, relative to the human race, the effect of redemption earned at such a high price is reduced almost to nothing?

But, your Grace, apart from the fact that I do not believe that good Theology does not provide any expedient for getting out of that difficulty, even if I agreed that baptism does not remedy the corruption of our nature, you still would not have reasoned any more soundly about it. You say we are sinners because of our first father's sin. But why was our first father himself a sinner? Why wouldn't the same reason by which you explain his sin apply to his descendants without original sin, and why must we impute an injustice to God by making ourselves sinners and punishable because of the vice of our birth, while our first father was a sinner

---

* If we were to say, along with Doctor Thomas Burnet,[26] that the corruption and mortality of the human race, in consequence of Adam's sin, was a natural effect of the forbidden fruit, that this food contained poisonous juices that upset the whole animal economy, irritated the passions, weakened the understanding, and carried the principles of vice and death throughout, then it would be necessary to agree that since the nature of the remedy has to relate to that of the illness, baptism ought to act physically on the body of man, give him back the constitution he had in the state of innocence, and if not the immortality that followed from it, at least all the moral effects of the restored animal economy.

and punished like us without that? Original sin explains everything except its own principle, and it is this principle that has to be explained.

You propose that with my principle* *one loses sight of that ray of light that lets us know the mystery of our own heart*. And you do not see that this principle, far more universal, illumines even the fault of the first man,** which yours leaves in obscurity. The only thing you can see is man in the hands of the Devil, while I see how he fell into them. The cause of evil, according to you, is corrupted nature, and this corruption itself is an evil whose cause had to be sought. Man was created good. We both agree on that, I believe. But you say he is wicked because he was wicked. And I show how he was wicked. Which of us, in your opinion, better ascends to the principle?

Yet you continue to exult at your pleasure, as if you had crushed me. You raise as an insoluble objection*** *this striking mixture of greatness and baseness, of zeal for truth and taste for error, of inclination to virtue and penchant to vice* that is found in us. *Astonishing contrast*, you add, *which disconcerts pagan philosophy and leaves it to wander in vain speculations!*

The Theory of man is not a vain speculation when it is founded on nature, proceeds with the support of facts by well-linked consequences, and in leading us to the source of the passions, teaches us to regulate their course. And if you call the Profession of Faith of the Savoyard Vicar pagan philosophy, I am unable to reply to that imputation, because I understand

---

* *Pastoral Letter*, in quarto, page 5; in duodecimo, p. xi [4 above].

** To resist a useless and arbitrary prohibition is a natural inclination, but one that, far from being vicious in itself, conforms with the order of things and the good constitution of man, since he would be incapable of preserving himself if he did not have a very lively love of himself and of the preservation of all his rights just as he has received them from nature. Someone who could do everything would want only what would be useful to him. But a weak Being, whose power is further restrained and limited by the law, loses a part of himself, and demands in his heart what is taken away from him. To impute this to him as a crime would be making it a crime for him to be himself and not someone else. It would be simultaneously wanting him to be and not to be. The order transgressed by Adam thus seems to me less a true prohibition than paternal advice. It is a warning to abstain from a pernicious fruit that brings death. This idea is surely more consistent with the idea one should have of God's goodness and even with the text of Genesis than the idea the Scholars are pleased to prescribe to us. Because, as for the menace of the double death, it has been shown that this term *morte morieris* does not have the emphasis they give it and is merely a hebraic turn of phrase used in other places where this emphasis cannot apply.

There is, moreover, such a natural motive of indulgence and commiseration in the tempter's ruse and in the woman's seduction that, considering Adam's sin in all its circumstances, it can be found to be only the slightest of faults. Yet according to them, what a fearful punishment! It is even impossible to conceive of a more terrible one. For what other castigation could Adam have sustained for the greatest crimes other than being condemned to death, himself and all his race, in this world and to spend eternity in the other one consumed by the fires of hell? Is that the penalty imposed by the God of mercy on a poor wretch for letting himself be fooled? How I hate the disheartening doctrine of our harsh Theologians! If I were tempted for a moment to acknowledge it, that is when I would believe I were blaspheming.

*** *Pastoral Letter*, in quarto, page 6; in duodecimo, page xi [4–5 above].

nothing about it.* But I find it amusing that you borrow almost his own terms** to say that he does not explain what he has explained best.

Allow me, your Grace, to place before your eyes again the conclusion you draw from such a well-discussed objection, and following that, the whole tirade relating to it.

****Man feels himself drawn by a fatal tendency, and how would he resist it if his childhood were not directed by teachers full of virtue, wisdom, vigilance, and if—during the entire course of his life—he himself, under the protection and with the grace of his God, did not make powerful and continual efforts?*

Which is to say: *We see that men are wicked even though constantly tyrannized since childhood. Therefore if they were not tyrannized from that time on, how could they be made wise, since even tyrannizing them constantly, it is impossible to make them so?*

Our reasonings about education may become clearer when they are applied to another subject.

Suppose, your Grace, that someone were to come and make this speech to men:

"You torment yourselves a great deal to seek equitable Governments and to give yourselves good laws. I am going to prove to you first of all that it is your very Governments that cause the evils you claim to remedy through them. I shall prove, in addition, that it is impossible for you ever to have either good laws or equitable Governments. And further I am going to show you the real way to prevent, without Governments and without Laws, all those evils about which you complain."

Let us suppose that after this he explains his system and proposes his alleged means. I am not examining whether this system would be solid and this means practicable. If it were not, perhaps people would be satisfied to lock the Author up with the madmen, and thereby do him justice. But if unfortunately it were, that would be far worse, and you can conceive, your Grace, or others will conceive for you, that there would not be enough stakes and racks to punish the wretch for having been right. That is not what is at issue here.

Whatever the fate of this man might be, it is certain that a deluge of writings would burst down on what he wrote. There would not be a single Scribbler who, to court the Powerful, and filled with pride at being published under royal authorization, would not hurl his pamphlet and his insults at him and boast of having reduced to silence a person who would

---

* Unless it relates to the accusation Monsieur de Beaumont makes against me later of having acknowledged several Gods.
** *Emile*, vol. III, pages 68 and 69, first edition [Bloom, 278–279].
*** *Pastoral Letter*, in quarto, page 6; in duodecimo, page xi [5 above].

not have deigned to reply or who would have been prevented from talking. But that again is not what is at issue here.

Let us suppose, finally, that a serious man, one who had an interest in the matter, believed that he, too, ought to do as the others did, and among many declamations and insults takes it upon himself to argue thus. *What, wretch! You wish to annihilate Governments and Laws? But Governments and Laws are the only brake on vice, and still have much trouble controlling it. What would it be like, great God, if we no longer had them? You take away the scaffolds and racks. You want to establish public brigandage. You are an abominable man.*[27]

If this poor man dared to speak, he would doubtless say: "Most excellent Sir, your Grace[28] is begging the question. I do not say that vice must not be curbed, but rather that it is better to prevent it from being born. I want to provide for the inadequacy of the Laws, and you cite the inadequacy of the Laws. You accuse me of establishing abuses because, instead of curing them, I prefer to see them prevented. What! If there were a way always to live in good health, must it be proscribed for fear of making the doctors idle? Your Excellency wants to see gallows and racks forever, whereas I would like to see no more evildoers. With all due respect, I do not believe I am an abominable man."

Alas, My Very Dear Brethren, despite the healthiest and most virtuous principles of education, despite the most magnificent promises of Religion and the most terrible threats, the follies of youth are still only too frequent, too manifold.[29] I proved that this education, which you call the healthiest, was the most senseless; that this education, which you call the most virtuous, was giving children all their vices. I proved that the entire glory of paradise tempted them less than a lump of sugar, and that they were far more afraid of being bored during Vespers than of burning in hell. I proved that the follies of youth, which people complain of being unable to repress by these means, were their product. *Left to itself, into what errors, what excesses would youth not throw itself.* Youth never goes astray on its own. All its errors come from being badly guided. Comrades and mistresses complete what has been started by Priests and Preceptors. I proved that. *It is a torrent that overflows despite the powerful dikes built to contain it. What would happen, then, if no obstacle stopped its flow and broke its force?* I could say: *it is a torrent that topples your impotent dikes and breaks everything. Broaden its bed and allow it to run without obstacle. It will never do harm.* But with such a serious subject, I am ashamed to use these schoolbook figures of speech, which everyone applies according to his whim and which prove nothing for either side.

Moreover, although according to you the follies of youth are still too frequent, too manifold, because of man's inclination toward evil, it appears that all things considered you are not too discontent with youth, that you rather take pleasure in the healthy and virtuous education currently given to it by your teachers full of virtues, wisdom, and vigilance; that, according to you, it would lose much in being raised in another manner, and that at bottom you do not think as ill of the present age—*the dregs of the ages*—as you affect to state at the beginning of your Pastoral Letter.

I agree it is superfluous to seek new plans of Education when one is so satisfied with the one that exists. But agree too, your Grace, that you are not very demanding in this matter. If you had been as accommodating in matters of doctrine, your Diocese would have been agitated by fewer disturbances. The storm you stirred up would not have fallen on the Jesuits. I would not have been crushed by association. You would have remained more tranquil, and I would have too.

You admit that, in order to reform the world as much as the weakness and, you claim, corruption of our nature permit, it would suffice to observe—under the direction and influence of grace—the first glimmers of human reason, grasp them with care, and direct them toward the path the leads to the truth.* *In that way*, you continue, *those minds, still exempt from prejudices, would always be on guard against error; those hearts, still exempt from the great passions, would acquire impressions of all the virtues*. We are in agreement on this point then, for I said nothing different. I did not add, I agree, that children had to be raised by Priests. I did not even think that was necessary to make Citizens and men out of them. And that error, if it is one, common to so many Catholics, is not such a great crime for a Protestant. I will not examine whether in your country the Priests themselves are considered such good Citizens. But since the education of the present generation is their handiwork, it is between you on one hand and your old Pastoral Letters on the other to decide whether their spiritual milk has truly benefited it, whether it has made such great saints from it,** *true adorers of God*,[30] and such great men, *worthy of being the support and ornament of the fatherland*. I can add one observation that ought to strike all good Frenchmen, and yourself as one. It is that, of the many Kings your Nation has had, the best is the only one who was not brought up by Priests.[31]

But what does all that matter, since I did not exclude them. Let them bring up the young people, if they are capable of doing so. I am not opposed to it. And what you say about that*** in no way works against my Book. Would you claim that my plan was bad merely because it can suit others besides the Clergy?

---

* *Pastoral Letter*, in quarto, page 5; in duodecimo, page x [4 above].
** Ibid.
*** Ibid.

If man is good by his nature, as I believe I have demonstrated, it follows that he remains so as long as nothing foreign to himself spoils him. And if men are wicked, as they have gone to the trouble of teaching me, it follows that their wickedness comes from elsewhere. Close the entrance to vice, then, and the human heart will always be good. On this principle, I establish negative education as the best or rather as the only good one. I show how all positive education, no matter how it is pursued, follows a path contrary to its goal. And I show how one tends to the same goal and how one reaches it by the route I have sketched.

What I call positive education tends to form the mind before maturity, and to give the child knowledge of the duties of the man. What I call negative education tends to perfect the organs, the instruments of our knowledge, before giving us this knowledge, and prepares for reason through the exercise of the senses. Negative education is far from idle. It does not produce virtues, but it prevents vices. It does not teach the truth, but it protects from error. It prepares the child for everything that can lead him to the true when he is capable of understanding it, and to the good when he is capable of loving it.

This process displeases and shocks you; it is easy to see why. You begin by slandering the intentions of the person who proposes it. According to you, *this idleness of the soul seemed necessary to me to prepare it for the errors I wanted to inculcate in it.* However it is not really clear what error someone wants to convey to his pupil when he teaches him nothing with more care than to feel his ignorance and to know that he knows nothing. You agree that judgment has its stages and forms only by degrees. *But does it follow,** you add, *that at age ten a child does not know the difference between good and evil, that he confuses wisdom with folly, goodness with barbarity, virtue with vice?*³² All that does follow no doubt, if at that age judgment has not developed. *What,* you continue, *he will not feel that obeying his father is a good, and that disobeying him is an evil?* Far from it. I maintain, to the contrary, that when he leaves his play to go study his lesson, he will feel that to obey his father is evil; and that to disobey him is good when he steals some forbidden fruit. He will also feel, I agree, that it is evil to be punished and good to be rewarded. And it is in balancing these contradictory goods and evils that his childish prudence is regulated. I believe I demonstrated this a thousand times in my first two volumes, and especially in the dialogue between master and child about what is evil.** As for you, your Grace, you refute my two volumes in two lines,

---

* *Pastoral Letter*, quarto, page 7; in duodecimo, page xiv [6 above].
** *Emile*, vol. I, page 189 [Bloom, 90].

and here they are*: *To claim that, My Very Dear Brethren, is to slander human nature, by ascribing to it stupidity it does not have.* There could be no more cutting refutation nor one conceived in fewer words. But this ignorance, which you are pleased to call stupidity, is constantly found in every mind constrained by imperfect organs or that has not been cultivated. It is easily observed and palpable to everyone. Attributing this ignorance to human nature is not slandering it then, and it is you who has slandered it by imputing to it a malignity it does not have.

You say further**: *Isn't wanting to teach man wisdom only at the time when he is dominated by the fire of the nascent passions to present it to him with the design that he will reject it?* Right at the outset you are good enough to ascribe to me this intention, which assuredly no one other than you will find in my Book. I showed, first, that a person who is brought up as I want will not be dominated by the passions at the time you say. I showed further how the lessons of wisdom could delay the development of those very passions. It is the bad effects of your education that you impute to mine, and you raise in objection to me the defects I teach you to prevent. I protected my pupil's heart from the passions until adolescence, and when they are ready to be born, I delay their progress further by efforts suited to curb them. Earlier, the lessons of wisdom signify nothing for the child, who is incapable of taking an interest in them and understanding them. Later, they no longer make an impression on a heart already abandoned to the passions. It is only at the moment I have chosen that they are useful, whether to arm him or to distract him. In either case, it is of equal importance for the young man to attend to them at that time.

You say***: *In order to find young people more docile for the lessons he prepares for them, this Author wants them to be devoid of any principle of Religion.* The reason for this is simple. It is that I want them to have a Religion, and I do not want to teach them anything whose truth their judgment is incapable of feeling. But your Grace, if I said: *In order to find young people more docile for the lessons being prepared for them, great care is taken to work with them before the age of reason*, would I be reasoning worse than you do, and would that be a very favorable prejudice toward what you teach children? According to you, I choose the age of reason to inculcate error, whereas you anticipate that age to teach the truth. You hurry to instruct the child before he can distinguish between true and false, and I wait to deceive him until he is capable of knowing it. Is this judgment natural, and which of

---

* *Pastoral Letter*, in quarto, page 7; in duodecimo, page xiv [6 above].
** *Pastoral Letter*, in quarto, page 9; in duodecimo, page xvii [7 above].
*** *Pastoral Letter*, in quarto, page 7; in duodecimo, page xiv [6 above].

the two appears to seek to seduce: the one who wants to speak only to men or the one who addresses himself to children?³³

You censure me for having said and shown that every child who believes in God is an idolater or an anthropomorphite, and you combat this by saying* that neither one nor the other can be assumed in a child who has received a Christian education. That is what is in question. The proof remains to be seen. Mine is that the most Christian education could not give the child understanding he does not have, nor detach his ideas from material beings, above which so many men can't raise their own. Moreover, I appeal to experience: I entreat each reader to consult his memory and to recall whether, when he believed in God as a child, he did not always form some image of him. When you say to him that *the divinity is nothing that can be perceived by the senses*,³⁴ either his troubled mind understands nothing or it understands that the divinity is nothing. When you speak to him about *an infinite intelligence*, he does not know what *intelligence* is, and he knows even less what *infinite* is. But you will make him repeat after you the words it pleases you to say to him. You will even make him add, if necessary, that he understands them; because that costs almost nothing, and he prefers saying he understands them to being scolded or punished. All the ancients, without excepting the Jews, represented God in a corporeal way, and how many Christians, especially Catholics, still do so today? If your children talk like men, it is because men are still children. That is why heaped up mysteries no longer pain anyone. Their terms are just as easy to pronounce as others. One of the conveniences of modern Christianity is to have made for itself a certain jargon of words without ideas, which satisfy everything except reason.³⁵

By examining the intelligence that leads to the knowledge of God, I find it is not reasonable to believe that this knowledge** is *always necessary for salvation*. I cite as examples madmen, children, and I put in the same class men whose minds have not acquired enough enlightenment to understand the existence of God. About this you say,*** *Let us not be surprised that the Author of Emile postpones the knowledge of God's existence to such a distant time. He does not believe it is necessary for salvation.* In order to make my proposition harsher, you begin by charitably suppressing the word *always*, which not only modifies it, but gives it another meaning, because according to my sentence this knowledge is ordinarily necessary for salvation, whereas it would never be so according to the phrase you attribute to me. After this little falsification, you continue as follows.

* *Pastoral Letter*, in quarto, page 7; in duodecimo, page xiv [6 above].
** *Emile*, vol. II, pages 352–353 [Bloom, 258].
*** *Pastoral Letter*, in quarto, page 9; in duodecimo, page xviii [8 above].

"It is clear," *he says through the organ of a chimerical character,* "it is clear that a man who has come to old age without believing in God, will not for that be deprived of his presence in the other" (you omitted the word *life*). If his blindness has not been voluntary, and I say that it is not always voluntary."

Before I transcribe your comment here, allow me to state mine. It is that this supposedly chimerical character is myself and not the Vicar. That this passage which you believed to be in the profession of faith is not, but in the body of the Book. Your Grace, you read very superficially and you cite very negligently the Writings you stigmatize so harshly. I find that a man in office who censures ought to examine his judgments more carefully. Now I return to your text.

Note, My Very Dear Brethren, that the issue here is not a man who would be deprived of the use of his reason, but solely of someone whose reason would not be aided by instruction. You affirm next* that *such a claim is supremely absurd. Saint Paul guarantees that among the pagan Philosophers, several arrived at knowledge of the true God through the strength of reason alone*[36]; and then you transcribe his passage about this.

Your Grace, it is often a small evil not to understand an Author one reads, but it is a great one when one is refuting him, and a very great one when one defames him. Now, you did not understand the passage of my Book that you attack here, just as you did not understand many others. The Reader will judge whether the fault is mine or yours when I have placed the whole passage before his eyes.

"We" (the Protestants) "hold that no child who dies before the age of reason will be deprived of eternal happiness. The Catholics believe the same thing of all children who have been baptized, even if they have never heard of God. There are therefore cases in which one can be saved without believing in God, and these cases have their place when the human mind is incapable—as in childhood or in madness—of the operations necessary to recognize the divinity. The whole difference I see here between you and me is that you claim that children have this capacity at seven, and I do not accord it to them even at fifteen. Whether I am wrong or right, it is a question here not of an article of faith but of a simple observation of natural history.

"By the same principle it is clear that some man who has come to old age without believing in God will not for that be deprived of his presence in the other life if his blindness was not voluntary, and I say that it is not always voluntary. You agree in the case of madmen whom an illness

---

* *Pastoral Letter*, in quarto, page 10; in duodecimo, page xviii [8 above].

deprives of their spiritual faculties but not of their quality of being men nor, consequently, of their right to the benefits of their creator. Why, therefore, do you not also agree in the case of those who would have been sequestered from all society from their childhood and would have led an absolutely savage life, deprived of the enlightenment which is acquired only in commerce with men? For it is a demonstrated impossibility that such a savage could ever raise his reflections up to the knowledge of the true God. Reason tells us that a man can be punished only for the mistakes of his will, and that an invincible ignorance could not be imputed to crime. From this it follows that before the bar of eternal justice every man who would believe if he had the necessary enlightenment is reputed to believe, and that the only unbelievers who will be punished are those whose heart closes itself to the truth." *Emile*, vol. II, page 352 and following [Bloom, 258–259].

That is my entire passage, about which your error leaps to the eyes. It consists in your having understood or making it be understood that according to me it is necessary to have been taught the existence of God to believe in it. My thought is quite different. I say that one must have an understanding developed and a mind cultivated to a certain point to be capable of comprehending the proofs of the existence of God, and above all to find them oneself without ever having heard of them. I am talking about barbarous or savage men; you allege that I am talking about philosophers. I say that it is necessary to have acquired some philosophy to raise oneself up to notions of the true God. You cite Saint Paul who acknowledges that a few pagan Philosophers raised themselves up to notions of the true God. I say that some crude man may not always be capable of formulating a just idea of the divinity on his own. You say that educated men are capable of forming a just idea of the divinity. And on this proof alone, my opinion appears *supremely absurd* to you. What! Because a Doctor of law should know the laws of his country, is it absurd to assume that a child who does not know how to read may be ignorant of them?

When an Author does not wish to repeat himself incessantly and has once clearly established his sentiment on a matter, he is not bound always to offer the same proofs when reasoning about the same sentiment. His Writings then explain each other, and the latest, when he is methodical, always presuppose the earliest. That is what I have always tried to do, and have done, above all on this occasion.

You suppose, as do those who deal with these matters, that man bears his reason fully formed with him, and that it is only a matter of putting it to work. Now that is not true; for one of man's acquisitions, and even one of the slowest, is reason. Man learns to see with the eyes of the mind as well as with the eyes of the body. But the former apprenticeship is far longer than the latter, because since the relations between intellectual objects are not measurable like extension, they are discovered only by estimation, and our first needs, our physical needs, do not make the examination of these same objects as interesting to us. We must learn to see two objects simultaneously. We must learn to compare them. We must learn to compare large numbers of objects, go back gradually to their causes, and follow them in their effects. We must have combined an infinity of relationships to acquire ideas of suitability, proportion, harmony, and order. That man who—deprived of the help of his fellows and constantly busy providing for his needs—is reduced to the sole progression of his own ideas in everything, makes a very slow progress in that direction. He grows old and dies before he has left the infancy of reason. Can you believe in good faith that out of a million men raised in that manner, there would be a single one who came to think of God?[37]

The order of the Universe, admirable as it is, does not strike all eyes equally. The people pay little attention to it, lacking the knowledge that makes this order palpable and not having learned to reflect on what they perceive. It is neither obduracy nor ill will. It is ignorance, numbness of the mind. The slightest meditation tires those people, just as the slightest manual work tires a studier. They have heard tell of the works of God and the marvels of nature. They repeat the same words without attaching the same ideas to them, and they are little moved by everything that can raise the wise man up to his Creator. Now if among us the people, within reach of so many teachings, are still so stupid, what of those poor people who are abandoned to themselves from childhood, and who have never learned anything from others? Do you believe that a Bantu or a Lapp philosophizes much about the working of the world and the generation of things? Yet the Lapps and Bantus, living in bodies of Nations, have multitudes of acquired and communicated ideas, with the help of which they acquire some crude notions of a divinity. They have their catechism, of a sort. But the savage man, wandering alone in the woods, has none whatever. This man does not exist, you will say. So be it. But he may exist in assumption. Some men certainly do exist who never had a philosophic discussion in their life, and whose entire time is consumed in seeking their food, devouring it, and sleeping. What shall we do with those men, Eskimos, for example? Shall we make Theologians out of them?

My sentiment, therefore, is that the mind of man—without progress, without instruction, without culture, and just as it comes from the hands of nature—is not capable by itself of raising itself up to sublime notions of the divinity; but that these notions present themselves to us in the proportion that our minds are cultivated; that in the eyes of every man who has thought, who has reflected, God manifests himself in his works; that he reveals himself to enlightened people in the spectacle of nature; that when our eyes are open, we must shut them in order not to see him there; that every atheistic philosopher is a reasoner in bad faith or is blinded by his pride; but also that any stupid and crude man, although simple and true, any mind without error and without vice, is capable — through involuntary ignorance — of not ascending to the Author of his being and not conceiving what God is, without having this ignorance make him punishable for a fault to which his heart did not consent. The latter is not enlightened; the former refuses to be. That seems to me quite different.

Apply your passage from Saint Paul to this sentiment and you will see that rather than opposing it, it favors it. You will see that this passage applies solely to those supposed wise men for whom *what may be known of God has been manifested*, to whom *the consideration of things that have been made since the creation of the world has made visible what is invisible in God*, but who *not having glorified him and given him thanks, are lost in the vanity of their reasoning*, and thus, remaining without an excuse, *calling themselves wise, have become mad*.[38] Since the reason the Apostle reproaches the philosophers for not having glorified the true God is not applicable to my assumption, it is the basis for an induction entirely in my favor. It confirms what I myself said, that any* *philosopher who does not believe is wrong, because he uses badly the reason he has cultivated and because he is in a position to understand the truth he rejects*.[39] It shows, finally, by the passage itself, that you have not understood me. And when you impute to me having said what I neither said nor thought — namely that people believe in God only on someone else's authority** — you are so wrong that, on the contrary, I only distinguished between the cases when we can know God by ourselves and those when we can do so only with the help of others.

Besides, even if your criticism were correct, even if you had solidly refuted my opinion, it would not follow from that alone that it was supremely absurd, as it pleases you to qualify it. Someone can be wrong without falling into extravagance, and not every error is an absurdity. My respect for you will make me less lavish with epithets, and it will not be my fault if the Reader chooses to apply them.

Still taking measures to censure without understanding, you shift from one serious and false imputation to another that is even more so, and after

* *Emile*, vol. II, page 350 [Bloom, 258].
** M. de Beaumont does not say precisely that. But it is the only reasonable meaning that can be given to his text supported by the passage from Saint Paul. And I can reply only to what I understand. (See his *Pastoral Letter*, in quarto, page 10; in duodecimo, page xviii [8 above].)

unjustly accusing me of having denied the evidence for the divinity, you accuse me even more unjustly of calling into question unity. You do even more. You take the trouble to discuss this, contrary to your usual process, and the only place in your Pastoral Letter where you are right is where you refute an extravagance I did not say.

Here is the passage you attack, or rather your passage when you cite mine, for the Reader must see me in your hands.

"I know,"* *he makes the assumed character who serves him as mouthpiece say*, "I know that the world is governed by a powerful and wise will. I see it, or rather, I sense it; and that is something important for me to know. But is this same world eternal or created? Is there a single principle of things? Or, are there two, or many of them, and what is their nature? I know nothing about all this, and what does it matter to me. . . .** I renounce idle questions which may disturb my amour-propre but are useless for my conduct and are beyond my reason."[40]

I observe in passing that this is the second time you refer to the Savoyard as a chimerical or assumed character. Tell me how you learned that, I beg of you. I affirmed what I knew; you deny what you do not know. Which of us is reckless? It is known, I agree, that few Priests believe in God; but it has not yet been proved that there are none at all. I return to your text.

*What*** *does this reckless Author want to say then? . . . the unity of God appears to him an idle question and beyond his reason, as though the multiplicity of Gods were not the greatest of absurdities.* "The plurality of Gods," Tertullian *states forcefully*, "is a nullifying of God"; *to acknowledge a God is to acknowledge a supreme and independent Being, to which all other Beings are subordinate.**** He implies then that there are several Gods.*

But who is saying there are several Gods? Ah, your Grace! How you wish I had said such foolish things. You would certainly not have gone to the trouble of issuing a Pastoral Letter against me.

I know neither why nor how what is, is, and many others who pride themselves on saying they do, know nothing more about it than I. But I see there is only one first moving cause, because everything palpably concurs toward the same ends. I therefore recognize a unique and supreme

* *Pastoral Letter*, in quarto, page 10; in duodecimo, page xix [8 above].

** These dots indicate an omission of two lines moderating the passage that M. de Beaumont did not want to transcribe. See *Emile*, vol. III, page 61 [Bloom, 276–277].

*** *Pastoral Letter*, in quarto, page 11; in duodecimo, page xx [9 above].

**** Tertullian commits a sophism here that was very common to the Church Fathers. He defines the word *God* according to the Christians, and then accuses the pagans of a contradiction because contrary to his definition they acknowledge several Gods. It would not be worth the trouble of imputing to me an error I did not commit solely in order to cite a sophism of Tertullian so inappropriately.

will that directs everything, and a unique and supreme power that executes everything. I attribute this power and this will to the same Being, because of their perfect harmony, which is conceived better in one than in two, and because beings must not be multiplied without reason. For even the evil that we see is not an absolute evil, and far from directly combatting the good, it contributes along with it to universal harmony.

But that by which things are is clearly separable into two ideas, namely the thing that makes and the thing that is made. Even these two ideas are not united in the same being without some effort at understanding, and one can hardly conceive a thing which acts without assuming another upon which it acts. Moreover, it is certain that we have an idea of two separate substances, namely mind and matter, what thinks and what is extended. And these two ideas can very well be conceived one without the other.

There are, therefore, two ways to conceive the origin of things; namely, either as residing in two separate causes—one alive and the other dead, one mover and the other moved, one active and the other passive, one efficient and the other instrumental; or residing in a single cause that derives from itself alone everything that is and everything that is made.[41] Neither of these two sentiments, debated by metaphysicians for so many centuries, has thereby become more believable to human reason, and if the eternal and necessary existence of matter has its difficulties for us, its creation has no fewer of them. For so many men and philosophers, who in all times have meditated on this subject, have all unanimously rejected the possibility of creation, except perhaps for a very small number who appear sincerely to have subjugated their reason to authority—a sincerity that motives of their interest, safety, and repose make very suspect, and about which it will always be impossible to be certain as long as one risks anything by speaking the truth.

Supposing that there is an eternal and unique principle of things, this principle, being simple in its essence, is not composed of matter and spirit, but is matter or spirit alone. From the reasons deduced by the Vicar, he cannot conceive that this principle is matter, and if it is spirit, he cannot conceive that matter received its being through it. For to do that, it would be necessary to conceive creation. Now the idea of creation, the idea according to which one conceives that by a simple act of will nothing becomes something, is, of all the ideas that are not clearly contradictory, the least comprehensible to the human mind.

Stopped on both sides by these difficulties, the good Priest remains undecided, and does not torture himself with a purely speculative doubt that in no way affects his duties in this world. For after all, what does it matter to me to explain the origin of beings, provided I know how they subsist, what place I have to fill among them, and by virtue of what this obligation is imposed on me?

But assuming two principles of things*⁴² — an assumption, however, that the Vicar does not make — is not for all that assuming two Gods; unless, like the Manicheans, we also suppose that both these principles are active, a doctrine absolutely contrary to that of the Vicar, who very positively acknowledges only one primary Intelligence, only one active principle, and consequently only one God.

I readily admit that since the creation of the world is clearly stated in our translations of Genesis, positively rejecting it would be in that respect rejecting the authority, if not of the Holy Scriptures, at least of the translations we are given of them; and this too maintains the Vicar in a doubt that he would perhaps not have without that authority. For in addition, the coexistence of two Principles** seems to explain the constitution of the universe better, and to remove difficulties that are hard to resolve without it, such as, among others, that of the origin of evil. Moreover, it would be necessary to understand Hebrew perfectly and even to have been a contemporary of Moses to know for certain what meaning he gave to the word translated for us by the word *created*. This term is too philosophical to have had at its origin the known and popular acceptation we give to it now based on faith in our Scholars.⁴³ This acceptation may have changed and deceived even the Septuagint, already imbued with the questions of Greek philosophy. Nothing is less rare than words that change their meaning over time and that make us attribute to the ancient Authors who used them ideas they did not have. It is very doubtful that the Greek word had the meaning we like to give it, and it is very certain that the Latin word did not have this same meaning, since Lucretius, who formally denies the possibility of all creation, nevertheless often uses the same term to express the formation of the Universe and its parts. Finally, M. de Beausobre⁴⁴ has proven*** that the notion of creation is not found at all in ancient Judaic Theology, and you are too educated, your Grace, to be unaware that many

---

* Someone who knows only two substances can imagine no more than two principles either, and the words *or many*, added in the quoted passage, are there only as a sort of expletive, serving at most to explain that the number of these principles is no more important to know than their nature.

** It is good to note that this question of the eternity of matter, which so greatly shocks our Theologians, shocked the Church Fathers, who were less removed from the sentiments of Plato, very little. Without mentioning Justin Martyr, Origen, and others, Clement of Alexandria takes the affirmative so strongly in his *Hypotiposes* that Photius would have it on this account that the Book was falsified. But the same sentiment appears again in the *Stromates*, where Clement presents the sentiment of Heraclitus without disapproval. In truth, this Father, in Book V, tries to establish a single principle, but that is because he refuses to give this name to matter, even while admitting its eternity.

*** *History of Manicheanism*, vol. II.

men, full of respect for our Holy Scriptures, nonetheless have not recognized the absolute creation of the Universe in the narrative of Moses. Thus the Vicar, who is not imposed on by the despotism of the Theologians, can very well doubt, without being any less orthodox because of it, whether there are two eternal principles of things or whether there is only one. It is a purely grammatical or philosophic debate, in which revelation plays no part.

Be this as it may, that is not the issue between us, and without supporting the sentiments of the Vicar, my only task here is to point out your errors.[45]

Now you are wrong to propose that the unity of God appears to me an idle question and beyond reason since, in the Writing you censure, this unity is established and supported by reasoning. And you are wrong to buttress yourself with a passage from Tertullian in order to conclude against me that it implies that there are several Gods, for without needing Tertullian, I too conclude that it implies that there are several Gods.

You are wrong to term me a reckless Author on that account, since where there is no assertion, there is no recklessness. It is inconceivable to consider an Author reckless solely for being less bold than you are.

Finally, you are wrong to believe you have justified very well the particular dogmas that give human passions to God — and, far from clarifying notions of the great Being, muddle and debase them — by falsely accusing me of muddling and debasing these notions myself; of directly attacking the divine essence which I did not attack at all; and of calling into doubt its unity which I did not call into doubt at all. If I had done so, what would follow? To recriminate is not to justify oneself. But a person whose sole defense is recriminating falsely, surely appears to be the only one guilty.

The contradiction for which you reproach me in the same place is fully as well founded as the preceding accusation. *He does not know,* you say, *what the nature of God is, and shortly thereafter he acknowledges that this supreme Being is endowed with intelligence, power, will, and goodness. Isn't that having an idea of the divine nature?*

Here, your Grace, is my reply to you on this point.

"God is intelligent, but in what way? Man is intelligent when he reasons, and the supreme intelligence does not need to reason. For it there are neither premises nor conclusions; there are not even propositions. It is purely intuitive; it sees equally everything which is and everything that can be. For it all truths are only a single idea, as all places are a single point, and all times a single moment. Human power acts by means; divine power acts by itself. God can because he wills. His will causes his power. God is good; nothing is more manifest. But goodness in man is love of his fellows, and the goodness of God is the love of order; for it is by order that he maintains what exists and links each part with the whole. God is just, I am convinced of it; it is a consequence of his goodness. The injustice of men is their work and not His. Moral disorder, which gives witness against providence in the eyes of the philosophers, only serves to demonstrate it in mine. But man's justice is to give each what belongs to him, and God's justice is to ask from each for an accounting of what he gave him.

"If I have just discovered successively these attributes of which I have no absolute idea. I have done so by compulsory inferences, by the good use of my reason. But I affirm them without understanding them, and at bottom that is to affirm nothing. I may very well tell myself, 'God is thus; I sense it. I prove it to myself.' I cannot conceive any the better how God can be thus.

"Finally, the more effort I make to contemplate His infinite essence, the less I can conceive it. But it is; that is enough for me. The less I can conceive it, the more I worship it. I humble myself and say to him, 'Being of beings, I am because you are; it is to lift myself up to my source to meditate on you ceaselessly. The worthiest use of my reason is for it to annihilate itself before you. It is my rapture of mind, it is the charm of my weakness to feel myself overwhelmed by your greatness.'"

There is my reply, and I believe it is unanswerable. Must I now tell you from where I have taken it? I took it word for word from the very place you accuse of contradiction.* You make use of it as do all my adversaries who, to refute me, only write the objections I raised for myself and suppress my solutions. The reply is already prepared; it is the work they have refuted.

Your Grace, we are about to reach the most important discussions.

After having attacked my System and my Book, you also attack my Religion, and because the Catholic Vicar raises objections against his Church, you seek to depict me as the enemy of mine, as if to propose difficulties about a sentiment were to renounce it; as if all human knowledge did not have its difficulties. As if Geometry itself did not have any or Geometers made a point of remaining silent about them in order not to damage the certitude of their art.

My ready reply to you is to declare with my usual frankness my sentiments in matters of Religion, just as I have professed them in all my Writings and just as they have always been in my mouth and in my heart. I will tell you, furthermore, why I published the profession of faith of the Vicar, and why, despite such an uproar, I will always consider it the best and

---

* *Emile*, vol. III, page 94 and following [Bloom, 285–286].

most useful Writing in the century during which I published it. Neither the stake nor arrest warrants will make me change my language. In ordering me to be humble, the Theologians will not make me false; and in taxing me with hypocrisy, the philosophers will not make me profess unbelief. I shall speak of my Religion, because I have one, and I shall speak of it loudly because I have the courage to do so and because it would be desirable for the good of men if it were that of the human race.

Your Grace, I am Christian, and sincerely Christian, according to the doctrine of the Gospel. I am Christian not as a disciple of the Priests, but as a disciple of Jesus Christ. My Master quibbled little over dogma and insisted much on duties. He prescribed fewer articles of faith than good works. He ordered belief only in what was necessary to be good. When he summed up the Law and the Prophets, it was more in acts of virtue than in formulas of belief,* and he told me himself and through his Apostles that the person who loves his brother has fulfilled the Law.**

As for myself, well-convinced of the essential truths of Christianity, which serve as the foundation of all good morality; seeking in addition to nourish my heart with the spirit of the Gospel without torturing my reason with what appears obscure to me in it: persuaded, finally, that whoever loves God above all things and his neighbor as himself is a true Christian, I strive to be one, leaving aside all these doctrinal subtleties, all this important gibberish with which the Pharisees muddle our duties and obfuscate our faith; and along with Saint Paul, placing faith itself beneath charity.***

Fortunate to be born into the most reasonable and holy Religion on earth, I remain inviolably attached to the worship of my Fathers. Like them, I take Scripture and reason for the unique rules of my belief. Like them, I challenge the authority of men and agree to submit to their formulas only to the extent I perceive their truth. Like them, I join in my heart with the true servants of Jesus Christ and the true adorers of God, to offer him the homages of his Church in the communion of the faithful. It is consoling and sweet for me to be counted among its members, to participate in the public worship they offer to the divinity, and to say to myself in their midst: I am with my brothers.

Filled with gratitude for the worthy Pastor[46] who, resisting the deluge of example and judging by truth, did not exclude a defender of God's cause from the Church, all my life I will preserve a tender memory of his truly Christian charity. I will always give myself glory in being counted

---

* Matthew VII: 12.
** Galatians V: 14.
*** First Corinthians XIII: 2, 13.

in his Flock, and I hope never to scandalize its members either by my sentiments or by my conduct. But when unjust Priests, claiming rights they do not have, will wish to make themselves arbiters of my belief and will come to me arrogantly to say: retract, disguise yourself, explain this, disavow that, their haughtiness will not impress me. They will not make me lie in order to be orthodox, nor say what I do not think in order to please them. And if my veracity offends them and they wish to exclude me from the Church, I will have little fear of this threat, the execution of which is not in their power. They will not prevent me from being joined in my heart to the faithful. They will not remove me from the ranks of the elect if I am inscribed there. They can deprive me of the consolations of this life, but not of hope for the life that must follow it, and it is there that my most ardent and sincere wish is to have Jesus Christ himself for arbiter and Judge between them and me.

Such are my true sentiments, your Grace, which I do not give as a rule for anyone, but declare to be mine, and they will remain so as long as it pleases not men but God, sole master of changing my heart and my reason. For as long as I shall be what I am and think as I think, I shall speak as I am speaking. Quite different, I admit, than your nominal Christians,[47] always ready to believe what must be believed or say what must be said for their interest or repose, and always sure they are good enough Christians provided no one burns their Books and there is no warrant out for their arrest. They live as people persuaded not only that they must confess such and such an article, but that to do so suffices for going to paradise. And I think, on the contrary, that what is essential in Religion consists in practice; and that not only must one be a good man, merciful, humane, and charitable, but that whoever is truly like that has enough belief for being saved. I admit, moreover, that their doctrine is more convenient than mine, and that it costs much less to join the faithful with opinions than with virtues.

Whether I ought to have kept these sentiments to myself, as they do not cease saying; whether when I had the courage to publish them and name myself, I attacked the Laws and disturbed public order, are issues I will examine shortly. But allow me first to beg you, your Grace, you yourself and all those who will read this writing, to place some faith in the declarations of a friend of truth, and not imitate those who, without proof, without probability, and on the sole testimony of their own heart, accuse me of atheism and irreligion contrary to such positive protestations, which nothing on my part has ever contradicted. I do not really have the air, it seems to me, of a man who disguises himself, and it is not easy to see what interest I would have in disguising myself that way. It ought to be presumed that someone who expresses himself so freely about what he does not believe is sincere about what he says he believes; and when his speech, his conduct, and his writings are always in agreement on this point, whoever dares to affirm that he is lying, and is not a God, is infallibly lying himself.

I have not always had the good fortune to live alone. I have frequented men of all kinds. I have seen people of all factions, Believers of all sects, free-thinkers of all systems. I have seen the great, the small, libertines, philosophers. I had reliable friends and those who were less so. I have been surrounded by spies and by the malicious; and the world is full of people who hate me because of the harm they have done me. I beseech them all, whoever they may be, to declare to the public what they know about my belief in the matter of Religion. Whether in the closest contact, the most intimate familiarity, the gaiety of dinner parties, the confidences of têtes-à-têtes, they ever found me different from myself. Whether when they wanted to dispute or jest, their arguments or their bantering ever perturbed me for a moment. Whether they discovered me shifting in my sentiments. Whether in the secrecy of my heart they penetrated what I was hiding from the public. If at any time whatever they found a shadow of falseness or hypocrisy in me, let them state it, let them reveal all, let them unveil me. I consent to it, I beg them to do it, I release them from the secrecy of friendship. Let them state loudly not what they wish I were, but what they know I am; let them judge me according to their conscience. I entrust my honor to them without fear, and I promise not to challenge them.

Let those who accuse me of being without Religion, because they cannot conceive of having one, at least agree among themselves if they can. Some of them find only a System of atheism in my Books, others say I pay homage to God in my Books without believing deep in my heart. They charge my writings with impiety and my sentiments with hypocrisy. But if I preach atheism in public, then I am not a hypocrite, and if I affect a faith I do not have, then I do not teach impiety. By heaping up contradictory imputations, the calumny reveals itself. But malice is blind and passion does not reason.

I do not have, it is true, that faith I hear so many people of such mediocre probity boast about; that robust faith which never doubts anything, believes without question everything presented to it for belief, and puts aside or dissimulates the objections it does not know how to resolve. I do not have the good fortune to see in revelation the evidence they find there, and if I decide in favor of it, it is because my heart leads me to do so, because it offers me nothing except what is consoling, and because the difficulties in rejecting it are no less great. But it is not because I see it proved, for most assuredly it is not proved in my eyes. I am far from being educated enough for a demonstration that requires such profound learning ever to be within my grasp. Isn't it amusing that I, who openly propose my objections and my doubts am the hypocrite, and that all these very determined people who say ceaselessly they firmly believe this and that; these people so certain about everything yet who are without better proofs than mine; these people, finally, most of whom are scarcely more learned than I and who, without removing my difficulties, reproach me for raising them are the people of good faith?

Why would I be a hypocrite, and what would I gain from being one? I attacked all particular interests, I aroused all factions against me, I upheld only the cause of God and humanity, and who cares about that? What I said about it did not even cause the slightest sensation, and not a soul was grateful to me for it. If I had openly declared myself in favor of atheism, the devout would not have done anything worse to me, and other no less dangerous enemies would not be dealing me their blows in secret. If I had openly declared myself in favor of atheism, the former would have attacked me with more reserve when they saw that I was defended by others and personally disposed to seek revenge. But a man who fears God is hardly to be feared. His faction is not formidable, he is alone or nearly so, and one is sure to be able to do him much harm before he dreams of reciprocating. If I had openly declared myself in favor of atheism, thereby separating myself from the Church, I would in one fell swoop have deprived its Ministers of the means to harass me incessantly, and to make me endure all their little tyrannies. I would not have suffered so many inept censures, and instead of blaming me so bitterly for having written, it would have been necessary to refute me, which is not quite so easy. Finally, if I had openly declared myself in favor of atheism, people would have protested a bit at first. But I would soon have been left in peace like all the others. The people of the Lord would not have assumed the task of inspection over me, and everyone would not have believed they were doing me a favor by not treating me as an excommunicated person. And I would have been quits with everybody. The saints of Israel would not have written me anonymous Letters, and their charity would not have been vented in pious insults. They would not have taken the trouble to assure me humbly that I was a scoundrel, an execrable monster, and that it would have been all too fortunate for the world if some good soul had taken the trouble to smother me in the cradle. Decent people, for their part, considering me then as a reprobate, would not torture themselves and me to lead me back to the right path. They would not pull me right and left, they would not smother me by the weight of their sermons, they would not force me to bless their zeal while cursing their importunity, and to acknowledge gratefully that they are called to make me die of boredom.

Your Grace, if I am a hypocrite, I am a madman, since for what I ask of men, it is great folly to put myself to the trouble of being false. If I am a hypocrite, I am a fool, for a person must be a great fool not to see that the road I have taken leads only to unhappiness in this life, and even if I could find some advantage in it, I could not profit from it without contradicting myself. It is true that there is still time. I only have to be willing to deceive men for a moment, and all my enemies will be at my feet. I have not yet reached old age. I may have a long time to suffer. I may see the public change its mind about me once again. But if I ever attain honors and wealth, by any route whatever, then I will be a hypocrite. That is certain.

The glory of the friend of truth is not attached to one opinion rather than some other. Whatever he says, provided he thinks it, he moves toward his goal. He who has no interest other than to be true is not tempted to lie, and there is no sensible man who does not prefer the simplest means when it is also the most certain. My enemies can insult me as much as they want. They will not deprive me of the honor of being a truthful man in all matters; of being the only Author of my century and many others who wrote in good faith and said only what he believed. They may momentarily sully my reputation by means of rumors and calumnies. But it will triumph sooner or later. For while they will vary in their ridiculous allegations, I will always remain the same. And with no other art than my frankness, I will always have the means to distress them.

But this frankness is misplaced with the public! But not every truth is good to state! But although all sensible men think as you do, it is not good for the rabble to think so also. That is what is shouted at me from all sides. That, perhaps, is what you yourself would say to me if we were tête-à-tête in your Study. Men are like that. They change their language as they change their clothes. They speak the truth only in dressing gowns. In formal garb, they know only how to lie, and not only are they deceivers and impostors to the face of the human race, but they are not ashamed to punish against their conscience whoever dares not to be an imposter and a public deceiver like them. But is that principle really correct that not every truth is good to state? If it were, does it follow that no error is good to destroy, and are all of men's follies so sacred that there is not one that should not be respected? That is what is proper to examine before presenting to me as a law a suspect and vague maxim that, even if it were true in itself, can trespass in its application.

I very much desire, your Grace, to follow my usual method here, and give the history of my ideas as my only reply to my accusers. I believe that

I cannot better justify all I have dared to say than by saying again everything I have thought.

As soon as I was capable of observing men, I watched them act and listened to them speak. Then, seeing that their actions bore little resemblance to their speeches, I sought the reason for this dissimilarity, and found that since being and appearing were two things as different for them as acting and speaking, this second difference was the cause of the first, and itself had a cause that remained for me to seek.

I found it in our social order which—at every point contrary to nature, which nothing destroys—tyrannizes over nature constantly and constantly makes nature demand its rights. I followed this contradiction to its consequences, and saw that by itself it explained all the vices of men and all the ills of society. From which I concluded it was not necessary to assume that man is wicked by his nature, when it is possible to indicate the origin and progression of his wickedness. These reflections led me to new research about the human mind considered in the civil state, and I found then that the development of enlightenment and of vices always occurred in the same ratio, not in individuals but in peoples, a distinction I have always carefully made and that none of those who have attacked me has ever been able to conceive.

I sought the truth in Books; I found only lies and error there. I consulted Authors. I found only Charlatans, who make a game of deceiving men, with no other Law than their interest, no other God than their reputation; quick to disparage leaders who do not treat them as they wish, quicker still to praise iniquity that pays them. Listening to the people who are allowed to speak in public, I understood that they dare or wish to say only what suits those who command; and being paid by the strong to preach to the weak, they know only how to speak to the latter about their duties and to the former about their rights. All public instruction will always tend to lies as long as those who direct it find lying to be in their interest, and it is only for them that the truth is not good to state. Why would I be the accomplice of those people?

There are prejudices that must be respected? That may be, but it is when everything else is in order, and it is impossible to remove these prejudices without also removing what compensates for them. Then the evil is left for love of the good. But when the state of things is such that there can be no change that is not for the better, are prejudices so respectable that reason, virtue, justice, and all the good that truth could do for men must be sacrificed to them? For myself, I have promised to speak it in every useful thing as long as it is in me. It is a commitment I have had to fulfill according to my talent, and that surely someone else cannot fulfill for me, since because each person is obligated to all, no one can pay for someone else. *Divine truth*, says Augustine, *is neither mine, yours, nor his, but ours, whom it calls upon forcefully to publish it together, on pain of being useless to ourselves if we do not communicate it to others. For whoever appropriates for himself alone a good that God wants everyone to enjoy loses through this usurpation what he hides from the public, and finds only error in himself for having betrayed the truth.**48

Men should not be half taught. If they must remain in error, why not leave them in ignorance? What good are so many Schools and Universities if they teach them nothing about what is important for them to know? What, then, is the object of your Colleges, your Academies, of so many learned establishments? Is it to mislead the People, modify its reason at the outset, and prevent it from proceeding to the truth? Professors of the lie, you pretend to instruct it in order to lead it astray, and like those brigands who place beacons on reefs, you enlighten it in order to destroy it.

That is what I thought in taking up my pen, and in setting it down I have no grounds for changing my sentiment. I have always seen that public education had two essential defects that were impossible to remove. One is the bad faith of those who give it and the other is the blindness of those who receive it. If men without passions taught men without prejudices, our knowledge would remain more limited but more certain, and reason would always reign. Now whatever one does, the interest of public men will always be the same, but the prejudices of the people, being without any fixed basis, are more variable. They can be modified, changed, increased, or diminished. It is only on this side, therefore, that education can gain some hold, and it is there that the friend of truth should aim. He can hope to make the people more reasonable but not those who lead it more honest.

I saw the same falseness in Religion as in politics, and that made me even more indignant. For the vice of Government can make its subjects unhappy only on earth, but who knows to what extent errors of conscience can harm unfortunate mortals? I saw that there were professions of faith, doctrines, forms of worship that were followed without belief, and that, since nothing of all that penetrated either heart or reason, it influenced conduct very little. Your Grace, I must speak straightforwardly to you. The true Believer cannot put up with all these affectations. He feels that man is an intelligent being who must have a reasonable form of worship, and a sociable being who must have a morality made for humanity. Let us first find this form of worship and this morality; it will be for all

---

* Aug. *Confes.* Book XII, chapter 25.

men. And then when national formulas are needed, we will examine their foundations, relations, and proprieties, and after saying what pertains to man, we will then say what pertains to the Citizen. Above all, let us not behave like M. Joli de Fleuri,[49] who, to establish his Jansenism, wants to uproot all natural law and all obligation that binds humans to one another. So that according to him, the Christian and the Infidel who enter a contract are bound to nothing at all toward one another, since there is no law common to them both.

I see then two ways to examine and compare the various Religions. One is according to what is true and false in them, either concerning the natural or supernatural facts on which they are established, or concerning the notions that reason gives us of the supreme Being and of the form of worship he wants from us. The other is according to their temporal and moral effects on earth, according to the good or evil they can do for society and the human race. One must not begin, in order to prevent this double examination, by deciding that these two things always go together, and that the truest Religion is also the most social. That is precisely what is in question. And one must not begin by shouting that someone who treats this question is impious, an atheist. For it is one thing to believe and another to examine the effect of what one believes.

It seems certain, however, I admit, that if man is made for society, the truest Religion is also the most social and the most humane. For God wants us to be as he made us, and if it were true that he had made us wicked, it would be disobeying him to want to cease being so. Moreover, considered as a relation between God and man, Religion can contribute to the glory of God only through the well-being of man, since the other term of the relation, which is God, is by its nature above everything man can do for or against him.

But for all its probability, this sentiment is subject to great difficulties from the historical account and the facts that contradict it. The Jews were born enemies of all other Peoples, and they began their establishment by destroying seven nations according to the express order they had received to do so. All the Christians have had wars of Religion, and war is harmful to men. All parties were persecutors and persecuted, and persecution is harmful to men. Several sects praise celibacy, and celibacy is so harmful* to

---

* Continence and purity have their function, even for population. It is always noble to be in command of oneself, and for those reasons the state of virginity is very worthy of esteem. But it does not follow that it is noble, or good, or praiseworthy to persevere through life in this state, offending nature and eluding its destination. A young nubile virgin is more respected than a young wife; but the mother of a family is more respected than an old maid, and that seems very sensible to me. Since people do not marry at birth and since it is not even proper to marry very young, virginity—which all have borne and honored—has its necessity,

the human species, that if it were followed everywhere, the species would perish. If that does not constitute the proof for deciding, it does constitute a reason for examining, and I was not asking for anything except that this examination be permitted.

I neither say nor think there is no good Religion on earth. But I do say, and it is only too true, that there is none among those that are or have been dominant that has not cruelly wounded humanity. All parties have tormented their brothers, all have offered to God sacrifices of human blood. Whatever the source of these contradictions, they exist. Is it a crime to want to eliminate them?

Charity is not murderous. Love of one's neighbor does not lead to massacring him. Thus zeal for the salvation of men is not the cause of persecutions. It is amour-propre and pride that are the cause. The less reasonable a form of worship is, the more its establishment is sought by force. A person who professes a senseless doctrine cannot tolerate its being seen for what it is. Reason then becomes the greatest crime. Whatever the cost, others must be deprived of it, because one is ashamed to be lacking it in their eyes. Thus intolerance and inconsistency have the same source. It is necessary to intimidate and frighten men ceaselessly. If you leave them to their reason for a moment, you are lost.

From that alone, it follows that a great good is accomplished for peoples in this delirium by teaching them to reason about Religion, for it is bringing them closer to the duties of man, removing the dagger from intolerance, giving back to humanity all its rights. But it is necessary to go back to principles that are general and common to all men. For if, by wanting to reason, you leave a foothold for the authority of Priests, you give fanaticism back its weapon, and you provide it with the means for greater cruelty.

A person who loves peace should not have recourse to Books. It is the way to finish nothing. Books are sources of inexhaustible disputes. Glance through the history of Peoples: those who have no Books do not dispute. Do you want to subject men to human authorities? One will be closer, another further from proof. They will be affected by it differently. Despite

---

its utility, its value, and its glory. But that is in order to go at the proper time and offer all one's purity in marriage. What! they say with their foolishly triumphant tone, bachelors are preaching the marriage bond! Why don't they get married?[50] Ah! Why? Because a state so sacred and so sweet in itself has become, through your foolish institutions, an unhappy and ridiculous state, in which it is henceforth almost impossible to live without being a rascal or a fool. Iron scepters, senseless laws! It is you we blame for our not having been able to fulfill our duties on earth, and it is through us that the cry of nature rises up against your barbarity. How dare you push it to the point of reproaching us for the wretchedness to which you have reduced us?

the most complete good faith and the best judgment in the world, it is impossible that they will ever be in agreement. Do not argue about arguments and do not base your position on speeches. Human language is not sufficiently clear. God himself, if he deigned to speak to us in our languages, would not say anything that could not be disputed.

Our languages are the work of men, and men are limited. Our languages are the work of men, and men are liars. Just as there is no truth so clearly enunciated that it cannot be quibbled with, there is no lie so crude that it cannot be buttressed with some false reason.

Let us assume that an individual comes at midnight to proclaim to us that it is daytime. He will be ridiculed. But give this individual the time and means to form a sect, sooner or later his partisans will succeed in proving to you that he told the truth. Because in fact, they will say, when he declared it was day, it was day somewhere in the world. Nothing is more certain. Others, having established that there are always some particles of light in the air, will maintain that in still another sense it is very true that night is day. Provided that subtle people get mixed up in it, they will soon make you see the sun at midnight. Everyone will not accept this evidence. There will be debates that degenerate, in accordance with custom, into wars and cruelties. Some will want explanations; others none at all. One will want to interpret the proposition figuratively, another literally. One will say: at midnight he said it was daytime, and it was night. Another will say: at midnight he said it was day, and it was day. Everyone will accuse the opposing party of bad faith and will see only obstinate people in it. People will end by fighting, by massacring each other. Rivers of blood will flow everywhere. And if the new sect is finally victorious, it will remain proved that night is day. That is approximately the history of all quarrels of Religion.

Most new forms of worship are established by fanaticism and maintained by hypocrisy. It follows from this that they offend reason and do not lead to virtue. Enthusiasm and delirium do not reason. While they last, everything is accepted and there is little haggling over dogmas. Besides, that is so convenient! It costs so little to follow doctrine and so much to practice morality that in joining the easier side, good works are ransomed by the merit of great faith. But whatever we do, fanaticism is a crisis state that cannot last forever. It has its fits that are more or less long, more or less frequent, and it also has its respites, during which people are composed. Returning to themselves at those times, people are completely surprised to see themselves fettered by so many absurdities. Yet the form of worship is organized, the forms prescribed, the laws established, the transgressors punished. Will anyone go alone to protest against all that, challenge the Laws of his country, and renounce the Religion of his father? Who would dare? People submit in silence; interest would have us share the opinion of the person from whom we inherit. One therefore does as the others do, except for laughing at one's ease in private about what one pretends to respect in public. That, your Grace, is how the majority of men in most Religions think, and above all in yours. And that is the key to the inconsistency that is noted between their morality[51] and their actions. Their belief is only appearance, and their morals are like their faith.

Why does one man have the right of inspection over another man's belief, and why does the State have it over the belief of the Citizens? It is because it is assumed that what men believe determines their morality, and that their conduct in this life is dependent on their ideas about the life to come. If this is not true, what difference does it make what they believe or what they pretend to believe? The appearance of Religion no longer serves any purpose except to absolve them from having one.[52]

In society, everyone has the right to find out whether another person believes himself obligated to be just, and the Sovereign has the right to examine the reasons on which each person bases this obligation. Moreover, national forms ought to be observed; I have insisted upon that greatly. But as for opinions that are not connected to morality, that do not influence actions in any way, and that do not tend to transgress Laws, each person has only his own judgment as a master on these, and no one has either right or interest in prescribing his way of thinking for others. For example, if someone, even someone constituted in authority, came to ask my sentiment about the famous question of hypostasis[53] about which the Bible does not say a word, but for which so many overgrown children have held Councils and so many men have been tortured, after telling him that I do not understand it and do not care about understanding it, I would ask him as decently as I could to mind his own business, and if he persisted, I would leave him there.

That is the only principle on which something stable and equitable can be established about disputes of Religion. Lacking that, everyone establishes on his own part what is in question, there will never be agreement on anything, people will never in their lives understand one another, and Religion, which ought to make men happy, will always cause their greatest ills.

But the older Religions become, the more their object is lost from sight. Subtleties multiply, people want to explain everything, decide everything, understand everything. Doctrine is incessantly refined and morality wastes ever farther away. There is surely a big gap between the spirit of Deuteronomy and the spirit of the Talmud and the Mishnah, between the spirit of the Gospels and the quarrels about the Constitution![54] St. Thomas asks* whether the articles of faith have multiplied by the succession of time, and he declares for the affirmative. That is to say that scholars, outdoing one another, know more than the Apostles and Jesus Christ said about them. St. Paul admits that he sees only obscurely and knows only in part.** Truly our Theologians are way ahead of that; they see everything, they know everything. They make clear to us what is obscure in the Scriptures. They pronounce about what was undecided. They make us feel with their usual modesty that the Sacred Authors had great need of their help to make themselves understood, and that the Holy Spirit would have been unable to explain himself clearly without them.

When people lose sight of the duties of man to attend only to the opinions and frivolous disputes of Priests, a Christian is no longer asked if he fears God, but rather if he is orthodox. He is made to subscribe to formulas about the most useless and often the most unintelligible questions, and when he has done so, all goes well. No one finds out anything more about him. Provided he does not get himself into trouble, he can live otherwise as he pleases. His morals are irrelevant; the doctrine is safe. When Religion has come to that, what good does it do for society, what advantage is it for men? It serves only to excite dissensions, turmoil, wars of all kinds among them; to set them at each other's throats about Word Puzzles. It would be better, then, to have no Religion than to have one that is so badly understood. Let us prevent it, if possible, from degenerating to that point, and be sure, despite the stake and chains, of deserving well from the human race.

Let us assume that, tired of the quarrels tearing it apart, the human race assembles to end them and agree on a Religion common to all Peoples. Everyone will begin, certainly, by proposing his own as the only true and reasonable and proven religion, the only one pleasing to God and useful to men. But since each one's proofs will fall short of his persuasion, at least in the opinion of the other sects, each party will obtain only its own vote. All the others will join against it; that is no less certain. The deliberation will make the rounds in this way, one alone proposing and all rejecting. This is not the way to reach agreement. It is believable that after much time lost in these puerile altercations, men of sense will seek means of conciliation. To do so, they will propose to begin by banishing all Theologians from the assembly, and it will not be hard for them to show how indispensable this preliminary step is. Once this good deed is done, they will say to the peoples: as long as you will not agree on some principle, it is not even

---

* *Secunda secundae Quaest.* I. Art. VII.
** I. Corinthians XIII: 9, 12.

possible for you to understand one another, and saying you are wrong because I am right is an argument that has never convinced anyone.

"You speak of what is pleasing to God. That is precisely what is in question. If we knew what form of worship is most pleasing to him, there would no longer be any dispute among us. You speak also of what is useful to men. That is a different matter. Men can judge about that. Let us take utility, therefore, as a rule, and then establish the doctrine that is most related to it. In that way we can hope to come as close to the truth as is possible for men. For it can be presumed that what is most useful to his creatures is what is most pleasing to the Creator.

"First let us consider whether there is some natural affinity between us, if we are anything to one another. Jews, what do you think about the origin of the human race? We think it came from one Father. And you, Christians? We think as the Jews do about that. And you, Turks? We think as the Jews and Christians do. So far so good: since men are all brothers, they should love each other as brothers.

"Tell us now from whom their common Father received his being? For he did not make himself all alone. From the Creator of Heaven and Earth. Jews, Christians, and Turks also agree on that. That is another very important point.

"And is this man, the work of the Creator, a simple or a mixed being? Is he formed of a single substance or of several? Christians, reply. He is composed of two substances, one which is mortal and another which cannot die. And you, Turks? We think the same. And you, Jews? Long ago our ideas about that were very confused, like the expressions in our Sacred Books. But the Essenes enlightened us, and on this point too we think as the Christians do."

Proceeding in this way from query to query about divine providence, the economy of the life to come, and all questions essential to the good order of the human race, these same men, having obtained nearly uniform replies from everyone, will say to them: (It will be recalled that the Theologians are no longer there.) "My friends, what are you torturing yourselves about? You are all in agreement about what is important to you. If you have differing sentiments about the rest, I see little problem with that. With this small number of articles, form a universal Religion that is, so to speak, the human and social Religion which every man living in society is obliged to accept. If someone dogmatizes against it, let him be banished from society as an enemy of its fundamental Laws. As for the rest, about which you do not agree, form from your particular beliefs so many national Religions, and follow them with sincerity of heart. But do not go torturing yourself to make other Peoples accept them, and be assured that

God does not require that. For it is as unjust to wish to subject them to your opinions as to your laws, and missionaries seem to me scarcely wiser than conquerors.

"As you follow your different doctrines, stop thinking they are so well proved that whoever does not see them as such is guilty of bad faith in your eyes. Do not believe that all those who weigh your proofs and reject them are therefore obstinate people whose incredulity makes them punishable. Do not believe that reason, love of truth, sincerity are yours alone. Whatever we do, we always tend to treat as enemies those whom we accuse of denying what is evident. We pity error, but we hate obstinacy. Give preference to your own reasons, well and good; but know that those who do not accept them have their own.

"Honor in general all the founders of your respective forms of worship. Let each person give to his own what he believes he owes him, but let him not scorn those of others. They have had great geniuses and great virtues. That is always worthy of respect. They have called themselves God's Messengers; that may or may not be so. The plurality cannot judge that in a uniform manner, the proofs not being equally at its disposal. But if it is not so, they must not be so lightly treated as impostors. Who knows to what extent continual meditations about the divinity and the enthusiasm of virtue have been able to disturb the didactic and pedestrian order of common ideas in their sublime souls? At heights that are too great, one's head swims and one no longer sees things as they are. Socrates believed he had a familiar spirit, and no one has dared accuse him of being an imposter on that account. Shall we treat the founders of Peoples, the benefactors of nations, with less regard than a private individual?

"Moreover, dispute no more among yourselves over the preference due to your forms of worship. They are all good when they are prescribed by the laws and when the essential Religion is found in them. They are bad when it is not found there. The form of worship is the regulation of Religions and not their essence, and it is the Sovereign's function to administer the regulations in his country."

I thought, your Grace, that someone who would reason that way would not be a blasphemer, an impious person; that he would propose a way of peace that was just, reasonable, and useful to men. And that this would not prevent him from having his particular Religion as others do, and from being completely as sincerely attached to it. The true Believer, knowing that the infidel is also a man, and perhaps a decent man, can be interested in his fate without committing a crime. He may justly prevent a foreign form of worship from entering his country; but let him not therefore damn those who do not think as he does. For whoever pronounces such a reckless judgment makes himself the enemy of the rest of the human race. I hear it said constantly that civil but not theological tolerance must be allowed.[55] I think it is just the opposite. I believe that a good man, in whatever Religion he lives in good faith, can be saved. But I do not therefore believe that foreign Religions can legitimately be introduced into a country without the permission of the Sovereign. For if that is not directly disobeying God, it is disobeying the Laws, and whoever disobeys the Laws disobeys God.

With regard to Religions that are established or tolerated in a country, I believe it is unjust and barbaric to destroy them there by violence, and that the Sovereign does wrong to himself in mistreating their sectaries. There is a great difference between embracing a new Religion and living according to the one into which we are born. Only the former is punishable. One should neither allow the establishment of a diversity of forms of worship nor proscribe those that have been established. For a son is never wrong to follow his father's Religion. The argument for public tranquillity works completely against persecutors. Religion never arouses disturbances in a State except when the dominant party wants to torment the weak party, or when the weak party, intolerant by principle, cannot live in peace with anyone at all. But every legitimate form of worship, that is every form of worship in which the essential Religion is found and consequently whose sectaries ask only to be tolerated and live in peace, has never caused either revolts or civil wars, except when it was necessary to defend oneself and repulse persecutors. The Protestants have never taken up arms in France except when they were prosecuted there. If it could have been resolved to leave them in peace, they would have remained there. I concur without hesitation that, at its birth, the reformed Religion had no right to establish itself in France, against the laws. But when, transmitted from Fathers to children, this Religion had become that of part of the French Nation, and when the Prince had solemnly concluded a treaty with that part in the Edict of Nantes, this Edict became an inviolable Contract that could no longer be annulled except by common consent of the two parties; and since that time, the exercise of the Protestant Religion is, in my opinion, legitimate in France.

If it were not, subjects would always have the alternatives of leaving the kingdom with their goods, or remaining there subject to the dominant form of worship. But compelling them to stay without wishing to tolerate them, wishing simultaneously that they be and not be, depriving them even of the right of nature, annulling their marriages,* declaring their

---

* In a decree of the Parlement of Toulouse concerning the matter of the unfortunate Calas,[56] the Protestants are reproached for contracting marriages among themselves, *which,*

children bastards . . . by merely stating what is I would say too much about it. I must be silent.

Here at least is what I can say. Considering only raison d'Etat, perhaps it was a good thing to remove all the leaders of the French Protestants, but that should have been the end of it. Political maxims have their applications and their distinctions. To prevent dissensions there is no longer any reason to fear, they deprive themselves of greatly needed resources. In a Kingdom such as France, what harm can be done by a party that has neither Grandees nor Nobility at its head? Examine all your preceding wars, called wars of Religion; you will find there was not one that did not have its cause at Court and in the interests of the Grandees. Ministerial intrigues embroiled matters, and then the Leaders stirred up the peoples in the name of God. But what intrigues, what cabals can Merchants and Peasants form? How will they go about setting up a party in a country where only Valets and Masters are desired, and where equality is unknown or loathed? A merchant who proposes to muster troops can make himself heard in England, but he will always make Frenchmen laugh.*

If I were King? no; Minister? Still less; but a powerful man in France, I would say: among us, everything leads to jobs, to expenses. Everyone wants to buy the right to do evil. Paris and the Court swallow up everything. Let us allow those poor people to fill the void of the Provinces. Let them be merchants and always merchants, farmers and always farmers. Not being able to change their status, they will draw from it as much as they can. They will replace our own in the deprived conditions we all seek to leave. They will make the most of commerce and agriculture, which

---

according to the Protestants, are only civil Acts, and consequently completely subject in their form and effects to the will of the King.

Thus, because according to Protestants marriage is a civil act, it follows that they are obliged to submit to the will of the King, who makes it an act of the Catholic Religion. In order to marry, the Protestants are legitimately constrained to become Catholics, given that, according to them, marriage is a civil act. That is how the Gentlemen of the Parlement of Toulouse reason.

France is such a vast Kingdom that the French have taken it into their minds that the human race ought to have no other laws than theirs. Their Parlements and Tribunals seem to have no idea of natural Right or the Law of Nations. And it is noteworthy that in all this great Kingdom where there are so many Universities, so many Colleges, so many Academies, and where so many useless things are so pretentiously taught, there is not a single professorship of natural Right. It is the only people in Europe who has considered this study as good for nothing.

* The only situation that forces a people thus stripped of Leaders to take up arms is when—reduced to despair by its persecutors—it sees the only choice it has left is how to perish. The war of the Camisards at the beginning of the century was like that. Then we are all amazed by the strength that a scorned faction draws from its despair. That is what persecutors have never been able to calculate in advance. Yet such wars cost so much blood that they really ought to think about it before making them inevitable.

everything makes us abandon. They will supply our luxury. They will work, and we will enjoy.

If this project were no more equitable than those that are being pursued, it would at least be more humane, and it would surely be more useful. It is less the tyranny and ambition of Leaders than their prejudices and short-sightedness that cause the unhappiness of Nations.

I will conclude by transcribing a sort of speech that has some relation to my subject and will not divert me from it for long.

A Parsi from Surat who had secretly married a Moslem was discovered, arrested, and having refused to embrace Mohammedenism, condemned to death. Before going to his execution, he spoke to his judges this way.

"What! You want to deprive me of life! But what are you punishing me for? I transgressed my law rather than yours. My law speaks to the heart and is not cruel. My crime has been punished by the blame of my brothers. But what have I done to you to deserve to die? I have treated you as my family, and have picked myself a sister from among you. I have left her free in her belief, and she has respected mine for her own interest. Restricted without regret to her alone, I have honored her as the instrument of the form of worship required by the Author of my being. Through her I have paid the tribute every man owes to the human race. Love gave her to me and virtue endeared her to me; she has not lived in servitude; she has possessed her husband's undivided heart. My fault has brought her no less happiness than it has me.

"To expiate such a pardonable fault, you wanted to turn me into an imposter and a liar. You wanted to force me to profess your sentiments without loving them and without believing them, as though the deserter from our laws would deserve to come under yours. You made me choose between perjury and death, and I made the choice, because I do not want to deceive you. I die then, because it must be; but I die worthy of living again and animating another just man. I die a martyr to my Religion, without fear of joining yours after my death. May I be reborn among Mohammedans, to teach them to become humane, clement, equitable. For in serving the same God we serve—since there are not two of them— you are blinded by your zeal when you torture his servants, and you are cruel and bloodthirsty only because you are inconsistent.

"You are children who know only how to do harm to men in your games. You believe yourselves learned, and you know nothing of what God is. Do your recent dogmas suit the one who is and would be adored forever? New peoples, how do you dare speak of Religion to us? Our rites are as old as the stars. The first rays of the sun shed light upon and received the homages of our Fathers. The great Zoroaster saw the infancy of the world. He predicted and described the order of the universe. And you, men of yesterday, want to be our prophets! Twenty centuries before Mohammed, before the birth of Ishmael and his father, the Magi were ancient. Our sacred books were already the Law of Asia and the world, and three great Empires had successively run their long course under our ancestors before yours had come out of nothingness.

"See the difference, prejudiced men, that exists between you and us. You say you are believers and you live like barbarians. Your institutions, your laws, your forms of worship, even your virtues torment man and degrade him. You have only sad duties to prescribe to him. Fasts, privation, struggles, mutilations, seclusions: you only know how to make a duty for him of what can afflict and constrain him. You make him hate life and the ways of preserving it: your women are without men; your lands are without cultivation; you eat animals and you massacre humans; you love blood, murders. All your establishments offend nature, debase mankind. And under the double yoke of Despotism and fanaticism, you crush it with its Kings and its Gods.

"As for us, we are men of peace, we do not do or wish any harm to anything that breathes, not even to our Tyrants. We give up the fruit of our efforts to them without regret, content to be useful to them and fulfill our duties. Our numerous flocks cover your pastures; the trees planted by our hands give you their fruits and their shade. Your lands that we cultivate feed you through our efforts. A simple and gentle people multiplies under your insults, and draws life and abundance for you from the bosom of our common mother where you are unable to find anything. The sun we take as witness to our works sheds light on our patience and your injustices. It never rises without finding us busy doing good, and when it sets, it brings us back into the bosom of our families to prepare for new labors.

"God alone knows the truth. If despite all that we are mistaken in our worship, it is still hardly believable that we, who do only good on earth, are condemned to hell, while you, who do only evil here, are God's elect. Even if we are in error, you ought to respect it for your own advantage. Our piety makes you fat, and your own consumes you. We repair the harm a destructive Religion does to you. Believe me, let us keep a form of worship that is useful to you. Be fearful that someday we might adopt yours. That is the worst thing that could happen to you."

I have tried, your Grace, to make you understand the spirit in which the profession of faith of the Savoyard Vicar was written, and the considerations that led me to publish it. I ask you now in what respect you can qualify his doctrine as blasphemous, impious, abominable, and what you find in it that is scandalous and pernicious to the human race? I ask the same of those who accuse me of having said what had to be kept silent and of having wanted to disturb public order — a vague and reckless accusation with which those who have reflected the least about what is useful or harmful set a credulous public against a well-intentioned Author with a single word. Is it teaching people to believe nothing to recall them to the true faith they forget? Is it disturbing order to refer everyone back to the laws of his country? Is it destroying all forms of worship to limit each people to its own? Is it depriving someone of his form of worship not to want him to change it? Is it making light of all Religion to respect all Religions? Finally, is it so essential to each religion to hate the others that, if this hatred is taken away, everything is taken away?

That, however, is what they persuade the People of when they want to make them take up hatred against their defender, and when they hold the power. Now, cruel men, your warrants, your stakes, your pastoral letters, your newspapers disturb and misinform the people about me. They believe I am a monster on the faith of your outcries. But your outcries will finally end. My writings will remain despite you, to your shame. The less prejudiced Christians will search them with surprise for the horrors you claim to find there. They will see in them, along with the morality of their divine master, only lessons of peace, harmony, and charity. May they learn from them to be more just than their Fathers! May the virtues they have garnered from them avenge me someday for your maledictions!

With regard to objections about the particular sects into which the universe is divided, would that I could give them enough strength to make each one less obstinate about his own and less hostile to the others, in order to lead each man to indulgence and gentleness, through the very striking and natural consideration that if he had been born in another country, into another sect, he would unfailingly take for error what he takes for truth, and for truth what he takes for error! It is so important for men to be attached less to the opinions that divide them than to those that unite them! And on the contrary, neglecting what they have in common, they cling to private sentiments with a kind of fury. The less reasonable these sentiments seem, the more strongly they are attached to them, and each person would like to compensate by dint of confidence for the authority that reason refuses to confer on his party. Thus, basically in agreement about everything that matters to us and that we do not take into account at all, we spend our lives arguing, quibbling, tormenting, persecuting, fighting each other for the things that are least understood and least necessary to understand. Decisions are piled on decisions in vain; in vain are their contradictions plastered over with unintelligible jargon. Each day we find new questions to resolve, each day new subjects for quarrels, because each doctrine has infinite branches, and each person, obstinate about his little idea, believes essential what is not at all so and neglects the truly essential. And if we propose to them objections they cannot resolve—which, given the structure of their doctrines, becomes easier from day to day—they sulk like children. And because they are more attached to their party than to the truth, and have more pride than good faith, it is on the basis of what they can least well prove that they are least forgiving of any doubt.

My own history characterizes better than any other the judgment one should make about today's Christians, but since it tells too much about them to be believed, perhaps someday it will lead to the very opposite judgment. Someday, perhaps, what is the shame of my contemporaries will be their glory, and the simple people who will read my Book will say with admiration: how angelic those times must have been when a book like that was burned as impious and its author pursued as an evildoer! Doubtless all Writings then were imbued with the most sublime devoutness, and the earth was covered with saints!

But other Books will remain. It will be known, for example, that this same era produced a panegyrist of the Saint Bartholomew massacre,[57] a Frenchman, a man of the Church as may well be thought, without Parlement or Prelate even thinking of disputing him. Then, by comparing the morality of the two Books and the wrong of the two Authors, people might change their language and draw another conclusion.

The abominable doctrines are those that lead to crime and murder, and make fanatics. Why, what in the world is more abominable than to reduce injustice and violence to a System, and make them flow from the clemency of God? I will abstain from drawing a parallel here that might displease you. Only agree, your Grace, that if France had professed the Religion of the Savoyard Priest—that Religion which is so simple and so pure, which makes people fear God and love men—rivers of blood would not have flooded French fields so often. This people so gentle and so gay would not have astonished others with its cruelties in so many persecutions and massacres, from the Inquisition of Toulouse* to the Saint Bartholemew and from the Albigensian wars to the Dragonades. The Councilor Anne du

---

* It is true that Dominick, a Spanish saint, played a big part in it. The Saint, according to a writer of his order, preaching against the Albigensians, had the charity to appoint as associates some devout individuals, zealous for the faith, who took the trouble to extirpate bodily and with a material sword the heretics he could not have vanquished with the sword of God's word. *Ob caritatem, praedicans contra Albienses, inadjutorium sumsit quasdam devotas personas, zelantes pro fide, quae corporaliter illos Haereticos gladio materiali expugnarent, quos ipse gladio verbi Dei amputare non posset.* Antonin, in *Chron.* P. III, tit. 23, c. 14 par.2. This charity hardly resembles the Vicar's, and its reward is very different too. One causes the arrest, the other the canonization of those who profess it.

Bourg would not have been hanged for having spoken out in favor of gentleness toward the Protestants. The inhabitants of Merindol and Cabrieres would not have been put to death by order of the Parlement of Aix[59]; and an innocent Calas tortured by executioners would not have died on the rack before our very eyes. Let us return now, your Grace, to your censures, and to the reasons on which you base them.

It is always men, says the Vicar, who attest to the word of God for us, and who do so in languages that are unknown to us. On the contrary, we would often greatly need God to attest to the word of men. It is at least quite certain that he could have given us his word without using such suspect organs. The Vicar complains that so many human witnesses are necessary to certify the divine word: *So many men*, he says, *between God and me!**

You reply, *For this complaint to make sense, My Very Dear Brethren, it would be necessary to be able to conclude that Revelation is false when it has not been made to each man individually. It would be necessary to be able to say: God cannot require me to believe what I am assured he said, unless he has addressed his word directly to me.***

And quite to the contrary, this complaint makes sense only by admitting the truth of Revelation. For if you assume it is false, how can you complain about the means God has used, since he has not used any? Is he accountable for the deceptions of an imposter? When you let yourself be duped, it is your fault and not his. But when God, master of the choice of his means, prefers to choose those that require so much knowledge and such deep discussions on our part, is the Vicar wrong to say: "Nevertheless let us see, examine, compare verify. Oh, if God had deigned to relieve me of all this labor, would I have served him any less heartily?"***

Your Grace, your minor premise is admirable. I must transcribe it here in its entirety. I like to quote your own words; it is my greatest unkindness.

But aren't there an infinite number of facts, even prior to that of Christian Revelation, that it would be absurd to doubt? By what means other than human testimony, then, has the Author himself come to know this Sparta, this Athens, this Rome whose laws, morals, and heroes he praises so often and with so much certainty? How many men there are between him and the Historians who have preserved the memory of these events![60]

If the subject were less serious and if I had less respect for you, this manner of reasoning would perhaps provide me with the occasion for entertaining my readers a bit. But God forbid that I should forget the tone suited to the subject I am treating, and the man to whom I am speaking.

---

* *Emile*, vol. III, page 141 [Bloom, 297].
** *Pastoral Letter*, in quarto, page 12; in duodecimo, page xxi [9 above].
*** *Emile, ubi sup.*

At the risk of being dull in my reply, I will be satisfied to show that you are mistaken.

I beg you to consider, then, that it is entirely appropriate for human facts to be witnessed by human testimonies. This cannot be done by any other way. I can know that Sparta and Rome existed only because contemporary Authors tell me so, and between me and another man who lived long ago there must necessarily be intermediaries. But why must there be some between God and me, and why must they be so remote, therefore needing so many others? Is it simple, is it natural that God should have sought out Moses in order to speak to Jean-Jacques Rousseau?

Moreover, no one is obliged on pain of damnation to believe that Sparta existed. No one will be devoured by eternal flames for doubting it. Every fact we do not witness is established for us only on the basis of moral proofs, and every moral proof is susceptible of more or less certainty. Shall I believe that divine justice will cast me into hell forever, solely because I was unable to determine very precisely the point where such a proof becomes invincible?

If there is a well-attested history in the world, it is that of the Vampires. Nothing is missing from it: interrogations, certifications by Notables, Surgeons, Parish Priests, Magistrates. The judicial proof is one of the most complete. And with all that, who believes in Vampires? Will we all be damned for not having believed?

However well-attested, even in the opinion of the incredulous Cicero, several of the prodigies related by Livy are, I consider them to be so many fables, and surely I am not the only one. My constant experience and that of all men is stronger in this regard than the testimony of a few. If Sparta and Rome were themselves prodigies, they were prodigies of the moral kind. And just as people in Lapland would be mistaken to establish four feet as the natural stature of man, we ourselves would be no less mistaken to establish the size of human souls on the basis of the people we see around us.

Please remember that I continue to examine your reasonings in themselves here, without defending those you attack. After this necessary reminder, I will permit myself still another assumption about your manner of arguing.

An inhabitant of the rue St. Jacques comes to make the following speech to the Archbishop of Paris. "Your Grace, I know you do not believe either in the beatitude of St. Jean de Pâris or in the miracles it pleased God to perform publicly on his tomb, in plain view of the most enlightened and populous City in the world. But I believe I should attest to you that I have just seen the Saint in person resuscitated at the place where his bones have been buried."[61]

The man from the rue St. Jacques adds to this the details of all the circumstances that might strike the spectator of such an event. I am persuaded that, on hearing this news, before explaining whether you place any faith in it, you will begin by questioning the person who attests to it about his station, his sentiments, his Confessor, and other similar articles. And when his manner as well as his speech have led you to understand that he is a poor Laborer without a certificate of confession to show you, he confirms your opinion that he is a Jansenist, "ah, ah," you will say to him in a bantering tone, "you are a convulsionist, and you have seen the resurrection of Saint Pâris? That is hardly surprising; you have seen so many other marvels!"

Continuing to follow my assumption, he will doubtless persist. He will say he was not the only one to see the miracle; there were two or three people with him who saw the same thing, and others whom he wanted to tell about it said they too had seen it themselves. On hearing that, you will ask whether all these witnesses were Jansenists. "Yes, your Grace," he will say; "but no matter; there are enough of them, people of good morals, good sense, and beyond reproach. The proof is complete and nothing is missing in our declaration to establish the truth of the fact."

Other less charitable Bishops would send for an Officer and consign to him the chap honored by the glorious vision to take him away to thank God from the insane asylum. You, your Grace, being more humane but not more credulous, after reprimanding him gravely, will be satisfied to say to him: "I know that two or three witnesses, decent and sensible people, can attest the life or death of a man. But I do not yet know how many are necessary to certify the resurrection of a Jansenist. While I am waiting to learn, go, my child; try to strengthen your empty brain. I dispense you from fasting, and here is something so you can make yourself some good soup."

That is approximately what you would say, your Grace, as would any other wise man in your place. From which I conclude that even according to you and any other wise man, the moral proofs sufficient to establish facts which are in the order of moral possibilities no longer suffice to verify facts of another order, purely supernatural. With this, I leave you to judge for yourself about the correctness of your comparison.

Yet here is the triumphant conclusion you draw against me. *His skepticism is based here, then, only on the interest of his unbelief.** Your Grace, if it ever procures for me a Bishopric with a hundred thousand pounds of income, you can speak of the interest of my unbelief.

---

* *Pastoral Letter*, in quarto, page 12; in duodecimo, page xxii [10 above].

Let us continue now to transcribe your writing, taking the liberty only of replacing when necessary the passages of my Book that you cut out.

"Let a man," *he adds later,* "come and use this language with us: 'Mortals, I announce the will of the Most High to you. Recognize in my voice him who sends me. I order the sun to change its course, the stars to form another arrangement, the mountains to become level, the waters to rise up, the earth to change its aspect.' At these marvels who will not instantly recognize the Master of nature." *Who would not believe, My Very Dear Brethren, that someone who expresses himself like that wants only to see miracles to become Christian?*

Much more than that, your Grace, since I do not even need miracles to be Christian.

Listen, however, to what he adds. He says, "The most important examination of the proclaimed doctrine remains. For since those who say that God performs miracles on earth also claim that the Devil sometimes imitates them, we are no farther advanced than before, even with the best-attested miracles; and since the magicians of Pharaoh dared, in the very presence of Moses, to produce the same signs he did by God's express order, why would they not in his absence have claimed, with the same credentials, the same authority? Thus, after the doctrine has been proved by the miracle, the miracle has to be proved by the doctrine, for fear of taking the Demon's work for God's work.* What can be done in such a case to avoid circular reasoning?[62] One thing only. Return to reasoning and leave aside the miracles. It would have been better not to have had recourse to them."

That is to say: show me miracles and I will believe. Yes, your Grace, that is to say: show me miracles and I will believe in miracles. *That is to say show me miracles and I will still refuse to believe.* Yes, your Grace, that is to say, according to the very precept of Moses**: even if I am shown miracles, I will still refuse to believe an absurd and unreasonable doctrine being propped up with them. I would rather believe in magic than recognize the voice of God in lessons contrary to reason.

I have said that that was the simplest good sense, which could only be obscured by very subtle distinctions at the very least. That is still one of my predictions. Here is its fulfillment.

When a doctrine is recognized to be true, divine, and based on sure Revelation, it is used to judge miracles, that is to say to reject the alleged marvels with which impostors would want to oppose this doctrine. When it is a matter of a new

---

* I am forced here to mix the note with the text, in imitation of M. de Beaumont. The reader can refer to them both in the book itself. Vol. III, page 145 and following [Bloom, 298–299].

** Deuteronomy XIII.

doctrine announced as emanating from God's bosom, miracles are produced as proofs. That is, the person who takes on the role of Envoy of the Most High confirms his Mission and his Preaching by miracles, which are the very testimony of the divinity. Thus doctrine and miracles are used respectively according to the differing points of view adopted in the study and teaching of Religion. There is in this neither abuse of reason, nor ridiculous sophism, nor vicious circle.*

The Reader will judge about this. As for me, I will not add a single word. I have sometimes replied above with my passages. But I want to reply to you here with yours.

Where then, My Very Dear Brethren, is the philosophic good faith which this Writer parades?

Your Grace, I have never prided myself on philosophic good faith, for I know of no such thing. I do not even dare speak very much any more about Christian good faith ever since the so-called Christians of our day find it so awful that we do not suppress the objections that perplex them. But as for pure and simple good faith, I ask which, yours or mine, is easier to find here?

The further I proceed, the more interesting the points to discuss become. I must continue transcribing from your letter, then. In discussions of this importance, I would not want to leave out a single one of your words.

One would believe that after the greatest efforts to discredit the human testimony attesting to Christian revelation, the same Author nonetheless defers to it in the most positive, most solemn manner.

That would doubtless be right, since I hold all doctrine to be revealed in which I recognize the spirit of God. It is necessary only to remove the ambiguity of your sentence. For if the relative verb *defers to it* refers to Christian Revelation, you are right. But if it refers to human testimony, you are wrong. However that may be, I take note of your testimony against those who dare to say I reject all revelation, as if it were rejecting a doctrine to recognize that it is subject to insoluble difficulties for the human mind; as if it were rejecting it not to accept it on the basis of the testimony of men, when there are other equivalent or superior proofs that dispense with that one. It is true that you say in the conditional mood *one would believe*; but *one would believe* signifies *one believes* when the reason that is the exception for not believing is reduced to nothing, as we shall see in what follows about yours. Let us begin with the affirmative proof.

To convince you of this, My Very Dear Brethren, and at the same time to edify you, this part of his work must be put before your eyes. "I admit that the

---

* *Pastoral Letter*, in quarto, page 13; in duodecimo, page xxiii [10 above].

majesty of the Holy Scriptures amazes me, and that the holiness of the Gospel* speaks to my heart. Look at the books of the philosophers with all their pomp. How petty they are next to this one! Can it be that a book at the same time so sublime and so simple is the work of men? Can it be that he whose history it presents is only a man himself? Is his the tone of an enthusiast or an ambitious sectarian? What gentleness, what purity in his morals! What touching grace in his teachings! What elevation in his maxims! What profound wisdom in his speeches! What presence of mind, what finesse, and what exactness in his responses! What a dominion over his passions! Where is the man, where is the sage who knows how to act, to suffer, and to die without weakness and without ostentation?** When Plato depicts his imaginary just man, covered with all the opprobrium of crime and worthy of all the rewards of virtue, he depicts Jesus Christ feature for feature. The resemblance is so striking that all the Fathers have sensed it: it is impossible to be deceived about it. What prejudices, what blindness one must have to dare to compare the son of Sophroniscus to the son of Mary? What a distance from one to the other! Socrates, dying without pain and without ignominy, easily sticks to his character to the end; and if this easy death had not honored his life, one would doubt whether Socrates, for all his intelligence, were anything but a sophist. He invented morality, it is said. Others before him put it into practice; all he did was to say what they had done; all he did was to draw the lesson from their examples. Aristides was just before Socrates said what justice is. Leonidas died for his country before Socrates had made it a duty to love the fatherland. Sparta was sober before Socrates had praised sobriety. Before he had defined virtue, Greece abounded in virtuous men. But where did Jesus find among his own people that elevated and pure morality of which he alone gave the lessons and the example? From the womb of the most furious fanaticism was heard the highest wisdom, and the simplicity of the most heroic virtues lent honor to the vilest of all peoples. The death of Socrates, philosophizing tranquilly with his friends, is the sweetest one could desire; that of Jesus expiring in torment, insulted, jeered at, cursed by a whole people, is the most horrible one could fear. Socrates, taking the poisoned cup, blesses the man who gives it to him and who is crying.

* The negligence with which M. de Beaumont transcribes me caused him to make two changes in one line here. He put *the majesty of the Holy Scripture* instead of *the majesty of the Holy Scriptures*; and he put *the holiness of the Holy Scripture* instead of *the holiness of the Gospel*. In truth, that does not make me say heresies, but it does make me talk very foolishly.

** As is my custom, I fill the gaps left by M. de Beaumont. Not that those he left here are absolutely insidious, as they are in other places, but because the lack of continuity and sequence weakens the passage when it is truncated. And also given that my persecutors carefully suppress everything I said so wholeheartedly in favor of Religion, it is good to restore it whenever the opportunity arises.

Jesus, in the midst of a frightful torture, prays for his relentless executioners. Yes, if the life and death of Socrates are those of a wise man, the life and death of Jesus are those of a god. Shall we say that the story of the Gospel was wantonly contrived? My friend, it is not thus that one contrives; the facts about Socrates, which no one doubts, are less well attested than those about Jesus Christ. At bottom, this is to push back the difficulty without doing away with it. It would be more inconceivable that many men in agreement had fabricated this book than that a single one provided its subject. Never would Jewish authors have found either this tone or this morality; and the Gospel has characteristics of truth that are so great, so striking, so perfectly inimitable that its contriver would be more amazing than its hero."*

***It would be difficult, My Very Dear Brethren, to pay a more beautiful homage to the authenticity of the Gospel.* I am obliged to you, your Grace, for this admission; you commit one injustice less than the others. Let us come now to the negative proof that makes you say *one would believe* rather than *one believes.*

However the Author believes this only as a result of human testimonies. You are mistaken, your Grace. I recognize it as a consequence of the Gospel and the sublimity I see in it, without anyone attesting to it. I do not need to have someone affirm for me that there is a Gospel when I am holding it. *It is always men who report to him what other men have reported.* Not at all. Someone doesn't report to me that the Gospel exists. I see it with my own eyes, and even if the whole Universe maintained to me that it does not exist, I would know very well that the whole universe is lying or is mistaken. *How many men are there between God and himself?* Not even one. The Gospel is the document that decides and that document is in my hands. However it came to be there and whatever Author wrote it, I recognize the divine spirit in it. That is as unmediated as it can be. There are no men between that proof and me. And in the sense in which there would be any, the historical account of this Sacred Book, of its authors, of the time when it was written, etc., returns to discussions of criticism where moral proof is admitted. Such is the reply of the Savoyard Vicar.

Behold him then, manifestly contradicting himself. Behold him, confounded by his own admissions. I allow you to enjoy all my confusion. *What strange blindness, then, enabled him to add:* "With all that, this same Gospel is full of unbelievable things, of things repugnant to reason and impossible for any sensible man to conceive or to accept! What is to be done amidst all these contradictions? One ought always to be modest and circumspect,

---

* *Emile*, vol. III, page 179 and following [Bloom, 307–308].
** *Pastoral Letter*, in quarto, page 14; in duodecimo, page xxv [11 above].

my child—to respect in silence* what one can neither reject nor understand, and to humble oneself before the great Being who alone knows the truth. This is the involuntary skepticism in which I have remained."[63] *But can skepticism, My Very Dear Brethren, be involuntary then, when one refuses to submit to the doctrine of a Book that cannot have been invented by men? When this Book bears such large, striking, perfectly inimitable hallmarks of truth that the book's inventor would be more astounding than its Hero? Surely here we may say that iniquity has given itself the lie.***

Your Grace, you accuse me of iniquity without cause. You often impute lies to me, and you show none of them. I impose on myself the opposite maxim with regard to you, and I sometimes have occasion to use it.

The Vicar's Skepticism is involuntary for the very reason that makes you deny it to be so. On the basis of the weak authorities one would give the Gospel, he would reject it by the reasons enumerated previously, if the divine spirit that shines in the morality and doctrine of that Book did not restore to it all the force lacking in the testimony of men on such a point. Therefore he acknowledges this Sacred Book with all the admirable things that it contains and that the human mind can understand. But as for the unbelievable things he finds in it, *which are repugnant to his reason and impossible for any sensible man to conceive or acknowledge*, he *respects them in silence without either understanding or rejecting them, and humbles himself before the great Being who alone knows the truth*. Such is his skepticism, and this skepticism is truly involuntary, since it is based on invincible proofs on both sides, which force reason to remain in suspense. This skepticism is that of every reasonable Christian of good faith, who wants to know only those things about Heaven that he can understand, those that are of importance to his conduct; and who rejects, with the Apostle, *foolish and uninstructive questions that only engender strife.****

First, you make me reject Revelation in order to confine myself to natural Religion, and in the first place I did not reject Revelation. Then you

---

* In order for men to impose on themselves this respect and this silence, someone must tell them just once the reasons to do so. A person who knows these reasons can state them, but those who censure and do not state them could remain silent. Speaking to the public with frankness, with firmness is a right common to all men, and even a duty wherever it is useful. But it is hardly permitted for a particular person to censure another publicly for it. That is arrogating to oneself too much superiority of virtues, talents, understanding. That is why I have never meddled with criticizing or reprimanding anyone. I have stated harsh truths to my century, but I have not said any to any particular person, and if it has happened that I have attacked and named some books, I have never talked about living Authors except with every kind of propriety and consideration. One sees how they return the favor. It seems to me that all those Gentlemen who so proudly step forward to teach me humility find the lesson easier to give than to follow.

** *Pastoral Letter*, in quarto, page 144; in duodecimo, page xxvi [11–12 above].

*** *Timothy* II: 23.

accuse me *of not acknowledging even natural Religion, or at least of not recognizing its necessity*. And your only proof is in the following passage which you relate. "If I am mistaken, it is in good faith. That is enough* for my error not to be imputed to a crime. If you were to be similarly mistaken, there would be little evil in that." *Which is to say,* you continue, *that according to him it is sufficient to be persuaded that one possesses the truth; that this persuasion, even if it were accompanied by the most enormous errors, can never be a subject of reproach. That one must always consider as a wise and religious man a person who, adopting the very errors of Atheism, will say he is of good faith.* Now isn't that opening the door to all superstitions, to all fanatical systems, to all the deliriums of the human mind?**

As for you, your Grace, you could not say here as the Vicar does: *If I am mistaken, it is in good faith.* For it is very clearly on purpose that you like to follow the wrong scent and make your Readers do so. That is what I take upon myself to prove beyond contradiction, and I take it upon myself thus in advance, so that you can keep a closer watch over it.

The Profession of the Savoyard Vicar is composed of two parts. The first part, which is the longer, the more important, the more filled with striking and new truths, is intended to combat modern materialism, to establish the existence of God and natural Religion with all the force of which the Author is capable. Neither you nor the Priests talk at all about that part, because it is extremely unimportant to you and because at bottom God's cause hardly affects you, provided the Clergy is safe.

The second part, very much shorter, less regular, and less thorough, raises doubts and difficulties about revelations in general, ascribing to ours, however, its true certitude in the purity and sanctity of its doctrine, and in the wholly divine sublimity of the person who was its Author. The object of this second part is to make each more circumspect from within his own Religion about accusing others of bad faith within theirs, and to show that the proofs of each one are not so conclusive to all eyes that those who do not see them with the same clarity as we do must be treated as guilty people. This second part, written with all proper modesty and respect, is the only one that has attracted your attention and that of the Magistrates. You have refuted my arguments only by the stake and insults. You saw the evil in doubting what is doubtful; you did not see the good in the proof of what is true.

In fact, this first part, which contains what is truly essential to Religion, is decisive and dogmatic. The Author does not waver or hesitate. His conscience and reason determine him invincibly. He believes, he affirms, he is powerfully persuaded.

* *Emile*, vol. III, page 21 [Bloom, 266]. M. de Beaumont wrote: *that is enough for me.*
** *Pastoral Letter*, in quarto, p. 15; in duodecimo, p. xxvii [12 above].

He begins the other part, in contrast, by declaring that *the examination remaining for him to make is very different; that he sees in it only perplexity, mystery, obscurity; that he brings to it only uncertainty and distrust; that only the authority of reason must be attributed to his discourse; that he himself does not know whether he is in error and that all his assertions here are only reasons for doubt.** Thus he proposes his objections, his difficulties, his doubts. He also proposes his great and powerful reasons for believing. And all this discussion results in certainty about essential dogmas and a respectful skepticism about the others. At the end of this second part, he emphasizes again the circumspection necessary for listening to him. *If I were more sure of myself,* he says, *I would have taken a dogmatic and decisive tone. But I am a man. I am ignorant and subject to error. What could I do? I have opened my heart to you without reserve. What I hold to be sure, I have told you as being sure. I have told you my doubts as doubts, my opinions as opinions. I have told you my reasons for doubting and for believing. Now it is for you to judge.***

Therefore, when in the same piece of writing the author says, *If I am mistaken, it is in good faith, that is enough for my error not to be imputed to crime*, I ask every reader who has common sense and some sincerity whether this suspicion of being in error must fall on the first or the second part; on the part where the author affirms, or the one where he hesitates? Whether this suspicion denotes fear of believing in God inappropriately, or fear of being wrong to have doubts about Revelation? You took the first option contrary to all reason, and with the sole desire of making me criminal. I defy you to give any other motive for it. Your Grace, where is, I do not say equity or Christian charity, but good sense and humanity?

Even if you could have been mistaken about the object of the Vicar's fear, the text alone to which you refer would have disabused you despite yourself. For when he says: *That is enough for my error not to be imputed to crime*, he recognizes that such an error could be a crime, and that he could be accused of such a crime if he did not proceed in good faith. But if there were not a God, what would be the crime in believing there is one? And if it were a crime, who could impute it to him? The fear of being in error can therefore not be applied to natural Religion, and the Vicar's speech would be true gibberish with the meaning you ascribe to it. It is therefore impossible to deduce from the passage you relate, that *I do not acknowledge natural Religion*, or that *I do not recognize its necessity*. It is also impossible to deduce from it that *one should always*—those are your terms—*consider as a wise and religious man someone who, adopting the errors of Atheism, will say he*

---

* *Emile*, vol. III, page 131 [Bloom, 295].
** Ibid., page 192 [Bloom, 310].

is of good faith. And it is even impossible that you believed this deduction to be legitimate. If that has not been demonstrated, nothing ever can be, or I must be a madman.

To show that one cannot found one's authority on a divine mission in order to spout absurdities, the Vicar pits an Inspired person, whom it pleases you to call a Christian, against a reasoner, whom it pleases you to call an unbeliever, and he makes them argue each in his own language, of which he disapproves and which is most assuredly neither his nor mine.* Based on that, you charge me *with glaring bad faith*,** and you prove that by the ineptness of the former's discourses. But if these discourses are inept, how do you recognize that he is Christian? And if the reasoner refutes only absurdities, what right do you have to accuse him of unbelief? Does it follow from the absurdities spouted by an Inspired man that he is a Catholic, and from those a reasoner refutes that he is a miscreant? Your Grace, you could very well have dispensed with identifying yourself with a language so full of anger and unreasonableness, for you had not yet issued your Pastoral Letter.

If reason and Revelation were opposed to each other, it is an certain fact, you say, *that God would be in contradiction with himself.*** That is an important admission you make there, for it is certain that God does not contradict himself. *You say, oh Impious people, that the dogmas we consider to be revealed combat the eternal truths; but saying that is not sufficient.* I agree. Let us try to do more.

I am sure you anticipate where this is leading me. It is apparent that you pass over the article on mysteries as if it were hot coals. You scarcely dare place a foot there. You force me, however, to stop you for a moment in this painful position. I will have the discretion to make this moment as brief as possible.

You will surely agree, I think, that one of those eternal truths that serve as elements of reason is that the part is less than the whole, and it is because he asserted the opposite that the Inspired man seems to you to make a speech full of stupidity. Now according to your doctrine of transubstantiation, when Jesus had the last Supper with his Disciples and, having broken bread, gave his body to each of them, it is clear that he held his whole body in his hand, and if he himself ate the consecrated bread, as he may have done, he put his head into his mouth.

There then, very clearly, very precisely, is the part greater than the whole, the container smaller than the contents. What do you say to that,

---

* *Emile*, vol. III, page 151 [Bloom 300–301].
** *Pastoral Letter*, in quarto, page 15; in duodecimo, page xxviii [12 above].
*** *Pastoral Letter*, in quarto, pages 15, 16; in duodecimo, page xxviii [13 above].

your Grace? For myself, I see no one but the Chevalier de Causans who can get you out of this difficulty.[64]

I know very well that you still have Saint Augustine as a resource, but that amounts to the same thing. After heaping up many unintelligible speeches about the Trinity, he agrees they have no meaning. *But,* says this Church Father naively, *we express ourselves this way not to say something, but in order not to remain silent.**

Considering everything, your Grace, I believe that the safest course you can adopt regarding this article and many others is the one you have adopted with M. de Montazet, and for the same reason.[65]

The bad faith of the author of Emile is no less revolting in the language he puts into the mouth of a supposed Catholic.** "Our Catholics," he has him say, "make a great to-do about the authority of the Church; but what do they gain by that, if they need as great an apparatus of proofs to establish this authority as other sects need for establishing their doctrine directly? The Church decides that the Church has the right to decide. Is that not an authority based on good proofs?"[66] *Hearing this imposter, who would not believe, My Very Dear Brethren, that the authority of the church is proved only by its own decisions, and that it goes about it this way: I decide that I am infallible; therefore I am? A slanderous imputation, My Very Dear Brethren.* That, your Grace, is what you assert. It remains for us to see your proofs. In the meantime, would you dare to affirm that Catholic Theologians have never established the authority of the Church by the authority of the Church, *ut in se virtualiter reflexam?* If they have, then I do not accuse them of a slanderous imputation.

****The constitution of Christianity, the spirit of the Gospel, even the errors and the weakness of the human mind lead to the demonstration that the Church established by Jesus Christ is an infallible Church.* Your Grace, you begin by fobbing us off with words that do not lead us astray. Vague discourses never constitute proof, and all those things that aim at demonstration, demonstrate nothing. Let us go straight to the body of the demonstration. Here it is.

We affirm that since this divine legislator has always taught the truth, his Church also teaches it always.****

But who are you, you who assert that to us as the entire proof? Wouldn't you be the Church or its leaders? From the ways you argue, you appear to count a great deal on the help of the Holy Spirit. What is it you say, then,

---

* *Dictum est tamen tres personae, non ut aliquid diceretur, sed ne taceretur.* Aug. *de Trinit.* Book 5, chapter 9.
  ** *Pastoral Letter,* in quarto, page 15; in duodecimo, page xxvi [13 above].
  *** *Pastoral Letter,* ibid. [13 above].
  **** Ibid. This passage deserves to be read in the *Pastoral Letter* itself.

and what did the Imposter say? I beg of you, look at that yourselves, for I do not have the courage to go all the way to the end.

However, I must note that the entire force of the objection you attack so well consists in this phrase which you took care to suppress at the end of the passage in question. *Step outside of that, and you return to all our discussions.* *

Indeed, what is the Vicar's reasoning here? To choose among various Religions, he says, it is necessary to do one of two things. Either understand the proofs of each sect and compare them or rely on the authority of those who teach us. Now the first method presumes knowledge that few men are in a position to acquire, and the second justifies each person's belief in the Religion into which he is born. He cites as an example the Catholic Religion in which the authority of the Church is given as law, and he bases this second dilemma on that. The Church either attributes this authority to itself and says: *I decide that I am infallible; therefore I am infallible*, and then it falls into the sophism called the vicious circle. Or it proves it has received this authority from God, and then it must have just as great an apparatus of proofs to show that indeed it has received this authority as other sects do to establish their doctrine directly. There is nothing to be gained, therefore, for ease of instruction, and the people are no more capable of examining the proofs of Church authority among Catholics than the truth of the doctrine among Protestants. How then will it decide in a reasonable manner other than by the authority of those who teach it? But then the Turk will decide in the same way. In what way is the Turk more guilty than we are? That, your Grace, is the reasoning to which you have not replied and to which I doubt one can reply.** Your Episcopal immunity extricates itself from the business by truncating the Author's passage in bad faith.

Thank Heaven I have finished this tedious task. I have followed your reasons, your citations, and your censures step by step, and shown that you have been wrong each time you attacked my book. Only the article on Government remains, for which I am willing to forgive you, feeling certain that when the person who deplores the miseries of the people, and

---

* *Emile*, vol. III, page 165 [Bloom, 303].

** This is one of those terrible objections which those who attack me carefully refrain from touching. There is nothing as convenient as replying with insults and pious declamations. One easily eludes everything awkward. It must also be admitted that, in their squabbles, Theologians have many resources they lack in relation to the ignorant, for which they must find whatever substitutes they can. They treat each other to a thousand gratuitous assumptions no one dares to reject when he has nothing better to offer himself. Such is the invention of some inborn faith or other which, to get out of their difficulty, they oblige God to transmit from father to son. But they reserve this jargon for their disputations with Scholars. If they used it with the rest of us lay people, they would be afraid of being ridiculed.

who experiences them, is accused by you of poisoning the sources of public felicity, there is no Reader who will not feel what such a discourse is worth. If the Treatise on the *Social Contract* did not exist and the great truths I develop in it had to be proved anew, the compliments you pay to the Powerful at my expense would be one of the facts I would cite as proof, and the fate of the Author would be another, even more striking. There is nothing left for me to say about this. My example alone has said everything, and the passion of private interest should not sully useful truths. It is the Warrant for my arrest, my Book burned by the executioner that I transmit to posterity as supporting documents. My sentiments are less well established by my Writings than by my misfortunes.

Your Grace, I have just discussed all your allegations against my Book. I have not let a single one of your propositions go unexamined. I have shown that you are not right about any point, and I am not afraid that my proofs will be refuted. Above all they are rejoinders where common sense reigns.

Yet if I had been wrong in some places, if I had always been wrong, what kind of indulgence did a Book in which one senses everywhere sincere love of good and zeal for truth, even in the errors, even in the evil that may be there, not deserve? A Book in which the Author—so unassertive, so indecisive—warns his readers so often to be wary of his ideas, to weigh his proofs, and to give them only the authority of reason? A Book that exudes only peace, gentleness, patience, love of order, obedience to the Laws in all things and even in the matter of Religion? Finally, a Book in which the cause of the divinity is so well defended, the utility of Religion so well established, in which morals are so respected, vice so deprived of the weapon of ridicule, wickedness depicted as so devoid of sense, and virtue so loveable? Ah! If this work did not contain a word of truth, its reveries should be honored and cherished as the sweetest chimeras that can soothe and nurture the heart of a decent man. Yes, I am not afraid to say it. If a single truly enlightened government existed in Europe, a government whose views were truly useful and healthy, it would have bestowed public honors on the Author of Emile, it would have erected statues to him. I knew men too well to expect gratitude from them. I did not know them well enough, I admit, to expect of them what they have done.

After having proven that you have reasoned badly in your censures, it remains for me to prove that you have slandered me with your insults. But since you insult me only by virtue of the wrongs you attribute to me in my Book, doesn't showing that my supposed wrongs are only yours sufficiently state that the insults following them must not be for me. You load my work with the most odious epithets, and call me an abominable man, reckless, impious, an imposter. Christian charity, what a strange language you have on the lips of the Ministers of Jesus Christ!

But you who dare reproach me for blasphemies, what are you doing when you take the Apostles for accomplices in the offensive propositions you enjoy making about me? To listen to you, one would believe that Saint Paul had done me the honor of thinking of me and of predicting my coming like that of the Antichrist. And how did he predict it, I ask you? Here it is. It is the beginning of your Pastoral Letter.

Saint Paul predicted, my very dear Brethren, that perilous days would come when there would be people, lovers of themselves, proud, haughty, blasphemous, impious, slanderers, bloated with pride, lovers of sensual pleasures rather than God; men of corrupt spirit and perverted faith.*

I assuredly do not contest that this prediction of Saint Paul has been fully accomplished. But if he had predicted, on the contrary, that there would come a time when none of those people would be seen, I admit I would have been much more struck by the prediction, and especially by its fulfillment.

Following such a well-applied prophesy, you have the goodness to paint a portrait of me in which your Episcopal gravity amuses itself with antitheses, and in which I find I am a very amusing character. That part, your Grace, seemed to me the prettiest section of your Pastoral Letter. No one could write a more pleasant satire, or defame a man with more wit.

From the bosom of error (It is true I spent my youth in your Church.) *there arose* (not very high) *a man full of the language of philosophy* (how could I use a language I do not understand at all?) *without being a true philosopher;* (Oh, I agree! I have never aspired to that title, to which I acknowledge I have no right; and I am surely not renouncing it through modesty.) *a mind endowed with a multitude of knowledge* (I have learned to be ignorant of multitudes of things I believed I knew.) *that did not enlighten him,* (It taught me not to think I was enlightened.) *and that spread darkness in other minds.* (The darkness of ignorance is preferable to the false light of error.) *A character given to paradoxes of opinions and conduct;* (Is there much to be lost in not acting and thinking like everyone else?) *alloying simplicity of morals with ostentation of thoughts,* (Simplicity of morals uplifts the soul; as for the ostentation of my thoughts, I do not know what that is.) *zeal for ancient maxims with the rage for establishing novelties;* (Nothing is newer for us than ancient maxims; there is no alloy in that, and I did not put any rage at all into it.) *the obscurity of retreat with the desire to be known by everyone.* (Your Grace, here you are like writers of Novels, who

---

* *Pastoral Letter*, in quarto, page 4; in duodecimo, page xvii [3 above].

guess everything their Hero did or said in his room. If it is this desire that made me take up my pen, explain how it came to me so late, or why I delayed so long to satisfy it?) *He has been seen to rail at the sciences he was cultivating;* (That proves I do not imitate your men of Letters, and that in my writings the interest of truth takes precedence over my own interest.) *extol the excellence of the Gospel,* (always, and with the truest zeal.) *whose dogmas he was destroying;* (No, but I was preaching its charity, quite destroyed by the Priests.) *depict the beauty of virtues he was extinguishing in the soul of his Readers.* (Honest souls, is it true that I extinguish the love of virtues in you!)

He made himself the Preceptor of the human race in order to deceive it, the public Monitor in order to lead everyone astray, the oracle of the century in order to complete its destruction. (I have just examined how you proved all that.) *In a work on the inequality of conditions,* (Why conditions? That is neither my subject nor my title.) *he lowered man to the level of the beasts;* (Which of the two of us raises or lowers him, when the choice is being stupid[67] or being wicked?) *in another, more recent production, he had introduced the poison of sensual pleasure.* (Ah, would that I could replace the horrors of debauchery with the charms of sensual pleasure! But be reassured, your Grace. Your Priests are safe from *Heloise*, they have *Aloisia* as a prophylactic.)[68] *In this work, he seizes upon man's first moments in order to establish the domain of irreligion.* (This imputation has already been examined.)

That, your Grace, is how you treat me, and much more cruelly still. I whom you do not know at all and whom you judge only on hearsay. Is this the morality of that Gospel, then, whose defender you claim to be? Let us grant that you want to protect your flock from the poison of my Book. Why make personal attacks against the Author? I am ignorant of the result you expect from conduct that is so unchristian, but I know that defending one's Religion with such weapons makes it very suspect to worthy people.

Yet it is I whom you call reckless. What! How have I deserved this name merely for proposing doubts and even doing that with so much reserve, putting forward only reasons, and that with so much respect; attacking no one, naming no one? And you, your Grace, how do you dare treat like this the person you speak of with so little justice and decorum, with so little propriety, with so much levity?

You call me an impious person. And of what impiety can you accuse me, I who have never spoken of the supreme Being except to render the glory that is its due, nor of the neighbor except to bring everyone to love him? The impious are those who unworthily profane God's cause by making it serve the passions of men. The impious are those who, daring to stand as interpreters of the divinity, as arbiters between it and men, demand for themselves the honors that are its due. The impious are those who arrogate to themselves the right of exercising the power of God on earth and want to open and close Heaven at their whim. The impious are those who have Libels read in churches.... My blood boils at this horrible idea, and tears of indignation flow from my eyes. Priests of the God of peace, you will account to him someday, you can be sure, for the use you dare make of his house.

You call me an Impostor! And why? In your manner of thinking, I err. But where is my imposture? To reason and be mistaken, is that imposture? Even a sophist who deceives without deceiving himself is not yet an impostor, as long as he confines himself to the authority of reason, even though he abuses it. An impostor wants to be believed on his word, he wants to make authority by himself. An imposter is a cheat who wants to impose on others for his profit; and where, I beg you, is my profit in this affair? According to Ulpian, impostors are those who perform magic tricks, imprecations, exorcisms. Now assuredly I have never done any of that.

How you talk away at your ease, you men established in high rank! Acknowledging no rights but your own, nor Laws but those you impose, far from making it your duty to be just, you do not even believe you are obliged to be humane. You proudly oppress the weak without answering to anyone for your iniquities. Outrages are no more costly to you than acts of violence. On the slightest expediencies of your interest or state policy, you sweep us before you like dust. Some banish and burn, others defame and dishonor without right, without reason, without scorn, even without anger, uniquely because it suits them and because the unfortunate man finds himself in their path. When you insult us with impunity, we are not even allowed to complain, and if we show our innocence and your wrongs, we are further accused of lacking respect for you.

Your Grace, you have publicly insulted me. I have just proved that you have slandered me. If you were a private individual like myself, whom I could bring before an equitable Tribunal where we could both appear—I with my Book, and you with your Pastoral Letter—you would certainly be declared guilty there, and condemned to make me a restitution that is as public as the offense has been. But you hold a rank in which one is dispensed from being just; and I am nothing. However, you who profess the Gospel, you a Prelate made to teach others their duties, you know your own in such a case. As for me, I have done mine, I have nothing more to say to you, and am silent.

Vouchsafe to accept, your Grace, my profound respect.

J.J. Rousseau

From Môtiers, November 18, 1762

Fragments of the Letter to Christophe de Beaumont

I

They must not imagine that by always telling me to be humble they will finally force me to be false, to retract what I think and to say what I do not think.

Your writings full of prejudices, of partiality, of bile are personal attacks[1]; they are not censures but satires, the most openly avowed enemy would judge with less passion. Based on your Pastoral Letter, based on this strange indictment, I myself would have been horrified by my book if I had not been acquainted with it.[2]

If I were founding a republic, I would like Religion and peace there. That is why I would banish the theologians from it with as much care as Plato banished the Poets from his.[3]

2

Judging him to be without defense anyone and everyone makes haste to give him the last kick.

An author who is Catholic and French the same as crowds of others has spoken in his books about kings and about your Church with a different freedom than I have. Instead of burning his book and issuing a warrant against his person, he was received for that very reason into the French academy. It is true that this was not a poor Foreigner.[4]

I acknowledge that you need very much to be enlightened, Your Grace, pardon my frankness; but your book appears to me to have been before the illumination.

3

Isn't it clear that he would have put his head into his mouth and that consequently the part was greater than the whole. This objection, Your

Grace, is clear, simple, and even crude. Nevertheless if you find some good solution to it have the charity to teach it to us; but for mercy's sake let it be clear, simple in its turn, in conformity with the Gospel, and intelligible to the poor in spirit.

With a peremptory word you deprive him of liberty, honor, you put his life in danger.

But what do I have to retract then? I have affirmed nothing but the existence of God, his attributes, his providence, everything that is essential to religion; doubtless that is not what they want me to retract. About all the rest I have only proposed objections and one does not retract objections, one resolves them. Now if I had known how to resolve mine I would not have made them.

They affirm that I make light of all religion and the sole proof is that I respect all religions. I do not despair of seeing someone who scoffs at them, who insults them, who despises all and above all his own, pass for an extremely pious man.

4

You deceive yourself, Your Grace, you yourself are mistaken, there is not a single point in your Pastoral Letter in which you are not wrong. Nevertheless that is not what I reproach you for.
It does not depend at all on us not to deceive ourselves but it does depend on us to be moderate and just. Why have you not been so toward me?
What, because there has been a redeemer for men they must be dragged to the torture, because the messiah has come to save them they must be persecuted?
Eh, is there anything more abominable in the world than to put injustice and violence into a system and to make them flow from God's clemency. Yes, all those who in the torments they cause men to suffer dare to mix the name of the supreme Being are monsters unworthy of living. And it is their bloody doctrines that are truly abominable.

5

Unable to resolve my objections you have attacked my person, you believed you degraded me by mistreating me and you were mistaken.

Without weakening my reasons, you have inspired good will toward my person in all generous hearts. You have made sensible people believe that by judging the author so badly one could judge the book badly; by wishing to complete my ruin you have made me famous. Yes, Your Grace, far from debasing me, persecution has raised up my soul, I feel myself honored to suffer for the truth.

If I deserved insults was it up to you to tell me some? You had only to abandon me to the disdain I had deserved. If I was worthy of you taking up the pen against me, I was worthy of you sparing me insults against my honor which do not leave yours without reproach. What, I am an imposter,[5] an abominable man [. . .][6] but how do you know that, Sir, or why do you affirm it?

Sir, I do not at all confuse the Pastoral Letter you have produced against my book with those crowds of violent and calumnious writings whose authors take advantage of my disgrace in order to overwhelm the oppressed man in safety. I believe that a zeal that was more pure than enlightened has led your pen and that considering your Church and your authority as having been attacked you believed you were fulfilling a duty by warning your flock of the danger.[7] Based on this opinion, I read your pastoral letter and I believed I owed you my remonstrances on the things that did not appear to me to answer to the praiseworthy goal that you propose for yourself. I will speak to you, Sir, with all the respect that I owe to your dignity and even more to your person. Bearing in mind that I am writing to a Bishop I will employ neither declamation nor antithesis and I hope that you will find in this writing the simplicity that I would have expected to find in yours.

I admit to you that it is not without surprise that I see myself summoned in some manner before you, and that I would not have understood very well on what grounds J. J. Rousseau, Citizen of Geneva, would have been accountable for his writings to a catholic Prelate. But I am being made familiar with stranger things and such new duties are being imposed on me each day that I no longer know with which competent judges I have to deal, [to] how many judges I have to answer.

There appears under the name of a Citizen of Geneva a book printed in Holland with privilege of the Estates General. Because this book is not found to be in conformity with the Religion of the Kingdom of France it is burned at the parlement of Paris and a warrant of arrest is issued against the said Citizen of Geneva without hearing him, without knowing whether he is really the author of the said book, whether he acknowledges it as his own, whether it is he who had it printed. I will not state at all what was done in other countries, that pertains to illusion. One saw the same man who, six months before, enjoyed some esteeem in Europe and even among your people, from the same writings that you decry; one saw, I say, this same man, infirm and hardly able to drag himself along, proscribed, pursued from State to State with a barbarism that has no precedent at all. Asylum[8] would have been refused to this unfortunate man, he would perhaps have been treated even more cruelly in the same country in which the atheist Spinoza lived and died peacefully and even honored, having his books printed and sold without any obstacle, while teaching his impious doctrine publicly.

Your pastoral duty was to resolve the difficulties I proposed and not to insult me because of them.

Nevertheless, Your Grace, you deceive yourself and you deceive them, and that error is no longer one of those that are indifferent to men and one that can be left to the Priests and Theologians to dispute.

If I was in fact an impious man, an imposter, an abominable author, you would have done better to prove it without saying it than to say it without proving it.

We are, you say, sinners because of the sin of our first father, but why was our first father himself a sinner? Why wouldn't the same reason by which you explain his sin be applicable to his descendants without original sin, and why must we impute to God an injustice by making us sinful and punishable through the vice of our birth, whereas our first Father was sinful and punished like us without that. Original sin explains everything except its principle, and it is this principle that must be explained. The true original sin is our body since without any other original vice the first man sinned. He sinned because he was enlightened by the knowledge of the law for as St. Paul says if he had not known the law at all he would not have sinned at all.

Were I a sophist I would not be an impostor for all that; the name of imposter was never given to a man who is deceived by the sole reason that he reasons badly. An impostor is a man who wishes to impose upon others for his own interest and where, I beg you, is my interest in this business?

As for me, I declare, that I acknowledge no other sovereign than the law, I was born free having only the law as master and so I always will remain. If I obey the Prince in the states in which I have the good fortune to live it is not because he is my master, but because the law wishes it and the same law that imposes obedience on me also fixes its limits and conditions.

Hardly any Citizen has been seen more zealous and who knew better the extent of his duties than the Abbé de St. Pierre and I have never said as much as he did.[9]

Although my book is made too famous it will be less known there perhaps and will surely do less evil there than your pastoral letter.

Although I do not call you Your Grace,[10] because you are not my Grace, perhaps I respect you more genuinely[11] than any of those who give you that name. For I know how to honor probity, morals, piety, virtue everywhere they are found, and even in my enemies.

Your Grace, I have to defend myself against you and before you. In this discussion I will feel more than once the almost insurmountable difficulties that make the case disappear in the face of persons.

If it were only a question between you and me of examining who is wrong and who is right, who is unjust and who is insulted, that would soon be done.

I have not made any declamations, Your Grace, I have not contrived any antitheses. Instead of insults and epithets, I have stated reasons and, although insulted and persecuted, I have stated them without bitterness. But it seems to me I have proven that you have calumniated me. Thus you, who are made to teach their duty to other people, you are not unaware of yours in such a case. I have nothing more to say to you, unless it is to assure you of my profound respect.

Obscure, isolated, a fugitive, and what is worse, poor, for if I had fifty thousand livres of income, that would already give me some influence, I would begin to be something for you and you would take on a slightly more moderate language when speaking to me. But in the Condition in which I am you can in complete safety calumniate me, insult me, publicly call me an impostor, an abominable man, you can impute to me every crime you please, you will not be cited before any tribunal, you will not be held at all accountable for your imputations. On the contrary the people will admire you, respect you[12] even for your lies, will regard you as a zealous defender of the faith and friend of the truth. Proscribed, pursued, stigmatized, having become through your word an object of horror for peoples [he] will not even have the liberty of raising his voice for his defense without being taken to task for insolence and temerity. What does it matter that my life and my liberty are compromised, I am only a man of the people, am I allowed to have an honor to defend, but you, you are a man constituted in dignity whose condition, rights, prerogatives are to be unjust with impunity, and who can never be in the wrong with the weak. I feel these difficulties, Your Grace, I feel them keenly, nevertheless I undertake to overcome them and to test at least once what justice and truth can do against violence and fanaticism. I will dare, then, to defend myself against you after having kept silence until now. For executioners, stakes, chains are objections to which the false and the true are equally without reply but as for epithets and insults one can respond to them with proofs and reasons.[13]

You begin, Your Grace, by telling us that St. Paul has predicted that perilous days would come in which there[14]

Never has a prediction been better verified but if St. Paul had announced to us a time in which there would not be any such people I believe he would have made a more remarkable one.

But St. Paul appears to me to cover with figurative language reasonings that are so sophistic that either his books must have been falsified or he must not always have been inspired. In fact his disagreements with St. Peter prove that each of the two did not believe that the other was guided by the Holy Spirit in everything; a Christian can doubt this without crime since J.C. did not say in any part of the Gospel that St. Paul was inspired.

They crucified my master and gave hemlock to a man who was worth more than I am.

Thus you are already barbaric and harsh, let us see whether you are at least equitable and truthful.

But do you consider that the more you extenuate the fault the more cruel you render the punishment, for what more terrible punishment could Adam have borne[15] for the greatest crimes than to be condemned with all his race to suffer and die in this world and to pass eternity in the other one consumed by eternal flames. Is this the penalty imposed by the God of Mercifulness upon a poor ignorant man for having let himself be fooled?

I will render to myself what I owe to myself because I owe it; but while not being unaware that the justification of an innocent man is a very insipid reading.

It is known that I have enemies from the evil that has been done to me, but not from that which I have done to anyone.

What do I say, doesn't the present quarrel over Jansenism prove that there is often as much perplexity among you to determine whether a dogma has been determined by the Church as to establish the right it has to determine it?

6

One would say that you approve of education beginning by making young people into libertines so that they might have the advantage of subsequently repenting. But these repentances that follow a criminal life are of little profit. Will they erase a thousand real evils by some goods in idea? The monuments of crime cover the earth, the regret of the dying is extinguished along with them.

As a result of enlarging the way of mercy you increase the resources of malefactors. You facilitate them, but no matter how cheaply you sell heaven to the wicked, you are deceiving yourself and you are deceiving them. According to me, lengthy heinous crimes are erased only by lengthy good works, and the one who hastens to repent at death in order to have absolution does not for all that evade the remorse that will punish him in the other life.

Not, says St. Augustine naively,* to say something, but so as not to be at a loss for words.   * *de Trinit.* L. V. c. 9

7

You make it understood that according to me one does not believe in God except through someone else's authority.

the multitudes of acquired and communicated ideas with the help of which they acquire some crude notion of the divinity. But let us suppose a savage man wandering alone in the woods from his birth and all of whose time is consumed in seeking his food, devouring it, and sleeping. Will you have the nerve to maintain that this poor unfortunate will be damned for all eternity for having closed his eyes to the light and for not having imagined your treatises *de Deo uno et trino* all by himself?

    The pagans also had their revelations.
    To believe them about it they had all useful knowledge from the Gods.

8

    I have demonstrated in my *Discourse on inequality* how gradual and slow the progress of human reason is, and certainly one must not be dull-witted in order to go back without help to the primary motor of things. This is the meaning that presents itself naturally at the point that is in question in the profession of faith of the Vicar. If, then, my thought were not explained there as clearly as it is, the meaning that you give it would not be that which you should attribute to the author if you were equitable, but the one that is determined by his own writings.

    for lack of being able to combat a new truth to rail stupidly at paradox as if a paradox were a lie; as if there were no paradoxes even in geometry, and as if these paradoxes were not demonstrated.

9

    My reason could have been more convinced, but my heart could not have been more persuaded.
    The belief that I give to revelation is not a feigned belief, a belief of bad faith, it is not the blind prejudice of a man who refuses to consider the objections out of fear of being shaken by them; who seeks to hide them from others in order to take advantage of them and who—loving his opinions better than the truth—would like people to see things as he depicts them rather than as they are. Far from me these base subterfuges.

10

    I said to myself, oh what good would be done for men by the one who would tell them the truth without disguise, without fear, without satire and without flattery, the one who, uprooting their base prejudices, would dry up the source of their miseries, the one who would make them see that they are wicked only because they are dupes, and unhappy only because they are foolish, the one who would teach them that they are made to be happy and good and what they have to do to be so.

I have tried to be that man; at least I dared to be him, and what is most difficult in this enterprise is courage. I kept quiet during my youth, the rage for reputation did not devour my heart. If I had received some talent I did not hurry to show it; I waited until mature age and reflection put me in a condition to make a good use of it. I believed I saw that use and then I spoke; I did not speak for my profit but for that of my fellows, I did not chase after the ordinary career of authors, I did not aspire to their honors, to their rewards, I did nothing to make my writings fashionable except to make them as good as was possible for me to do. Perhaps I put as many errors into them as they put into theirs. But what I certainly put more of into them is a sincere desire to be useful and true, disinterestedness, and good faith. There is the glory to which I laid claim, I deserve it, I will obtain it, for the public's errors have their limit and all their cabals will not deprive me of it.

I love liberty, nothing is more natural; I was born free, each is allowed to love the government of his country and if we give leave to the subjects of Kings to speak ill of Republics with so much stupidity and impertinence, why would they not give us leave, with so much justice and reason, to speak ill of royalty. I hate servitude as the source of all the ills of the human race. Tyrants and their flatterers ceaselessly shout: peoples bear your chains without murmur because the first of goods is repose; they lie: it is liberty. In slavery there is neither peace nor virtue. Whoever has other masters than the laws is a wicked man.[16]

I penetrated the secret of governments, I revealed it to peoples not so that they might shake off the yoke, which is not possible for them, but so that they might become men again in their slavery, and, enslaved to their masters, they might not also be enslaved to their vices. If they can no longer be Citizens, they can still be wise men. The slave Epictetus was one. Whoever acknowledges only the laws of virtue and those of necessity is no longer enslaved to men. That one alone knows how to be free and good in chains.

II

It is suitable, they say, to deceive the people; but whom does it suit? The authors who deceive it and the leaders who torment it. Am I paid to be the accomplice of those people? Whoever wants to deceive wants thanks, I do not know any axiom more certain. There are prejudices that must be respected, that may be, but it is when everything is in order otherwise and when one cannot remove these prejudices without also removing what compensates for them. Then one leaves the evil for love of the good. But when the state of things is such that nothing could change anymore except for the better, are prejudices so respectable that equity, reason, virtue, and all the good that truth could do for men must be sacrificed to them? What would one say about an unfaithful servant who, seeing robbers enter the house of his master, would let them peacefully make their strike in order not to trouble his rest? If one paid for his discretion with the galleys, in my opinion, one would not be doing him a great wrong.

One vainly affects to despise the people, they have more sense than those who esteem themselves above them, and some simpleton who, with his carriage and his lackeys, talks with disdain about the people he sees in the street, would gain a great deal if he were worth as much as the least among them. The people is not as much a dupe as one thinks. If one did not use force with them, ruse would hardly serve for anything. The way one goes about it, one might just as well leave it there, one might just as well ask very openly for money for one's pleasures and for one's rogues as to ask for it with bowmen[17] for the good of peoples.[18] For they are convinced that it is their goods that one wants for their good. In this, therefore, there is no longer any secret to keep nor truths to keep silent about. The lowest peasants know as much about this as the greatest ministers do. My writings will not teach them anything about the iniquity of the stronger and my example can teach them to console themselves for it. The true springs of governments are in the cowardice of men, that cowardice adheres to roots that my books will not uproot and if they could uproot them they would do more good for men than all their legislators have done. As long as they are vicious they will be led by their vices. When they no longer are so they will no longer be led; it is true, but they will be virtuous.[19] Which is better then, that they be wicked and subjected or good and free? Answer, grave magistrates, but be clear.

12

I will be asked why then, loving Republics so much, I have always lived in the countries of Kings. To that I answer that I have lived in monarchies because I loved liberty. Let whoever can, understand this new paradox, I leave my former fellow citizens the trouble of explaining it. I further answer that the one who depends in no way on what enchains the hearts of men is free everywhere. In whatever place he is allowed to live he acknowledges no other laws than those of duty and of necessity.

The conclusion offers itself. Spare us the trouble of drawing it.

* * *

To believe that I myself am without passion in speaking to men and without any other love than that of the truth, that is assuredly neither what I do nor want to be done. I am willing, on the contrary, that people read at the bottom of my heart all the pride that animates me. I am willing that people see there all the energy of the most noble passion that can swell the heart of a good man. Doubtless I aspire to glory; after good witness of oneself it is the most worthy recompense for virtue. But this glory to which I aspire, and which I will obtain in spite of you and all my contemporaries is the only one to which opinion has not given being[20] and which draws a value from itself. All prejudices can change, entire peoples have been seen to despise riches and detest conquerors. Some have been seen among whom great talents were without honor and without practice, but none have been seen among whom zeal for justice was not esteemed and among whom true courage was despised. None have been seen who did not honor frankness and good faith when they were known to it. My own interest is to say what is useful to others without regard to my own utility, and that honor which I alone will have among the authors of my century will always cause me to be distinguished from them all and will compensate me for all their advantages. If one wishes they will be better philosophers and finer wits, they will be more profound thinkers, more precise reasoners, more pleasing writers; but I, I will be more disinterested in my maxims, more sincere in my sentiments, more an enemy of satire, bolder in speaking the truth, when it is useful to others without troubling myself about my fortune nor about my safety. They may deserve pensions, employments, places in academies, and I, I will have only insults and slights; they will be decorated and I, I will be stigmatized, but it does not matter, my disgrace will honor my courage, it will be seen that I did not deserve it at all and that I knew how to endure it, it will be seen that I did not repel outrages except by my conduct and calumny except by reasons, in sum whatever place I might obtain now, I will be alone in it and I do not want anything in common with those who deceive us, not even popular favor acquired at that price. The people hate me, I know it, but that is not their fault; this hatred is again the work of its tyrants: it is not me that it hates, it is what it has been told I was. Cruel men, self-interested and jealous men, your warrants, your stakes, your pastoral letters, your newspapers disturb and deceive them. They believe me to be a monster on the trustworthiness of your outcries. But your outcries will finally end and my writings will remain to your shame. Less prejudiced Christians will search them with surprise for the horrors you claim to find there. They will find in them along with the morality of their divine master only lessons of concord and of charity, they will learn from them to be more just than their fathers, and may their virtues someday avenge me for your maledictions.

13

Where do these contradictions come from, Your Grace? From a clear enough cause, in my opinion, it is that men have always wanted to mix their work with the work of God and spoil the purity of his worship by a thousand inventions according to their fancy based on which it is impossible for them ever to agree. What has resulted from that is that they have abandoned the essential and have attached themselves to apish antics. They have ceaselessly added, retrenched, corrected, changed; they have reduced everything to formulas, they have put everything into articles of faith. As a result of talking about what must be believed they have forgotten what must be done, doctrine has absorbed everything, it has no longer been a question of morality, and religion has no longer consisted in anything but putting on a mask in a certain manner, of taking a certain posture at a certain hour and in pronouncing certain words in certain places.

Is it surprising that in this condition faith not be in agreement with actions, that one speak in one manner and act in another, that one be a Hebrew in mouth and uncircumcised in heart, that one preach continence while sleeping with other people's wives?

From this furor to settle everything, to explain everything, to pronounce upon what one understands the least; from this audacity to make God speak incessantly

While always settling, explaining, pronouncing, one has made one's way

As a result of advancing and of settling one has contradicted oneself one time, and one has never been able to remove these contradictions, because having always made God speak, his interpreters have not been able to retract what they have said in his name. In order to sanctify the foolishness of men one has made the divinity responsible for them, and one has made it speak the most palpable absurdities that had indeed to be received in silence when an arrogant priest

Thus the vehicle for every extravagance has been the *submit, for God has spoken*.

Whoever says that he believes absolutely everything that we are taught and that he believes it without seeing the slightest difficulty in it is certainly either a liar or a fool.

There are liars who say they believe, and imbeciles who believe they believe.

It is to represent God as a poor workman who is forced at every moment to make alterations in his machine for lack of knowing how to set it up all at once as it should be.

all the miracles he goes about doing here and there as if to pass his time. Agree for example that those of your correligionists are funny miracles, and that if God amuses himself with such conjuring tricks he must be very much at loose ends.

Of all the Religions of the world yours is the most tormenting, precisely because it is the least reasonable. One must incessantly intimidate, frighten men. If you leave them to their reason for a moment you are lost.

But human reason is not governed as men are, it is free by its essence, one cannot tyrannize over it, authority has no hold upon it at all, one can sooner annihilate it than enslave it. One can well retail absurdities to a reasonable man and order him to believe them, all he can do is to lower his head in silence but his mind does not consent. You can force him to speak but you can not force him to acquiesce within himself; he can only lie in order to please you. To convince him one must begin by making him mad.

This is the case of fanaticism. But fanaticism is a state of crisis among a people or in a sect; it cannot last forever, it has fits but it calms itself and reason takes back its rights. It is then that, coming back to itself, it sees with surprise this labyrinth of aberrations into which one has entered during one's delirium, having become more reasonable one is completely astonished at having been so little so; but it is no longer time to take it back. Religion is established, formulas are drawn up, laws are passed, transgressors are punished, who would dare to clamor against it if the very one who respects them while weighing them is treated this way. Thus one submits to them in appearance, one pretends to believe what the citizens say they believe, in order to be one. One professes one's father's religion in order to inherit his property. One does what is necessary in order not to be punished, even more and when one can speak in liberty one laughs at one's ease about everything one has the appearance of respecting in public. Those who have a particular interest in the thing, those who deal in selling paradise keep their merchandise in credit as much as they can. But their crude zeal deceives no one. That is the system one wishes to treat with consideration because it is useful for those who lead the others, I am not paid to deceive the public in favor of those people.

14

Our doctrines are imperfect in every respect and our discussions are misunderstandings. For what is more imperfect than Religions that do not teach their sectary to do good and what is a greater misunderstanding than discussions that do not lead to conviction. Those are the great objects of investigations and very important to the human race.[21]

Various and hardly reasonable Religions will always exist on the earth, and in these religions there will always be people who profess them without believing in them. When these people make up the majority then the Religions become more pernicious than useful, they do not do any good for anyone and their cloak serves to cover infinite evils. In this condition one is attached all the more to the forms because these forms are the only thing left, they have particular interests as support, and these particular interests are the most powerful ones in the State.

In everything the false appearance of order is worse than an absolute disorder.

It is a very great temerity in the Fathers who explained and in the Councils who settled everything to have wanted to make clear what was obscure in scripture and to pronounce about what was unsettled, as if the sacred authors did not know how to explain themselves more clearly without them if they had wanted to.[22] For example why this word of trinity which is not in the bible? Why these decisions upon the manner in which God and man are joined in J.C. since neither the Gospel nor the apostles have said anything about it? Your theologians, having the rage of explaining everything up to the mystery, take delight in a certain gibberish that accustoms them to talk nonsense ceaselessly, to be understood neither among themselves nor by others and to explain everything without knowing anything. St. Paul himself admits he knew only in part what your Doctors claim to know in everything. I Cor. XIII: 8 and following.

The one who claims to see clearly what they have seen obscurely is a heretic from the very fact that he meddles in seeing things differently or better than they have seen them.

I do not know, Your Grace, whether I deceive myself, but my own history appears to me to characterize my century regarding the condition of

Religion very well. I admit that I have only the proof of sentiment for this, but I am strongly affected by it. The public has the piece in its hands in order to judge about what I see. I think, then, and it is an idea it would be cruel to deprive me of, for it makes up the consolation of my life, I think that every man who believes in God, of whatever religion he might be, will never read the profession of the Savoyard vicar without being moved by it, without feeling that the author's heart has spoken to his, without experiencing some benevolence for him, without saying to himself if I do not think the way that man does, I would at least want everyone to think as he does. That, according to me, is what every true believer reading that writing must say in himself if he has a soul as pure as his faith. Instead of this . . . let us not retrace the history of my miseries.[23] One day perhaps what is the shame of my century will be its glory, and those who will read my book will say with admiration: How angelic those times must have been in which a book like that was regarded as impious, doubtless then all writings breathed the most sublime devoutness and the earth was covered with nothing but saints.

If the peoples no longer have any religion it is the fault of the Clergy, they have demanded so much faith that one could not find enough of it to satisfy them, and soon one abandoned everything. If they had eased up over some articles perhaps they might have preserved the rest but when one demands all or nothing the choice of the one who cannot give all is soon made.

Every doctrine that prescribes more articles of belief than motives for virtue is bad.

15

How can it happen that all those people so zealous for the dogmas of Christianity follow its morality so poorly, and that with such an ardent faith they have so little charity?

We believe revelation, not because it is demonstrated to us, which according to me is very far from being true; but because it would be desirable that it be so, because we love to believe it, because our heart is touched by the great things it proclaims to us, by the great lessons it gives us and that we would discover with greater difficulty without that, and because without it we would have more difficulty in practicing.

* * *

I who never offended anyone, what enemies can I have other than those who have offended me; but they are all the more implacable the more unjust they are. For sometimes the offended person forgives, but the offender never forgives.

The certitude of moral proofs cannot bear on any facts except those that are in the order of moral possibilities.

And just as people in Lapland would be mistaken to establish 4 feet as the natural stature of man, we ourselves would be no less mistaken to establish the size of human souls on the basis of those of the people we see around us.

not ceding anymore to their prejudices than to their wills, and keeping mine as free as my reason.

16

A miracle is indeed a supernatural thing, but not absurd nor contradictory in itself. Hence I have not absolutely rejected miracles, although I do not quite know what proof is sufficient to verify one of them well; for to content oneself with a proof similar to the one that verifies a natural event, that is foolishness. Thus I could see a miracle and believe it. But never will one make me believe an absurdity by virtue of this miracle, unless it began by making me go mad. I do not see in this where the inconsistency and absurdity is that you find in it.

17

In order to understand the language of inspired men it would be necessary to be inspired oneself. Without which everything obscure and inconceivable they say to us is for us only words without ideas. It is as if they were saying nothing to us.

18

Such are my sentiments, Sir, which I do not give as a rule for anyone but which I declare to be my own and which will remain such not as long as it will please men, but until it pleases God to change my heart or my reason. For as long as I will be what I am and I will think as I am thinking, I will speak as I am speaking. Very different I admit from your Christians in effigy always ready to believe what must be believed, to say what must be said for their interest, their repose, very sure of always being good enough Christians[24] as long as their books are not burned and a warrant is not issued for their arrest. Whether I should have kept these sentiments to myself alone as they do not stop saying; whether when I had the courage to publish them, to name myself, I attacked[25] the laws and violated public order is what I will soon examine. In the mean time

[On Proceedings against Writers]

. . . From that alone falls, with regard to the whole profession of faith of the Vicar, the advantage that is drawn against me from the fact that I put my name at the head of the book. For with regard to that writing[26] the author is as it were anonymous, the public can very well presume that this author is that of the book; but if such presumptions sufficed before Tribunals to issue a warrant against a man in a free country where would justice be, or where would liberty be?

I do not say that one can print with impunity every bad book as long as one is not its author; but I say that although one might be able to impute to the Editor the evil done by the sentiments he publishes, one cannot nevertheless impute these sentiments to him unless he has expressly adopted them. From that follows an essential difference in the procedure about which I will speak below.

And what a door wouldn't one be opening to violence and persecution[27] if one could equally impute to the author all the propositions he gives as his own and all those that he puts into the mouth of someone else.[28] It would follow that every time he established contradictory discussions one could impute[29] to him the pro and the con[30] above all when the question is not clear enough to admit an unanswerable solution. One could charge him at pleasure with the one out of the two sentiments that make him guilty, and under the pretext that he had not combatted it invincibly enough, maintain that it is the one he secretly favors. It is that way, for example, that decent censors certify that in *Julie*[31] I establish suicide and attack prayer because one of the correspondents who is refuted by others advances these opinions[32] in fact.[33] That my enemies reason this way, that is their trade; and I am not seen to rouse myself very much to answer them. But that someone might take it into his head to enter the above as a serious accusation against me in a legal proceeding,[34] this would certainly be a new jurisprudence that would never have taken place except against me.

Among a thousand examples, I take only one. If there has ever been a

Book that must have displeased the Clergy it was certainly the one by Baron de la Hontan.[35] You know that these Gentlemen are not depicted to their advantage in it and that objections against Religion are neither rare nor weak in it. Nevertheless have you ever heard it said that anyone picked a fight with the Baron de la Hontan about his book? If someone had wouldn't he have made fun of his Judges, wouldn't he have said to the[36]

BOOKS I AND II
History of the Government of Geneva

In order to know the constitution of the Republic of Geneva well, it is necessary to go back to its origins. It is necessary to find what the political State of that City was when the present government was instituted.[1]

It is known that under Catholicism the Bishop exercised sovereignty. To look for how he had acquired it is a labor of pure erudition that is not at issue here. To find the extent of his power and to show where the distribution of his rights came from, is to clarify by means of principles the transmission of this power and of these rights from the Prince to the Republic. After the fall of the western Empire and the extinction of the two Kingdoms of Burgundy several Bishops, alone keeping an independent power, had no trouble extending it over the debris of the one that no longer existed. The people, prey to brigands and no longer being able to do without masters, submitted without trouble to the only men who conserved any rights over it. The ambition of the pastor and the need of the flock cooperated in this change. Reason itself wished peoples — for lack of Princes powerful enough to protect them — to give themselves by preference to leaders whose station took the place of force.

Let us limit ourselves to practice and to the distribution that the Prince made of his rights in order to see the true foundations of the establishment that still exists. It would be superfluous for our object to burrow beyond this.

I do not believe that the Bishops of Geneva ever enjoyed an absolute power, regarding either independence or authority. At first they acknowledged the jurisdiction of the Emperors, before long that of the Popes, and afterward both to some degree at the same time, which often caused revocations, contradictions, and conflicts over competency. They acknowledged in the people some rights and franchises that were not simple voluntary concessions and that they could not revoke. Finally they had as vassals the Counts of the Genevese and the Dukes of Savoy who followed them so that the sovereign himself could not take back the portion of power he had alienated to these princes; in spite of him they were his officers and enjoyed by right of birth a part of the executive power.

But without entering into these discussions of antiquity, let us suppose that at first the sovereignty of the Bishop was absolute and begin from there. We will find in the condition of things alone the reason for all the concessions of the Prince and for all the modifications that his authority susequently received. So that if the Bishop had begun by being a despot he would necessarily have finished by having only a tempered power. The force of things alone would have reduced him to the same point to which the defense and extension of the rights of others could have reduced him.

[Book I]

Geneva is a very old city. Caesar went there and does not speak of it as a recent city. But it is not the history of this city that I am undertaking to expose here.

After the destruction of the Roman Empire, the Allobrogians, of whom Geneva made up a part, fell under the domination of the Kings of Burgundy. After the destruction of the Kings of Burgundy, the conquerors invaded their States. What they could not seize or conserve fell into anarchy. Finally, the power of Charlemagne passed in a flash, all the parts of this vast empire fell scattered into a thousand hands and finished destroying themselves between the hands that sought to wrest them from one another.

Modern Governments have not been, as those of ancient peoples were, formed in one piece and founded so to speak in a single stroke. Formerly States that were new or reborn through sudden revolutions sometimes gave themselves a master and sometimes a Constitution. A single man whose functions were well beyond those of Kings was in this latter case charged with the enterprise, and adopted by the nation, his labor formed a regular system all of whose parts cooperated toward the same end since they were made for each other. This is no longer the case among the moderns, all our governments—built up successively out of pieces related less in accordance with the public needs than in accordance with private aims—in their irregularities show only the peculiarity of the events that caused them. Among us the name of Legislator is no longer anything but an abstract word more fit to represent the one who gives force to the laws than the one who drafts them. There is no longer any other Legislator than force nor other laws than the interest of the more powerful. And if sometimes one sees a body of laws issuing from the same hand being passed by a people, they are no longer anything but civil laws that have no bearing on the government.

It follows from this that in order to study the political laws of a modern State well one must not begin by taking them as a body in order then to analyze them, but on the contrary one must take them at their origin and follow the order of their composition. For one cannot clearly fathom their spirit except with the aid of the circumstances that have produced them and of the effects that those who made them anticipated would arise from them.

This is true above all for small Governments which, like that of Geneva, always agitated but sheltered from violent storms, have lasted in the midst of continual agitations without experiencing great revolutions. And in fact we will see that the most marked revolution experienced by that City and the one that gave birth to the Republic left it in several respects as it was beforehand and raised liberty itself only on the basis of the Episcopal Government. Thus in order to explain the present Government I am obliged to go back to its source and often to clarify what exists by means of what happened a long time ago. My plan is not however to plunge into antiquities; I will leave behind everything that is merely critical or erudite research in order to limit myself to what pertains most closely to my subject.

Geneva was formerly subject to two sorts of authority, between which sovereignty was as it were divided, namely that of the Bishops and that of the Counts. These two authorities equally emanated from imperial concessions; but they differed both in the order of antiquity and in the use the concessionaries made of them. The counts, who were at first only officers of the Emperors and whose high rank was only for life and even revocable, took advantage of the empire's disorders in order to render it hereditary and independent.

Too weak and too occupied elsewhere to be able to repress this usurpation at that time, the Emperors preferred to alienate to the Bishop the sovereignty that was slipping away from them rather than to abandon it to rebels. Since the favor of the people was for its pastor, at least in the city it was easy for the Bishop to secure a power that he had legitimately acquired; while the count, master of the castles and of the countryside, conserved the one he had usurped no less easily. From that came the natural division of their power. From that came the frequent contentions between the Bishop and the count, from that came the often contradictory judgments of the Imperial Court depending on which one of them was more in favor. For, because the supreme right of the Empire had always been held in reserve, neither of the two competitors ever dared decisively to disregard it, and the weaker always made it into a resource to stop the undertakings of the more powerful.

It seems also that the people had acquired or preserved some rights whose origin one cannot see in history, but which one can find by induction. For it seems to me hardly probable that it would not have lost under so many masters the use of a right that all peoples have naturally.

Thus there was a perpetual dispute among three parties, the best founded of which was ordinarily the weakest. By a sort of compensation, this formed an equilibrium among all of them and prolonged the dissensions without it being possible to see the end of them. Such was just about the political condition of the city of Geneva for almost five centuries from the end of the second Kingdom of Burgundy up to the extinction of the episcopacy.

In a rather simple manner one can acquire an exact conception of this Government without entering into the examination of facts disputed among the parties. To do so it is enough to assume that the Bishops at first enjoyed absolute power. Whether this was by a concession of the Emperors or by their own usurpation, as is more likely, does not matter. It does not even matter that the fact be true. It is enough that from this sole hypothesis well applied one can deduce the whole system of the constitution. If one does not know from this how it was established, at least one will know very exactly what it was, and that is the sole object that I am proposing for myself in this writing.

Let the sovereign authority then have been at first entirely in the hands of the Bishops, I say that it should naturally be divided and tempered as it was: for, since by his station the Bishop was not able to hold either the military sword or the criminal sword by himself, he had to put both into other hands, but always in a manner so that the depositories made use of it only under his authority.

The manner in which this division was made depends on the times, on places, and on the situation of the country. When the temporal authority of the Bishops was established they had for neighbors, not great Princes, but lords powerful enough to make themselves feared without being powerful enough to subjugate them. To protect their territory from these plunderers, they gave the guardianship of it to the one who could protect them or hurt them the most, and in order to make him take an interest in their defense it was necessary to cede him a portion of their rights. From that came those of the Counts, who exercised the executive power in the State; but under the authority of the Bishop, of whom they acknowledged themselves feudatories and to whom they gave homage as to their suzerain, for the Bishop himself was a vassal of the Empire.

The Diocese of Geneva was large, which made the power of the count very formidable, and under the name of defender—that is what was called in other places advocate, *advocatus*—of the Church, he could easily have been its oppressor. As a matter of good policy it was necessary to give his power a counterweight. This counterweight could only be the City itself, the only refuge where the force of the Count could not be extended under cover of the castles and fortresses he occupied in the country. But the City was small in proportion to the territory. Too weak to hold his own against a Count armed with such a great power, the Bishop was constrained to allow him to exercise it in the city itself. With more limited possessions the Bishops would have maintained themselves better. Once it passed into other hands, their own power was one of the instruments of their ruin.

Another cause was in the difference between the isolated, precarious, and individual state of the Bishop and the state of the count who by his temporal power, by his family and his alliances, had a solid and permanent base which the Episcopacy did not have. If the Bishops had been married, it is to be presumed that then their power, having become hereditary, would have maintained itself better and that they would not have needed the Counts or that they would have kept them in their dependence. But the celibacy of Priests which is believed to be so useful to the clergy has often been harmful to it, above all on the occasions similar to the one at issue: for in opposition to a house forever existing whose interests did not change at all and whose projects and intentions were transmitted from Father to children, the Bishops, taken successively from various countries and from various families, and whose interests, feelings, and maxims changed with each mutation, could not sustain a too unequal competition for very long, and insensibly themselves returned to the dependency in which they had at first put the counts.

It is true that the first counts were for life, as were the Bishops, and even revocable, which the Bishops were not, but the high rank of the counts having become hereditary as a result of the weakening of the Empire, their power increased all the more rapidly since, often having the influence to have the Bishops chosen from among their families, they were then favored by them in their usurpations.

Since this double defect in the sovereign authority, a defect that depended on the one side on the site of the territory and on the other on the episcopal state, could not be corrected, it forced the Prince always to lean on the weaker party against the stronger and to oppose the City to the Count in all the latter's usurpations. From that came the system rather consistently followed by the Bishops of favoring the people on every occasion and returning to it in small portions what they had usurped all at once under the Emperors. From that came the great concessions they made to it, the franchises they gave or confirmed to it at different times, and which made the City free and almost republican under the authority of a sovereign. Moreover, to me it seems rather unreasonable to make these franchises go back to times anterior to the Bishops, no monument worthy of faith authorizes this opinion. What rights could be claimed by peoples accustomed for numerous centuries to constantly carrying the yoke of the strongest? At that time there were only nobles and villains, that is to say conquerors and conquered peoples. Like all the ancient cities, Geneva was always in the latter class and in those unfortunate times one does not see the vestige of a single Republic. Thus the idea of going to look for some image of liberty under the kings of Burgundy and under Charlemagne is chimerical. Liberty sprang up only under the Episcopacy, and the Bishops, whom the people of Geneva regard as the ancient tyrants of their fatherland, were in fact its fathers and Benefactors.

Nevertheless, neither all the measures of the Bishops nor the sort of league they had with the City could shield them from the usurpations of the Counts whose undertakings, having become unbearable, forced the Bishop to look outside for a support against the Tyranny of his vassal.

Here begins to figure in the history of Geneva the warlike and wise house whose noble origin is lost in the night of times, whose genealogy offers a continuous succession of great men, and which marches with slow and steady steps for eight centuries toward an eminence whose limit is not to be seen.

After long wars almost always to the disadvantage of the counts of the Genevese, the last among them sold his heritage and his rights to the celebrated Amadeus VIII. Fortified by the vicarage of the Empire, the princes of Savoy, longtime rivals and finally successors of the Counts of the Genevese, then knew so well how to extend and make the most of their pretensions that they were on the point of making themselves completely sovereigns of Geneva. That would infallibly have happened in spite of the assistance of the Swiss and above all of the canton of Fribourg, if the unforeseen revolutions brought about by the Reformation had not rescued that city at the moment when it was already under the yoke.

That is the key to the old Government of Geneva; let us now set forth the system it opened up, and let us enter into the details of the administration.

That of the city and that of the territory were always distinct and separate. In them justice was administered neither in the same manner, nor by the same authority. The country was subject to two different powers: that of the Bishop and that of the Count. At first only two authorities were recognized in the City also, namely that of the Bishop and that of the community. Later on the Count also introduced his own and three authorities were recognized there. The Bishop was very much the only sovereign everywhere, but the exercise of power was divided, and he could not claim the parts of it that had been alienated to others.

THE BISHOP

After having been the most free of all peoples the Romans became the most enslaved; their servitude was that of the whole empire; the very idea of liberty was effaced under the Emperors. It seems that it should have been reborn under the barbarians. Not at all. Only domination and slavery, conquerors and conquered peoples were seen. Aristotle's division came back in an opposite sense. The Greeks and Romans were low commoners, the Goths and Lombards were the nobles.[2] Natural law gave way to the law of the conquerors. The feudal system degraded human nature and there were no longer any men properly speaking.

Between these two classes, the one debased and the other ennobled, a third was formed that served as a connection between them and without which it would have been difficult for this strange division to continue to exist. This intermediate estate was the clergy. Christianity was opportunely established in Europe to moderate the ferocity of the peoples ready to subjugate it. If the Romans, fiercely against the Christians, had had the misfortune to destroy them, they would soon have been destroyed by the barbarians themselves. But this new form of worship that they were persecuting was their safeguard, the law of Christ—which is the law of humanity—was the only thing that could restrain men when governments and their laws no longer existed.

This was one of the causes of the great authority taken on by the Clergy at that time. Mediator between the conquerors and the conquered, they often saved the latter from the cruelty of the others. In times of calamities and aggression the people had no protector other than its priests. They alone could speak for it; such a noble function made their station respectable even to pagans. They abused their influence in order to extend their power, but let us agree that one could not have based it on a finer title. The leaders of the Clergy, more heeded by Princes and more in a condition to protect the peoples, had the trust of both of them. Thus the great authority of the Bishops established itself. Call them usurpers, I consent to it; but admit that under their usurpation the people were a hundred times happier than under the Princes.

In this way was formed the temporal authority of a great number of Bishops in Germany and of those of Basel, Sion, Lausanne, and Geneva in Switzerland.

At first founded solely on the respect one had for them and on the favor of the people, the power of these last maintained itself. It increased under the Kings of Burgundy through the unrest, the murders, the revolutions that often made the interposition of these Prelates necessary. Finally, under Charlemagne and his successors, it acquired a fixed and legal footing from the enfeoffment made to them by these Emperors of the temporal authority over their diocese with which they found themselves vested.

I am speaking only about the temporal here. I am leaving aside the purely episcopal authority common to all Bishops.

The Bishop of Geneva was sole Prince and sovereign in his City and in his diocese, within the immediate jurisdiction of the Empire of which nevertheless his State never formed an active part, because he was never recognized a member of the Germanic body nor admitted to the diet either in person or through his deputies.

His vassalage was even of a rather singular sort: for although he acknowledged the authority of the Empire and of the imperial Bulls, he conferred neither faith nor homage upon the Emperor, did not receive investiture from him, did not render him any obeisance, and did not even take part in his election. This appears to prove in favor of those Genevans who claim that their city has always been free and imperial. In effect the Bishop, considered not as sovereign but as leader of an Imperial City, did not need any investiture and was not any less obligated to acknowledge the Emperor's authority. If his deputies did not enter into the college of the cities, it is because it was not precisely a member of the Empire, but under its protection.

Not only as Bishop but also as Prince, the Bishop also acknowledged the authority of the Pope, who by his bulls, by his stewards, or by himself rather frequently delivered judgments about his disputes as much with the Count and the neighboring Princes as with the City itself. Often appeal about civil business was brought to the archbishop[3] and subsequently to Rome, and these appeals finally became so frequent and so inconvenient that this abuse very much facilitated the progress of the reformation.

Since the power of the Prince was mixed it was not really well known to whom the right of electing him belonged. The clergy, the people, and the Pope claimed it. At first the Bishop was elected by the people, in accordance with the practice of the primitive church, afterward he was by the people and by the clergy jointly, afterward by the clergy alone, and finally the election was made by the canons alone. The consent and the Bulls of the Pope were always necessary, he did not refuse them, but sometimes he named a Bishop himself, and one saw three Bishops at the same time, one named by the Pope, another by the People, and another by the clergy. Influence and intrigue, as one might believe, always played a large part in these elections. It seems that at the beginning the counts were for life and, as officers of the Bishops, were chosen and named by them or at least by the Emperors at their solicitation and then it was natural that the choice of the Bishop fell upon his brother or on one of his relatives. As soon as the Countship, having become hereditary, was the appanage of one family, it was reciprocally natural that the count endeavored to have his son, his brother, or someone from his house elected Bishop. With the aid of this policy, the old counts of Geneva had already usurped very many of the rights of the Prince, but these usurpations became larger and more rapid when the countship of the Genevese, having passed into the house of Savoy, put it in the position to employ all its power to dispose of the Episcopacy. For then, the Bishops, almost all poor or subject to the Dukes, hardly ever failed to favor their enterprises at the expense of their own successors.

Although the real power of the Bishops increased or diminished in accordance with the times, in the City they constantly enjoyed the royal rights[4] of sovereignty: that of coining money and that of pardoning criminals. Civil justice was exercised in their name, they had numerous officers whose authority and superiority were acknowledged throughout the city, as Princes and independent of the officiality they had their own private prisons; the *lods* and confiscations belonged to them in large measure. They had the right to have the general council assembled, to have the matters that pleased them proposed there, and the Syndics could not convoke it without the Bishop's permission.

But their spiritual authority, which had acquired the temporal power for them, always limited it. They never had a garrison in the city, nor their own troops, nor authority of arms; they never imposed capital punishments either by themselves or by their immediate officers. Their only de facto proceeding was excommunication, and the effect it had against the city in 1309 proves that it was more effective than that of arms; but in the end their sovereignty, which came from ecclesiastic authority, depended enough on it so that at all times the Prince would have been insignificant if the Bishop did not protect him.

THE COUNT

It is to be presumed that the Counts of the Genevese received their high rank from the Emperors as all the others did, since the first time these counts are spoken of is to obtain the confirmation of their titles from the Emperor. Nevertheless, far from being above the Bishops, they were their vassals. It is proven by various acts that they gave homage to them from the first times. They even held a portion of their rights from the Bishops. Numerous ancient titles give credence to this and, among others, an act of 1124 between Bishop Wido and his brother Aymon, count of the Genevese.

Formerly the Counts had no authority in the city, and in place of the title of Counts of Geneva, which they took later on, at first they had only that of Counts in the territory of the Genevese: *Comes in pago Gehennensi*; this part of the Diocese, which they possessed in fief within the jurisdiction of the Bishop, became a special province under the name of *Genevese*, which it still bears today even though it is independent of the Republic. Even though the lords of this Province sometimes affected to qualify themselves as *Counts of Geneva*, they were never qualified in the City as anything but *Counts of the Genevese*.

Continuing to take advantage of the favor of time, their successors little by little acquired some authority in Geneva, and, transmitted to the Counts of Savoy, this authority increased rapidly in their hands. One even sees the counts of Savoy and of the Genevese each have their castle and their garrison in the city at the same time.

It is true that, by an agreement, these two castles were to have been demolished and that the one belonging to the count of Geneva (which was in the Borough of Four) was in fact demolished, but the one belonging to the count of Savoy (which was on the Isle) remained standing and it was there that until the reformation he kept an Officer who is spoken of in the following chapter.

The counts of Geneva had occupied castles and maintained garrisons in the city. But they had never had such officers there. It was only through the treaty of 1290 that the count of Savoy, having become lord of the countship of the Genevese, for which he paid homage to the Bishop, stipulated this new right. And as the name of count had become odious to the people of Geneva, his lieutenant did not take the name of viscount, but that of vidomne,[5] *vice dominus*. The Genevans maintain that it was the count of Savoy himself who bore this title of vidomne, a title that his lieutenant, who at first had only that of castellan, took only a long time afterward. Thus according to the Writers of Savoy, the count was lord of his chief, and according to those of Geneva he was only the lieutenant of the Bishop, and his castellan in Geneva was properly only the lieutenant of the lieutenant.

At first this officer was established only to render justice to the subjects of the Duke who were present in the city. Afterward he was also charged with the custody of prisoners and the execution of criminal judgments rendered by the episcopal judges or by the Syndics. By putting the executive power into the hands of the vidomne, this right, which did not appear very honorable, became the instrument used by the Dukes to extend their power.

Finally, in more recent times the House of Savoy, having added to the ancient rights of the counts those that it held from the bulls of the Emperors, and moreover, having subjugated the Bishops whom it had elected as it pleased, succeeded in leaving them only the name of Princes and in exercising an almost arbitrary power in the city. But since that was never done without opposition on the part of the people, these usurpations were unable to ordain contrary to its franchises nor to abolish its right to liberty.

Consider what peace, what security, what public order could reign in a city whose administration was constantly disputed among four authorities and in which two enemy Princes each had a castle from which—endlessly at war against each other—they cooperated only to lay waste to the inhabitants together.

THE FRANCHISES

The origin of the franchises and liberties of the people of Geneva is lost in the mists of time. In the famous act of the Bishop Ademarus Fabri, this Bishop himself acknowledges that these franchises that he sanctions exist from times immemorial. Still, one cannot assume that in the disorders brought about by the fall of the Roman Empire any people or any city preserved the slightest shadow of liberty. The feudal system founded on the enslavement of the conquered was not suited to giving birth to it again. The Bishops, the only protectors of the People, extricated it from its degradation, and the municipal rights of the city of Geneva were established only on those of the Clergy. The Prince who owed his power to the people paid his debt with usury, he founded liberty. It came from the side from which one would least have expected it.

Geneva had just about the same rights under its Bishops as Neufchâtel has under its Princes. The honor and inconvenience of government were for the Prelate, the advantage and security were for the people. Protected from the outside by his sovereign, from the inside by his franchises, the Genevan feared neither his master nor his neighbors, he was much more free than if he had been completely Republican.

His municipal administration was as democratic as possible. The people acknowledged neither classes nor privileges nor any inequality among its members; it acted either by itself in general council, or by its procurators called Syndics whom it elected annually, and who accounted to it for their administration; no intermediary order interposed itself between them and it, and that is the true characteristic of Democracy. We shall see how this characteristic changed little by little by the establishment of a Council.

One can well imagine that by the People I understand only the body of the bourgeoisie, as it also is understood in the Edicts of the Republic in which this word is employed in the same sense. It is not known when the true right of Bourgeoisie began, it is known only that it is extremely old and that the title of Bourgeois of Geneva was very honorable for the Bishops. When Pope Martin V passed through Geneva in 1418 the city gave Letters of Bourgeoisie to four of his cardinals, and the last Bishop, Pierre de la Baume, asked the general council to be admitted to the Bourgeoisie, which was granted him. This fact is one of the most remarkable ones and pertains too much to the subject of this chapter not to be clarified in it.

At first being vassals of the Bishops, the Princes of Savoy, having little by little made the Bishops dependent on them, wished to extend their own authority over the city under cover of the episcopal authority. In spite of some apparent successes, they did exactly the opposite of what they wanted: because they wanted to enhance the sovereignty of the Bishop in order to appropriate it for themselves and on the contrary they weakened it without acquiring it. They wanted to enslave the people by means of the Bishop, and on the contrary by resisting them in this the people also learned to resist the Bishop who supported them, so that the closer servitude was seen to approach, the more steps were made toward liberty. The fact cited above is an example of this. In accordance with ancient agreements the city could not make a treaty with any power without the consent of the Bishop, but near the end of the fifteenth century, pressed by necessity, it made a treaty on its own authority and, once usurped, this right furnished it with the means to maintain itself in it. From this resulted the treaties of co-bourgeoisie with Fribourg and Berne. Not being able to break apart this alliance, and wishing at least to reduce its advantage by dividing it, the Bishop found no other means but to be admitted to the Bourgeoisie. He was, but one sees from the consequences of this step that he had acquired nothing and ceded a great deal.

I have said that there was no inequality of rights in the Bourgeoisie. For at that time the difference between Citizens and Bourgeois did not exist* and everyone could equally attain offices. Nevertheless there were inhabitants who were not bourgeois; newcomers were not supposed at first to share the rights of the children of the house. But the sons of the inhabitants became bourgeois by their birth, and the word *native*[6] was no more known than that of citizen.

---

* The word *citizen*, which one finds in ancient acts is only a literal translation of the word *cives*, and has no other meaning than that of the word *Bourgeois*, which cannot be rendered in Latin.

Sometimes even the inhabitants entered into the general Council, above all when it was composed only of heads of families; for then all those who were heads entered it indiscriminately. But if the people was hardly jealous of its exclusive rights, it was very much so of its franchises because it did not lose its rights by sharing them, whereas the slightest inroad on its franchises was one on its liberty. Rights were for the community, the franchises belonged to persons, it is by them that each enjoyed his belongings in peace and slept in safety under his roof.

The various articles of these franchises are expressed in several declarations of the Bishops and notably in that of Ademarus Fabri in 1387. This Document, authentic and regarded by the bourgeoisie of Geneva as the foundation of its liberty, contains a large number of articles that are trivial, but there are some extremely important ones in it. In it the Bishop declares that he is only gathering together or confirming franchises so old that there is no memory to the contrary, he confirms them in such a way that non-usage cannot prescribe against them and that he leaves neither to his successors nor to anyone the right of revoking them. For them to be abolished it would be necessary for the People of Geneva to renounce them by an act as solemn as the one by which they are ensured of them.

ON THE VIDOMNE

The Vidomne, *Vice Dominus*, officer of the Bishop, receiving orders from him, judging in his name, was nevertheless subject to the Duke of Savoy, named by him, bearing his arms and occupying his castle on the Island. One conceives how under cover of this equivocal State the Dukes of Savoy, little by little making the vidomne to be considered as their own officer, finally passed themselves off as sovereigns in Geneva.

But one does not conceive at first how the Duke named an officer of the Bishop. The vidomnate, whose origin is very obscure, pledged itself, sold itself, and passed from hand to hand like an inheritance. Now it appears that at first this office belonged to the counts of the Genevese. It was pledged for sixty livres to Bishop Humbert de Grammont, it is not known by whom. Bishop Pierre de Sessons wanted to cede it for thirty livres to Pierre de Confignon, who was laying claim to it by right of inheritance, but the Chapter was opposed to it. In 1285, Amé 5, count of Savoy, having entered a league with the city against the count of the Genevese, seized the castle of the Island and that office which was afterward ceded to him in fief by the Bishop Guillaume de Conflans for the expenses of the war, which could not be paid to him. This is how the vidomnate passed into the house of Savoy.

THE MAGISTRATES

The City had no magistracy for life, but every year the people assembled in general council took back the powers it had given and entrusted them anew to whomever it pleased, and the depositaries of these powers were called syndics.

The Syndics have always been four in number elected annually by the people to be its procurators and to act in its name in all the community's business. Every year upon leaving office they reported on their administration in general council, standing up and bare-headed in front of the assembly, which was wearing hats and seated.

Their power was great, as will be said below; it is also one of the characteristics of Democracy that the more free the people is, the more the authority of the leaders it elects ought to be extended. Each carried a black stick decorated with silver as a sign of his dignity. These sticks were extremely respected. This custom appears old. Leti says that these sticks were invented in 1450 on the occasion of a procession in which, since all the bodies had some distinctive mark, the canon Montelli imagined this one for the syndics. Although rather an enemy of the Clergy, this author had a singular taste for ecclesiastical ceremonies. The syndics always took them when it was a question of pacifying some insurrection and often the sight of this scepter alone impressed more than the magistrate who was carrying it.

Sometimes syndics were removed from office, even all four of them were in 1519. But that was never done except with violence and in an illegal manner. A syndic cannot be removed from office without giving him a trial, and during the year of his reign—this word is consecrated by custom at Geneva and they say, "the reigning syndics"—he cannot lose his place except with his head.

A Treasurer and a secretary were also elected in general Council, and since these offices involved no jurisdiction, the people gave them for three years and sometimes confirmed them for three more.

The Syndics had Councilors or assessors of their choice, who had only an advisory voice: for, not being named by the people, they were nothing for it but simple private men without Tribunal, without jurisdiction, without authority. Each Syndic chose four or five of them from among the citizens and their functions ended with his. Sometimes there were sixteen of them, sometimes eighteen, sometimes twenty. Their number was not fixed and depended absolutely on the will of the Syndics. Nevertheless since they were the elite of the citizens and they acquired experience in business from their function, it very often happened that the newly elected Syndics kept the councilors of their predecessors. In this way little by little their positions became permanent. Henri called l'Espagne was the first councilor for life in [1487][7] but he was elected in general council.

DETAILS OF ADMINISTRATION

After having made known the three principal jurisdictions among which the administration was divided, it remains for me to state what this division was and in what each department consisted.

All civil cases passed to the tribunal of the vidomne with the possibility of appeal and they were pleaded and judged summarily in common language, without writings or formal pleading; afterward they passed by appeal to the official, then in things important to Vienna to the metropolitan and even to Rome, very inconvenient appeals that, having become too frequent, were one of the motives for the Reformation.

The vidomne had two canons and four citizens of his choice as assistant judges in his tribunal. He could pass as sentence some small fines, up to sixty sous, one third of which belonged to him.

The syndics, assisted by four citizens named by the former, were sole judges in criminal cases and they alone could order torture. The vidomne had custody of prisoners and it does not even seem that the city had any prisons of its own. After the expulsion of the Bishop, the Bishop's prisons were made into those of the city, which leads me to presume that it did not have any previously. After having prepared the trial with the assistant judges mentioned, the syndics alone judged the guilty in the midst of the people, on a tribunal set up in the street, and then delivered him to the vidomne, who had the judgment executed in the city when the penalty did not go as far as death; but when it was a question of the extreme penalty, the Vidomne had the condemned man led out of the city and delivered to the castellan of Gaillard, reading him the sentence that the castellan had executed. As sovereign, the Bishop not only had the right of pardoning but that of removing to himself both civil and criminal cases before they were judged.

With regard to Ecclesiastics, they were not under the jurisdiction of the vidomne nor even under that of the syndics; as for criminal jurisdiction, they depended on a judge established by the Bishop who was called the Judge of excesses, from whom the matter was brought to the Episcopal council if it was serious.

The civil order was divided among the three jurisdictions, but the syndics had the greatest share in it. The protection of the city and the right of imprisoning belonged to them alone during the night; during the day this right belonged to the bishop, to the vidomne, or to both, for this article is not very clear. The walls of the city, the gates, the towers, the artillery, the munitions, the bourgeois militias, and in general everything that pertained to the right of arms was also in the department of the syndics, and the fourth of them had the particular direction of it as the first had that of the civil government.

Because of these franchises, one could not either arrest or detain in the city and the neighborhood any citizen, bourgeois, inhabitant, or juryman, except in a judicial manner based on a denunciation that was formal and not ex officio. If one of them was exposed to some violence, from whatever side it came, everyone was permitted and prescribed to protect him or deliver him from it by force, even to close the Gates, to tighten the chains, and to seize the aggressors. Nor could one cite any of said citizens and Bourgeois outside of the city, not even by authority of the Bishop, and if one of them was arrested out of the neighborhood neither the Bishop nor his Council could judge the affair except with the assistance of the citizens. Neither the Bishop nor his vidomne could inflict any personal punishment on any delinquent for the case of rebellion, but could only impose a fine, which could not surpass sixty gros. One could neither deliver a prisoner nor bring him out of the city without formal consent of the citizens. They alone, presiding through their syndics, could order torture and they were obliged to be present. Finally the rate of the price of commodities belonged to citizens alone. One could not impose any tax without their consent. No one's goods were subject to confiscation, and everything that was not specified by the franchises was supposed to be judged by Roman law.

In addition to all these Jurisdictions, the Dukes of Savoy sometimes exercised one of them in the city over their subjects but always by a particular commission from the Bishop and the citizens, which—being for a term—needed to be renewed every time these princes wished to exercise anew the same jurisdiction.

The expenses of administration were not great either on the part of the Bishop, who paid his ecclesiastical officers by means of benefices and his Vidomne by means of some rights, or on the part of the city, which paid wages to only six magistrates and, having no regular Troops, had almost no other expense than the upkeep of the walls of the city and public buildings. The revenues destined to this use were those of Customs, two thirds of which belonged to the Bishop and the other third to the city.

Nevertheless there did not fail to be several sorts of rights independent of the ecclesiastic revenues that yielded a good profit to the Bishop and of which the city also had some part, such as *lods* and fishing.

ON THE TERRITORY

Although the Diocese of Geneva was very extensive, the city's territory was very small, or to state it more accurately it was nothing; for the private individuals had land, but the city had no power outside its walls. Everything depended on the castles that surrounded it and these very numerous castles belonged to the Bishop, to the counts of Geneva, to the counts of Savoy, and to other lords who looked unfavorably upon a free city and did not treat the inhabitants very considerately.

The Genevans, as if imprisoned in their walls, depended on their neighbors for their subsistence; these neighbors, being precisely the ones who had undertaken to enslave them, were not inclined to facilitate the extraction of commodities for them; in spite of treaties, the dukes of Savoy often interdicted it and perhaps would never have permitted it if it had been less useful to their subjects. It is to this difficulty of subsisting that one must attribute the famines and plagues that so often desolated the city before it had public storehouses and before the importation of provisions was more consistently free because of more secure treaties.

It is not possible for Geneva ever to be truly free because it cannot be self-sufficient and because it will always be at the discretion of someone else for its subsistence. Knowing that the Savoyards cannot do without them in order to pay their tax, the Genevans think that the dependence disappears because it is reciprocal; in which they deceive themselves because it is easier to do without money than without bread.

PRETENSIONS OF THE HOUSE OF SAVOY

Geneva was so extremely at the Discretion of the Dukes of Savoy that it was not possible for them not to have some rights over her. They acquired real ones by bringing about and seizing upon all favorable occasions. They lost them by rushing too much to abuse them.

They classified their pretensions under several headings all of which were related to the sovereignty of Geneva.

1. As replacements for the rights of the Counts of Geneva whose heirs they were.
2. As vicars of the Empire.
3. As established on their authority by various bulls of the Emperors and even of the Popes.
4. As assignees of the Bishops with regard to temporal matters.
5. Finally as acknowledged by the Genevans themselves by the fact of

a long possession as much on their own authority as by the assignment made to them by the Duke of Zeringhen of the one that he had obtained from the Emperor.

1. As to the first point, which lays down as a fact the sovereignty of the former counts of Geneva, they said they were replacements for these Princes through the sale that Odo de Villars, last count of Geneva, had made to Amé VIII of all his rights for the sum of 800 golden marcs.

2. As to the second, they adduced various bulls of the Emperors who established the counts of Savoy as vicars of the Empire on this side as well as that side of the mountains, in a number of which Geneva was specifically named, and notably that of Charles IV of August 18, 1356, which declares that the appeals of cases in the City of Geneva must be brought to the count of Savoy in his capacity as Vicar of the Empire as if it was to the Emperor himself, and that of Maximilian in 1501, of Charles V in 1527, 1530, which all confirm to the Dukes of Savoy the Vicarage of the Empire with mandates to the Bishop, to the syndics, and to the citizens to acknowledge these princes and to obey them in this capacity.

3. As to the third point, they cited an act of October 14, 1423, by which the Emperor Sigismond conveyed to count Amedée of Savoy the county of Geneva, which had reverted to the Empire by the death of the last count, another act of May 29, 1424, by which the same Emperor removed from the Prince of Orange all equality of rights with the count of Savoy on the subject of said county. And another act of Charles V of December 4, 1528, by which he ordered the Bishop and the Citizens of Geneva to obey the Duke of Savoy as their Prince.

[4.] As proof of the fourth article they adduced the surrender made in 1513 by the Bishop Jean de Savoy to Duke Charles of the temporal power of the Bishopric, approved in 1515 by Pope Leon X and rendered even more authentic by that of the Bishop Pierre de la Baume in [1523].

And as to the exercise of their sovereignty in Geneva they said they had enjoyed it peacefully and legitimately both from the consent of the Bishops and from that of the Syndics and Citizens, sometimes even at their own demand, making use of royal rights, possessing a fortified castle in the city, establishing Governors, officers, sergeants there, administering justice there through their vidomne, setting up their armories there, coining money there, making their public entrances there, holding their court and their council there, and in a word conducting themselves as sovereign Princes in everything there, not only without any opposition, but with the tacit and formal assent of the Bishop, of the people, and of the magistrates.

THE RESPONSE OF THE GENEVANS

It always appears peculiar to me to ask a free people why it is free. It is as if one asked a man who has his two arms why he is not one-armed. The right to liberty is born from itself, it is the natural state of man. This is not the case for domination, its right needs to be proved when it exists. When it no longer exists, it no longer has any right.

Thus the Genevans had only to respond to the Dukes of Savoy: You are, you say, the legitimate sovereigns of our fathers. So be it, go then to rule over our Fathers, as for us we are[8] born free and we wish to remain so.

That is what they also did say through their behavior; through their writings they said in addition:

1. That Geneva had always been a free and imperial city, acknowledged as such by the Emperors and other sovereigns of Europe, without excepting even the Counts and Dukes of Savoy.

2. That the counts of the Genevese, having never been sovereigns, could not transmit to others a right that they themselves did not have.

3. That the vicarage of the Empire did not at all remove from States that took over from the Empire the sovereignty that they previously enjoyed.

4. That neither the Emperors nor the Popes, being unable to give what did not belong to them, had themselves revoked these abusive donations.

5. That the Bishops of Geneva never had the power to alienate their sovereignty, that this alienation, contrary to their oath, of the rights of the city expressly acknowledged and confirmed by them and even to Papal bulls, was illegitimate and void.

6. And as to the fact, the Genevans denied that the Princes of Savoy ever exercised a sovereign authority in the city, but only some acts of violence proven illegitimate by the very declarations of the Princes who did them.

[1.] To establish their first assertion, they adduced their alleged ancient name of *Colonia equestris*,[9] an inscription on stone, an imperial eagle, engraved over the portal of their Church, and other proofs of similar stuff more capable of harming their case than of supporting it; but in ages of ignorance people always have a rage for imaginary antiquities. The Genevans believed they could not be free unless they had always been so.

[2.] That the counts of Genevese had never been sovereigns of Geneva is proven by their own declarations at all times, by the transactions they had completed with the Bishops, by the homages they had rendered to them. All that is founded on authentic acts from the one of 1124 up to the one of 1346.

And as proof that neither the Duke nor even the Bishop had ever had a Governor in Geneva, they cited the nomination the latter made in 1518 of Master De Salleneuve as his temporal lieutenant, and which the citizens rejected, saying that it was a new and unheard of thing and that they had never had any other governor than their Bishop. Nevertheless Master Sorlin was subsequently acknowledged as lieutenant of his brother Pierre de la Baume.

[3., 4.] The third and fourth Articles are proved both by the example of Italy, of which the Dukes of Savoy had not become sovereign even though they were vicars of the Empire, and by the express revocation made of said vicarage over the City of Geneva by the Emperors Charles IV and Sigismond and by Popes Gregory XII and Sixtus IV as having been obtained by surprise and invalid, since the Emperors could not dispose of someone else's property, nor despoil of a dependent sovereignty of the Empire those to whom it belonged in order to give it others.*

5. The Alienation of sovereignty by the Bishop was contrary to right, because this sovereignty did not belong to the Bishop but to the Bishopric, and one did not dispose of an elective sovereignty as one does of one's patrimony. Moreover, a similar alienation, having been censured by the college of Cardinals as contrary to the constitutions of the Church, could not be adduced as legitimate by a Catholic Prince, since that was simultaneously to admit and reject the right that established it.

6. That the Dukes of Savoy would never have exercised sovereignty in Geneva is proved by the records of the city and of the Bishopric, where the royal rights had always belonged to the Bishop. He alone had enjoyed that of coining money and that of pardoning and the Dukes could not adduce an example of a similar right exercised by them in the city. If the vidomnate belonged to the Dukes of Savoy, it was as vassals of the Bishops, and that is proved by the jurisdiction itself from which one appealed to the Bishop and not to the Duke. As to the frequent sojourns that these Princes had made in Geneva, the councils they had held there, the justice they had sometimes rendered to their subjects there, it was always subsequent to requests made on their part, to permissions granted by the Bishop or by the city and to formal declarations that these permissions would be of no consequence at all and that the acts that resulted from them were from

* Letter of Charles V to the duke of Savoy of April 1, 1527, by which the Emperor orders him to give up his pretensions over Geneva (Spon, t.1, p. 409). In another directly opposed letter from the end of the same year (p. 411), there are strange variations that cast great suspicion on the authenticity of all these acts, which might very well have been fabricated after the fact by one party or the other, or perhaps by both of them.

favor and not from right. So that everything that the Dukes adduced to establish their possession invincibly proved that they had never had it.

Book II

We have seen that during the Episcopacy Geneva was a free city under the authority of its Bishops, but oppressed and tormented by a powerful neighbor. In their liberty the Genevans suffered all the evils of slavery, and—what is perhaps an example unique in history—they had their own Prince as the defender of their rights and a foreign Prince as usurper.

Everything changed in the sixteenth century. Reduced almost to the last extremity by the most violent crisis, Geneva performed an act of vigor that saved it. After having shaken off the yoke of its terrible neighbor, enticed by this success, it also shook off that of the Church. Having become independent of all foreign power, is it more free than before? It would not seem that that should be a question. Nevertheless it is a question that one must not be in a hurry to pronounce upon.

The Genevans, more struck with the latter revolution than the former, usually mix them up. They believe that the expulsion of the Duke of Savoy and of his vidomne was that of the Bishop and his clergy; they are mistaken. These two revolutions have neither the same dates nor the same causes; they were very close to each other but they were very distinct, and it is important to make that distinction to see clearly the influence of each of them on the subsequent state of the Genevans.

The project of seizing hold of their city had been formed by the house of Savoy almost from its birth. It followed this project without respite for three centuries; the means were different in accordance with the various characters of the Princes but all went toward the same goal and Duke Philibert was finally quite close to attaining it when other concerns caused him to miss the moment.

The first step toward reaching it was to take up the defense of the Bishop and the City against the Count of Geneva. This well-managed step yielded them a castle in the City and the Vidomnate. Then, seeing the House of Geneva in its decline and ready to die out, they took their measures to obtain its inheritance or rather its Rights, for they had already almost entirely despoiled it of its possessions. Having joined to their pretensions those of the counts of Geneva, they put into establishing them the same vigor and the same success that they had put into combatting them. Supported from the outside by great alliances, they seized every favorable moment to obtain bulls and declarations from the Popes and the Emperors which they knew how to turn to account in spite of the revocations with which they hardly troubled themselves. It did not matter whether their titles were legitimate, it was enough for them to have some. Usurpation needs only a pretext, and a poorly founded right serves it as well as a good one. In taking their measures in this way on the outside, they did not neglect the interior of the city and their security was strengthened there day by day. The greatest obstacle came from the Bishops, much more difficult to subjugate than the counts, and whose authority—more powerful than force—defended their state better than soldiers. They adopted the course of opposing the Church to itself and the interest of the Bishop to that of the Episcopate. They won over these prelates by means of rich abbeys whose revenues corresponded to their docility, they gave advancement to their relatives, and they favored their families. This was still not enough. Since the episcopal seat was elective, what they had done for one Bishop was useless for another; they always had to begin all over again. They took care to win over the Electors also. The Chapter was composed of the nobility of the vicinity, and consequently in large part of subjects of the Duke. Through them he succeeded in making himself master of the elections. Then, having the Bishop always chosen from within his family or within his states, he lacked nothing to assure himself of it as far as it was possible and to destroy the rights of the seat by those whom he took care to place in it. Add to this that, since the city had no territory, the citizens could not acquire any land except among their neighbors; and since they did not fail to favor these acquisitions, since three quarters of the citizens' property was in Savoy, they were very careful not to offend its sovereign, and thus they refused him nothing of what he demanded. They were content to protest that they were granting it freely and not out of duty. They asked him for a similar declaration and he never refused it. For what did it matter to him in what manner he was the master provided he became so in fact?

All these means combined, and followed with the prudence and firmness that have put the house of Savoy in the condition in which it is, seemed to assure the success of this undertaking so much that it appears surprising that it failed just when it neared its end, for it is certain that only the title of sovereign was still lacking to Duke Charles 3; he had all the authority in Geneva.

Two principal causes brought about the revolution that deprived him of it. The first came from the wars that broke out between Charles the Fifth and François the first and that, setting Italy ablaze, forced the Duke of Savoy to bring his attention to bear on that side. The other was the prosperity of the Swiss after the defeat of Charles the Bold. For, seeing themselves then in a condition to resist the Princes who made them anxious, they set themselves to making leagues not only among themselves but with their neighbors, and Geneva took advantage of this.

Thus the liberation of that city came from the wars of the Milanese and from its alliance with Fribourg and Berne, both of which were catholic at that time. Before the reformation was even an issue, Geneva was united with two free cities and was itself free. The Duke and his [vidomne] having been expelled from it, one scarcely knew that there were Lutherans in the world. Thus Religion had no part in its emancipation. If it did, this was in a very contrary sense because all the means that facilitated the establishment of the Republic came to it from the catholics and would have been lacking to it if the citizens had not been catholic. It was the Bishops who, moved by a very natural policy, put the city in a condition to shake off first the yoke of the Duke and finally their own. Wish as it might to assure itself of them, the House of Savoy could not prevent the interest of their authority being contrary to its undertakings, and the less they dared to resist it face to face, the more they needed to put a barrier between its pretensions and their rights. This barrier was the city and its privileges; that explains how one saw these privileges being extended in measure as the danger became more pressing.

This system of the Bishops, remarkable in all their conduct, is the only key to the historical account and to the facts, which, without it, offer only an inexplicable enigma. When the older Bishops resisted the counts of Geneva and Savoy with vigor and forced them to render homage to them, it was only a question of the rights of the Church: the Genevans were scarcely spoken of; but as soon as the house of Savoy disposes of the Episcopacy everything changes. The Bishop scarcely dares to show himself; it is the city that shows itself then. As soon as some Bishop feels himself strong enough to act alone, he resists by himself, the city—which he no longer needs—returns to dependency, and the citizens no longer say anything. Such was the case of Jean Louis de Savoy, so intrepid and proud, who, being too closely related to the Dukes, did not fear them at all and had his own way with them, and who, not needing to make the Genevans act, treated them with little consideration. Nevertheless it was this Prelate who founded the Republic by a treaty that he made with the Swiss in the name of the city and his own, and the Genevans were so stupid at that time that this treaty was made almost in spite of them and they did not want to make it perpetual.

All the Bishops of recent times, people of good sense in spite of their faults, followed the same maxims. They all constantly favored the city and supported its franchises in proportion to the powerlessness they felt in themselves to support their own rights. One must except from this only

Jean de Savoy, vile debauched man, servile tyrant, and greedy without ambition, who, far from having the honor of being from the house of Savoy whose name he dared to bear, was only a bastard of a bishop and by his tastes perfectly supported the morals that had caused him to be born.

Pierre de la Baume, his successor and last Bishop of Geneva, was accused of inconstancy. But this so-called inconstancy was less in his character than in his situation. No Bishop more favored the city and its privileges than he did. He approved the alliance with the two cantons, he wanted to be included in it. He had himself received as Bourgeois, he gave the syndics cognizance of civil cases. Every time he acted of his own accord it was always to the profit of his subjects; but, seeing himself through his property and above all through his Abbey of Pignerol at the mercy of the Duke whose power moreover was very frightening, he was often forced to gratify him in spite of himself; still he could not avoid offending this Prince who more than once wanted to have him seized. Piere de la Baume never lost his favorable dispositions toward the Genevans, until he saw them abandoned to the new doctrine and ready to repudiate his authority. It was only then that he abandoned them. Thus it is unjust to attribute to his inconstancy fluctuations that were the product of necessity. But it is true that it sometimes pushed him to very ridiculous measures, to the point of sending two Deputies to the same diet charged with completely opposite instructions and each of which contradicted everything that the other had said.

I have said that it was a Bishop who made the first alliance with the two cities almost in spite of the Citizens; I will add that it was the one with Fribourg that saved the nascent Republic from the hands of the Duke and that forced him to leave Geneva, into which he had entered with a formidable display of force, resolved not to leave it except as acknowledged sovereign. That was the decisive moment. Having left Geneva, the Duke never re-entered it again. Having been set free in this way, at last feeling the utility of co-bourgeoisie with Fribourg, the city took advantage of it until the reformation and always found in the Fribourgeois sure friends and faithful co-bourgeois who served it with more affection, zeal, and disinterestedness than the Genevans have found since in any other ally.

Add that the establishment of the council of the two hundred, of that of the sixty, the settled form and the election of the small council, the institution of the lieutenant and of the auditors, the interdiction of the appeal to Vienna and to Rome, in sum the whole present constitution, existed before the Reformation, and you will admit that these two revolutions, far from being linked in the way people imagine, were so in an opposite sense and that the prior establishment of liberty produced that of the reformation. For, having begun to taste independence, the Genevans wished to have it whole and turned against the Church the arms it had given them against the Dukes.

Without the prior establishment of liberty, that of the reformation could not have been brought about. This latter revolution set against Geneva everything that had favored it in the former. Fribourg abandoned it, France supported it only reluctantly, the Pope did not cease sounding the tocsin against it. The Duke, charmed at no longer having the Bishop between it and him, set himself at ease in his project and, far from acting secretly, again made it into an affair of conscience in which all catholic princes ought to cooperate. From that time Geneva, supported almost solely by one ally, not less to be feared than its enemies themselves, always saw itself within an inch of its ruin until the recent treaties. All it could do in this condition was to maintain its liberty; a more favorable one was needed in order to acquire it.

Why then did Geneva reform itself? For this very thing, to affirm the liberty it had acquired before the Reformation. If Geneva had remained catholic, it is probable that it would have had the fate of Strasbourg,[10] for it appears certain to me that the Dukes of Savoy would have had less of an advantage against it than they have had since the Reformation. Reformed, Geneva has remained more united to the protestant Cantons, which is the reason for circumspection on the part of France. The rights of the Bishop having been mixed up with those of the Duke, Louis XIV, in spite of his zeal, not daring to re-establish the former from fear of also re-establishing the latter, preferred to leave Geneva as it was. Thus on the one side the Reform gave more of an advantage to the house of Savoy, which already was no longer to be feared, and on the other it forced France to treat it with more consideration. By favoring the weaker and containing the stronger, it put between these two formidable neighbors precisely the equilibrium necessary to contain both of them. Geneva, which could not have freed itself except as Catholic, could hardly maintain itself except as Reformed, and that is how fortune has always made it adopt the course that was best for its preservation.

But did political liberty increase civil liberty, did the independence of the State extend to all of its members, and was the establishment of the Republic favorable or the opposite to the franchises of the Citizens? This is a question that cannot be resolved except by examining the Government that was established and comparing it with the one that had preceded it. For this I am going to take up again in a few words the historical account of the changes brought about by the revolution.

The first of these changes was the abolition of the Vidomnate, the second was the concession made to the Syndics by the Bishop of the judgment of civil cases that belonged to his officers. The competence of all civil cases had previously been divided between the vidomne and the official in such a way that neither the people nor its syndics had any sort of authority in that regard.

The city having divided itself into two factions concerning the treaty of co-bourgeoisie with Fribourg and Berne, and the Eignots (partisans of the alliance) having the advantage, the Ducals or mammelus were ill-treated, which frightened the Vidomne Verneau so much that he left the City in 1526, leaving only a secretary who did not stay there for long after him. They seized the occasion of this desertion to convey to the syndics the authority of the execution of criminal sentences, which they already alone had the right to pronounce, and to add to it that of judging civil cases, which was previously in the vidomne's cognizance. The following year, the Bishop having conveyed to the syndics the right of judging all civil cases by a properly formal act, they thus found themselves fully invested with the two jurisdictions.

In order to put some order into the procedures, from the month of February 1529, the council of the two hundred, which will be spoken about immediately below, had named a syndic and six assistants, as many from the small council as from its own body, to make up a Tribunal that was supposed to expedite the small cases and take the place of that of the vidomne. However, since civil cases were a matter in which neither the syndics nor the council were versed at all; since the multitude of pieces of public business deprived them of the time necessary for the investigation of trials; since, moreover, this partial tribunal, not having at all been approved in general council, was not adequately authorized; the same Council of the Two Hundred resolved on September 7 of the same year to propose the fixed and irrevocable establishment of a Court of justice composed of a Lieutenant, the Syndics, and of four assistants or Auditors where justice would be administered in a summary and simple manner in accordance with the franchises. These resolutions were approved in general council, where on the 14th of the same month were elected Claude Richardet, Lieutenant, Nicolin du Crest, Girardin de la Rive, Claude Savoye and Jean Balard, Auditors. They sent a deputation to the Bishop to ask him for confirmation of this institution, which he granted secretly, not wanting the Duke of Savoy to be informed of it.

The second and more considerable change was the institution of the political orders or intermediate bodies between the general council and the syndics. I put these establishments of councils after that of courts of justice. For although the sixty and the two hundred were named previously, they did not have their fixed and precise form until two years after the institution of this Tribunal.

I have said that under the Episcopal government the small Council was a free and precarious establishment dependent almost absolutely on the choice and the will of the syndics, thus the addition of these assessors did not have as its object to diminish the power of those who named them but to clarify its usage. When it was a question of passing resolutions that required longer deliberations than could be made in general council, they formed extraordinary Councils to which the former handed over its power of acting.

Nevertheless one does not see that anything of any significance was ever done in these councils that did not pass afterward in the general council.

LETTERS WRITTEN FROM THE MOUNTAIN

LETTERS
WRITTEN FROM THE
MOUNTAIN
By J. J. ROUSSEAU

IN TWO PARTS

VITAM
IMPENDERE
VERO.¹

AT AMSTERDAM,
By MARC-MICHEL REY.
MDCCLXV

Foreword

This is a belated return, I feel, to an overly hackneyed and already nearly forgotten subject. My condition, which no longer permits me any continuous work, and my aversion for the polemical genre have caused my slowness to write and my aversion to publishing. I would even have suppressed these Letters completely, or rather I would not have written them, if it concerned only myself. But my Fatherland has not become so foreign to me that I can calmly see its Citizens oppressed, especially when they have compromised their rights only in defending my Cause. I would be the most worthless of men if on such an occasion I heeded a sentiment that is no longer either gentleness or patience, but weakness and cowardice in the one whom it prevents from fulfilling his duty.

Nothing is less important for the public, I agree, than the subject matter of these Letters. The Constitution of one small Republic, the fate of one small private individual, the exposition of a few injustices, the refutation of a few sophisms: all that is not in itself important enough to merit many Readers. But if my subjects are small, my objects are large, and worthy of the attention of every decent man. Let us leave Geneva in its place and Rousseau in his humiliation. But Religion, but liberty, justice! There are things that are not beneath you whoever you might be.

Let no one even seek in the style here for compensation for the dryness of the subject matter. Those who have been so strongly annoyed by a few fortunate strokes of my pen, will find wherewithal to appease themselves in these Letters. The honor of defending an oppressed person might have set my heart aflame if I had spoken on someone else's behalf. Reduced to the sad task of defending myself, I had to confine myself to reasoning. To get excited would have been to debase myself. I will have found favor for this, then, from those who imagine it is essential for the truth to be stated coldly, an opinion I nonetheless can hardly understand. When a strong persuasion moves us, how is it possible to use frigid language? When Archimedes all ecstatic ran naked through the streets of Syracuse, had he found the truth any less because he was enthusiastic about it? Quite the contrary, the person who feels it cannot refrain from adoring it; the person who remains cold has not seen it.

However that may be, I beg the Readers to be willing to put my fine style aside, and examine only whether I reason well or badly. For in the end, I do not see how it can follow solely from the fact that an Author expresses himself in good terms that this Author does not know what he is saying.

FIRST PART

First Letter

No, Sir, I do not blame you at all for not having joined the Remonstrators[2] to uphold my cause. Far from having approved this step myself, I opposed it with all my power, and my relatives withdrew from it at my request. People were silent when it was necessary to speak; they spoke when there was nothing left to do but remain silent. I foresaw the uselessness of the remonstrances. I anticipated their consequences. I judged that their inevitable results would disturb the public peace or change the constitution of the State. The event has justified my fears only too well. There you are, reduced to the alternative I feared. The crisis you are in requires another deliberation of which I am no longer the object. On the basis of what was done, you ask what you ought to do. You consider that the effect of these steps, being related to the entire body of the Bourgeoisie, will fall no less on those who abstained from them than on those who took them. Thus, whatever the various opinions were at first, the common interest ought to bring them all together here. Your rights claimed and attacked can no longer remain in doubt. They must either be recognized or abolished, and it is their obviousness that places them in danger. The torch should not have been brought close during the storm. But today, the house is on fire.

Although my interests are no longer at issue, my honor still involves me in this affair. You know that, yet you consult me as a neutral man. You suppose that prejudice will not blind me, and passion will not make me unjust. I hope so too. But in such delicate circumstances, who can answer for himself? I feel it is impossible for me to forget myself in a quarrel of which I am the subject, and which has my misfortunes as its original cause. What will I do then, Sir, to reply to your confidence and justify your esteem as well as I can? This. With proper distrust for myself, I will tell you not so much my opinion as my reasons. You will weigh them, you will compare them, and you will choose. Do more. Always distrust, not my intentions,—God knows they are pure—but my judgment. When he is deeply wounded, the most just man rarely sees things as they are. I surely do not want to deceive you, but I can deceive myself. I could do so in any other matter, and the probability is all the greater that it has to happen here. Be on your guard then, and if I am not right ten times over, do not grant that I am right once.

There, Sir, is the precaution you ought to take, and here is the one I want to take in turn. I will start by talking to you about me, my grievances, the harsh proceedings of your Magistrates. When that has been done and my heart is well eased, I will forget myself. I will talk to you about yourself, about your situation, which is to say about the Republic. I do not believe I am expecting too much of myself if I hope, by means of this arrangement, to treat the question you ask me with equity.

I have been all the more cruelly outraged because I flattered myself that I deserved well of my Fatherland. If my behavior had needed pardon, I could reasonably hope to obtain it. Yet, with unprecedented haste, without warning, without summons, without examination, they rushed to stigmatize my Books. They did more. Without regard for my misfortunes, my ills, my condition, they issued a warrant against my person with the same precipitation. They did not even spare me the terms used for criminals. These Gentlemen have not been indulgent; have they at least been just? That is what I want to seek out with you. Don't take flight, I beg you, at the length I am forced to give to these Letters. In the multitude of questions that arise, I would like to be sober with words; but Sir, whatever one does, they are needed for reasoning.

Let us first gather together the motives they gave for this procedure, not in the indictment, not in the decree transmitted in secret and remaining in the shadows*; but in the replies of the Council to the Remonstrances of the Citizens and Bourgeois, or rather in the *Letters Written from the Country*, a work that serves as their manifesto and in which alone they deign to reason with you.

"My books," they say, "are impious, scandalous, reckless, full of blasphemies and calumnies against Religion. Disguised as doubts, the Author has gathered in them everything that can tend to undermine, unsettle, and destroy the fundamental principles of the revealed Christian Religion.

"They attack all Governments.

"These Books are all the more dangerous and reprehensible because they are written in French, in the most seductive style; they appear under the

---

* My family made a formal request for the communication of this decree. Here is the reply:
June 25, 1762
"*In ordinary council in reference to the present Request, it is decreed that there is no cause to concede the petitioners claims therein.*" Lullin

The Decree of the Parlement of Paris was printed as soon as it was passed. Imagine what a free State must be where such Warrants against the honor and freedom of Citizens are kept hidden!

name and title of a Citizen of Geneva; and, according to the Author's intention, *Emile* ought to serve as a guide for fathers, mothers, and preceptors.

"In judging these Books, it was not possible for the Council not to cast a glance upon the person who was presumed to be their Author."

Moreover, the Warrant issued against me, they continue, "is neither a judgment nor a sentence, but a simple provisional evidentiary ruling that left my exceptions and defenses intact and that, in the anticipated case, served as preparation for the procedure prescribed by the Edicts and by the ecclesiastical Statute."

To that, the Remonstrators, without going into the examination of the doctrine, objected: "that the Council had judged without preliminary formalities; that Article 88 of the ecclesiastical Statute had been violated in this judgment; that the procedure carried out in 1562 against Jean Morelli under this Article clearly showed its usage and, through this example, established a jurisprudence that they ought not to have disdained; that this new manner of proceeding was even contrary to the rule of natural Right acknowledged among all peoples, which requires that no one be condemned without having his defense heard; that one cannot stigmatize a work without at the same time stigmatizing the Author whose name it bears; that it is not clear what exceptions and defenses remain for a man who has been declared impious, reckless, scandalous in his writings, and after the sentence has been rendered and executed against these same writings, since as objects are not susceptible to infamy, what results from the burning of a Book by the hand of the Executioner necessarily rebounds upon the Author. From which it follows that it was not possible to deprive a Citizen of his most precious possession, honor; it was not possible to destroy his reputation, his status, without starting by hearing him; that the condemned and stigmatized works deserved at least as much support and tolerance as various other writings in which there are cruel satires about Religion and that have been distributed and even printed in the City; that finally in relation to Governments, it has always been allowed in Geneva to reason freely about this general matter, no Book that deals with it is forbidden, no Author is stigmatized for having discussed it whatever his sentiment may be; and that far from attacking the Government of the Republic in particular, I let no opportunity escape for praising it."

To these objections, the Council replied, "that it is not at all violating the rule stating that no one be condemned without a hearing to condemn a Book after having undertaken its reading and having examined it sufficiently; that Article 88 of the Statutes is applicable only to a man who dogmatizes and not to a Book that is destructive of the Christian Religion; that it is not true that the stigmatization of a book carries over to its

Author, who may have been only imprudent or blundering; that with regard to the scandalous works tolerated or even printed in Geneva, it is not reasonable to claim that because a Government has sometimes dissimulated, it is obliged always to dissimulate; that besides, the Books in which Religion is only ridiculed are not by far as deserving of punishment as those in which it is directly attacked by reasoning; that finally, what the Council owes to the maintenance of the Christian Religion in its purity, to the public good, to the Laws, and to the honor of the Government having caused it to pass this sentence, does not allow it either to change or to weaken it."

Those are not all the reasons, objections, and replies that have been alleged by each side, but they are the principal ones and they suffice to establish the question of fact and of right in relation to me.

However, since the object thus presented still remains a little vague, I am going to try to establish it with more precision, for fear you might extend my defense to the part of that object I do not want to include in it.

I am a man and I have written books. I have therefore also made errors.* I perceive a rather large number of them myself. I have no doubt that others see many more of them, and that there are still more that neither I nor others see. If one says only that, I agree with it.

But what Author is not in the same situation or dares flatter himself that he is not in it? There is, then, no dispute on this point. If someone refutes me and is right, the error is corrected and I remain silent. If someone refutes me and is wrong, I still remain silent. Should I answer for someone else's act? Whatever the situation, after hearing the two Parties, the public is judge, it pronounces, the Book triumphs or fails, and the trial is finished.

The errors of Authors are often very indifferent, but there are also some that are prejudicial, even contrary to the intention of the person who commits them. One can be mistaken to the detriment of the public just as to one's own. One can harm innocently. Controversies about matters of jurisprudence, of morality, and of Religion frequently fall into that case. One of the two disputants is necessarily wrong, and error about these important matters always becomes a fault. However, it is not punished when it is presumed to be involuntary. A man is not guilty for doing harm when he wanted to serve, and if an Author were criminally prosecuted for mistakes of ignorance or inadvertence, for bad maxims that could be

---

* Exceptions, if you wish, are Books of Geometry and their authors. Furthermore, if there are no errors in the propositions themselves, who will assure us there are none in the order of deduction, in the selection, in the method? Euclid demonstrates and attains his goal, but what path does he take? How much does he wander on his way? Science may well be infallible; the man who cultivates it is often mistaken.

derived from his writings very consistently but against his will, what Writer could shelter himself from prosecutions? One would have to be inspired by the Holy Spirit to turn Author and have only people inspired by the Holy Spirit as judges.

If only faults like those are imputed to me, I will not defend myself against them any more than simple errors. I cannot affirm not having committed such, because I am not an Angel. But those faults that one claims to find in my Writings may very well not be there, because those who find them there are not Angels either. Men and subject to error like myself, on what basis do they claim that their reason is the arbiter of mine, and that I am punishable for not having thought like them?

The public is therefore also the judge of similar faults. Its blame is the only punishment for them. No one can escape from this Judge, and for myself, I do not make any appeal from it. It is true that if the Magistrate finds these faults harmful, he can proscribe the Book that contains them. But I repeat: he cannot for that reason punish the Author who committed them, for that would be punishing an offense that may be involuntary, and one ought to punish only the will to do evil. Thus this is still not what is at issue.

But there is a great difference between a Book that contains harmful errors and a pernicious Book. Established principles, a chain of coherent reasoning, consequences deduced manifest the Author's intention, and this intention, dependent on his will, falls under the jurisdiction of the Laws. If this intention is evidently bad, it is no longer error or fault, but crime. That changes everything. It is no longer a matter of a literary dispute about which the public judges according to reason, but of a criminal trial that must be judged in Courts according to the full rigor of the Laws. Such is the critical position into which I have been thrust by Magistrates who call themselves just, and by zealous Writers who find them too clement. As soon as prisons, executioners, and chains are made ready for me, whoever accuses me is an informer. He knows that it is not merely the Author he is attacking, but the man; he knows that what he writes can influence my fate.*[3] It is no longer only my reputation he has designs upon, but my honor, my freedom, my life.

---

* When a famous Book first appeared a few years ago, I resolved to attack its principles, which I found dangerous. I was carrying out this enterprise when I learned that the Author was being prosecuted. Instantly, I threw my sheets of paper into the fire, judging that no duty could authorize the baseness of joining the crowd to overwhelm an oppressed man of honor. When calm was restored, I had occasion to state my sentiment about the same subject in other Writings. But I stated it without naming the Book or the Author. I believed I ought to add this respect for his misfortune to the esteem I always had for his person. I do not believe that this way of thinking is unique to me. It is shared by all decent people. As soon as a matter becomes a criminal charge, they ought to keep silent, unless they are called to testify.

First Letter (Pl., III, 692–694)

This, Sir, brings us back all at once to the state of the question from which it seems to me the public is straying. If I wrote reprehensible things, they can blame me for it, they can suppress the Book. But to stigmatize it, to attack me personally, there must be more. The fault does not suffice; there must be an offense, a crime. It must be that I wrote a pernicious Book with bad intent, and that must be proved, not as one Author proves that another Author is mistaken, but as an accuser must convict the accused before the Judge. To be treated as a malefactor, I must be convicted of being one. That is the first question that has to be examined. The second, assuming that the offense has been established, is to determine its nature, the place where it was committed, the tribunal that must judge it, the Law that condemns it, and the penalty that ought to punish it. Once resolved, these two questions will determine whether or not I have been treated justly.

In order to know if I have written pernicious Books, one must examine their principles, and see what would result from these principles if they were accepted. Since I dealt with many matters, I must confine myself to those for which I am prosecuted, namely Religion and Government. Let us start with the first point, following the example of the judges who did not explain themselves regarding the second.

In *Emile* one finds the profession of faith of a Catholic Priest, and in *Heloise* that of a pious woman.

These two Pieces are sufficiently in accord that one can explain one of them by the other, and from this agreement it can be presumed with some likelihood that if the Author who published the Books that contain them does not adopt both of them in their entirety, he at least favors them greatly. Of these two professions of faith, the first—being the most extensive and the only one in which the body of the offense was found—ought to be preferred for examination.

In order to attain its goal, this examination necessitates one more clarification. For note well that to clarify and to distinguish the propositions that my accusers muddle and confuse is to reply to them. Since they argue contrary to the evidence, when the question is well posed, they are refuted.

I distinguish two parts of Religion, in addition to the form of worship, which is only ceremonial. These two parts are dogma and morality. I divide dogmas further into two parts, namely the one which in setting forth the principles of our duties serves as a foundation for morality, and the one which, purely of faith, contains only speculative dogmas.

From this division, which appears precise to me, results the division of sentiments about Religion into on the one hand true, false, or doubtful, and on the other good, bad, or indifferent.

Judgment about the former belongs to reason alone, and if the Theologians have seized hold of it, it is as reasoners, as professors of the science by which one arrives at the knowledge of the true and false in matters of faith. If error in this part is harmful, it harms only those who err, and it is only prejudicial to the afterlife, over which human Tribunals cannot extend their competence. When they take cognizance of this matter, it is no longer as Judges of the true and false, but as Ministers of the civil Laws regulating the external form of worship. This part is not yet in question here. It will be dealt with later on.

As for the part of Religion that deals with morality, that is to say justice, the public good, obedience to the natural and positive Laws, the social virtues and all the duties of man and Citizen, it is the business of Government to take cognizance of them. It is on this point alone that Religion falls directly under its jurisdiction, and that it must banish not error, of which it is not the judge, but every harmful sentiment that tends to cut the social knot.

That, Sir, is the distinction you have to make in order to judge this Piece of writing taken before the Tribunal not of Priests, but of Magistrates. I admit that it is not all affirmative. Objections and doubts are seen in it. Let us posit what is not true, that these doubts are negations. But it is affirmative in its greatest part. It is affirmative and demonstrative about all the fundamental points of civil Religion. It is so decisive about everything that relates to eternal Providence, to love of one's neighbor, to justice, to peace, to the happiness of men, to the Laws of society, to all the virtues, that the objections and even the doubts in it have some advantage as their object, and I challenge anyone to show me a single point of doctrine attacked in it that I do not prove to be harmful to men either in itself or in its inevitable effects.

Religion is useful and even necessary for Peoples. Isn't that stated, maintained, proved in this same Writing? Far from attacking the true principles of Religion, the Author sets them forth, strengthens them with all his power. What he attacks, what he fights, what he must fight is blind fanaticism, cruel superstition, stupid prejudice. But, they say, one has to respect all that. But why? Because that is how Peoples are led. Yes, that is how they are led to their doom. Superstition is the most awful scourge of the human race. It brutalizes the simple, it persecutes the wise, it puts Nations in chains, it does a hundred horrible evils everywhere. What good does it do? None. If it does some, it is for Tyrants. It is their most terrible weapon, and that in itself is the greatest harm it has ever done.

They say that, in attacking superstition, I want to destroy Religion itself. How do they know that? Why do they confound these two causes, which I distinguish with so much care? Why don't they see that this imputation is thrown back against them with all its force, and that Religion has no enemies more terrible than the defenders of superstition? It would be very cruel for it to be so easy to inculpate the intention of a man, when it is so difficult to justify it. By the very fact that it has not been proved bad, it must be judged good. Otherwise, who could be safe from the arbitrary judgments of his enemies? What! Their affirmation alone constitutes proof of what they cannot know, and mine, together with all my behavior, does not establish my own sentiments? What means do I have left, then, to make them known? I cannot show the good I feel in my heart, I admit; but who is the abominable man who dares boast of seeing in it the evil that never was there?

The more guilty a person would be of preaching irreligion, M. d'Alembert states very well, the more criminal it is to accuse of irreligion those who do not in fact preach it.[4] Those who judge my Christianity publicly, only show what kind theirs is, and the only thing they have proved is that they and I do not have the same Religion. That is precisely what makes them angry. One has the sense that the supposed evil embitters them less than the good itself does. This good that they are forced to find in my Writings vexes and bothers them. Reduced to converting it into evil too, they feel they are exposing themselves too much. How much more comfortable they would be if this good were not there!

When they do not judge me on what I said but on what they assert I wanted to say, when they seek in my intentions the evil that is not in my Writings, what can I do? They give the lie to my discourses by my thoughts. When I said white, they assert that I wanted to say black. They put themselves in the place of God to do the work of the Devil. How can I shield my head from blows delivered from such a height?

I see only one way to prove that the Author did not have the horrible intention they attribute to him. It is to judge it by the Work. Ah! Let them judge it in that way, I agree to it. But this task is not mine, and a sustained examination from this point of view would be an indignity on my part. No, Sir, there is no misfortune or stigmatization that can reduce me to this abasement. I would believe I was insulting the Author, the Publisher, even the Reader by a justification that is all the more shameful for being simple. It is degrading virtue to show that it is not a crime. It is obscuring the evidence to prove it is the truth. No, read and judge for yourself. Woe to you if, during this reading, your heart does not bless a hundred times the virtuous and firm man who dares instruct humans in this way!

Oh, how would I resolve to justify this work? I, who believe that through it I expunge the faults of my entire life. I, who accept the evils it brings me as compensation for those I have done. I who, full of confidence, hope to say to the Supreme Judge someday: Deign in your clemency to judge a weak man. I did evil on earth, but I published this Writing.

My dear Sir, allow my heavy heart to breathe its sighs from time to time. But be assured that, in my discussions, I will mix in neither declamations nor lamentations. I will not even put into them the vivacity of my adversaries. I will always reason coolly. I continue, then.

Let us try to find a setting that is satisfactory to you and does not debase me. Let us suppose for a moment that the profession of faith of the Vicar has been adopted in a corner of the Christian world, and let us see what good and evil would result from it. This will be neither attacking nor defending it; it will be judging it by its effects.

First I see the newest things without any appearance of novelty: no change in form of worship and great changes in hearts, conversions without show, faith without disputes, zeal without fanaticism, reason without impiety, few dogmas and many virtues, the tolerance of the philosopher and the charity of the Christian.

Our proselytes will have two rules of faith that make up only one, reason and the Gospel. The latter will be all the more immutable because it will base itself only on the former and not at all on definite facts that, because they need to be attested, put Religion back under the authority of men.

The entire difference there will be between them and other Christians is that the latter are people who dispute a great deal about the Gospel without bothering to practice it, whereas our people will be very attached to its practice, and will not dispute at all.

When the disputatious Christians will come and say to them: You call yourselves Christians without being so. For to be Christians, it is necessary to believe in Jesus Christ, and you do not believe in him at all. The peaceful Christians will reply to them: "We are not too sure whether we believe in Jesus Christ according to your idea, because we do not understand it. But we try to observe what he prescribes to us. We are each Christians in our own way; we by observing his word, and you by believing in him. His charity would have us all be brothers; we follow it in acknowledging you as such. For love of him, do not deprive us of a title we honor with all our strength and that is as dear to us as to you."

The disputatious Christians will no doubt persist. In using the name of Jesus, you have to tell us by what title? You observe his word, you say, but what authority do you give it? Do you acknowledge Revelation? Do you not acknowledge it? Do you accept the Gospel in its entirety? Do you accept it only in part? On what do you base these distinctions? Ridiculous

Christians, who bargain with the master, who choose from his doctrine what they choose to accept and to reject!

To that, the others will say peacefully, "My brothers, we do not bargain. For our faith is not a commerce. You suppose it depends on us to accept or reject as we please. But that is not so, and our reason does not obey our will. No matter how much we might wish that what appears false to us appear true, it would appear false to us despite ourselves. All that depends on us is to speak according to our thought or contrary to our thought, and our only crime is not to want to deceive you.

"We recognize the authority of Jesus Christ because our intelligence acquiesces to his precepts and discovers their sublimity for us. It tells us that it is suitable for men to follow these precepts, but that it was beyond men to find them. We accept Revelation as emanating from the Spirit of God, without knowing how and without tormenting ourselves to discover it. Provided we know that God has spoken, it matters little to us to explain how He went about making himself understood. Thus, recognizing divine authority in the Gospel, we believe that Jesus Christ is cloaked in that authority. We recognize a more than human virtue in his behavior, and a more than human wisdom in his teachings. That is what is very settled for us. How did that happen? That is not settled, that is beyond us. That is not beyond you. Wonderful. We congratulate you wholeheartedly. Your reason may be superior to ours. But that is not to say it ought to serve as our Law. We consent to your knowing everything. Allow us to be ignorant of something.

"You ask us if we accept the entire Gospel. We accept all the teachings given by Jesus Christ. The utility, the necessity of most of these teachings strikes us, and we try to conform to them. A few are not within our grasp. They were doubtless given for more intelligent minds than ours. We do not believe we have attained the limits of human reason, and deeper men need loftier precepts.

"Many things in the Gospel go beyond our reason and even shock it. Yet we do not reject them. Convinced of the weakness of our understanding, we know how to respect what we cannot conceive, when the association with what we do conceive causes us to judge it superior to our understanding. Everything necessary for us to know to be holy appears clear to us in the Gospel. What need do we have to understand the rest? On this point, we remain ignorant but exempt from error, and that will not make us any less good men. This humble reserve itself is the spirit of the Gospel.

"We do not respect this Sacred Book precisely as a Book, but as the word and life of Jesus Christ. The character of truth, of wisdom, and of sanctity found in it teaches us that this history has not been essentially tampered with,* but according to us it has not been proven that it has not been tampered with at all. Who knows whether the things in it we do not understand are not mistakes slipped into the text? Who knows whether Disciples so greatly inferior to their master understood and represented him well throughout? We do not decide about that, we do not even presume, and we offer you conjectures only because you demand it.

"We may be mistaken in our ideas, but you may also be mistaken in yours. Why could that not be, since you are men? You may have as much good faith as we, but you cannot have more. You may be more enlightened, but you are not infallible. Who will judge between the two parties, then? Will it be you? That is not just. Far less will it be we who are so wary of ourselves. Let us leave this decision, then, to the common judge who hears us, and since we are in agreement about the rules of our reciprocal duties, put up with us on the rest, as we put up with you. Let us be men of peace; let us be brothers. Let us unite in the love of our common master, in the practice of the virtues he prescribes to us. That is what makes the true Christian.

"And if you persist in refusing us this precious title, after having done everything to live fraternally with you, we will console ourselves for this injustice by considering that words are not things, that the first disciples of Jesus Christ did not take the name of Christians at all, that the martyr Stephen never bore it, and that when Paul was converted to the faith of Christ, there were not yet any Christians** in the world."

Do you believe, Sir, that a controversy handled like that will be very animated and very long, and that one of the Parties will not soon be reduced to silence when the other will not want to dispute at all.

If our Proselytes are masters in the country in which they live, they will establish a form of worship as simple as their belief, and the Religion that will come of all that will be the most useful to men by its very simplicity. Freed from all they put in the place of virtues, and having neither superstitious rites nor subtleties in the doctrine, it will go entirely to its true goal, which is the practice of our duties. The words *devout* and *orthodox* will not be in use there. The monotony of certain articulated sounds will not constitute piety. The only impious people there will be the wicked, and the only faithful, good people.

Once this institution is accomplished, everyone will be obliged by the Laws to submit to it, because it is not founded on the authority of men,

---

* What would become of the simple faithful, if that were knowable only by critical discussions or by the authority of Pastors? By what impudence does one dare make faith dependent on so much science or so much submission?

** This name was given to them for the first time a few years later at Antioch.

there is nothing in it that is not in the order of natural enlightenment, it contains no article that does not relate to the good of society, and it is not mixed with any dogma useless to morality or any point of pure speculation.

Will our Proselytes be intolerant on that account? On the contrary, they will be tolerant by principle, they will be more tolerant than it is possible to be with any other doctrine, because they will accept all the good Religions that do not accept each other, that is to say, all those that, possessing the essential that they neglect, make an essential point of what is not. By devoting themselves to the essential alone, our proselytes will let others make it an accessory as they wish, provided they do not reject it. They will let the others explain what they do not explain, decide what they do not decide. They will leave to each one its rites, its formulas of faith, its belief. They will say: accept with us the principles of the duties of the man and the Citizen. For the rest, believe whatever you please. As for the Religions that are essentially bad, that bring man to do evil, they will not tolerate them at all, because that in itself is contrary to genuine tolerance, which has as its goal only the peace of the human race. The genuinely tolerant person does not tolerate crime; he does not tolerate any dogma that makes men wicked.

Now suppose, on the contrary, that our Proselytes are under the domination of others. As people of peace, they will be subject to the Laws of their masters, even in matters of Religion, unless this Religion is essentially bad. For in such a case, without offending those who profess it, they would refuse to profess it. They would say to them: since God calls us to servitude, we want to be good servants, and your sentiments would prevent us from being so. We know our duties, we love them, we reject what detaches us from them. It is in order to be faithful to you that we do not adopt the Law of iniquity.

But if the Religion of the country is good in itself, and what is bad about it lies only in individual interpretations or in purely speculative dogmas, they will cling to the essential and tolerate the rest, as much out of respect for the Laws as out of love for peace. When they are called to declare their belief expressly, they will do it because one must not lie. They will state their sentiment, if need be, with firmness, even with force. They will defend themselves by reason if they are attacked. Moreover, they will not dispute against their brothers, and without persisting in wanting to convince them, they will remain united with them by charity, they will attend their assemblies, they will adopt their formulas, and not believing themselves more infallible, they will subject themselves to the opinion of the greatest number concerning what does not involve their conscience and does not appear to them to matter for salvation.

That is the good, you will say; let us see the bad. It will be stated in a few words. God will no longer be the organ of the wickedness of men. Religion will no longer serve as the instrument of the tyranny of the Clergy and of the vengeance of usurpers. It will no longer be useful except for making believers good and just. That is not to the advantage of those who lead them. It is worse for them than if it served no purpose.

Thus the doctrine in question is good for the human race and bad for its oppressors. In what absolute category must it be put? I have faithfully stated the pros and cons. Compare and choose.

When all is well examined, I believe you will agree on two things. One is that these men I hypothesize would behave in this matter very consistently with the Vicar's profession of faith. The other is that this behavior would be not only irreproachable, but truly Christian, and that it would be wrong to refuse these good and pious men the name Christians. For they would deserve it perfectly by their behavior, and they would be less opposed in their sentiments to many sects who take it and for whom it is not contested, than several of these same sects are opposed to one another. They would not be, if you will, Christians in the manner of Saint Paul who was naturally a persecutor, and who had not heard Jesus Christ himself. But they would be Christians in the manner of Saint James, chosen by the master in person, who had received from his own lips the instructions he transmits to us. This entire argument is very simple, but it appears to me conclusive.

You will perhaps ask me how this doctrine can be reconciled with that of a man who says the Gospel is absurd and pernicious for society? In admitting frankly that this reconciliation appears difficult to me, I will ask you in turn where is this man who says the Gospel is absurd and pernicious? Your Gentlemen accuse me of having said it. And where? In the *Social Contract*, in the Chapter on civil religion. That is strange! In this same Book, and in this same Chapter, I think I said precisely the opposite. I think I said that the Gospel is sublime and the strongest bond of society.*
I do not want to accuse these Gentlemen of lying. But admit that two such contrary propositions in the same Book and in the same Chapter must constitute a rather extravagant whole.

Might there not be some new ambiguity here, by means of which I was portrayed as more guilty or crazier than I am? This word *Society* offers a slightly vague meaning. There are many types of societies in the world, and it is not impossible that what is useful to one is harmful to another. Let us see. My aggressors' favorite method is always artfully to offer inde-

---

* *Social Contract*, Book IV, chapter 8, pages 310–311 in the edition in octavo.

terminate ideas. As my only response, let us continue to try to establish them.

The chapter I am speaking of is intended, as can be seen from the title, to examine how religious institutions can be a part of the constitution of the State. Thus what is at issue here is not at all to consider Religions as true or false, nor even as good or bad in themselves, but to consider them uniquely in relation to political bodies and as parts of Legislation.

From this perspective, the Author shows that all ancient Religions, without excepting the Jewish one, were national in their origin, appropriated by and incorporated into the State, and forming the foundation or at least being part of the legislative System.

Christianity, on the contrary, is in its principle a universal Religion, which has nothing exclusive in it, nothing local, nothing suited to one country rather than another. Embracing all men equally in his limitless charity, its divine Author came to lift the barrier that was separating Nations, and to unite the whole human race in a people of brothers: *for in every Nation, the one who fears him and devotes himself to justice is pleasing to him.** Such is the true spirit of the Gospel.

Those, then, who wanted to make Christianity into a national Religion and introduce it as a constitutive part of the system of Legislation have in so doing made two mistakes, one of which is harmful to Religion and the other to the State. They deviated from the spirit of Jesus Christ, whose kingdom is not of this world, and mingling the interests of Religion with earthly ones, they have defiled its celestial purity, they have made it the weapon of tyrants and the instrument of persecutors. They have done no less injury to the healthy maxims of politics, since instead of simplifying the machine of Government, they have complicated it; they have given it superfluous foreign springs; and subjecting it to two different driving forces, often in contradiction, they have caused the wrangling that is felt in all Christian States where Religion has been made to enter into the political system.

Perfect Christianity is the universal social institution. But in order to show that it is not a political establishment and does not contribute to good specific institutions, it was necessary to remove the Sophisms of those who mix religion with everything, like a hold with which they take possession of everything. All human establishments are based on the human passions and preserved by means of them. What fights and destroys the passions is therefore not suited to fortifying these establishments. How would what detaches hearts from the earth increase our interest

---

* Acts X: 35.

in what happens there? How would what preoccupies us uniquely with another Fatherland attach us more to this one?

National religions are useful to the State as parts of its constitution, that is undisputable. But they are harmful to the human Race, and even to the State in another sense. I have shown how and why.

Christianity, on the contrary, making men just, moderate, and friends of peace, is very favorable to the general society. But it weakens the force of the political spring, it complicates the movements of the machine, it breaks the unity of the moral body, and since it is not sufficiently suited to it, it must either degenerate or remain a foreign and cumbersome component.

There, then, are a detriment and some disadvantages from both sides relative to the body politic. Yet it is important for the State not to be without Religion, and it is important for serious reasons, upon which I have strongly insisted throughout. But it would be still better to have none at all than to have a barbarous and persecuting one that, tyrannizing the Laws themselves, would thwart the duties of the Citizen. It is as if everything that has happened with respect to me in Geneva occurred only in order to establish this Chapter as exemplary, to prove by my own story that I have reasoned very well.

What ought a wise Legislator to do with these alternatives? One of two things. The first is to establish a purely civil Religion, which includes all fundamental dogmas of every good Religion, all dogmas truly useful to either a universal or a particular society, and leaves out all the others, which may be important to faith but not at all to wordly well-being, the unique object of Legislation. For how can the mystery of the Trinity, for example, contribute to the good constitution of the State; in what way will its members be better Citizens when they have rejected the merit of good works; and what does the dogma of original sin have to do with the bond of civil society? Although true Christianity is an institution of peace, who does not see that dogmatic or theological Christianity, by the multitude and obscurity of its dogmas and above all by the obligation to accept them, is a permanent battlefield between men; and that without our being able, by dint of interpretations and decisions, to prevent fresh disputes about those very decisions?

The other expedient is to leave Christianity as it is in its genuine spirit: free, disengaged from all bonds of flesh, with no other obligation than that of conscience, no other constraint in its dogmas than morals and Laws. The Christian Religion, through the purity of its morality, is always good and healthy in the State, provided that it is not made a part of its constitution, provided that it is allowed there uniquely as Religion, sentiment, opinion, belief. But as political Law, dogmatic Christianity is a bad establishment.

That, Sir, is the most powerful conclusion that can be drawn from this Chapter, in which far from taxing the *pure Gospel** with being pernicious for society, I find it in a sense too sociable, encompassing all of the human race too much for a Legislation that has to be exclusive; inspiring humanity rather than patriotism, and tending to fashion men rather than Citizens.** If I am mistaken, I have made an error in politics, but where is my impiety?

The science of salvation and that of Government are very different. Wanting the former to embrace everything is a fanaticism of a small mind. It is thinking like the Alchemists who also see universal medicine in the art of making gold, or like the Muslims who claim to find all the sciences in the Koran. The doctrine of the Gospel has only one aim: it is to call and save all men. Their freedom, their well-being here below has no part in it. Jesus said so a thousand times. To mix worldly concerns with this aim is to alloy its sublime simplicity, to sully its sanctity with human interests. That is what is truly an impiety.

These distinctions have always existed. They have been confounded for me alone. In removing the Christian Religion from national Institutions, I establish it as the best for the human race. The Author of *The Spirit of the Laws* went further. He said the Muslim religion was best for Asiatic countries. He reasoned as a political thinker, and so do I. In what country have they picked a fight, I do not say with the Author, but with the Book.*** Why, then, am I guilty, or why wasn't he?

Sir, that is how an equitable critic, by means of faithful excerpts, achieves an understanding of the true sentiments of an Author and of his intent in composing his Book. Let all of mine be examined by this method; I have no fear of the judgments any decent man could reach about them. But this is not how these Gentlemen go about it. They are far from it, they would not find in it what they seek. With the plan of making me guilty at any cost, they set aside the true goal of the work. They confer

---

* *Letters Written from the Country*, page 30.

** It is amazing to see the collection of fine sentiments that are heaped up for us in Books. Only words are necessary for this, and virtues on paper are cheap. But they do not combine themselves quite like that in the heart of man, and paintings are a far cry from realities. Patriotism and humanity, for example, are two virtues incompatible in their energy, and especially among an entire people. The Legislator who wants them both will get neither one nor the other. This compatibility has never been seen and never will be, because it is contrary to nature, and because one cannot give the same passion two aims.

*** It is good to note that the Book *The Spirit of the Laws* was originally printed in Geneva without the Scholarques finding anything in it to retract and that it was a Pastor who checked the proofs of the Edition.

on it as a goal each error, each negligence that has eluded the Author, and if by chance they leave an equivocal passage, they do not fail to interpret it with the meaning it does not have. In a huge field covered with a fertile harvest, they carefully sort out a few bad plants, in order to accuse the person who planted it of being a poisoner.

My propositions could do no harm in context. They were true, useful, decent in the meaning I gave them. It is their falsifications, their misrepresentations, their fraudulent interpretations that make them punishable. They must be burned in their Books, and awarded a prize in mine.

How often have defamed Authors and the indignant public not protested against this odious manner of hacking up a work, disfiguring all its parts, judging it by shreds picked from here and there at the whim of an unfaithful accuser who produces the evil himself by detaching it from the good that corrects and explains it, by twisting the true meaning throughout? Let La Bruyere or La Rochefoucault be judged on isolated maxims, well and good. Still it will be just to compare and count. But in a Book of reasoning, how many different meanings can the same proposition not have according to the manner in which the Author uses it and has it be considered? There is perhaps not one of those imputed to me for which in the place I put it the preceding or following page does not serve as a reply, and which I did not take in a sense different than that given it by my accusers. Before the end of these Letters, you will see proofs of that which will surprise you.

But if there are false, reprehensible, intrinsically blameworthy propositions, does that suffice to make a Book pernicious? A good Book is not the one that contains nothing bad or nothing that one could interpret as bad. Otherwise, there would be no good Books at all. But a good Book is the one that contains more good things than bad, a good Book is the one whose overall effect is to lead to good, despite the evil that may be found in it. My God, what would happen if, in a great work full of useful truths, lessons of humanity, piety, and virtue, one was allowed to go looking with a malicious precision for all the errors, all the equivocal, suspect, or ill-considered propositions, all the inconsistencies that amid the detail can elude an Author overburdened with his material, overwhelmed by the numerous ideas it suggests to him, distracted from some by the others, and who can hardly assemble in his head all the parts of his vast plan? If one were allowed to heap up a collection of all his faults, to aggravate some by means of others by bringing together what is separated and linking what is isolated; then passing over in silence the multitude of good and praiseworthy things that contradict them, explain them, redeem them, that show the Author's true goal, to present this horrible collection as that

First Letter (Pl., III, 707–709)

of his principles, to assert that this constitutes the summary of his true sentiments, and to judge him on the basis of such a selection? To what desert would one have to flee, in what cavern would one have to hide in order to escape the pursuits of such men, who under the guise of evil would punish the good, who would count as nothing the heart, intentions, and rectitude that are apparent throughout, and would treat the slightest and most involuntary fault like the crime of a scoundrel? Is there a single Book in the world, however true, however good, however excellent it may be, that could escape this infamous inquisition? No, Sir, there is not one, not a single one, not even the Gospel. For they would know how to place in it the evil that is not there by their unfaithful excerpts, by their false interpretations.

We submit to you, they would dare to say, *a scandalous, reckless, impious Book, whose morality is to enrich the rich and despoil the poor,* to teach children to repudiate their mother and their brothers,** to seize without scruple what belongs to another,*** not to teach the wicked, for fear they will correct themselves and be pardoned,**** to hate father, mother, wife, children, all one's relations.***** A Book in which the fire of discord is breathed everywhere,****** where one boasts of arming the son against the father,******* relatives one against the other,******** servants against their masters.********* Where violation of the Laws is approved,********** where persecution is imposed as a duty.*********** Where to induce people to engage in brigandage, eternal happiness is made the reward of force and the conquest of violent men.*************

Picture an infernal soul analyzing the entire Gospel this way, creating from this slanderous analysis an essay under the name *Evangelical Profession of Faith*, a Writing that would inspire horror, and the devout Pharisees promoting this Writing in a triumphant manner as the abridged lessons of Jesus Christ. Yet that is where this unworthy method can lead. Whoever will have read my Books and will read the imputations of those who accuse me, who judge me, who condemn me, who pursue me, will see that this is how they have all treated me.

* Matthew XIII: 12; Luke, XIX: 26.
** Matthew XII: 48; Mark, III: 33.
*** Mark XI: 2; Luke, XIX: 30.
**** Mark IV: 12; John, XII: 40.
***** Luke XIV: 26.
****** Matthew X: 34; Luke, XII: 51, 52.
******* Matthew X: 35; Luke, XII: 53.
******** Ibid.
********* Matthew X: 36.
********** Matthew XII: 2 and following.
*********** Luke XIV: 23.
************ Matthew XI: 12.

I believe I have proved to you that these Gentlemen have not judged me according to reason. Now I have to prove to you that they have not judged me according to the Laws. But let me take a moment to catch my breath. To what sad undertakings am I reduced at my age? Did I have to learn to make my apology so late? Was it worth starting?

Second Letter

I assumed, Sir, in my preceding Letter that I had in fact committed the errors against the faith of which I am accused, and I caused it to be seen that because these errors are not at all harmful to society they were not punishable before human justice. God has reserved for himself his own defense and the punishments of faults that offend only him. It is a sacrilege for some men to make themselves into the avengers of the divinity, as if it needed their protection. Magistrates, Kings have no authority over souls, and as long as one is faithful to the Laws of society in this world, it is not at all up to them to meddle with what will happen to one in the other, where they have no inspectorship. If this principle were lost from sight, Laws made for the happiness of the human race would soon be its torment, and under their terrible inquisition, men, judged by their faith more than by their deeds, would all be at the mercy of whoever would want to oppress them.

If the Laws do not have any authority over the sentiments of men in what pertains uniquely to Religion, they do not have any either over writings in which these sentiments are manifested. If the Authors of these Writings are punishable, it is never precisely for having taught error, because neither the Law nor its ministers judge about what is precisely only an error. The Author of the *Letters Written from the Country* appears to agree with this principle.* Perhaps he would even push it too far by granting that *Politics and Philosophy could maintain the liberty of writing everything.*** That is not what I wish to examine here.

But here is how your Gentlemen and he twist the thing in order to authorize the judgment rendered against my Books and against me. They judge me less as a Christian than as a Citizen; they regard me less as impious toward God than as a rebel against the Laws; in me they see sin less than crime, and heresy less than disobedience. According to them I have attacked the Religion of the State; thus I have incurred the penalty provided by the Law against those who attack it. There, I believe, is the sense of what is intelligible in what they have said to justify their proceeding.

---

* *In this regard*, he says on page 22, *I recognize my maxims well enough in those of the remonstrances*; and on page 29, he regards as *incontestable that no one can be prosecuted for his ideas about Religion.*
** Page 30.

I see in that only three little difficulties. The first, to know what that Religion of the State is; the second, to show how I attacked it; the third, to locate that Law in accordance with which I have been judged.

What is the Religion of the State? It is the holy evangelical Reformation. Without contradiction these are very striking words. But what is the holy evangelical Reformation at Geneva today? Would you know, Sir, by any chance? In that case I congratulate you for it. As for me, I do not know. I used to believe I did know it; but I was mistaken as were many others, more learned than I on every other point, and not less ignorant on this one.

When the Reformers separated from the Roman Church they accused it of error; and in order to correct that error at its source, they gave to Scripture a different meaning than the one the Church gave it. They were asked by what authority they thus deviated from the accepted doctrine? They said that it was by their own authority, by that of their reason. They said that since the meaning of Bible was intelligible and clear to all men in what concerned salvation, each was a competent judge of doctrine and could interpret the Bible, which was its rule, in accordance with his individual mind; that all would agree this way about the essential things, and that those upon which they could not agree were not at all essential.

Thus the individual mind is established as the sole interpreter of Scripture; thus the authority of the Church is rejected; thus each is put under his own jurisdiction for doctrine. Such are the two fundamental points of the Reform: to acknowledge the Bible as rule of one's belief, and not to admit any other interpreter of the meaning of the Bible than oneself. Combined, these two points form the principle on which the Reformed Christians separated from the Roman Church, and they could not do any less without falling into contradiction; for what interpretive authority could they have reserved for themselves, after having rejected that of the body of the Church?

But, it will be said, how could the Protestants have been able to unite based on such a principle? Wanting each to have his manner of thinking, how did they constitute a body against the Catholic Church? They had to do it: they united in this, that all acknowledged each of them as competent judge for himself. They tolerated and they ought to tolerate all interpretations except one, namely that which removes liberty of interpretation. Now that single interpretation which they rejected was that of the Catholics. Thus they had to proscribe in concert Rome alone, which equally proscribed all of them. The very diversity of their manners of thinking about all the rest was the common bond that united them. It was so many small States leagued against a great Power, and the general confederation of which removed nothing from the independence of each.

That is how the evangelical Reformation was established, and that is how it must preserve itself. It is very true that the doctrine of the majority can be proposed to all, as the most probable or the most authorized. The Sovereign can even draw it up in a formula and prescribe it to those it charges with teaching, because some order, some rule, is needed in public instruction, and because at bottom this does not obstruct anyone's liberty, since no one is forced to teach in spite of himself: but it does not follow from this that private individuals are obliged to admit precisely those interpretations given to them and that doctrine taught to them. Each remains the sole judge of them for himself, and does not acknowledge any authority in them other than his own. Good instruction ought less to fix the choice we ought to make than to put us in a condition to choose well. Such is the genuine spirit of the Reformation; such is its true foundation. Individual reason pronounces in it, by drawing faith from the common rule it establishes, namely the Gospel; and it is so much of the essence of reason to be free, that even if it wished to subject itself to authority, it would not be able to do so. Make the slightest infringement of this principle and all evangelism instantly collapses. Let someone prove to me today that in matters of faith I am obliged to submit to someone else's decisions, beginning tomorrow I will become Catholic, and every consistent and true man will act as I do.

Now the free interpretation of Scripture entails not only the right to explain passages from it, each in accordance with its particular sense, but that of remaining in doubt over those that one finds doubtful, and that of not understanding those one finds incomprehensible. That is the right of each of the faithful, a right that neither Pastors nor Magistrates have anything to do with. As long as one respects all of the Bible and one is in accord on the capital points, one lives in accordance with the evangelical Reformation. The oath of the Bourgeois of Geneva entails nothing more than that.

Now I already see your Doctors triumphing over these capital points, and claiming that I deviate from them. Slowly, Gentlemen, for mercy's sake; I am not yet the issue, you are. Let us know first what these capital points are according to you, let us know what right you have to constrain me to see them where I do not see them, and perhaps where you do not see them yourselves. Do not forget at all, if you please, that to give me your decisions as laws is to deviate from the holy evangelical Reformation, it is to unsettle its true foundations; it is you who deserve punishment by Law.

Whether one considers the political state of your Republic when the Reformation was established, or one ponders the terms of your old Edicts in relation to the Religion they prescribe, one sees that the Reformation is everywhere put into opposition with the Roman Church and that the Laws have as their object only to abjure its principles and form of worship, which are destructive of liberty in every sense.

In this particular position the State existed, so to speak, only by the separation of the two Churches, and the Republic was annihilated if Papism reacquired the upper hand. Thus the Law that settled the evangelical form of worship, in doing so, considered only the abolition of the Roman form of worship. This is attested to by the (even indecent) invectives that one sees against it in your first Ordinances, and that subsequently were wisely excised, when the same danger no longer existed: This is attested to also by the oath of the Consistory, which consists solely in preventing *all acts of idolatry, blasphemy, dissolution, and other things contravening the honor of God and of the Reformation of the Gospel.* Such are the terms of the Ordinance passed in 1562. In the review of the same Ordinance in 1576 they put at the head of the oath, *to watch out for all scandals**: which shows that in the first formula of the oath they had only the separation from the Roman Church as object; later on they provided in addition for public order: that is natural when an establishment begins to take on consistency: But, in sum, neither error nor heresy is a question in either one or the other reading, nor in any oath of Magistrates, or Bourgeois, of Ministers. Far from that having been the object of the Reformation or the Laws, that would have been to put oneself in contradiction with oneself. Thus, under this word *Reformation*, your Edicts have not fixed anything but the points debated with the Roman Church.

I know that your history, and that of the Reform in general, is full of facts that show a very severe inquisition, and that, from being persecuted the Reformers soon became persecutors: but this contrast, so shocking in all the history of Christianity, does not prove anything in yours but the inconsistency of men and the rule of passions over reason. As a result of disputing against the Catholic Clergy, the Protestant Clergy acquired the disputing and touchy spirit. It wanted to determine everything, regulate everything, pronounce about everything: each modestly proposed his sentiment as the supreme Law for all the others; this was not the way to live in peace. Calvin, doubtless, was a great man; but in the end he was a man, and what is worse, a Theologian: moreover he had all the pride of the genius who feels his superiority, and is indignant that anyone disagree with him: the majority of his colleagues were in the same position, all of them all the guiltier in this as they were more inconsistent.

---

* Ordon. Eccles. Tit. III. Art. LXXV.

Thus what a hold they gave to the Catholics on this point, and what a pity it is to see in their defenses these learned men, these enlightened minds who reasoned so well on every other article, talking nonsense so stupidly on that one? Nevertheless these contradictions did not prove anything other than that they followed their passions much more than their principles. Their harsh orthodoxy was itself a heresy. That was very much the spirit of the Reformers, but it was not that of the Reformation.

The Protestant Religion is tolerant by principle; it is tolerant essentially; it is as much so as it is possible to be, since the only dogma it does not tolerate is that of intolerance. That is the insurmountable barrier that separates us from the Catholics and unites the other communions among themselves. Each one indeed views the others as being in error. But none views or ought to view that error as an obstacle to salvation.*

The Reformed people of our day, at least the Ministers, no longer know or no longer love their Religion. If they had known and loved it, they would have shouted with joy in unison at the publication of my Book; they would all have joined with me, who attacked only their adversaries. But they prefer abandoning their own cause to sustaining mine. With their laughably arrogant tone, with their rage for quibbling and intolerance, they no longer know what they believe, nor what they want, nor what they say. I no longer see them as anything except bad valets of the Priests, who serve them less out of love for them than out of hatred for me.**[5] When they have disputed well, squabbled well, caviled well, pronounced well, at the very height of their little triumph, the Roman Clergy—who laugh now and leave them alone—will come to chase them out, armed with arguments *ad hominem* to which there is no reply; and beating them with their own weapons, the clergy will say to them: *that is fine; but now get out, evil intruders that you are. You have worked only for us.* I return to my subject.

As a Reformed church, the Church of Geneva, then, does not and should not have any profession of faith that is precise, articulated, and common to all its members. If people wished to have one, for that very reason, they would offend evangelical freedom, they would renounce the principle of the Reformation, violate the Law of the State. All the Protestant Churches

---

* Of all the Christian sects, the Lutheran appears the most inconsistent to me. It has gratuitously collected against itself alone all the objections of the sects to each other. It is in particular intolerant like the Roman Church. But it lacks the great argument of the latter: it is intolerant without knowing why.

** It is rather superfluous, I believe, to give notice that I make an exception here for my Pastor and those who think as he does on this point. Since writing this note, I have learned to make exceptions for no one, but I am leaving it as I have promised, for the instruction of any decent man who may be tempted to praise the Clergy.

that have drawn up formulas for a profession of faith, all the Synods that determined points of doctrine, wanted only to prescribe to ministers the one they ought to teach, and that was good and proper. But if these Churches and these Synods claimed to do more by means of these formulas and to prescribe to the faithful what they ought to believe, then by such decisions these assemblies proved nothing other than that they were ignorant of their own Religion.

For a long time the church of Geneva appeared to stray less than the others from the genuine spirit of Christianity, and it is on the basis of this misleading appearance that I honored its Pastors with praises of which I believed they were worthy, for my intention was assuredly not to mislead the public.[6] But today who can see these same Ministers, formerly so accommodating and suddenly having become so rigid, quibble about the orthodoxy of a Layman and leave their own in such scandalous uncertainty? One asks them if Jesus Christ is God, they dare not reply. One asks them what mysteries they recognize, they dare not reply. To what will they reply then, and what will be the fundamental articles, different from mine, on which they want people to decide, if those are not included?

A Philosopher gives them a quick glance. He sees through them. He sees them to be Arians, Socinians. He says so and thinks he honors them. But he does not see that he is exposing their temporal interest, the only thing that generally determines the faith of men here below.

Immediately alarmed and frightened, they gather, they discuss, they fidget, they do not know where to turn.[7] And after many consultations,* deliberations, conferences, everything ended with a piece of nonsense in which they said neither yes or no, and in which it is as impossible to understand anything as in Rabelais' two speeches for the defense.**[8] Isn't the orthodox doctrine perfectly clear, and isn't it in safe hands?

Yet because one of them, compiling many scholastic jokes as benign as they are elegant, in order to judge my Christianity does not fear abjuring his own, altogether charmed by their colleague's knowledge and above all by his logic, they endorse his scholarly work and thank him for it through a deputation. In truth, these Gentlemen your Ministers are singular men! We know neither what they believe nor what they do not believe. We do not even know what they pretend to believe. Their only manner of establishing their faith is by attacking that of others. They do as the Jesuits do, who, it is said, forced everyone to sign the constitution[9] without wanting

---

* *When one is well resolved about what one believes*, said a Journalist dealing with this subject, *a profession of faith ought to be quickly made.*

** There would perhaps have been some difficulty in explaining themselves more clearly without having to retract certain things.

to sign it themselves. Instead of explaining themselves about the doctrine imputed to them, they think they put the other churches off the scent by picking a fight with their own defender. They want to prove through their ingratitude that they did not need my efforts, and believe they look Orthodox enough by looking like persecutors.

From all this, I conclude that it is not easy to say what composes the holy Reformation in Geneva today. The only thing that can be said with certainty about this point is that it has to consist mainly in rejecting the points contested against the Roman Church by the first Reformers, and especially by Calvin. That is the spirit of your institution. That is what makes you a free people, and it is in this respect alone that among you Religion is part of the Law of the State.

I pass from this first question to the second, and ask how it is possible in a Book where the truth, utility, and necessity of Religion in general is established with the greatest force; where, without making any exception,* the Author prefers the Christian Religion to any other worship and the evangelical Reformation to any other sect, for this same Reformation to be attacked? That appears difficult to conceive. However, let us see.

I have already proved above in general and will later prove in more detail that it is not true that Christianity is attacked in my Book. Now when the common principles are not attacked, any sect in particular can be attacked only in two ways, namely indirectly, by supporting the distinctive dogmas of its adversaries, or directly, by attacking its own.

But how would I have supported the distinctive dogmas of the Catholics since, on the contrary, they are the only ones I have attacked, and since it is that attack itself that aroused the Catholic party against me, without which it is certain the Protestants would have said nothing? That, I admit, is one of the strangest things anyone ever heard of, but it is nonetheless true. I am a communicant of the protestant faith in Paris; that is why I am still one in Geneva.

And how would I have attacked the distinctive dogmas of the Protestants since, on the contrary, they are what I have supported with the most force, since I have not stopped insisting on the authority of reason in matters of faith, the free interpretation of the Scriptures, evangelical tolerance, and obedience to the Laws, even in matters of worship, all of which are distinctive and radical dogmas of the Reformed church, without which, far from being solidly established, it could not even exist.

There is more. See what force the very form of the Work adds to the arguments in favor of the Reformed. It is a Catholic Priest who is talking,

* I entreat every equitable reader to reread and weigh in *Emile* what immediately follows the profession of faith of the Vicar, and where I resume talking.

and this Priest is neither impious nor a libertine. He is a believing and pious man, full of candor, rectitude, and despite his difficulties, his objections, and his doubts, nurturing at the bottom of his heart the truest respect for the worship he professes. A man who, in his most intimate effusion, declares that having been called to the service of the Church in this worship, he fulfills the tasks prescribed to him with all possible exactitude; that his conscience would reproach him for voluntarily failing in the slightest detail; that in the mystery that most shocks his reason, he collects his thoughts at the moment of consecration in order to do it with all the dispositions the Church and the greatness of the sacrament require; that he pronounces the sacramental words with respect; that he confers on their effect all the faith of which he is capable; and that, whatever the case for this inconceivable mystery, he does not fear that on the day of judgment he will be punished for having ever profaned it in his heart.*

That is the way of talking and thinking of this venerable, truly good, wise, truly Christian man, the most sincere Catholic who perhaps ever existed.

Listen, however, to what this virtuous Priest says to a young Protestant man who had become Catholic and to whom he gives advice. "Go back to your Fatherland, return to the religion of your fathers, follow it in the sincerity of your heart and never leave it again. It is very simple and very holy. I believe that of all the religions on earth it is the one which has the purest morality and which is most satisfactory to reason." **

He adds a moment later: "If you wish to listen to your conscience, countless vain obstacles will disappear at its voice. You will sense that in the uncertainty in which we dwell, it is an inexcusable presumption to profess a religion other than that in which we were born, and a falseness not to practice sincerely the religion which we profess. For if we go astray, we deprive ourselves of a great excuse at the tribunal of the Sovereign Judge. Will He not pardon the error on which we were weaned sooner than the error we dared to choose ourselves?" ***

A few pages earlier he had said: "If I had Protestants in my neighborhood or in my parish, I would not distinguish them at all from my true parishioners in everything connected with Christian charity. I would bring them all to love one another without distinction and to regard one another as brothers, to respect all religions, and to live in peace, with each observing his own. I think that to urge someone to leave the religion in which he was born is to urge him to do evil, and consequently is to do evil

---

* *Emile*, T. III, p. 185 and 186 [Bloom, 308–309].
** Ibid., page 196 [Bloom, 311, translation altered].
*** Ibid., page 195 [Bloom, 311].

oneself. While waiting for greater enlightenment, let us protect public order. In every country let us respect the laws, let us not disturb the worship they prescribe; let us not lead the citizens to disobedience. For we do not know with certainty whether it is a good thing for them to abandon their opinions in exchange for others, and we are very certain that it is an evil thing to disobey the laws."[10]

That, Sir, is how a Catholic Priest talks in a Writing where I am accused of having attacked the worship of the Reformed, and where nothing else is said about it. What I might have been reproached for, perhaps, was excessive partiality in their favor, and a lack of propriety in making a Catholic Priest talk the way no Catholic Priest has ever talked. Thus in everything I did precisely the opposite of what I am accused of having done. It is as if your Magistrates behaved on a wager. If they had bet on judging against the evidence, they could not have been more successful.

But this book contains objections, difficulties, doubts! And why not, I beg you? What is the crime for a Protestant to propose his doubts about what he finds doubtful and his objections about what he finds admits of some? If what appears clear to you appears obscure to me, if what you judge demonstrated does not seem demonstrated to me, by what right do you claim to subject my reason to yours and to give me your authority as Law, as if you claimed the Pope's infallibility? Isn't it amusing that it is necessary to reason like a Catholic to accuse me of attacking the Protestants?

But these objections and these doubts touch on the fundamental points of faith? Under the appearance of these doubts, everything that can tend to undermine, unsettle, and destroy the principal foundations of the Christian Religion has been assembled? That changes the thesis, and if that is true, I may be guilty. But it is also a lie, and a very imprudent lie on the part of people who themselves do not know what constitutes the fundamental principles of their Christianity. For myself, I know very well what constitutes the fundamental principles of mine, and I have said so. Almost all of Julie's profession of faith is affirmative, the entire first part of the Vicar's is affirmative, half of the second part is also affirmative, a part of the chapter on civil Religion is affirmative, the Letter to the Archbishop of Paris is affirmative. There, Sirs, are my fundamental articles. Let us see yours.

They are skillful, these Gentlemen. They establish the method of discussion that is newest and most convenient for persecutors. They artfully leave all the principles of the doctrine uncertain and vague. But if an Author has the misfortune to displease them, they go rummaging through his Books to find out what his opinions might be. When they believe they have verified them well, they take the opposite of these opinions and make them into so many articles of faith. Then they rail about impiety, blasphemy, because the Author did not introduce in his Books ahead of time the supposed articles of faith that they constructed after the fact to torment him.

How is it possible to follow them in these multitudes of points on which they attacked me, to bring together all their personal attacks, to read them? Who can go sort out all these fragments, all these rags among the junk dealers of Geneva, or in the rubbish of the Mercurey of Neufchâtel? I get lost, I get bogged down in the midst of so many stupidities. Let us select from this trash a single article to serve as an example, their most triumphant article, the one for which their preachers* entered the fray and about which they have made the most noise: miracles.

I am entering a lengthy examination. I beg you to forgive me for its tiresomeness. I do not want to discuss this awful point except to spare you those upon which they insisted less.

They say then, "J. J. Rousseau is not Christian although he presents himself as such. For we, who certainly are, do not think as he does. J. J. Rousseau does not believe in revelation at all, although he says he believes in it. Here is the proof of that.

"God does not reveal his will directly to all men. He speaks to them through his Messengers, and his Messengers have miracles as proof of their mission. Therefore, whoever rejects miracles rejects the Messengers of God, and whoever rejects the Messengers of God rejects Revelation. Now Jean-Jacques Rousseau rejects miracles."

First let us grant both the principle and the fact as if they were true. We will return to them later. That supposed, the preceding reasoning has only one fault, which is that it works directly against those who use it. It is very good for the Catholics, but very bad for the Protestants. It is my turn to prove.

You will find that I repeat myself often, but what does that matter? When I need the same proposition for totally different arguments, do I have to avoid taking it up again? That affectation would be childish. The issue is not variety, but truth, and correct, conclusive reasonings. Forget the rest and consider only that.

When the first Reformers began to make themselves heard, the universal Church was at peace. All sentiments were unanimous. There was not one essential dogma debated among Christians.

In this tranquil situation, suddenly two or three men raise their voices and shout throughout Europe: Christians, be on your guard. You are

---

* I would not have used this term, which I found disparaging, if the example of the Council of Geneva, who used it in writing to the Cardinal de Fleury, had not taught me that my scruple was badly founded.

being deceived, you are being led astray, you are being taken on the road to hell. The Pope is the Antichrist, the instrument of Satan; his Church is the school of lies. You are lost if you do not listen to us.

At these first clamors, an astonished Europe remained silent for some moments, waiting to see what would happen. Finally the Clergy, recovered from their initial surprise and seeing that these newcomers were forming Sectaries as every man who dogmatizes always does, understood that it was necessary to have it out with them. They began by asking them who they were after with all this racket. The others respond proudly that they are the apostles of truth, called to reform the Church and bring the faithful back from the road to perdition where the Priests were leading them.

But, they were answered, who gave you this fine errand to come disturb the peace of the Church and the public tranquillity? Our conscience, they said, reason, the inner light, God's voice which we cannot resist without committing a crime. It is He who calls us to this sacred ministry, and we follow our vocation.

You are Messengers of God, then, the Catholics continued. In that case, we agree that you ought to preach, reform, teach, and that one ought to listen to you. But to obtain this right, start by showing us your credentials. Prophesy, heal, enlighten, perform miracles, display the proofs of your mission.

The reply of the Reformers is beautiful and is well worth the trouble of transcribing.

"Yes, we are the Messengers of God. But our mission is not extraordinary. It is in the impulse of an upright conscience, in the enlightenment of a healthy understanding. We do not bring you a new Revelation. We limit ourselves to the one that has been given to you and that you no longer hear. We come to you not with marvels that can be deceptive and with which so many false doctrines have propped themselves up, but with the signs of the truth and of reason that do not deceive; with this holy Book that you disfigure and that we explain to you. Our miracles are invincible arguments, our prophesies are demonstrations. We predict to you that if you do not listen to the voice of Christ which speaks to you through our mouths, you will be punished like unfaithful servants who are told the will of their masters and who do not want to carry it out."

It was not natural for Catholics to admit the evidence of this new doctrine, and that is just what the majority of them were careful not to do. Now it can be seen that, being reduced to this point, the dispute could no longer be brought to a close and that each one had to carry his point; the Protestants always maintaining that their interpretations and their proofs were so clear that one had to act in bad faith to reject them. And the Catholics, for their part, finding that the petty arguments of a few private individuals, which were not even unanswerable, should not win out over the authority of the entire Church, which had in all ages determined the debated points otherwise.

That is the state in which the quarrel has remained. People have not ceased disputing over the force of the proofs, a dispute that will never come to an end as long as men do not all have the same head.

But that was not the issue for the Catholics. They were put off the scent, and if, without being diverted by quibbling about the proofs of their adversaries, they had limited themselves to disputing their right to prove, they would have confounded them, it seems to me.

"In the first place," they would have said to them, "your manner of reasoning only begs the question. For if the force of your proofs is the sign of your mission, it follows for those whom they do not convince that your mission is false, and that therefore we, the whole lot of us, can legitimately punish you as heretics, as false Apostles, as disturbers of the Church and the human Race.

"You do not preach new Doctrines, you say. What are you doing then when you preach your new explanations to us? Isn't giving a new meaning to the words of the Scripture establishing a new doctrine? Isn't it making God speak altogether differently than He spoke? It is not the sounds but the meanings of words that are revealed. Changing these meanings that are recognized and established by the Church is changing Revelation.

"Furthermore, see how unjust you are! You agree there must be miracles to authorize a divine mission, and yet, though you are simple private individuals by your own admission, you come to speak to us imperiously and as the Messengers of God.* You demand the authority to interpret Scripture at your whim, and you claim to deprive us of the same freedom. You arrogate to yourselves alone a right you refuse both to each one of us and to all of us who compose the Church. What title do you have, then, to subject our common judgments in this way to your individual mind? What intolerable conceit to claim always to be right, and right alone against the whole world, without wanting to leave alone in their sentiment those

---

* Farel declared in his own words in Geneva before the Episcopal Council that he was the Messenger of God, which made one of the Council members quote these words of Caiaphas: "He blasphemed. What need is there for other testimony? He deserved death." In the doctrine of miracles, other testimony was necessary to reply to that. Yet Jesus performed none on that occasion, nor did Farel either. Froment declared likewise to the Magistrate who forbade him to preach, "that it was better to obey God than men," and continued to preach, despite the interdiction, behavior that could certainly not be authorized except by an express order from God.

who do not share yours and who think they are right too!* The distinctions with which you put us off would be at most tolerable if you simply stated your opinion and left it at that. But not so. You wage open war on us. You breathe fire everywhere. To resist your lessons is to be rebellious, idolatrous, worthy of hell. You want absolutely to convert, to convince, even to constrain. You dogmatize, you preach, you censure, you anathematize, you excommunicate, you punish, you put to death. You exercise the authority of Prophets and present yourselves as mere private individuals. What! You Innovators, on your opinion alone, supported by a few hundred men, you burn your adversaries and we with fifteen Centuries of antiquity and the votes of a hundred million men, we will be wrong to burn you? No, stop talking and acting like Apostles or show your titles; or when we are the stronger, you will be very justly treated as imposters."

Do you see, Sir, what solid reply our Reformers could have made to this discourse? For myself, I do not see it. I think they would have been reduced to silence or to performing miracles. A sad recourse for friends of truth!

I conclude from this that establishing the necessity of miracles as proof of the mission of the Messengers of God who preach a new doctrine, is turning the Reformation upside down. It is to do, in order to fight me, what I am falsely accused of having done.

I have not said all there is to say on this subject, Sir. But what remains to be said cannot be divided and will only make an overly long Letter. It is time to finish this one.

---

* What man, for example, was ever more trenchant, more imperious, more decisive, more divinely infallible as he pleased than Calvin, for whom the slightest opposition, the slightest objection someone dared to make to him was always a work of Satan, a crime worthy of the fire? It was not only Servet who paid with his life for daring to think differently from him.

Third Letter

I take up again, Sir, this question of miracles that I have undertaken to discuss with you, and after having proved that to establish their necessity was to destroy Protestantism, I am now going to seek what their use is for proving revelation.

With heads so variously organized, men cannot all be equally affected by the same arguments, above all in matters of faith. What appears evident to one does not even appear probable to the other. By his turn of mind, one is struck only by one type of proof, the other is struck only by a very different kind. All can indeed agree sometimes on the same things, but it is very rare that they agree for the same reasons. This, it should be said in passing, shows how little sense dispute itself makes. We might as well want to force someone else to see through our eyes.

Thus when God gives men a Revelation that all are obliged to believe, he must establish it on proofs that are good for all, and that consequently are as diverse as the ways of seeing of those who must adopt them.

On this reasoning, which seems just and simple to me, it was found that God had given various characteristics to the mission of his Messengers that made this mission recognizable to all men, small and great, wise and foolish, learned and ignorant. The one among them who has a flexible enough brain to be moved by all these characteristics at the same time is fortunate, no doubt. But the one who is struck only by some is not to be pitied, provided he is sufficiently struck to be persuaded.

The first, most important, and most certain of these characteristics is derived from the nature of the doctrine; that is from its utility, its beauty,* its sanctity, its truth, its depth, and from all the other qualities that can announce to men the instructions of supreme wisdom and the precepts of the supreme goodness. This characteristic, as I have said, is the most

---

* I do not know why people want to attribute the beautiful morality of our Books to the progress of philosophy. This morality, taken from the Gospel, was Christian before it was philosophic. The Christians teach it without practicing it, I admit. But what more do the philosophers do, except to give themselves a great deal of praise, which since it is not repeated by anyone else does not prove much, in my opinion?

Plato's precepts are often very sublime, but doesn't he go greatly astray sometimes, and don't his errors go far? As for Cicero, can we believe that without Plato this Rhetorician would have found his treatise on duties? Concerning morality, the Gospel alone is always reliable, always true, always unique, and always resembles itself.

reliable, and most infallible; it bears within itself a proof that makes all others unnecessary. But it is the least easy to verify. In order to be felt, it requires study, reflection, knowledge, discussions suited only to wise men who are educated and know how to reason.

The second characteristic is in that of the men chosen by God to announce his word. Their sanctity, their veracity, their justice, their pure and spotless morals, their virtues inaccessible to the human passions, along with the qualities of understanding, reason, mind, knowledge, prudence, are as many respectable indications whose combining, when nothing gives it the lie, forms a complete proof in their favor and says they are more than men. This is the sign that especially strikes good and upright people, who see the truth everywhere they see justice, and hear the voice of God only from the mouth of virtue. This characteristic has its certainty, too, but it is not impossible for it to deceive, and it is no marvel for an imposter to fool good people, nor for a good man to fool himself, carried away by the ardor of a holy zeal that he mistakes for inspiration.

The third characteristic of the Messengers of God is an emanation of divine Power, which can interrupt and change the course of nature at the will of those who receive this emanation. This characteristic is indisputably the most brilliant of the three, the most striking, the quickest to leap to the eyes, the one that, being distinguished by a sudden and perceptible effect, seems to require the least examination and discussion. Because of that, this characteristic is also the one that particularly strikes the people, incapable of coherent reasoning, slow and reliable observations, and in all things the slave of its senses. But that is what makes this same characteristic equivocal, as will be proved below. And indeed, so long as it strikes those for whom it is intended, what difference does it make whether it is apparent or real? That is a distinction they are incapable of making, which shows there is no truly certain sign except the one derived from doctrine, and that consequently only good reasoners can have a solid and sure faith. But divine goodness lends itself to the weaknesses of the vulgar, and wishes to give them proofs that work for them.

I stop here, without seeking whether this enumeration can go further. It is a discussion of no use to ours, for it is clear that when all these signs are combined, it is sufficient to persuade all men: the wise, the good, and the people. Everyone with the exception of madmen, incapable of reason, and the wicked, who do not want to be convinced of anything.

These characteristics are proofs of the authority of those in whom they reside. They are the reasons for which people are obliged to believe them. When all that is done, the truth of their mission is established. They can then act with right and power in their quality as Messengers of God. Proofs are the means; the faith owed to doctrine is the end. Provided we accept the doctrine, it is the most futile thing to argue about the number and choice of proofs, and if one alone convinces me, it is wasted effort to want to make me adopt others. It would at least be very ridiculous to maintain that a man does not believe what he says he believes because he does not believe it for precisely the same reasons we say we have to believe it too.

These, it seems to me, are clear and incontestable principles. We come now to their application. I declare myself Christian. My persecutors say that I am not. They prove that I am not Christian because I reject Revelation, and they prove I reject Revelation because I do not believe in miracles.

But for this consequence to be just, one of two things would have to be true: either that miracles were the unique proof of Revelation or that I rejected the other proofs that bear witness to it. Now, it is not true that miracles are the unique proof of Revelation, and it is not true that I reject the other proofs, since on the contrary they are found established in the very work cited to accuse me of destroying Revelation.*

That is precisely where matters stand. Determined to make me reject Revelation in spite of myself, these Gentlemen count as nothing the fact that I accept it based on the proofs that convince me, if I do not also accept it based on those that do not convince me; and because I cannot do so, they say I reject it. Can one conceive of anything more unjust and more extravagant?

And see if I am making too much of this, please, when they accuse me of a crime for not accepting a proof that not only did Jesus not give but that he expressly rejected.

He did not proclaim himself at first by miracles, but by preaching. At the age of twelve, he was already disputing in the Temple with the Learned, sometimes questioning them and sometimes surprising them by the wisdom of his answers. That was the beginning of his functions, as he stated himself to his mother and Joseph.** In the countryside, before he performed any miracle, he started to preach the Kingdom of Heaven to the peoples,*** and he had already gathered several disciples without having obtained their sanction by any sign, since it is said that he made the first at Cana.****

---

* It is important to note that the Vicar could find many objections as a Catholic that are null for a Protestant. Thus the skepticism in which he remains does not prove mine in any way, especially after the very express declaration I made at the end of this same Writing. It is clearly seen in my principles that several of the objections it contains are beside the mark.

** Luke XI: 46, 47, 49.

*** Matthew IV: 17.

**** John II: 11. I cannot think that anyone wishes to count among the public signs of his mission the temptation of the devil and the forty-day fast.

When he subsequently performed miracles, it was most often on particular occasions whose choice did not proclaim a public testimony, and whose goal was so little to manifest his power that he was never asked to do it for that purpose without his refusing. Look at the whole history of his life in this regard. Listen above all to his own statement. It is so decisive that you will find nothing in it to reply to.

His career was already well advanced when the Learned, seeing him acting in earnest as a Prophet in their midst, took it into their heads to ask him for a sign. What should Jesus have replied to that, according to your Gentlemen? "You ask for a sign; you have had a hundred of them. Do you believe I came to proclaim myself to you as the Messiah without beginning by bearing witness about myself, as if I wanted to force you to mistake me and cause you to err despite yourselves? No. Cana, the Centurion, the Lepers, the blind men, the paralytics, the multiplication of the loaves, all Galilee, all Judea vouch for me. Those are my signs. Why do you pretend not to see them?"

Instead of that reply, which Jesus did not make at all, here, Sir, is the one he did give.

The wicked and adulterous Nation demands a sign, and none will be given to it. Elsewhere he adds, *No other sign will be given to it than that of Jonah the Prophet. And turning his back to them, he went away.**

See first how, blaming this mania for miraculous signs, he treats those who ask for them? And that does not happen to him only once, but many times.** Within the system of your Gentlemen, this request was very legitimate. Why, then, insult those who made it?

See next in whom we have to prefer to trust: in those who maintain it is rejecting Christian Revelation not to accept the miracles of Jesus as the signs that establish him, or in Jesus himself, who declares that he has no sign to give.

They will ask what, then, is the sign of Jonah the Prophet? I will reply to them that it is his preaching to the Ninevites, precisely the same sign Jesus used with the Jews, as he himself explains.*** The second passage can only be given a meaning that refers back to the first, or else Jesus would have contradicted himself. Now in the first passage where a miracle is requested as a sign, Jesus says positively that none will be given. Therefore the meaning of the second passage indicates no miraculous sign.

A third passage, they will insist, explains this sign by the resurrection of

---

* Mark VIII: 12; Matthew XVI: 4. For brevity, I have combined these two passages, but I have preserved the distinction essential to the question.

** Examine the following passages: Matthew XII: 39, 41; Mark VIII: 12; Luke XI: 29; John II: 18, 19; IV: 48; V: 34, 36, 39.

*** Matthew XII: 41; Luke XI, 30, 32.

Jesus.* I deny it. It explains it at best by his death. Now the death of a man is not a miracle. It is not even a miracle that after lying in the earth for three days, a body is taken out of it. In this passage, there is not a word about resurrection. Besides, what kind of proof would it be to claim authority during one's lifetime based on a sign that will not happen until after one's death? It would be wanting to find only non-believers. It would be hiding one's light under a bushel. Just as this behavior would be unjust, so this interpretation would be impious.

Moreover, the invincible argument returns again. The meaning of the third passage should not undermine the first, and the first affirms that no sign at all will be given, none whatever, none. Finally, whatever the case may be, it remains always proved by the testimony of Jesus himself, that if he performed miracles during his lifetime, he did not do so as a sign of his mission.

Every time the Jews insisted on this type of proof, he always sent them away scornfully, without ever deigning to satisfy them. He did not even approve of having his works of charity taken in this sense. *If you do not see marvels and miracles, you do not believe at all*, he said to the person who begged him to cure his son.** Is that how someone speaks who wants to offer marvels as proofs?

Wasn't it very astounding that if he performed so many of these, people incessantly continued to ask him for them? *What miracle do you perform*, the Jews said to him, *such that having seen it we believe in you? Moses gave manna in the desert to our fathers. But what work do you do?*** It is just about in the sense of your Gentlemen and setting aside royal Majesty, as if someone came to say to Frederick: *They say you are a great Captain. And why so? What have you done that shows you to be such? Gustave won at Leipzig, at Lutzen, Charles at Frawstat, at Narva; but where are your monuments? What victory did you win, what Stronghold did you take, what march have you undertaken, what Campaign covered you with glory? By what right do you bear the name Great?* Is the impudence of such a speech conceivable, and in the entire world would we find a man capable of making it?

Yet without putting to shame those who spoke to him like this, without granting them any miracle, without edifying them at least about those he had performed, Jesus, in reply to their question, is satisfied to allegorize about the bread of Heaven. So it was that far from winning him new Disciples, his reply deprived him of many of those he had and who, no doubt, thought as your Theologians do. The desertion was such that he said to

* Matthew XII: 40.
** John IV: 48.
*** John VI: 30, 31, and following.

the twelve: *And you, don't you, too, want to go away?* It does not appear that he had his heart set on preserving those whom he could retain only with miracles.

The Jews were asking for a sign from Heaven. In their system, they were right. For them, the sign that was to verify the coming of the Messiah could not be too manifest, too decisive, too much above suspicion, nor have too many eye witnesses. Since the direct testimony of God is always worth more than that of men, it was safer to believe it by the sign itself than by the people who said they had seen it, and for that purpose, heaven was preferable to earth.

The Jews were right in their view, then, because they wanted a manifest and entirely miraculous messiah. But Jesus said after the Prophet that the Kingdom of Heaven does not come manifestly, that the person who proclaims it does not debate at all, does not shout at all, that one cannot at all hear his voice in the streets. All that does not evince the ostentation of miracles, nor was that the goal he had in mind for his own. He placed in them neither the apparatus nor the authenticity necessary to verify true signs, because he did not offer them as such. On the contrary, he recommended secrecy to the sick people he cured, to the lame he made to walk, to the possessed he freed from the Demon. It was as though he was afraid to have his miraculous virtue known. One will admit that this was a strange way to make this the proof of his mission.

But all that is self-explanatory, as soon as it is conceived that the Jews went looking for this proof where Jesus did not want it to be. *The person who rejects me,* he said, *has a judge.* He added, *Will the miracles I have performed condemn him?* No, but *the word I have brought will condemn him.* The proof is in the word, then, and not in the miracles.

One sees in the Gospel that those of Jesus were all useful, but they were without luster, without affectation, without pomp; they were simple like his discourses, like his life, like all his behavior. The most manifest, the most palpable he performed was indisputably that of the multiplication of the five loaves and two fish that fed five thousand men. Not only had his disciples seen the miracle, but it had so to speak passed through their hands. And yet they did not think about it, they almost were not aware of it. Can you conceive it is possible to give as well-known signs to the human Race for all time facts to which the most immediate witnesses scarcely pay attention?*

And it was so far from the truth that the real object of Jesus' miracles was to establish the faith, that on the contrary he began by requiring faith

---

* Mark VI: 52. It is said that was because their hearts were stupid. But who would dare boast of having a heart more intelligent about sacred things than the disciples chosen by Jesus.

before performing the miracle. Nothing occurs so frequently in the Gospel. It is precisely because of that, it is because a prophet is without honor only in his own country, that he performed very few miracles in his.* It is even said that he could not perform any because of their incredulity.** What? It was because of their incredulity that he had to perform some to convince them, if his miracles had had that purpose. But they did not. They were simply acts of goodness, charity, kindness, which he performed for the benefit of his friends and those who believed in him. And such acts constituted the works of mercy truly worthy of being his, which he said bore witness to him.*** These works denoted the power to do good rather than the will to astonish; they were virtues**** more than miracles. And how could the supreme wisdom have used means so contrary to the end it proposed for itself? How could it not have foreseen that the miracles with which it supported the authority of its Messengers would produce a completely opposite effect, that they would make the truth of the story suspect as much concerning the miracles as the mission, and that among so many solid proofs, that one would only make enlightened and true people more demanding about all the others? Yes, I will always maintain it: the support we want to give belief is its greatest obstacle. Take the miracles out of the Gospel and the whole world will be at the feet of Jesus Christ.*****

You see, Sir, that it is attested by Scripture itself that, in the mission of Jesus Christ, miracles are not a sign so necessary to faith that we cannot have it without accepting them. Let us grant that other passages present a meaning contrary to these, and these in turn present a meaning contrary to the others; and so I chose, making use of my right, the one of these meanings that appeared to me the most reasonable and the most clear. If I had the pride of wanting to explain everything, I could twist and turn each passage to my meaning, like a true Theologian. But good faith does not allow me these Sophistic interpretations. Sufficiently authorized in my sentiment****** by what I understand, I remain at peace regarding what

---

* Matthew XIII: 58.
** Mark VI: 5.
*** John X: 25, 32, 38.
**** That is the word used in the Scripture. Our translators render it by the word miracles.
***** Paul preaching to the Athenians was listened to very peaceably until he spoke to them about a resuscitated man. At that point, some started to laugh. The others said to him, *That is enough. We will hear the rest another time.* I do not know very well what these good, fashionable Christians think deep in their hearts. But if they believe in Jesus through his miracles, I believe in him despite his miracles; and to my mind, my faith is worth more than theirs.
****** This sentiment is not so unique to me that it is not also shared by several Theologians whose orthodoxy is better established than that of the Genevan Clergy. Here is what one of those gentlemen wrote me on February 28, 1764.

Whatever the throng of modern apologists for Christianity say, I am persuaded there is not a word in the sacred Books from which one can legitimately conclude that miracles

I do not, and what those who explain it to me make me understand even less. I do not give the authority I give the Gospel to the interpretations of men at all, and I do not intend to subject them to mine any more than I subject myself to theirs. The rule is common, and clear about what is important. The reason that explains it is individual, and each has his own that constitutes authority only for him. Allowing oneself to be led by another in this matter is substituting the explanation for the text; it is subjecting oneself to men and not to God.

I take up my train of reasoning again, and after having established that miracles are not a necessary sign for faith, I am going to show in confirmation of this that miracles are not an infallible sign about which men can judge.

Regarding a specific fact, a miracle is an immediate act of divine power, a tangible change in the order of nature, a real and visible exception to its Laws. That is the idea one must not stray from if one wants to understand one another in reasoning about this matter. This idea offers two questions to resolve.

The first: can God perform miracles? That is, can he depart from the Laws he has established? Seriously treated, this question would be impious if it were not absurd. It would be too great an honor to the person who would resolve it negatively to punish him. It would suffice to lock him up. But also what man has ever denied that God could perform miracles? It was necessary to be a Hebrew to ask whether God could erect tables in the desert.

Second question: Does God want to perform miracles? That is a different matter. This question, in itself and abstracting from all other considerations, is completely indifferent. It does not in any way concern the glory of God, whose plans we cannot fathom. I will say even more. If there could be some difference as to faith in the manner of responding to it, the greatest ideas we could have of divine wisdom and majesty

---

were destined to serve as proof to men of all times and all places. Far from that, it was not in my opinion the principal object for those who were eye witnesses to them. When the Jews asked Saint Paul for miracles, his only answer was to preach Jesus' crucifixion to them. Certainly if Grotius, the Authors of the Boyle society, Vernes, Vernet, etc. had been in this Apostle's place, they would have had nothing more urgent to do than send for a stage to satisfy a request that squares so well with their principles. Those people believe they perform marvels with their mass of arguments. But someday, I hope, people will question whether they were not compiled by a society of unbelievers, without needing to be Hardouin to do so.

Let it not be thought, moreover, that the Author of this Letter is my partisan. Far from it. He is one of my adversaries. He finds only that the others do not know what they are saying. He suspects perhaps worse, for the faith of those who believe based on miracles will always be very suspect to enlightened people. That was the sentiment of the most illustrious reformers. *Non satis tuta fides eorum qui miraculis nituntur. Beze in Joan*, c. II, v. 23.

would favor the negative. Only human pride is against that. That is as far as reason can go. Moreover, this question is purely idle, and it would be necessary to read the eternal decrees to resolve it. For as we shall soon see, it is impossible to decide by the facts. Let us be careful, then, not to dare cast a curious eye on these mysteries. Let us pay this respect to the infinite essence to make no pronouncements about it. We know only its immensity.

However, when a mortal boldly comes and asserts to us that he has seen a miracle, he clearly cuts this great question short. Judge whether we should believe him at his word! If there were a thousand of them, I would not believe them.

I leave aside the crude sophism of using moral proof to verify naturally impossible facts, because then the very principle of credibility based on natural possibility is lacking. If in such cases men are willing to accept this proof regarding matters of pure speculation, or regarding facts whose truth hardly touches them, we can be assured that they would be more demanding if their slightest temporal interest were at stake. Let us suppose a dead man came to demand his property back from his inheritors, affirming that he has been resuscitated and requesting the opportunity to prove it,* do you believe there would be a single tribunal on earth where that would be granted to him? But once again, let us not open up this debate here. Let the facts retain all the certainty given to them, and let us be satisfied to distinguish between what the senses can attest and what reason can conclude.

Since a miracle is an exception to the Laws of nature, to judge one it is necessary to know those Laws, and to judge one reliably, it is necessary to know them all. For a single law that is not known could, in certain cases unknown to the spectators, change the effect of those that are known. Thus the person who proclaims that such and such an act is a miracle declares that he knows all the Laws of nature and that he knows this act is an exception to them.

But who is this mortal who knows all the Laws of nature? Newton did not boast of knowing them. A wise man who has witnessed an unheard of fact can attest that he has seen this fact and one can believe him. But neither this wise man nor any other wise man on earth will ever affirm that this fact, however astonishing it may be, is a miracle. For how can he know that?

All that can be said of the person who boasts of performing miracles is that he does very extraordinary things. But who denies that very extra-

---

* Note carefully that in my supposition, it is a genuine resurrection and not a false death that has to be verified.

Third Letter (Pl., III, 737–739)

ordinary things are done? I have seen those things myself, and have even done some.*[11]

The study of nature leads to new discoveries every day. Human industry perfects itself every day. Curious Chemistry has transmutations, precipitations, detonations, explosions, phosphoruses, pyrophoruses, earthquakes, and a thousand other marvels to make the people who would see them cross themselves a thousand times. Oil of guaiacum and nitric acid are not terribly rare substances. Mix them together, and you will see what happens. But do not do this experiment in a room, because you may well set the house on fire.** If the priests of Baal had had M. Rouelle[12] in their midst, their pyre would have caught fire on its own, and Elijah would have been taken for a dupe.

Pour water into water, behold ink. Pour water into water and make a hard substance. A Prophet from the College of Harcourt goes to Guinea and says to the people: acknowledge the power of the one who sends me. I am going to transform water into stone. By means known to the least Schoolboy, he makes ice. Behold the Negroes ready to worship him.

Formerly, Prophets made fire come down from Heaven at the sound of their voice. Today children do as much with a small piece of glass. Joshua made the Sun stop. An almanac writer is going to have it eclipsed. The marvel is even more striking. The workroom of the Abbé Nollet[13] is a laboratory of magic; mathematical games are a collection of miracles. What am I saying? Even fairs will be swarming with them. People like Brioché are not a rarity at fairs. The peasant of North Holland by himself, whom I have seen twenty times light his candle with his knife, is capable of subjugating all the People, even in Paris. What do you think he would have done in Syria?[14]

These Paris fairs are a rather unusual spectacle. There is not one of them where one does not see the most amazing things, without the public deigning to pay them almost any attention, so accustomed is one to amazing things, and even to those that one cannot conceive! At the very moment

---

* In Venice in 1743, I saw a rather novel method of telling fortunes, stranger than those at Praenestum. The person who wanted to consult them entered a room, and stayed there alone if he desired. There, from a Book full of blank pages, he selected one. Then, holding this sheet, he asked—not aloud but mentally—what he wanted to know. Then he folded his empty sheet, placed it in an envelope, sealed it, placed it in a Book similarly sealed. Finally, after reciting certain very baroque formulas without losing sight of his Book, he withdrew the paper from it, recognized the seal, opened it, and found his answer in writing.

The magician who told these fortunes was the first Secretary of the Ambassador of France. His name was J. J. Rousseau.

I was content to be a sorcerer because I was modest. But if I had the ambition to be a Prophet, who would have prevented me from becoming one?

** There are precautions to take to succeed in this operation. I will be excused, I think, from giving the recipe here.

I am writing this, two separate portable machines can be seen there, one of which walks or stops exactly according to the will of the person who makes the other one walk or stop. I saw a talking wooden head there, about which people did not talk as much as about that of Albert the Great.[15] I saw an even more surprising thing, which was many heads of men, of scientists, of Academicians who rushed to the miracles of the convulsions,[16] and came back all amazed.

With the cannon, optics, the magnet, the barometer, what marvels are not performed among the ignorant? The Europeans with their arts were always held to be Gods by the barbarians. If in the very bosom of the Arts, the Sciences, colleges, and Academies; if in the middle of Europe, in France and in England, a man had come in the last century armed with all the miracles of electricity that our physicists perform today, would he have been burned as a sorcerer, would he have been followed as a Prophet? It can be presumed one or the other would have been done. It is certain a mistake would have been made.

I do not know if the art of curing has been found or if it ever will be. What I do know is that it is not outside of nature. It is just as natural for a man to get well as it is for him to fall sick. He can just as easily get well suddenly as die suddenly. All that can be said about certain cures is that they are surprising, but not that they are impossible. How will you prove, then, that they are miracles? There are however, I admit, things that would astonish me greatly if I witnessed them. It would not be as surprising to see a lame man walk as to see a man walk who had no legs; nor to see a paralytic move his arm, as a man who has only one get both again. That would strike me even more, I admit, than to see a dead man resuscitated. For indeed a dead man can be not dead.* See Mr. Bruhier's book.[17]

Besides, however striking such a spectacle might appear to me, I would not want to witness it for anything in the world. For what do I know could happen as a result? Instead of making me a believer, I would greatly fear it would only make me insane. But this is not about me. Let us return.

We have just learned the secret of reviving the drowned. We have already sought that of reviving the hanged. Who knows whether in other types of deaths, we will not succeed in restoring life to bodies we thought

---

* *Lazarus was already in the earth?* Would he be the first man who had been buried alive? *He had been in it for four days?* Who counted them? Not Jesus, who was absent. *He was already stinking?* What do you know about that? His sister says so, that is the entire proof. Fright, disgust would have caused any other woman to say as much, even if it was not true. *Jesus only calls him and he emerges.* Be careful not to reason badly. It was a matter of physical impossibility, which is no longer so. Jesus made more of a fuss in other cases that were no more difficult. See the next note. What accounts for this difference, if everything was equally miraculous? This can be an exaggeration, and it is not the biggest Saint John made. I cite as evidence the last verse of his Gospel.

were deprived of it. We used not to know how to remove a cataract. It is a simple thing now for our surgeons. Who knows if there is not some secret that can be found to make it suddenly go away? Who knows if the possessor of such a secret cannot do with simplicity what an ignorant spectator will take for a miracle, and what a biased Author can present as such?* All that is not likely, so be it. But we have no proof it is impossible, and the issue here is physical impossibility. Without that, God displaying his power before our eyes could have given us only probable signs, simple probabilities. And the result of this would be that the authority of miracles being based only on the ignorance of those for whom they were performed, what would be miraculous in one era or for one people would no longer be so for others. So that lacking universal proof, the system established on it would be destroyed. No, give me miracles that will remain so whatever happens, at all times and in all places. If several of those that are related in the Bible appear to fall into this category, others also appear not to. Answer me then, Theologian. Do you require that I let the lot of them pass as a whole, or do you allow me to sort them out? When you have made a decision about this, we will see what happens after that.

Note well, Sir, that in supposing at most some amplification of the circumstances, I do not establish any doubt concerning the foundation of all the facts. That is what I have already said, and it is not superfluous to restate it. Enlightened by the spirit of God, Jesus had understanding so superior to that of his disciples that it is not surprising he performed many extraordinary feats in which the spectators' ignorance saw a marvel that was not there. To what extent, by virtue of this understanding, could he act by natural ways unknown to them and to us?** That is what we do

---

* We sometimes see in the details of reported facts a gradation that is not suited to a supernatural operation. A blind man is introduced to Jesus. Instead of healing him at the moment, he leads him out of the village. There he anoints his eyes with saliva and places his hands on him. After that, he asks him if he sees something. The blind man replies that he sees men walking who appear to him like trees. Thereupon, judging that the first operation is not sufficient, Jesus starts over, and finally the man is healed.
Another time, instead of using pure saliva, he mixes it with earth.
Now I ask what is the good of all that for a miracle? Is nature arguing with her master? Does he need effort and persistence to make himself obeyed? Does he need saliva, earth, ingredients? Does he even need to talk, and isn't it sufficient that he wills? Or rather will one dare to say that Jesus, certain of his success, does not fail to resort to a petty trick of a charlatan, as if to look more impressive and amuse the spectators? In the system of your Gentlemen, it must be one or the other, however. Choose.

** Our men of God wish with all their might that I have made Jesus an Imposter. They get angry in order to respond to this ignoble accusation, so it will be thought that I made it. They assume it with an air of certainty. They insist on it, they return to it affectionately. Ah, if these gentle Christians could finally extract some blasphemy from me, what a triumph it would be! What contentment, what edification for their charitable souls! With what holy joy they would bring the embers lighted by the fire of their zeal to burn me at the stake!

not know at all, and what we cannot know. The spectators of marvelous things are naturally inclined to describe them with exaggeration. About that we can in very good faith deceive ourselves as we deceive others. If a fact is a bit beyond our understanding, we suppose it is beyond reason, and the mind finally sees a marvel where the heart makes us strongly desire to do so.

Miracles, as I have said, are the proofs of simple people, for whom the Laws of nature form a very tight circle around them. But the sphere expands as men learn more and sense how much more there is for them to know. The great Physicist sees the limits of that sphere as so far away that he is unable to discern a miracle beyond them. *That cannot be*, is a phrase that rarely comes from the lips of wise men. They more often say, *I do not know.*

What ought we to think, then, of so many miracles related by Authors, truthful, I have no doubt, but of such crass ignorance and so full of zeal for the glory of their master? Must we reject all these facts? No. Must we accept them all? I am unaware.* We ought to respect them without making pronouncements about their nature, were a warrant issued against us a hundred times. For in the end, the authority of the Laws cannot extend to forcing us to reason badly. And yet this is what must be done to find a miracle necessarily where reason can see only an amazing fact.

Even if it were true that the Catholics have a sure means to make this distinction for themselves, what would be the consequence of that for us? In their system, when the Church once recognized has determined that such a fact is a miracle, it is a miracle. For the Church cannot be mistaken. But I am not dealing with the Catholics here, but with the Reformed. The latter have refuted very well some parts of the Vicar's profession of faith that, being written only against the Roman church, neither could nor had

---

* There are some in the Gospel that it is not even possible to take Literally without renouncing good sense. Such, for example, are those of the possessed. We recognize the Devil by his works, and the truly possessed are the wicked. Reason will never acknowledge any others. But let us move on. Here is more.

Jesus asks a group of Demons its name. What! Demons have names? Angels have names? Pure spirits have names? No doubt to call to one another or to hear when God is calling them? But who gave them these names? In what language are the words? What mouths pronounce these words; what ears are struck by their sound? This name is *Legion*, for they are many, which Jesus apparently did not know. These Angels, these Intelligences sublime in evil as in goodness, these Celestial Beings who have been able to revolt against God, who dare to fight his eternal Decrees, lodge themselves in a crowd inside the body of a man. Forced to leave this wretch, they ask to throw themselves into a flock of pigs. They are granted this. These pigs rush into the sea. And those are the august proofs of the mission of the Redeemer of the human race, the proofs that have to bear witness to it to all the peoples of all times, and of whom none can be in doubt on pain of damnation! Just God! One's head spins; one does not know where one is. Are those, then, the foundations of your faith, Sirs? Mine has some that are safer, it seems to me.

to prove anything against them. In the same way, the Catholics will easily be able to refute these Letters, because I am not dealing in any way here with Catholics, and our principles are not theirs. When it is a matter of showing that I do not prove what I did not want to prove, that is where my adversaries triumph.

From everything I have just set forth, I conclude that the best attested facts, even if all their circumstances were accepted, would prove nothing, and one can even suspect exaggeration regarding the circumstances without impugning the good faith of those who relate them. Continual discoveries being made about the laws of nature, those that probably will still be made, those that will always be left to make; the past, present, and future progress of human industry; the various limits people place on what is possible according to whether they are more or less enlightened; everything proves to us that we cannot know these limits. Yet for a miracle to be truly a miracle, it must go beyond them. Therefore whether there are miracles or whether there are not, it is impossible for the wise man to be certain that any fact, whatever it might be, is one.

Independently of the proofs of this impossibility I have just established, I see another that is no less powerful in the supposition itself. For let us grant that there might be true miracles, what good will they do us if there are also false miracles from which it is impossible to differentiate them? And note carefully that here I am not calling a false miracle a miracle that is not real, but an act that is really supernatural performed to support a false doctrine. As the word *miracle* in this sense can wound pious ears, let us use another word and give it the name *magic trick*.[18] But let us remember that it is impossible for the human senses to differentiate between a magic trick and a miracle.

The same authority that attests miracles also attests magic tricks, and this authority proves again that the appearance of magic tricks is in no way different from that of miracles. How then can they be distinguished from each other, and what can the miracle prove if the person who sees it cannot discern by any mark that is certain and drawn from the thing itself whether it is the work of God or whether it is the work of the Demon? There would have to be a second miracle to certify the first.

When Aaron threw down his rod in front of Pharaoh and it was changed into a serpent, the magicians also threw down their rods and they were changed into serpents. It makes no difference whether this change was real on both sides, as it is said in Scripture, or whether only Aaron's miracle was real and the magic trick of the magicians was only an appearance as some Theologians say. This appearance was exactly the same. Exodus does not note any difference between them, and if there had been, the magicians would have been careful not to expose themselves to the comparison, or if they had, they would have been confounded.

Now men can judge miracles only by their senses, and if the sensation is the same, the real difference they cannot perceive means nothing to them. Thus the sign, as sign, proves nothing more for one side than for the other, and in this regard the Prophet has no advantage over the Magician. If this once again is some of my fine style, agree that it will take a far finer one to refute it.

It is true that Aaron's serpent devoured the Magicians' serpents. But forced for once to acknowledge Magic, Pharaoh could well conclude nothing from it except that Aaron was more skilful than they in that art. Thus it was that Simon, enchanted with the things Philip was doing, wanted to buy from the Apostles the secret of doing as much as they did.[19]

Besides, the Magicians' inferiority was due to Aaron's presence. But in Aaron's absence, by making the same signs, they had the right to claim the same authority. The sign in itself therefore proved nothing.

When Moses changed water into blood, the Magicians changed water into blood. When Moses produced frogs, the Magicians produced frogs. They failed at the third plague, but let us confine ourselves to the first two, which God himself had made the proof of Divine power.* The magicians also made that proof.

As for the third plague, which they could not imitate, one does not see what made it so difficult, to the point of signifying that *the finger of God was there*. Why were those who could produce an animal unable to produce an insect, and how was it that after making frogs they could not make lice? If it is true that in those things only the first step is hard, that was assuredly stopping right in the middle.

The same Moses, having learned from these experiences, orders that if a false Prophet comes to proclaim other Gods—that is to say a false doctrine—and if this false Prophet gives authority to his statements by predictions or marvels that succeed, he must not be heeded but put to death. It is possible, then, to use true signs for the benefit of a false doctrine. A sign in itself proves nothing, then.

The same doctrine of signs through magic tricks is established in a thousand parts of the Scripture. Beyond that, after having declared that he will not make any signs, Jesus announces false Christs who will make them. He says *that they will make great signs, miracles capable of seducing even the elect, if that were possible.*** Wouldn't this language make it tempting to take signs as proofs of falseness?

* Exodus VII: 17.
** Matthew XXIV: 24; Mark XIII: 22.

What! God, master of the choice of his proofs when he wants to speak to men, prefers to choose those that assume knowledge he knows they do not have! In order to teach them he takes the same path he knows the Demon will take to deceive them! Would this course then be that of the divinity? Is it possible that God and the Devil follow the same route? That is what I cannot conceive.

Our Theologians, better reasoners but of less good faith than the ancients, are greatly perplexed by this magic. They would very much like to free themselves from it entirely, but they do not dare. They sense that denying it would be denying too much. These people who are always so decisive change their language here. They do not deny it, nor do they acknowledge it. They adopt the course of equivocating, of looking for subterfuges; they stop at each step. They do not know which leg to stand on.

I believe I have given you a sense, Sir, of where the difficulty lies. In order to make it perfectly clear, here it is stated as a dilemma.

If one denies magic tricks, one cannot prove miracles, because they are both founded on the same authority.

And if one accepts magic tricks along with miracles, one has no sure, precise, and clear rule for distinguishing between them. Thus miracles prove nothing.

I know well that our people pressed in this way come back to the doctrine. But they simply forget that if the doctrine is established, the miracle is superfluous, and that if it is not, it cannot prove anything.

I beg you not to be led astray, and from the fact that I have not regarded miracles as essential to Christianity, do not go concluding that I have rejected miracles. No, Sir, I have not and do not reject them. While I have stated reasons for having doubts about them, I have not dissimulated the reasons for believing in them. There is a big difference between denying something and not affirming it, between rejecting it and not acknowledging it; and I am so undecided on this point that I dare someone to find a single place in all my writings where I am affirmative against miracles.

Ah, how could I have been so despite my own doubts, since in all the places where I see myself most decided, I still affirm nothing. See what affirmations a man can make who speaks like this right from his Preface.*

"As to what will be called the systematic part, which is here nothing but the march of nature, it is the point that will most put the readers off, and doubtless it is here that I will be attacked. And perhaps it will not be wrong to do so. It will be believed that what is being read is less an educational treatise than a visionary's dreams about education. What is to be

---

* Preface of *Emile*, page iv [Bloom, 34].

done about it? It is on the basis not of others' ideas that I write but on that of my own. I do not see as do other men. I have long been reproached for that. But is it up to me to provide myself with other eyes or to affect other ideas? No. It is up to me not to go overboard, not to believe that I alone am wiser than everybody. It is up to me not to change sentiments but to distrust mine. That is all I can do; and that is what I do. If I sometimes adopt an assertive tone, it is not for the sake of making an impression on the reader but for the sake of speaking to him as I think. Why should I propose as doubtful what, so far as I am concerned, I do not doubt at all? I say exactly what goes on in my mind.

"In expounding freely my sentiment, I so little expect that it be taken as authoritative that I always join to it my reasons, so that they may be weighed and I be judged. But although I do not wish to be obstinate in defending my ideas, I nonetheless believe that it is my obligation to propose them; for the maxims concerning which I am of an opinion different from that of others are not matters of indifference. They are among those whose truth or falsehood is important to know and which make the happiness or the unhappiness of mankind."[20]

An Author who does not know himself whether he is in error; who fears that everything he says is a web of reveries; who, being unable to change his sentiments, is wary of his own; who does not adopt an assertive tone to advance it, but to speak as he thinks; who, not wishing at all to play the authority, always states his reasons so that he can be judged, and who does not even want at all to persist in defending his ideas; does an Author who talks in that way at the beginning of his Book want to pronounce oracles in it? Does he want to give decisions, and by this preliminary declaration, doesn't he place his strongest assertions among the doubts?

And let it not be said that I break my promises by persisting in defending my ideas here. That would be the height of injustice. It is not my ideas I defend, it is my person. If only my Books had been attacked, I would constantly have remained silent. That was a settled point. Since my declaration in 1753,[21] have I been seen to respond to someone, or was I silent for want of aggressors? But when I am prosecuted, when a warrant is issued against me, when I am dishonored for having said what I did not say, to defend myself I really have to show that I did not say it. It is my enemies who place the pen back in my hand in spite of myself. Ah! Let them leave me in peace, and I will leave the public in peace. I gladly give my word to do so.

This already serves as a reply to the retort I foresaw, of wanting to play the reformer myself while defying the opinions of my entire era. For nothing has less of an air of bravado than such language, and to speak with so much circumspection is assuredly not to adopt a Prophet's tone. I considered it as a duty to state my sentiment about important and useful things. But have I said a word, have I taken a step to have it adopted by others? Has anyone seen in my behavior the look of a man who was seeking to make sectaries for himself?

In transcribing the particular Writing that makes so many unexpected zealots for the faith, I warn the reader again that he has to be wary of my judgments, that it is for him to see if he can derive some useful reflections from this Writing; that I propose to him neither someone else's sentiment nor mine as a rule; that I present it to him to examine.*

And when I resume speaking, here is what I put in additionally at the end.

"I have transcribed this writing not as a rule for the sentiments that one ought to follow in religious matters, but as an example of the way one can reason with one's pupil in order not to diverge from the method I have tried to establish. So long as one concedes nothing to the authority of men or to the prejudices of the country in which one was born, the light of reason alone cannot, in the education founded by nature, lead us any farther than natural religion. This is what I limit myself to with my Emile. If he must have another religion, I no longer have the right to be his guide in that. It is up to him alone to choose it."**

After that, what man is impudent enough to dare accuse me of having denied miracles that are not even denied in this Writing? I have not spoken of them elsewhere.***

What! Because the Author of a Writing published by another person introduces into it a reasoner of whom he disapproves**** and who in an argument rejects miracles, does it follow from this that not only the Author of this Writing but the Editor also rejects miracles? What a web of reckless acts! That one permits oneself such presumptions in the heat of a literary quarrel is very blameworthy and too common. But to take them as proofs in Tribunals! That is jurisprudence to give the shivers to the most just and firm man who has the misfortune to live under such magistrates.

The Author of the profession of faith raises objections as much about the utility as about the reality of miracles, but these objections are not at all negations. Here is the strongest thing he says concerning this. "It is the unalterable order of nature which best shows the Supreme Being. If many

---

* *Emile*, vol. II, page 360 [Bloom, 260].
** Ibid., vol. III, page 204 [Bloom, 313–314].
*** I have spoken of them since in my *Letter to M. de Beaumont*. But beside the fact that no one has said anything about that letter, its contents cannot serve as the basis for proceedings that occurred before it appeared.
**** *Emile*, vol. III, page 151 [Bloom, 300–301].

exceptions took place, I would no longer know what to think; and as for me, I believe too much in God to believe in so many miracles that are so little worthy of Him."[22]

Now I ask you, what does that say? That too great a multitude of miracles would make them suspect to the Author. That he does not indiscriminately accept every kind of miracle, and that his faith in God makes him reject all those that are not worthy of God. What then? Does someone who does not accept all miracles reject all miracles, and is it necessary to believe in all those in the Legend to believe the ascension of Christ?

As the last straw, far from being able to understand the doubts contained in this second part of the profession of faith as negations, on the contrary the negations it may contain ought to be understood only as doubts. That is what the Author declares in beginning it about the sentiments he is going to dispute. He says, *Attribute to my discourse only the authority of reason. I do not know whether I am in error. It is difficult in discussion not to adopt an assertive tone sometimes. But remember that all my assertions here are only reasons for doubt.** Is it possible to speak more positively?

As for myself, I see facts attested in the holy Scriptures. That suffices to settle my judgment on this point. If they were elsewhere, I would reject these facts or I would remove the name miracles from them. But because they are in the Scriptures I do not reject them at all. I do not accept them either, because my reason refuses to do so and because my decision on this matter does not concern my salvation. No judicious Christian can believe that everything in the Bible is inspired, even the very words and errors. What we ought to believe inspired is everything that relates to our duties. For why would God have inspired the rest? Now the doctrine of miracles is in no way related to that. That is what I have just proved. Thus the sentiment we may have about that has no bearing on the respect we owe to the sacred Books.

Besides, it is impossible for men to ascertain that any fact whatever it might be is a miracle.** That is what I also proved. Thus, in acknowledging all the facts contained in the Bible, one can reject miracles without impiety and even without inconsistency. I did not go that far.

That is how your Gentlemen derive from miracles—which are not certain, which are not necessary, which prove nothing, and which I did not reject—the evident proof that I destroy the foundations of Christianity and that I am not Christian.

* *Emile*, vol. III, page 131 [Bloom, 295].
** If these gentlemen say that is determined in the Scripture and I ought to recognize as a miracle what it presents to me as such, I reply that this is what is at issue, and I add that this reasoning on their part is a vicious circle. For since they want the miracle to serve as proof of Revelation, they ought not to use the authority of Revelation to verify the miracle.

Boredom would prevent you from following me if I went into the same detail about the other accusations they heap up in the attempt to offset by their number the injustice of each one in particular. They accuse me, for example, of rejecting prayer. Look at the Book and you will find a prayer in the very place that is at issue. The pious man who is speaking* does not believe, it is true, that it is absolutely necessary to ask God for one particular thing or another.** He does not disapprove at all of doing that. For myself, he says, I do not do it, being convinced that God is a good father who knows better than his children what suits them. But cannot one worship him in other ways that are as worthy of him? The homage of a heart filled with zeal, the adorations, the praises, the contemplation of his greatness, the admission of our nothingness, the resignation to his will, the submission to his laws, a pure and saintly life, aren't all these things worth as much as self-interested and mercenary wishes? Near a just God, the best way to ask is to deserve to receive. Do the Angels who praise him surrounding his Throne pray to him? What would they have to ask of him? This word *prayer* is often used in the Scriptures for *homage, adoration*, and whoever does the greater is discharged from the lesser. For myself, I reject none of the ways of honoring God. I have always approved of joining the Church which prays to him. I do so. The Savoyard Priest did so himself.*** The Writing so violently attacked is full of all that. No matter. I reject prayer, they say. I am an impious man to be burned. Thus am I judged.

They say further that I accuse Christian morality of making all our duties impracticable by carrying them to excess. Christian morality is that of the Gospel. I do not recognize any other at all, and my accuser understands it in this same way, since it is from imputations where that is included that he concludes, a few lines after, that I call the Gospel divine by derision.****

* A minister from Geneva, most assuredly demanding about Christianity in the judgments he brings to bear on mine, affirms that I said—I, J. J. Rousseau—that I did not pray to God. He asserts it in so many words, five or six times in a row, and always naming me. I want to be respectful toward the Church, but would I dare ask him where I said that? Every scribbler is permitted to reason badly and chatter as much as he wants. But a good Christian is not permitted to be a public slanderer.

** *When you pray*, Jesus says, *pray like this*. When words are used to pray, it is well to prefer those. But I do not see here at all the order to pray with words. Another prayer is preferable. It is to be disposed toward everything God wants. *Here I am, Lord, to do your will.* Of all the formulas, the Lord's Prayer is, indisputably, the most perfect. But what is still more perfect is complete resignation to what God wills. *Not what I want, but what you want.* What am I saying? That is the Lord's Prayer itself. It is entirely in these words: *Thy will be done.* All other prayer is superfluous and only contradicts that one. It is possible that someone who thinks like this may be mistaken. But is the person who publicly accuses him on that account of destroying Christian morality and not being Christian a very good Christian himself?

*** *Emile*, vol. III, page 185 [Bloom, 308–309].

**** *Letters Written from the Country*, page 11.

Now see whether a blacker falsehood could be proposed, or more marked bad faith shown, since in the passage of my Book where this is reported, it is not even possible that I wanted to talk about the Gospel.

Here is this passage, Sir. It is in the fourth volume of *Emile*, page 64. "By enslaving decent women only to gloomy duties, we have banished from marriage everything which could make it attractive to men. Ought we to be surprised if the taciturnity they see reigning at home drives them from it or if they are scarcely tempted to embrace so unpleasant a condition? By exaggerating all duties, Christianity makes them impracticable and vain. By forbidding women song, dance, and all the entertainments of the world, it makes them sullen, shrewish, and unbearable in their homes."[23]

But where does the Gospel forbid women to sing and dance? Where does it subject them to sad duties? Completely to the contrary, the duties of husbands are discussed in it, but not a word is said about those of wives. Therefore it is wrong to have me say about the Gospel what I said only about the Jansenists, the Methodists, and other sanctimonious people today, who make Christianity a Religion as awful and unpleasant,* as it is pleasant and gentle under the true law of Jesus Christ.

I would not want to adopt the tone of Father Berruyer,[24] whom I hardly like and even find in very bad taste. But I cannot keep myself from saying that one of the things that charms me in Jesus' character is not only the gentleness of morals, and simplicity, but ease, grace, and even elegance. He did not flee from either pleasures or celebrations; he went to weddings, he visited women, he played with children, he liked perfumes, he dined at the homes of financiers. His disciples did not fast. His austerity was not at all troublesome. He was simultaneously indulgent and just, gentle with the weak and terrible with the wicked. His morality had about it something attractive, affectionate, tender. He had a sensitive heart. He was a man of good company. If he had not been the wisest of mortals, he would have been the most lovable.

Certain passages of Saint Paul, exaggerated or misunderstood, have produced many fanatics, and these fanatics have often disfigured and dishonored Christianity. If people had held closer to the spirit of the Master, that would never have happened. Let them accuse me of not always shar-

---

* The first Reformed people initially let themselves go to this excess with a harshness that produced many hypocrites, and the first Jansenists did not fail to imitate them in that. A preacher from Geneva named Henri de la Marre maintained from the pulpit that it was a sin to go to a wedding more joyously than Jesus Christ went to his death. A Jansenist curate similarly maintained that wedding feasts were an invention of the Devil. Someone objected to him concerning this that Jesus Christ had nevertheless attended them, and that he had even deigned to perform his first miracle at one in order to prolong the gaiety of the festivities. The curate, a little embarrassed, replied, grumbling: *That is not the best thing he did.*

ing Saint Paul's opinion, I can be reduced to proving that I am sometimes right not to do so. But it will never follow from this that I find the Gospel divine by derision. Yet that is how my persecutors reason.

Forgive me, Sir. I tire you with these lengthy details. I feel it, and I bring them to an end. I have already said only too much in my defense, and I bore myself by always replying with reasons to unreasonable accusations.

Fourth Letter

I have made you see, Sir, that the imputations drawn from my Books as proof that I was attacking the Religion established by the laws were false. It is, however, by these imputations that I have been judged guilty and treated as such. Let us assume now that I was in fact guilty, and let us see what punishment was owed me in that situation.

Like virtue, vice has its degrees.

Being guilty of one crime does not make someone guilty of them all. Justice consists in tailoring the punishment exactly to the fault, and extreme justice is itself a wrong when it pays no heed to the reasonable considerations that ought to temper the rigor of the law.

Assuming the offense is real, it remains for us to seek what its nature is and what procedure is prescribed by your laws in such cases.

If I violated my oath of the Bourgeois, as I am accused of doing, I committed a crime against the State, and cognizance of this crime belongs directly to the Council. That is incontestable.

But if my entire crime consists in error about doctrine, this error was itself an impiety. That is a different thing. According to your Edicts, it belongs to another Tribunal to take cognizance of it in the first instance.

And even if my crime were a crime against the State, if a prior decision about doctrine must be made in order to declare it as such, it is not up to the Council to make it. It is very proper for it to punish the crime, but not to establish it. That is explicit according to your Edicts, as we shall see later.

The first thing is to know whether I violated my oath of the Bourgeois, that is to say the oath my ancestors swore when they were admitted to the Bourgeoisie. Because for myself, not having lived in the Town, and not having performed any function as Citizen, I have not sworn the oath at all. But let it go at that.

In the formulation of this oath, there are only two articles that could concern my offense. By the former, one promises, *to live in accordance with the Reformation of the Holy Gospel*; and by the latter, *not to make, nor to allow any intrigues, machinations, or undertakings against the Reformation of the Holy Gospel.*

Now far from infringing the first article, I have conformed to it with a fidelity and even a boldness that have few examples, openly professing my Religion among the Catholics, although I previously lived in theirs; and one cannot cite that lapse from my childhood as an infraction from the oath, above all since my authentic rejoining of your Church in 1754[25] and my reestablishment in my rights of Bourgeoisie, well known to all Geneva, and of which moreover I have proofs positive.

One could not say, either, that I have infringed this first article by the condemned Books; since in them I have not ceased to declare myself to be a Protestant. Furthermore, conduct is one thing, Writings are something else. To live in accordance with the Reformation is to profess the Reformation, although by error one could lapse from its doctrine in blameworthy Writings, or commit other sins that offend God, but which by the fact alone does not cut the offender off from the Church. That distinction, if one could dispute it in general, is present in the oath itself; since in it they separate into two articles what could make only one, if the profession of the Religion was incompatible with every undertaking against the Religion. One swears by the first to live in accordance with the Reformation, and one swears by the last not to undertake anything against the Reformation. These two articles are very distinct and even separated by many others. Thus in the meaning of the Legislator these two things are separable. Thus if I had violated this last article, it does not follow that I have violated the first.

But have I violated this last article?

Here is how the Author of the *Letters Written from the Country* establishes the affirmative, page 30.

"The oath of the Bourgeois imposes on them the obligation *not to make, nor to allow any intrigues, machinations, or undertakings against the Reformation of the Holy Gospel*. It seems that it is to intrigue and machinate against it *a little** to seek to prove in two such seductive Books that the pure Gospel is absurd in itself and pernicious to society. The Council was thus obliged to cast a glance upon the one whom so many vehement presumptions accused of that undertaking."

See first how agreeable these Gentlemen are! It seems to them that they catch a glimpse of *a little* intrigue and machination from afar. Based on this remote semblance of a little maneuver, they cast a glance upon the one whom they presume to be its Author; and this glance is a warrant for his arrest.

---

* This *a little*, so humorous and so different from the serious and decent tone of the remainder of the Letters, since it has been cut out of the second edition, I abstain from going in search of the claw to whom this little tip, not of an ear, but of a fingernail, belongs.

It is true that the same Author subsequently amuses himself by proving that it is out of pure kindness toward me that they issued a warrant for me. *The Council,* he says, *could have personally summoned M. Rousseau, it could have subpoenaed him in order to hear him, it could have issued a warrant for him. . . . Of these three choices the last was incomparably the most gentle. . . . at bottom this was only a warning not to return, if he did not want to expose himself to a proceeding, or if he did want to expose himself to one to prepare his defenses well.**

Brantome says that the executioner of the unfortunate Don Carlos, Infant of Spain, joked this way. As the Prince was crying out and wanted to struggle, *Peace, My Lord,* he said to him while strangling him, *everything that is being done is only for your good.*[26]

But what then are these intrigues and machinations of which they accuse me? *To intrigue,*[27] if I understand my language, is to contrive secret intelligence for oneself; *to machinate,* is to engage in secret schemes, it is to do what certain people do against Christianity and against me. But I conceive of nothing less secret, nothing less hidden in the world than to publish a Book and to put one's name on it. When I have stated my sentiment on any matter whatsoever, I have stated it openly, to the public's face, I have named myself, and then I have remained tranquil in my retreat: it will be difficult to persuade me that that resembles intrigues and machinations.

In order to understand well the spirit of the oath and the meaning of the terms, one must transport oneself to the times when its formulation was set up and when it was essentially an issue for the State not to fall back under the double yoke that they had just shaken off. Every day they discovered some new plot in favor of the house of Savoy or the Bishops under pretext of Religion. That is clearly what the words *intrigues* and *machinations* concern, which, as long as the French language has existed have certainly never been used for the general sentiments that a man publishes in a Book in which he names himself, without plan, without object, without particular intention, and without a reference to any Government. That accusation appears so little serious to the very Author who dares to make it, that he acknowledges me to be *faithful to the duties of the Citizen.*** Now how could I be so, if I had infringed my oath of Bourgeois?

Thus it is not true that I have infringed this oath. I add that if that were true, nothing would be more unheard of in Geneva in things of that sort, than the proceeding brought against me. There is perhaps not a Bourgeois who does not infringe this oath in some point,*** without them taking it

---

* Page 31.
** Page 8.
*** For example, to not leave the Town in order to go to live elsewhere without permission. Who asks for that permission?

into their heads to pick a quarrel with him for that, and much less to issue a warrant for him.

One cannot say, either, that I attack morality in a Book in which I establish with all my power the preference for the general good over the private good and in which I relate our duties toward men to our duties toward God; the only principle upon which morality can be founded, in order to be real and go beyond appearance. One cannot say that this Book tends in any way to disturb the established form of worship nor the public order since, on the contrary, in it I insist upon the respect one owes to the established forms, upon obedience to the laws in everything, even in matters of Religion, and since it is for that prescribed obedience that a Preacher of Geneva has most bitterly reproached me.

This terrible offense about which they are making such a fuss is reduced, then, admitting it to be real, to some error over faith which, if it is not advantageous to society, is at least a matter of great indifference to it; the greatest evil that results from it being tolerance for the sentiments of others, consequently peace in the State and in the world over matters of Religion.

But I ask you, you, Sir, who knows your Government and your Laws, to whom it belongs to judge, and above all in the first instance, about errors over faith that a private individual can commit? Is it to the Council, is it to the Consistory? There is the nub of the question.

First it was necessary to reduce the offense to its type. Now that it is known, the proceeding must be compared to the Law.

Your Edicts do not settle the penalty due to the one who errs in matters of faith and who publishes his error. But by Article 88 of the Ecclesiastical Ordinance, in the Chapter on the Consistory, they regulate the Order of the proceeding against the one who dogmatizes. That Article is couched in these terms.

If there is someone who dogmatizes against the received doctrine, let him be summoned to confer with him: if he falls into line, let him be supported without scandal or defamation: if he is stubborn, let him be admonished several times in order to attempt to constrain him. If one finally sees that there is need for greater severity, let him be prohibited from Holy Communion, and let the Magistrate be notified in order to provide for it.

One sees from that. 1st. That the first inquisition of this sort of offense belongs to the Consistory.

2nd. That the Legislator does not intend that such an offense be irremissible, if the one who has committed it repents and falls into line.

3rd. That he prescribes the means that ought to be followed to lead the guilty one back to his duty.

4th. That these means are full of gentleness, of consideration, of commiseration; such as it is fitting for Christians to make use of, after the example of their master, in faults that do not disturb civil society at all and only concern Religion.

5th. That finally the last and greatest penalty that he prescribes is drawn from the nature of the offense, as that always ought to be, by depriving the guilty person of the Holy Communion and the communion of the Church, which he has offended, and which he wants to continue to offend.

After all that, the Consistory denounces him to the Magistrate who then ought to provide for it; because the Law, allowing only a single Religion in the State, the one who persists in wanting to profess and teach another one ought to be cut off from the State.

One sees the application of all the parts of that Law in the form of the procedure followed in 1563 against Jean Morelli.

Jean Morelli, an inhabitant of Geneva, had written and published a Book in which he attacked the ecclesiastical discipline and which was censured at the Synod of Orléans. The Author, complaining very much about this censure and having been summoned by the Consistory of Geneva for this same Book, did not want to appear there and took flight. Then, having come back with the permission of the Magistrate in order to be reconciled with the Ministers, he disregarded to speak with them and to go to the Consistory, until being cited anew, he finally appeared, and after long disputes, having refused every sort of satisfaction, he was handed over and cited to the Council, where, instead of appearing, he had an excuse in writing presented by his wife, and once again took flight from the Town.

Proceedings were finally held against him, that is against his Book, and since the sentence delivered on this occasion is important, even concerning its terms, and little known, I am going to transcribe it here in its entirety. It may have its utility.

*"We, Syndics Judges of criminal cases in this City, having heard the report of the venerable Consistory of this Church concerning the proceedings held against Jean Morelli, an inhabitant of this City, inasmuch as he has now abandoned this City for the second time and instead of appearing before us and our Council when he was remanded to it, has shown himself to be disobedient; with these and other just causes guiding us, sitting as a Tribunal in the place of our Ancestors, according to our ancient customs, after good participation in Council with our Citizens, having God and his Holy scriptures before our eyes and invoking his Holy name in order

---

* Excerpt from the proceedings brought and held against Jean Morelli. Printed in Geneva by Francois Perrin, 1563, page 10.

to make upright judgment, say: in the name of the Father, and of the Son, and of the Holy Spirit, Amen. Through this, our definitive sentence, which we offer here in writing, we have decided with mature deliberation to proceed further as in a case of contempt against the said Morelli: above all, in order to warn all those concerned to be wary of his Book so as not to be misled by it. Being then duly informed about the reveries and errors that are contained in it, and above all that said Book tends to create schisms and disturbances in the Church in a seditious manner, we have condemned it, and do condemn it as a harmful and pernicious Book, and to make an example of it have ordered and do order that one copy be burned presently. Forbidding all Booksellers to keep any or present any for sale, and all Citizens, Bourgeois, and Inhabitants of this Town of whatever class they might be to buy or have any to read. Commanding all those who would have any to bring them to us, and those who would know where there are some, to reveal that to us in twenty-four hours, on pain of being rigorously punished.

"And you, our Lieutenant, we order to put our present sentence into due and complete execution."

Pronounced and executed on Thursday the sixteenth day of September one thousand five hundred sixty-three.

"Thus signed by P. Chenelat."

Sir, you will find observations of more than one kind to make at their time and place about this document. For the present, let us not lose sight of our object. That was the procedure at the judgment of Morelli, whose Book was burned only at the end of the trial, with no talk of Executioner or stigmatization, and against whose person a warrant was never issued, although he was obstinate and in contempt.

Rather than that, everyone knows how the Council proceeded against me at the moment the Work appeared and without any mention even being made of the Consistory. To receive the book by mail, to read it, to examine it, to submit it for judgment, to burn it, to issue a warrant against me, all that was a matter of eight or ten days. One could not imagine a more expeditious proceeding.

I assume here that I fit the legal case, the sole case in which I am punishable. For otherwise, by what right would faults be punished that attack no one and about which the Laws have stated nothing?

Was the Edict observed, then, in this matter? You other People of good sense would imagine in examining it that it was violated gratuitously in all its parts. "The Said Rousseau," say the Remonstrators, "has not been called before the Consistory, but the magnificent Council has first proceeded against him. He ought to have been *supported without scandal*, but his Writings have been treated in a public judgment as *reckless, impious, scandalous*. He ought to have been *supported without defamation*. But he has been stigmatized in the most defamatory manner, his two Books having been lacerated and burned by the hand of the Executioner.

"The Edict has therefore not been observed," they continue, "both with regard to the jurisdiction that belongs to the Consistory and relative to the Said Rousseau, who ought to have been called, supported without scandal or defamation, admonished a few times, and who could not be judged except in the case of obstinate stubbornness."

That, no doubt, is as clear as day to you and to me too. Well, no. You are going to see how these people who know how to show the Sun at midnight know how to hide it at noon.

The usual skill of sophists is to heap up many arguments in order to cover their weakness. To avoid repetitions and gain time, let us divide those in the *Letters Written from the Country*. Let us confine ourselves to the most essential, let us leave aside those I have refuted above, and in order not to alter the others at all, let us relate them in the Author's terms.

It is according to our Laws, he says, *that I ought to examine what was done with respect to M. Rousseau.* Very well, let us see.

The first Article of the oath of the Bourgeois obligates them to live in accordance with the Reformation of the Holy Gospel. Now I ask, is it living according to the Gospel to write against the Gospel?

First sophism. To see clearly whether that is my case, put back into the minor clause of this argument the word *Reformation* which the Author removes from it, and which is necessary for his reasoning to be conclusive.

Second sophism. In this article of the oath it is not a question of writing in accordance with the Reformation, but of living in accordance with the Reformation. As has been seen above, a distinction is made between these two things in the oath itself. And it has been seen also whether it is true that I have written either against the Reformation or against the Gospel.

The first duty of the Syndics and Council is to maintain the pure Religion.

Third sophism. Their duty is certainly to maintain the pure Religion, but not to pronounce on what is or is not the pure Religion. The Sovereign has certainly charged them with maintaining the pure Religion, but it did not on that account make them judges of doctrine. It is another body that it charged with this task, and it is this body they must consult on all matters of Religion, as they have always done since your Government has been in existence. In the case of an offense in these matters, two Tribunals are established, one to establish it, the other to punish it. That is evident in the terms of the Ordinance. We will return to that below.

The imputations examined above follow, and for that reason I will not repeat them. But I cannot forbear from transcribing here the article that ends them. It is strange.

It is true that M. Rousseau and his partisans claim that these doubts do not really attack Christianity, which with that exception he continues to call divine. But if a Book, characterized the way the Gospel is in the works of M. Rousseau, can still be called divine, let someone tell me then the new meaning attached to this term? In truth, if it is a contradiction, it is shocking. If it is a joke, agree that it is quite out of place in such a subject.*

I understand. Spiritual form of worship, purity of heart, works of charity, confidence, humility, resignation, tolerance, the forgetting of insults, forgiving of enemies, the love of one's neighbor, universal brotherhood, and the union of the human race through charity are so many inventions of the devil. Would that be the sentiment of the Author and his friends? One would say so judging by their arguments and above all by their works. In truth, if it is a contradiction, it is shocking. If it is a joke, agree that it is quite out of place in such a subject.

Add that joking on such a subject is so much to the taste of these Gentlemen that, according to their own maxims, it should, if I had done it, have caused me to find favor with them.**

After the exposition of my crimes, listen to the reasons for which they have so cruelly outdone the rigor of the Law in pursuit of a criminal.

These two Books appear under the name of a Citizen of Geneva. Europe bears witness to its scandal. The first Parlement of a neighboring realm prosecutes Emile *and its Author. What will the government of Geneva do?*

Let us stop a moment. I believe I perceive some lie here.

According to our Author the scandal of Europe forced the Council of Geneva to deal severely against the Book and the Author of *Emile*, following the example of the Parlement of Paris: but on the contrary, it was the warrants of these two Tribunals that caused the scandal of Europe. The Book had been in public in Paris for only a few days when the Parlement condemned it[28]***; it had not yet appeared in any other country, not even in Holland, where it was printed; and there was only an interval of nine days between the warrant of the Parlement of Paris and that of the Council of Geneva****; just about the time that was needed to have notice of what was happening at Paris. The frightful uproar that was made in Switzerland about this affair, my expulsion from the home of my friend, the attempts made at Neuchâtel and even at the Court to deprive me of my last refuge,

---
* Page 11.
** Page 23.
*** That was an arrangement made before the Book appeared.
**** The warrant of the Parlement was issued June 9 and that of the Council, the 19th.

all that came from Geneva and the environs, after the warrant. It is known who the instigators were, it is known who the emissaries were, their activity was unprecedented; it is not their fault that I was not deprived of fire and water in all of Europe, that a piece of earth was not left to me as a bed, a stone for a headrest. Let us then not transpose things here, and let us not give as the motive for the warrant of Geneva the scandal that was its effect.

The foremost Parlement of a neighboring Kingdom prosecuted Emile *and its Author. What will the Government of Geneva do?*

The answer is simple. It will do nothing, it ought not to do anything, or rather it ought to do nothing. It would overturn all judicial order, it would defy the Parlement of Paris, it would dispute its competence by imitating it. It was precisely because a warrant was issued for my arrest at Paris that one could not be at Geneva. The offense of a criminal certainly has a place and a unique place; he can no more be guilty of the same offense in two States at the same time than he can be in two places at the same time, and if he wants to appear in response to the two warrants, how do you want him to divide himself? In effect, have you ever heard it said that a warrant was issued against the same man in two countries at the same time for the same deed? This is the first example of it, and probably this will be the last. In my misfortunes I will have the sad honor of being in all respects a unique example.

The most atrocious crimes, even murders, are not and ought not to be prosecuted before any Tribunals other than those of the places in which they have been committed. If a Genevan killed a man, even another Genevan, in a foreign country, the Council of Geneva would not be able to appropriate cognizance of this crime to itself: it could hand over the guilty man if he was laid claim to, it could solicit his punishment, but unless the judgment along with the documents of the proceeding was voluntarily remitted to it, it would not judge it, because it does not belong to it to take cognizance of an offense committed in the territory of another Sovereign, and because it cannot even give orders for the information necessary to establish it. There is the rule and there is the answer to the question. *What will the Government of Geneva do?* These are the simplest concepts of public Right that it would be shameful for the lowest Magistrate to be ignorant of. Will it always be necessary for me to teach at my own expense the elements of jurisprudence to my Judges?

Following the Authors of the Remonstrances, it ought to have limited itself to prohibiting sale in the Town provisionally.* That is, in fact, all that it could legitimately do to satisfy its animosity; that is what it had already done for

---

* Page 12.

Fourth Letter (Pl., III, 764–766)

the New Heloise, but seeing that the Parlement of Paris did not say anything, and that a similar prohibition was not made anywhere, it was ashamed of it and very quietly withdrew it.* *But wouldn't such a weak disapproval be accused of being secret connivance?* But the Council of Geneva has been accused for a long time of a rather unsecret connivance with other, much less tolerable Writings, without being overly troubled about this judgment. *No one, they say, could have been scandalized by the moderation they would have practiced.* The public outcry teaches you how scandalized they are by the contrary. *In good faith, if it had been a question of a man as disagreeable to the public as M. Rousseau was dear to it, wouldn't what they call moderation have been accused of being indifference, of an unpardonable lukewarmness?* It would not have been such a great evil as all that, and one does not give such decent names to the harshness they are practicing toward me for my Writings, nor to the support that they are lending to those of someone else.

Continuing to assume me to be guilty, let us assume further, that the Council of Geneva had the right to punish me, that the procedure had been in conformity to the Law, and that nevertheless, without even wanting to censure my Books, it had received me peacefully arriving from Paris; what would decent people have said? Here it is.

"They have closed their eyes, they should have. What could they do? To employ rigor on this occasion would have been barbarism, ingratitude, even injustice, since genuine justice repays evil with good. The guilty man loved his Fatherland tenderly, he deserved well from it; he honored it in Europe, and while his compatriots were ashamed of the name Genevan, he gloried in it, he rehabilitated it among foreigners. He previously gave useful advice, he wanted the public good, he was mistaken, but he was pardonable. He gave the greatest praises of the Magistrates, he sought to restore the confidence of the Bourgeoisie in them; he defended the Religion of the Ministers, he deserved some return on behalf of everyone. And with what countenance would they have dared to deal severely for some errors with the defender of the divinity, with the apologist of Religion which is so generally attacked, when they tolerated, when they permitted even the Writings that are the most odious, the most indecent, the most insulting to Christianity, to good morals, the most destructive of all virtue, of all morality, the very ones that Rousseau believed he ought to refute? One would have looked for the secret motives for such a shocking partiality; one would have found them in the zeal of the accused for liberty and in

---

* It must be agreed that if *Emile* ought to be prohibited, *Heloise* at least ought to be burned. Above all its notes are of a boldness that the profession of faith of the Vicar certainly does not approach.

the Judges' plans to destroy it. Rousseau would have passed for the martyr of the laws of his fatherland. Upon putting on the mask of hypocrisy on this occasion alone, his persecutors would have been accused of making light of Religion, of making it into the weapon of their vengeance and the instrument of their hatred. In sum by means of that haste to punish a man whose love for his fatherland is his greatest crime, they would have only made themselves odious to good people, suspect to the bourgeoisie and despicable to foreigners." That, Sir, is what they could have said; there is all the risk the Council would have run in the assumed case of offense, by abstaining from taking cognizance of it.

Someone was right to say that either the Gospel or the Books of M. Rousseau should have been burned.

The convenient method that these Gentlemen always follow against me! If they must have proofs, they multiply assertions and if they must have testimony, they make Somebody or other speak.

This one's apothegm has only one meaning that is not preposterous and this meaning is a blasphemy.

For isn't it blasphemy to assume that the Gospel and the collection of my Books are so similar in their maxims that they mutually replace each other, and that one could indifferently burn one as superfluous, provided that one preserved the other? Doubtless, I have followed the doctrine of the Gospel as closely as I could; I have loved it, I have adopted, extended, explained it without pausing over the obscurities, the difficulties, the mysteries, without turning myself away from what is essential: I attached myself to it with all the zeal of my heart; I became indignant, I cried out at seeing that Holy doctrine so profaned, debased by our so-called Christians, and above all by those who make a profession of teaching it to us. I even dare to believe, and I pride myself on it, that none of them spoke more worthily than I did about true Christianity and about its Author. On that I have the testimony, even the applause of my adversaries, not of those in Geneva, in truth, but of those whose hatred is not at all a fury, and from whom passion has not removed every feeling of equity. There is what is true. There is what proves it: my response to the King of Poland, and my letter to M. d'Alembert, and Heloise, and Emile, and all my Writings, which breathe the same love for the Gospel, the same veneration for Jesus Christ. But that it follows from that that I can approach my Master in anything and that my Books can take the place of his lessons, that is what is false, absurd, abominable. I detest this blasphemy and disavow this recklessness. Nothing can be compared to the Gospel. But its sublime simplicity is not equally within the grasp of everyone. Sometimes in order to put it there it is necessary to expose it under many lights. This sacred Book must be preserved as the rule of the Master, and mine as the commentaries of the Student.

Up to this point I have treated the question in a slightly general manner; let us now bring it closer to the facts, by means of the parallel of the proceedings of 1563 and 1762, and of the reasons they give for their differences. As this is the decisive point in relation to me, I cannot, without neglecting my cause, spare you these details, perhaps unpleasant in themselves, but of interest, in many respects, for you and for your Fellow Citizens. This is another discussion that cannot be interrupted and that will form a long Letter by itself. But, Sir, a little more courage; this will be the final one of this sort in which I will converse with you about myself.

Fifth Letter

After having established, as you have seen, the necessity of dealing severely with me, the Author of the Letters proves, as you are going to see, that the procedure followed against Jean Morelli, although exactly in conformity with the Ordinances, and in a case similar to mine, was not an example to follow with regard to me; considering, first, that the Council, being above the Ordinance, is not at all obliged to conform with it; that besides, my crime being more serious than Morelli's offense ought to be treated more severely. To these proofs the Author adds that it is not true that they judged me without hearing me, since it was enough to hear the Book itself and since the stigmatization of the Book does not fall in any manner on the Author; since finally the works that they reproach the Council for having tolerated are innocent and tolerable in comparison to mine.

As to the first Article, perhaps you will have difficulty believing that they dared to set the small Council above the Laws without further ado. I know nothing more certain to convince you of it than to transcribe for you the passage in which this principle is established, and out of fear of changing the meaning of this passage by cutting it, I will transcribe all of it.

*"Did the Ordinance want to tie the hands of the civil power and oblige it not to repress any offense against Religion until after the Consistory took cognizance of it? If that were so, it would result from it that one could write against Religion with impunity, that the Government would be impotent for repressing that license, and for stigmatizing any Book of that sort; for if the Ordinance wants the delinquent to appear first at the Consistory, the Ordinance does not any less prescribe that *if he falls into line, he is to be supported without defamation.* Thus, whatever his offense against Religion might have been, the accused will always be able to escape by putting up a show of falling into line; and the one who would have defamed Religion throughout the world ought to be supported *without defamation* by means of a simulated repentance. Could those who are acquainted with the spirit of severity, to say nothing more, that reigned

---

* Page 4.

when the Ordinance was compiled, believe that that was the meaning of Article 88 of the Ordinance?

"If the Consistory does not act, will its inaction chain the Council? Or at least will it be reduced to the function of informer to the Consistory? That is not what the Ordinance intended, when, after having treated the establishment of the duty and of the power of the Consistory, it concludes that the civil power remains in its entirety, in such a manner that nothing be derogated from its authority nor from the ordinary course by means of any ecclesiastical remonstrances. Thus this Ordinance does not assume, as it is made to do in the Remonstrances, that in this matter the Ministers of the Gospel are more natural judges than the Councils. Everything that is within the jurisdiction of authority in matters of Religion is within the jurisdiction of the Government. This is the principle of the Protestants, and it is particularly the principle of our Constitution, which in cases of dispute attributes to the Councils the right of deciding about dogma."

You see, Sir, in these final lines the principle upon which what precedes them is founded. Thus to proceed with order in this examination, it is fitting to begin at the end.

Everything that is within the jurisdiction of authority in matters of Religion is within the jurisdiction of the Government.

There is an equivocation in this word *Government* here that it is very important to clarify, and I advise you, if you love the constitution of your fatherland, to be attentive to the distinction that I am going to make; you will soon feel its utility.

The word *Government* does not have the same meaning in every country, because the constitution of States is not the same everywhere.

In Monarchies, where the executive power is joined to the exercise of sovereignty, the Government is nothing but the Sovereign itself, acting by means of its Ministers, by means of its Council, or by means of Bodies that depend absolutely on its will. In Republics, above all in Democracies, where the Sovereign never acts immediately by itself, it is something different. Then the Government is only the executive power, and it is absolutely distinct from sovereignty.

This distinction is very important in these matters. In order to have it thoroughly present in one's mind one ought to read with some care the first two Chapters of the third Book in the *Social Contract*, in which I attempted to fix by means of a precise meaning expressions that they artfully leave uncertain, in order to give them at need the acceptation they want. In general, the Leaders of Republics are extremely fond of employing the language of Monarchies. Under cover of terms that seem consecrated, they know how to introduce little by little the things that these words signify. This is what the Author of the Letters does very skillfully here, by taking the word, *Government*, which has nothing frightening in itself, for the exercise of sovereignty, which would be shocking, attributed straightforwardly to the small Council.

This is what he does even more openly in another passage* in which, after having said that *the Small Council is the Government itself*, which is true taking this word *Government* in a subordinate sense, he dares to add that by this title it exercises all the authority that is not attributed to other Bodies of the State; thus taking the word of Government in the sense of sovereignty, as if all the Bodies of the State, and the general Council itself, were instituted by the small Council: for it is only under cover of this assumption that it can appropriate to itself alone all the powers that the Law does not give expressly to anyone. I will take up this question again below.

This equivocation made clear, one sees the Author's sophism laid bare. In effect, to say that everything that is within the jurisdiction of authority in matters of Religion is within the jurisdiction of the Government is a genuine proposition, if by this word Government one understands the legislative power or the Sovereign; but it is very false if one understands the executive power or the body of Magistrates; and one will never find in your Republic that the general Council has attributed to the small Council the right to rule without appeal over everything that concerns Religion.

A second even more subtle equivocation comes to the support of the first in what follows. *This is the principle of the Protestants, and it is particularly the principle of our Constitution, which in cases of dispute attributes to the Councils the right of deciding about dogma.* This right, whether there is a dispute or whether there isn't one, belongs without contradiction *to the Councils* but not *to the Council*. See how one could change the constitution of a State with a letter more or less!

In the Principles of the Protestants, there is no Church other than the State and no ecclesiastical Legislator other than the Sovereign. This is what is manifest, above all at Geneva, where the ecclesiastical Ordinance has received from the Sovereign in the general Council the same sanction as the civil Edicts.

Having thus prescribed under the name of Reformation the doctrine that ought to be taught at Geneva and the form of worship one ought to follow there, the Sovereign has divided among two bodies the effort of maintaining that doctrine and that worship as they have been fixed by the Law. To the one it has handed over the matter of public instructions, the decision of what is in conformity with or contrary to the State's Religion,

---

* Page 66.

the suitable warnings and admonitions, and even spiritual punishments, such as excommunication. It has charged the other with providing for the execution of the Laws on this point as on every other one, and of giving a civil punishment to obstinate prevaricators.

Thus every regular proceeding on this matter ought to begin by the examination of the fact; namely, whether it is true that the accused is guilty of an offense against Religion, and by Law that examination belongs to the Consistory alone.

When the offense is established and it is of a nature to deserve a civil punishment, then it is up to the body of Magistrates alone to render justice, and to order that punishment. The ecclesiastical Tribunal denounces the guilty man to the civil Tribunal, and that is how the competence of the Council over this matter is established.

But when the Council wants to pronounce as a Theologian over what is or isn't dogma, when the Consistory wants to usurp the civil jurisdiction, each of these bodies leaves its area of competence; it disobeys the Law and the Sovereign who declared it, which is no less Legislator in ecclesiastic matters than in civil matters, and ought to be recognized as such by the two sides.

The body of Magistrates is always the judge of the Ministers in all that regards the civil, never in what regards dogma; that is the Consistory. If the Council pronounced the judgments of the Church it would have the right of excommunication, and on the contrary its members are subject to it themselves. A very humorous contradiction in this business is that I have had a warrant issued against me for my errors and that I have not been excommunicated; the Council prosecutes me as an apostate and the Consistory leaves me in the ranks of the faithful! Isn't that peculiar?

It is very true that if dissensions happen among the Ministers over doctrine, and out of the obstinacy of one of the parties they cannot come to an agreement either among themselves or by the intercession of the Elders, it is said by Article 18, that the cause ought to be brought to the body of Magistrates *to put order into it*.

But to put order into the quarrel is not to decide about dogma. The Ordinance itself explains the motive for recourse to the body of Magistrates; it is the obstinacy of one of the Parties. Now the public order in every State, inspection over quarrels, the maintenance of peace and of all public functions, the reduction of the obstinate, are incontestably within the jurisdiction of the body of Magistrates. It will not for all that judge doctrine, but it will re-establish in the assembly the order suitable for it to be able to judge it.

And if the Council were judge without appeal of doctrine, it would still not be allowed to invert the order established by Law, which attributes to the Consistory the first cognizance in these matters; in the same manner that it is not permitted, even though it is supreme judge, to remove to itself civil trials, before they have passed to the first appeals.

Article 18 does say that in case the Ministers cannot come to an agreement, the trial ought to be brought to the body of Magistrates to put order into it; but it does not say at all that the first cognizance of the doctrine can be taken away from the Consistory by the body of Magistrates, and there is not a single example of a similar usurpation as long as the Republic has existed.* The Author of the Letters appears to agree with this himself when he says that *in case of dispute* the Councils have the right to decide over dogma; for that is to say that they do not have this right until after the examination of the Consistory, and that they do not have it at all when the Consistory is in agreement.

These distinctions of the civil jurisdiction and the ecclesiastical jurisdiction are clear, and founded, not only on the Law, but on reason, which does not want the Judges, upon whom the fate of private individuals depends, to be able to decide on any other basis than on constant facts, on bodies of positive, well-established offenses, and not on imputations as vague, as arbitrary, as those of errors about Religion. What security would Citizens enjoy, if, among so many dogmas that are obscure and susceptible of various interpretations, the Judge could, at the caprice of his passion, choose the one that would indict or disculpate the Accused, in order to condemn or absolve him?

---

* In the sixteenth century there were many disputes over predestination, which should have been made into the amusement of schoolchildren, and which they did not fail, according to practice, to make into a great State affair. Nevertheless it was the Ministers who decided it, and even contrary to the public interest. Never, that I know of, since the Edicts has the small Council taken it into its head to pronounce on dogma without their agreement. I am acquainted with only one judgment of that sort, and it was rendered by the Two-Hundred. It was in the great quarrel of 1669 over particular grace. After long and vain debates in the Company and in the Consistory, the Professors, not being able to come to an agreement, brought the affair to the small Council, which did not judge it. The Two-Hundred removed it and judged it. The important question that was at issue was to know whether Jesus had died only for the salvation of the elect, or whether he had died also for the salvation of the damned. After many sessions and mature deliberations, the Magnificent Council of the Two-Hundred pronounced that Jesus had died only for the salvation of the elect. One conceives very well that this judgment was a business of favor, and that Jesus would have died for the damned, if Professor Tronchin had had more influence than his adversary. Doubtless all that is extremely ridiculous: one can say nevertheless that it was not an issue here of a dogma of faith, but of the uniformity of public instruction the inspection of which belongs without contradiction to the Government. One can add that this fine dispute had excited so much attention that the whole Town was in an uproar. But it doesn't matter; the Councils ought to have pacified the quarrel without pronouncing on doctrine. The decision of all questions that interest no one and in which no one whatsoever understands anything ought always to be left up to the Theologians.

The proof of these distinctions is in the institution itself, which would not have established a useless Tribunal; since if the Council was able to judge ecclesiastical matters, above all in first jurisdiction, the institution of the Consistory would not serve any purpose.

It also occurs in a thousand places in the Ordinance, where the Legislator distinguishes the authority of the two Orders so carefully; a very vain distinction, if in the exercise of its functions one is subject to the other in everything. See in Articles XXIII and XXIV, the specification of crimes punishable by the Laws, and of those whose *first inquisition belongs to the Consistory*.

See the end of the same Article XXIV, which requires that in the latter case, after the conviction of the guilty person, the Consistory make a report about it to the Council, adding its advice to it. *So that*, the Ordinance says, *the judgment concerning the punishment might always be reserved to the Seignory*. Terms from which one ought to infer that judgment concerning doctrine belongs to the Consistory.

See the oath of the Ministers, who swear for their part to make themselves subject and obedient to the Laws; and to the body of Magistrates to the extent that their Ministry leads to it: that is to say without being prejudicial to the liberty that they ought to have to teach in accordance with what God commands them. But where would that liberty be, if by the laws they were subject for that doctrine to the decisions of a body other than their own?

See Article 80, in which the Edict not only prescribes to the Consistory to watch over and provide against general and particular disorders of the Church, but in which the Edict institutes it for that purpose. Does that article have a meaning or doesn't it have one? Is it absolute, is it only conditional; and would the Consistory established by Law have only a precarious existence, dependent on the good pleasure of the Council?

See Article 97 of the same Ordinance, in which, in cases that require civil punishment, it is said that, once the Consistory has heard the Parties and made the ecclesiastical remonstrances and censures, it ought to report the whole to the Council, which *based on its report*, note well the repetition of this word, *will consider how to order and pass judgment, in accordance with the exigency of the case*. See, finally, what follows in the same Article, and do not forget that this is the Sovereign who is speaking. *For however conjoined and inseparable are the Seignory and superiority that God has given us, and the spiritual Government that he has established in his Church, they ought not to be confused in any way; since he, who has complete empire of commanding and to whom we want to render all subordination as we ought, wishes to be so acknowledged as Author of the political and ecclesiastical Government, both the vocations and the administration of each of which he has nevertheless expressly distinguished.*

But how can these administrations be distinguished under the common authority of the Legislator, if one can encroach upon that of the other at will? If there is no contradiction there, I cannot see one anywhere.

To Article 88, which expressly prescribes the order of procedure that one ought to observe against those who dogmatize, I join another one that is no less important; that is article 53 under the title *on the Catechism*, in which it is ordained that those who contravene good order, after having been remonstrated with sufficiently, if they persist, are called to the Consistory, *and if then they do not wish to comply* with the remonstrances that will be made to them, *that it be reported to the Seignory*.

What good order is being spoken about there? The Title says it; it is good order in the matter of doctrine, since it is only a question of the Catechism, which is its summary. Besides, the maintenance of good order in general appears to belong much more to the Magistrate than to the ecclesiastical Tribunal. Nevertheless, see what a gradation! First, *it is necessary to remonstrate*; if the guilty man persists, *he must be called before the Consistory*; finally if he does not want to comply, *it is necessary to make a report to the Seignory*. In all matters of faith the final jurisdiction is always attributed to the Councils; such is the Law, such are all your Laws. I am waiting to see some article, some passage in your Edicts, in virtue of which the small Council attributes to itself also the first jurisdiction, and can suddenly make such an offense into the subject of a criminal proceeding.

This step is not only contrary to the Law, it is contrary to equity, to good sense, to universal practice. In all the countries of the world the rule requires that, in what concerns a science or an art, before pronouncing one takes the judgment of the Professors in that science or Experts in that art; why, in the most obscure, in the most difficult of all the sciences, why, when it is a question of the honor and liberty of a man, of a Citizen, would the Magistrates neglect the precautions they take in the most mechanical art on the subject of the most base interest?

Once again, what Law, what Edict does one oppose to so much authority, to so many reasons that prove the illegality and irregularity of such a procedure in order to justify it? The only passage the Author of the Letters could have cited is this one, whose terms he again transposes in order to alter its spirit.

*Let all ecclesiastical remonstrances be made in such a manner that by the Consistory nothing be derogated from the authority of the Seignory nor of ordinary law courts; but that the civil power remain in its entirety.**

---

* Ecclesiastical Ordinances Art. XCVII.

Now here is the conclusion that he draws from it: "This Ordinance, then, does not assume, as they do in the Remonstrances, that the Ministers of the Gospel are more natural Judges than the Councils in these matters." Let us begin first by returning this word Council to the singular, and for a reason.

But where is it that the Remonstrators have assumed that the Ministers of the Gospel are more natural Judges than the Council in these matters.*

According to the Edict the Consistory and the Council are each natural Judges in their parts, the one of the doctrine, and the other of the offense. Thus the civil and the ecclesiastical power each remains in its entirety under the common authority of the Sovereign; and what would this very word of *civil Power* mean here, if there was not another *Power* understood? As for me, I do not see anything in this passage that changes the natural meaning of the ones I have cited. And very far from that; the lines that follow confirm them, by determining the state into which the Consistory ought to have put the proceeding before it is brought to the Council. This is precisely the opposite conclusion from the one that the Author wanted to draw from it.

But see how, not daring to attack the Ordinance by means of the terms, he attacks it by means of the consequences.

"Did the Ordinance want to tie the hands of the civil power and oblige it not to repress any offense against Religion until after the Consistory took cognizance of it? If that were so, it would result from it that one could write against Religion with impunity, the accused could always escape by putting up a show of falling into line; and the one who would have defamed Religions throughout the world ought to be supported without defamation by means of a simulated repentance."**

Thus it is to avoid this horrible misfortune, this scandalous impunity, that the Author does not want the Law to be followed to the Letter. Nevertheless, sixteen pages later, the same Author speaks to you this way.

"Politics and Philosophy will be able to support this liberty of writing everything, but our Laws have rejected it: now it is a question of knowing whether the judgment of the Council against the Works of M. Rousseau

---

* *The examination and the discussion of this matter*, they say on page 42, *belong more to the Ministers of the Gospel than to the Magnificent Council*. What is the matter that is at issue in this passage? It is the question whether under the appearance of doubts I have gathered in my Book everything that can tend to undermine, unsettle, and destroy the principal foundations of the Christian Religion. The Author of the Letters departs from that to make the Remonstrators say that in these matters the Ministers are more natural judges than the Councils. Without contradiction they are the most natural Judges of the question of Theology, but not of the penalty due to the offense, and that is also what the Remonstrators have neither said nor caused to be understood.

** Page 14.

and the warrant against his person are contrary to our Laws, and not to know whether they are in conformity with philosophy and politics."*

Elsewhere, again this Author, agreeing that the stigmatization of a Book does not destroy its arguments and can even give them a greater publicity, adds: "In that regard, I recognize my maxims well enough in those of the Remonstrances, but these maxims are not those of our Laws."**

By compressing and linking together all these passages, I find in them just about the sense that follows.

Although Philosophy, Politics, and reason can maintain the liberty of writing everything, in our State one ought to punish that liberty, because our Laws reject it. But nevertheless one must not follow our Laws to the Letter, because then one would not punish that liberty.

To speak truly, I catch a glimpse in this of some gibberish or other that shocks me; and nevertheless the Author seems to me to be a man of intelligence: thus in this summary I incline to believe that I am mistaken without being able to see wherein. Compare yourself, then, pages 14, 22, 30; and you will see whether I am wrong or right.

Whatever may be the case, while waiting for the Author to show us these other Laws where the precepts of Philosophy and of Politics are rejected, let us take up the examination of his objections against this one.

First, far from it being permitted in a Republic for the Magistrate to make the Law harsher out of fear of leaving an offense unpunished, it is not even permitted for him to extend it to offenses about which it is not explicit, and it is known how many guilty people escape in England under cover of the smallest subtle distinction in the terms of the Law. *Whoever is more severe than the Laws*, says Vauvenargue, *is a Tyrant.*[29]***

But let us see whether the consequence of impunity, of the sort at issue, is as terrible as the Author of the Letters makes it.

In order to judge the spirit of the Law well, one must remember this great principle, that the best criminal Laws are always those that draw from the nature of the crimes the punishments that are imposed on them. Thus murderers ought to be punished by death, thieves, with the loss of their property, or, if they do not have any, with that of their liberty, which is then the only property they have left. In the same way, in offenses that

---

* Page 30.
** Page 22.
*** Since at Geneva there are no penal Laws properly speaking, the Magistrate arbitrarily imposes the penalty for crimes; which is certainly a great defect in the Legislation and an enormous abuse in a free State. But that authority of the Magistrate extends only to crimes against natural law and acknowledged as such in every society, or to things especially forbidden by positive law; it does not go to the point of fabricating an imaginary offense where there is none at all, nor, based on whatever offense there may be, to the point of overturning the procedure fixed by the Law out of fear that a guilty person might escape.

are uniquely against Religion, the penalties ought to be drawn uniquely from Religion; such is, for example, the deprivation of the proof by oath in things that require it; such is also excommunication, prescribed here as the greatest penalty against whoever has dogmatized against Religion. Aside from the transfer to the Magistrate afterward, for the civil penalty owed to the civil offense, if there is one.

Now it must be remembered that the Ordinance, the Author of the Letters, and I, are speaking here only about a simple offense against Religion. If the offense were complex, as if, for example, I had printed my Book in the State without permission, it is incontestable that, by being absolved before the Consistory, I would be absolved before the Magistrate.

This distinction being made, I come back and I say: there is this difference between offenses against Religion and civil offenses, that the latter commit against men or against the Laws a wrong, a real harm for which the public safety necessarily requires reparation and punishment; but the others are only offenses against the divinity, whom no one can harm and who pardons upon repentance. When the divinity is appeased, there is no longer an offense to punish, aside from the scandal, and the scandal is set right by giving the repentance the same publicity that the fault had. Then Christian charity imitates divine clemency, and it would be an absurd inconsistency to avenge Religion by means of a rigor that Religion rejects. Human justice has and ought to have no regard for repentance, I admit it; but that is precisely why, in a sort of offense that repentance can set right, the Ordinance has taken measures so that the civil Tribunal did not take cognizance of them first.

The terrible inconvenience that the Author finds in leaving offenses against Religion without civil punishment thus does not have the reality he gives it, and the conclusion he draws from it in order to prove that this is not the spirit of the Law, is not just, against the explicit terms of the Law.

Thus, whatever the offense against Religion might have been, he adds, *the accused will always be able to escape by putting up a show of falling into line*. The Ordinance does not say, *if he puts up a show of falling into line*, it says, *if he falls into line*, and there are rules as certain as one can have in any other case to distinguish reality from false appearance here, above all with regard to exterior effects, alone understood under this remark, *if he falls into line*.

If the offender having fallen into line, relapsed, he commits a new more serious offense that deserves a more rigorous treatment. He is a relapsed heretic, and the means of restoring him to his duty are more severe. On this point the Council has as model the judicial forms of the inquisition,*

---

* See the *Manual of the Inquisitors*.

and if the Author of the Letters does not approve of the Council being this gentle, he ought at least always to leave it the distinction of cases; for it is not permitted, from fear that an offender might relapse, to treat him in advance as if he had already relapsed.

It is nevertheless upon these false consequences that this Author relies in order to affirm that in this Article the Edict did not have as its object regulating the procedure and establishing the competence of the Tribunals. What, then, did the Edict want, according to him? Here it is.

It wanted to prevent the Consistory from dealing severely with people to whom one might impute what they had perhaps not said, or whose lapses might have been exaggerated; that it might not deal severely, I say, with those people without having conferred about it with them, without having attempted to win them over.

But what is dealing severely, on the part of the Consistory? It is to excommunicate, and to hand over to the Council. Thus, out of fear that the Consistory might hand over a guilty person too easily, the Edict delivers him all at once to the Council. This is a completely new sort of precaution. It is admirable that, in the same case, the Law takes so many measures to prevent the Consistory from dealing severely in a precipitate manner, and that it does not take any to prevent the Council from dealing severely in a precipitate manner; that it brings such a scrupulous attention to preventing defamation, and that it gives none to preventing physical punishment; that it provides for so many things to keep a man from being excommunicated inappropriately, and that it does not make any provision to keep him from being burned at the stake inappropriately; that it fears the rigor of the Ministers so much, and that of the Judges so little! It was certainly well done to take so much account of the communion of the faithful; but it was not well done to take so little account of their safety, their liberty, their life; and that very Religion that prescribed so much indulgence to its guardians ought not to give so much barbarity to its avengers.

There, however, according to our Author, is the solid reason why the Ordinance did not want to say what it does say. I believe that to set it forth suffices for answering it. Let us now turn to the application; we shall not find it any less curious than the interpretation.

Article 88 has for its object only the one who dogmatizes, who teaches, who instructs. It does not speak at all about a simple Author, about a man who does nothing but publish a Book, and who, what is more, keeps himself at rest. To speak the truth, that distinction appears to me a little subtle; for, as the Remonstrators say very well, one dogmatizes by means of writing, just as one does by the living voice. But let us accept this subtlety; in it we will find a distinction of favor for making the Law more gentle, not of rigor for making it more harsh.

In all the States of the world the officers of public order watch over those who instruct, who teach, who dogmatize with the greatest care; they do not allow these sorts of functions except to authorized people. It is not even allowed to preach the right doctrine if one is not recognized as a preacher. The blind People is easy to seduce; a man who dogmatizes gathers a crowd, and soon he can stir it up. The smallest undertaking on this point is always regarded as a punishable attempt, because of the consequences that can result from it.

It is not the same for the Author of a Book; if he teaches, at least he does not gather a crowd, he does not stir it up, he does not force anyone to listen to him, to read him; he does not seek you out, he comes only when you seek him out yourself; he leaves you to reflect on what he says to you, he does not argue with you, does not grow heated, does not become obstinate, does not alleviate your doubts, does not resolve your objections, does not pursue you; if you want to leave him, he leaves you, and, what is the important point here, he does not speak to the people.

Therefore never has the publication of a Book been regarded by any Government in the same way as the practices of a dogmatizer. There are even countries in which the liberty of the press is complete; but there is none in which it is indifferently permitted to everyone to dogmatize. In the countries in which it is forbidden to print Books without permission, those who disobey are sometimes punished for having disobeyed; but the proof that at bottom they do not consider what a Book says to be very important is, the ease with which they allow to enter the State these same Books which, in order not to appear to approve their maxims, they do not allow to be printed there.

All this is true, above all, of Books that are not written for the people such as mine have always been. I know that your Council affirms in its responses that, *in accordance with the intention of the Author, Emile ought to serve as a guide to fathers and to mothers**: but this assertion is not excusable, since, in the preface and several times in the Book, I indicated a completely different intention. It is a question of a new system of education the plan of which I offer to the examination of the wise, and not of a method for fathers and mothers, about which I never dreamed. If sometimes, through a rather common figure of speech, I appear to address them, it is either to make myself better understood, or to express myself in fewer words. It is true that I undertook my Book at the solicitation of a mother; but that

---

* Pages 22 and 23 of the printed Remonstrances.

mother, as young and amiable as she is, has philosophy and knows the human heart; in looks she is an ornament of her sex, and in genius an exception.[30] It is for minds of her caliber that I took up the pen, not for Mister such and such, nor for other Gentlemen of similar stuff, who read me without understanding me, and who insult me without getting me angry.

It results from the assumed distinction that if the procedure prescribed by the Ordinance against a man who dogmatizes is not applicable to the Author of a Book, it is because it is too severe for this latter. This very natural conclusion, this conclusion that you and all my readers surely draw, as well as I do, is not at all the conclusion of the Author of the Letters. He draws a completely opposite one. It is necessary to listen to his very words: you would not believe me if I paraphrased him.

"It is only necessary to read this Article of the Ordinance to see clearly that it has in view only that order of person who spread by means of their discourses principles considered to be dangerous. It is said there, *If these persons fall into line, let them be supported without defamation.* Why? It is because then one has a reasonable security that they will no longer spread those tares, it is because they are no longer to be feared. But what does the true or simulated retraction matter of the person who has imbued the whole world with his opinions by the route of printing? The offense has been consummated; it will always subsist, and in the eyes of the Law, this offense is of the same sort as all the others, in which repentance is useless as soon as justice has taken cognizance of it."

There is something to be disturbed about in this, but let us calm ourselves and reason. As long as a man dogmatizes, he does evil continuously; until he has fallen into line this man is to be feared; his very liberty is an evil, because he uses it to do evil, to continue to dogmatize. That he does fall into line in the end, never mind; the teachings he has given are always given, and the offense in this regard is as consummated as it can be. On the contrary, as soon as a Book is published, the Author does not do any more evil, it is the Book alone that does it. Whether the Author be free or be arrested, the Book goes on at its own pace. The detention of the Author can be a punishment that the Law pronounces, but it is never a remedy to the evil he has done, nor a precaution to stop its progress.

Thus the remedies to these two evils are not the same. In order to dry up the source of the evil that the dogmatizer does, there is no means as prompt and certain as to arrest him: but to arrest the Author is to remedy nothing at all; on the contrary it is to increase the publicity for the Book, and consequently to make the evil worse, as the Author of the Letters says very well elsewhere. Thus that is not a preliminary to the proceedings, it is not a precaution that is suitable to the thing; it is a penalty that ought to be inflicted only by a judgment, and that has no utility but the punishment of the guilty person. Thus, unless his offense is a civil offense, it is necessary to begin by reasoning with him, admonishing him, convincing him, exhorting him to set right the evil he has done, to give a public retraction, to give it freely so that it might have its effect, and to state the reasons for it so well that his final sentiments lead back those whom the first have led astray. If, far from falling into line, he grows obstinate, only then must one deal severely with him. That is certainly the course to take to go to the benefit of the matter; such is the aim of the Law, such will be that of a wise Government, which *ought much less to propose to itself to punish the Author than to prevent the effect of the work.**

How would it not be so for the Author of a Book, since the Ordinance, which follows in everything the ways suitable to the spirit of Christianity, does not even want one to arrest the dogmatizer before having exhausted all means possible for leading him back to duty? It prefers to run the risks of the evil he may continue to do than to be lacking in charity. Find out how, for pity's sake, from that alone one can conclude that the same Ordinance wants one to begin against the Author with a warrant for his arrest?

Nevertheless the Author of the Letters, after having declared that he recognized his maxims well enough on that point in those of the Remonstrators, adds: *but these maxims are not those of our Laws*, and a moment afterward he adds further that, *those who incline to a full tolerance could at the most criticize the Council for not having silenced in this case a Law whose exercise did not appear suitable to them.*** That conclusion ought to surprise, after so many efforts to prove that the only Law that appears to apply to my offense does not necessarily apply to it. What the Council is reproached for is not to have not silenced a Law that exists, it is to have made one speak that does not exist.

The Logic employed here by the Author always appears new to me. What do you think of it, Sir? Do you know many arguments in the form of this one?

The Law forces the Council to deal severely with the Author of the Book.

And where is it, this Law that forces the Council to deal severely with the Author of the Book?

It does not exist, in truth: but another one does exist, which, ordering to treat with gentleness the one who dogmatizes, consequently, orders to treat with rigor the Author, about whom it does not speak at all.

This reasoning becomes even much stranger for anyone who knows

---

* Page 25.
** Page 23.

that it was as an Author and not as a dogmatizer that Morelli was prosecuted; he had also written a Book, and it was for this Book alone that he was accused. The body of the offense, according to the maxim of our Author was in the Book itself, the Author did not need to be heard; nevertheless he was, and not only did they hear him, but they waited for him; they followed from point to point the whole procedure prescribed by this very article of the Ordinance that we are told regards neither Books nor Authors. They did not even burn the Book until after the Author's withdrawal, a warrant was never issued against him, they did not speak about the Hangman;* finally all that was done under the eyes of the Legislator, by the drafters of the Ordinance, at the moment it had just passed, in the very times in which there reigned that spirit of severity that, according to our Anonymous fellow, had dictated it, and that he alleges in very clear justification of the rigor exercised today against me.

Now listen to the distinction he makes about this. After having set forth all the gentle ways they made use of toward Morelli, the time they gave him to fall into line, the slow and regular procedure they followed before his Book was burned, he adds, "All that proceeding was very wise. But must it be concluded from it that in all cases and in very different cases, a similar one absolutely must be kept to? Should one proceed against an absent man who attacks Religion in the same manner that one would proceed against a man who is present who censures the discipline."** That is to say in other terms: "Should one proceed against a man who does not attack the Laws, and who lives outside of their jurisdiction, with as much gentleness as against a man who lives under their jurisdiction and who does attack them?" In fact, it would not seem that there should be any question about it. This, I am sure of it, is the first time it has entered the human mind to make the crime of a guilty person harsher because the crime was not committed inside the State.

"In truth," he continues, "they remark in the Remonstrances to the advantage of M. Rousseau that Morelli had written against a point of discipline, while M. Rousseau's Books, in the sentiment of his Judges,

---

* Add the circumspection of the body of Magistrates in all this business, its slow and gradual course in the proceeding, the report of the Consistory, the display of the judgment. The Syndics ascend onto their public Tribunal, they invoke the name of God, they have the holy Scripture under their eyes; after a mature deliberation, after having taken council from the Citizens, they pronounce their judgment before the people so that it might know its causes, they have it printed and published, and all that for the simple condemnation of a Book without stigmatization, without warrant against the obstinate and contumacious Author. Since then, these Gentlemen have learned to dispose less ceremoniously of the honor and the liberty of men, and above all of Citizens: For it should be remarked that Morelli was not one.

** Page 17.

attack Religion as such. But this remark could very well not be generally adopted, and those who regard Religion as the Work of God and the support of the constitution might think that it is less permitted to attack it than some points of discipline, which, only being the Work of men, can be suspected of error, and at least susceptible of an infinity of different forms and combinations."*

This discourse, I admit it to you, at the most would appear acceptable from the mouth of a Capuchin monk, but it would shock me extremely from the pen of a Magistrate. What does it matter if the remark of the Remonstrators is not generally adopted, if those who reject it do so only because they reason badly?

To attack Religion is without contradiction a greater sin before God than to attack the discipline. It is not so before human Tribunals that are established to punish crimes, not sins, and that are not the avengers of God, but of the Laws.

Religion can never form part of Legislation except in what concerns the actions of men. The Law orders to do or to abstain, but it cannot order to believe. Thus whoever does not attack the practice of Religion does not attack the Law at all.

But the discipline established by the Law essentially forms a part of Legislation, it becomes Law itself. Whoever attacks it attacks the Law and does not tend to anything less than disturbing the constitution of the State. Although that constitution was, before having been established, susceptible of several different forms and combinations, is it less respectable and sacred under one of these forms, once it has been vested with it to the exclusion of all the others; and from that time isn't the political Law as constant and fixed as the divine Law?

Thus those who would not adopt the remark of the Remonstrators in this business would be all the more wrong since that remark was made by the Council itself in the sentence against Morelli's Book, which it accuses above all of *tending to cause schism and disturbance in the State in a seditious manner*; an imputation that it would be hard to accuse mine of.

What the civil Tribunals have to defend is not the Work of God, it is the Work of men; it is not souls they are charged with, it is bodies; it is of the State and not of the Church that they are the true guardians, and when they meddle with matters of Religion, it is only to the extent that they are within the jurisdiction of the Laws, to the extent that these matters are important for good order and for public safety. There are the healthy maxims of the Magistracy. This is not, if one wants, the doctrine of absolute

---

* Page 18.

power, but it is that of justice and of reason. One will never deviate from it in civil Tribunals without giving way to the most fatal abuses, without putting the State into combustion, without making the Laws and their authority into the most odious brigandage. I am sorry for the people of Geneva that the Council despises it enough to dare to delude it by such discourses, of which the most limited and the most superstitious peoples of Europe are no longer the dupes. On this Point your Remonstrators reason as Statesmen, and your Magistrates reason as Monks.

In order to prove that the example of *Morelli* does not constitute a rule, the Author of the Letters opposes to the proceeding made against him the one that was made in 1632 against *Nicolas Antoine*, a poor madman whom the Council had burned for the good of his soul at the solicitation of the Ministers. These Auto-da-fès were not rare formerly at Geneva, and it appears by what is happening to me that these Gentlemen do not lack the taste to begin them anew.

Let us always begin by faithfully transcribing the passages, in order not to imitate the method of my persecutors.

"Look at the trial of Nicolas Antoine. The ecclesiastical Ordinance existed, and they were close enough to the time when it had been drafted to be acquainted with its spirit. Was Antoine cited at the Consistory? Nevertheless among so many voices that were raised against this sanguinary Decree, and in the midst of the efforts that humane and moderate people made to save him, was there anyone who cried out against the irregularity of the proceeding? Morelli was cited at the Consistory, Antoine was not; thus citation at the Consistory is not necessary in all cases." *

From that you will believe that the Council proceeded right away against Nicolas Antoine as it did against me, and that it was not even a question of the Consistory nor of the Ministers: You are going to see.

Nicolas Antoine having been, in one of his fits of rage, on the point of throwing himself into the Rhône, the Magistrate resolved to take him out of the public lodging where he was in order to put him in the Hospital, where the Doctors treated him. He remained there for some time loudly uttering various blasphemies against the Christian Religion. "The Ministers saw him every day, and tried, when his rage appeared slightly calmed, to make him recover from his errors, which came to nothing, Antoine having said that he would persist in his sentiments until death, that he was ready to suffer for the glory *of the great God of Israel*. Not having been able to prevail over him, they informed the Council, where they represented him as worse than Servet, Gentilis, and all the other Antitrini-

---

* Page 17.

tarians, concluding in favor of putting him into a locked room; which was put into effect."*

First you see from that why he was not cited at the Consistory; that is because, since he was gravely ill and in the hands of the Doctors, it was impossible for him to appear there. But if he did not go to the Consistory, the Consistory or its members went to him. The Minsters saw him every day, exhorted him every day. Finally, not having been able to prevail over him in anything, they denounce him to the Council, represent him as worse than others whom they had punished with death, demand that he be put into prison, and on their demand that is put into effect.

In the very prison the Ministers did their best to bring him back, entered along with him into discussion of various passages of the old Testament, and entreated him by all the most touching things they could imagine to renounce his errors,** but he remained firm. He was so also before the Magistrate, who made him undergo the ordinary interrogations. When it was a question of judging this affair, the Magistrate consulted the Ministers again, who appeared in Council to the number of fifteen, both Pastors and Professors. Their opinions were divided, but the advice of the larger number was followed and Nicolas executed. So that the trial was entirely ecclesiastical, and Nicolas was, so to speak, burned by the Ministers' hands.

Such was, Sir, the order of the proceeding in which the Author of the Letters assures us that Antoine was not cited at the Consistory. From which he concludes that this citation is thus not always necessary. Does the example appear to you as well chosen?

Let us assume that it is, what will follow from it? The Remonstrators concluded from a fact in confirmation of a Law. The Author of the Letters concludes from a fact against that same Law. If the authority of each of these two facts destroys that of the other, the Law remains in its entirety. Although infringed one time, is that Law any less explicit because of that, and would it be enough to have violated it once to have the right to violate it always?

Let us conclude in our turn. If I have dogmatized, I am certainly within the case of the Law: if I have not dogmatized, what do they have to say to me? No Law has spoken about me.*** Thus they have transgressed the Law that exists, or assumed the one that does not exist.

---

* *History of Geneva*, in duodecimo. Vol. 2, page 550 and following at the note.

** If he had renounced them, would he still have been burned? According to the maxim of the Author of the Letters he should have been. Nevertheless, it appears that he would not have been; since, in spite of his obstinacy, the Magistrate did not fail to consult the Ministers. He regarded him, in some fashion, as still being under their jurisdiction.

*** Nothing that offends against no natural Law becomes criminal until it is forbidden by some positive Law. That remark has as its goal to make superficial reasoners feel that my dilemma is precise.

It is true that in judging the Work they have not judged the Author definitively. They have not yet done anything but issue a warrant against him, and they count that for nothing. That appears harsh to me, nevertheless; but let us never be unjust, even toward those who are so toward us, and let us not look for iniquity where there might not be any. I do not treat as a crime on the part of the Council, nor even on the part of the Author of the Letters, the distinction they put between the man and the Book in order to exonerate themselves of having judged me without hearing me. The Judges might have seen the thing the way they show it, so in that I do not accuse them either of fraud or of bad faith. I only accuse them of having deceived themselves at my expense on a very serious point; and to deceive oneself in order to absolve is pardonable, but to deceive oneself in order to punish is a very cruel error.

In its responses the Council advanced that, in spite of the stigmatization of my Book, I remained, as to my person, in possession of all my exceptions and defenses.

The Authors of the Remonstrances reply that one does not understand what exceptions and defenses are left for a man declared impious, reckless, scandalous, and even stigmatized by the hand of the Hangman in works that bear his name.

"You are assuming something that does not exist," says the Author of the Letters to that; "namely, that the judgment bears on the one whose name is borne by the Work: but this judgment has not yet grazed him, thus his exceptions and defenses are left for him in their entirety." *

You yourself are deceived, I would say to that writer. It is true that the judgment that characterizes and stigmatizes the Book has not yet attacked the life of the Author, but it has already destroyed his honor: his exceptions and defenses are still left for him in their entirety for what concerns the afflictive penalty, but he has already received the infamatory penalty: He is already stigmatized and dishonored, to the extent that it depends on his judges: The only thing that remains for them to decide is whether he will be burned or not.

The distinction on this point between the Book and the Author is inept, since a Book is not punishable. A Book is not in itself either impious or reckless; these epithets can fall only upon the doctrine it contains, that is to say upon the Author of that doctrine. When one burns a Book, what does the Hangman do? Does he dishonor the pages of the Book? Who ever heard it said that a Book had any honor?

There is the error; here is its source: a poorly understood practice.

---

* Page 21.

Fifth Letter (Pl., III, 790–793)

Many Books are written; few are written with a sincere desire to further the good. Out of a hundred Works that appear, at least sixty have motives of interest or ambition as their object. Thirty others, dictated by the spirit of party, by hatred, proceed, under the cover of anonymity, to bring into public the poison of calumny and satire. Ten, perhaps, and that is much, are written with good intentions: one says in them the truth that one knows, one seeks in them the good that one loves. Yes; but where is the man in whom one pardons the truth? Thus one must hide oneself in order to say it. In order to be useful with impunity, one lets one's Book loose among the public, and one ducks.

Out of these various Books, some of the bad ones and just about all of the good are denounced and proscribed in the Tribunals: the reason for that is seen without my stating it. Moreover this is only a formality, in order not to appear to approve these Books tacitly. Moreover, provided that the names of the Authors are not on them, these Authors, although the whole world knows them and names them, are not known by the Magistrate. Several are even in the practice of avowing these Books in order to do themselves honor with them, and of disavowing them in order to put themselves under cover; the same man will be or will not be the Author, in front of the same man depending whether they are at a hearing or at a supper. It is alternately yes or no, without difficulty, without scruple. In that manner safety costs vanity nothing. There is the prudence and skillfulness that the Author of the Letters reproaches me for not having had, and that nevertheless, it seems to me, one does not go to great expense in intelligence in order to have.

That manner of proceeding against anonymous Books whose Authors one does not want to know has become a judicial practice. When one wants to deal severely against the Book one burns it, because there is no one to hear, and because one sees very well that the Author who is hiding is in no mood to avow it; aside from laughing with him in the evening about the investigations against him that one just ordered in the morning. Such is the practice.

But when a clumsy Author, that is to say, an Author who knows his duty, who wants to fulfill it, believes himself obliged to say nothing to the public without avowing it, without naming himself, without showing himself in order to respond, then equity, which ought not to punish the clumsiness of a man of honor as a crime, wants one to proceed with him in another manner. It wants one not to separate the trial of the Book from that of the man, since by putting his name on it he declares that he does not want them separated. It wants one not to judge the work, which cannot respond, until after having heard the Author who responds for it.

Thus, although to condemn an anonymous Book might in fact be only to condemn the Book, to condemn a Book that bears the name of the Author, is to condemn the Author himself, and when one does not put him in a position to respond, it is to judge him without having heard him.

The preliminary summons, even, if one wishes, the warrant for arrest is thus indispensable in such a case before proceeding to the judgment of the Book, and vainly would one say along with the Author of the Letters that the offense is obvious, that it is in the Book itself; that does not dispense one from following the judicial form that one follows in the greatest crimes, in the most confirmed ones, in the best proven ones: For if the whole Town has seen a man murdering another one, the murderer still would not be judged without being heard, or without having been put into a position to be heard.

And why does this frankness of an Author who names himself turn against him this way? Shouldn't it, on the contrary, earn him some consideration? Shouldn't it impose upon the Judges more circumspection than if he did not name himself? Why would he expose himself this way when he treats some bold questions, if he was not reassured against the dangers, because of the reasons he can offer in his favor and which, based on his conduct itself, one can presume are worth the trouble of hearing? For all that the Author of the Letters will characterize this conduct as imprudence and clumsiness; it is not any less that of a man of honor, who sees his duty where others see that imprudence, who feels that he has nothing to fear from anyone who wants to proceed justly with him, and who regards publishing things that one does not want to acknowledge as a punishable act of cowardice.

If it is only a question of reputation as an Author, does one need to put one's name on one's Book? Who doesn't know how to set about it in order to have all the honor for it without risking anything, in order to glorify oneself for it without answering for it, in order to take on a humble aspect as a result of vanity? Which Authors of a certain rank are unaware of this little trick of sleight of hand? Who among them does not know that it is even beneath dignity to name oneself, as if everyone ought not to guess upon reading the Work the Great man who composed it?

But these Gentlemen have not seen anything but the ordinary practice, and far from seeing the exception that acted in my favor, they have made it serve against me. They ought to have burned the Book without making mention of the Author, or if they bore the Author a grudge, they ought to have waited until he was present or contumacious in order to burn the Book. But not at all; they burn the Book as if the Author was not known, and issue a warrant against the Author as if the Book was not burned. To issue a warrant against me after having defamed me! What else did they want to do to me then? What worse thing did they reserve for me afterward? Didn't they know that the honor of a decent man is more dear to him than life? What harm is left to do to him when one has begun by stigmatizing him? What use is it for me to present myself as innocent before the Judges, when the treatment they give me before hearing me is the cruelest punishment they could impose on me if I was judged criminal?

They begin by treating me in every respect as a malefactor who has no more honor to lose and whom one can punish only corporally from now on, and then they tranquilly say that I remain with all my exceptions and defenses! But how will these exceptions and defenses erase the ignominy and the evil that they will have made me suffer in advance both in my Book and in my person, when I will have been paraded in the streets by archers, when to the ills that are crushing me they will have taken care to add the rigors of prison? What then! In order to be just should one mix together all faults and all men in the same class and in the same treatment? For an act of frankness called clumsiness, must one begin by dragging an irreproachable Citizen into the prisons like a scoundrel? And what advantage will public esteem and the integrity of an entire life have then before the judges, if fifty years of honor over against the slightest evidence do not save a man from any affront?*

"The comparison of *Emile* and the *Social Contract* with other Works that have been tolerated, and the partiality with which they take the occasion to reproach the Council do not seem to me to have any foundation. It would not be reasoning well to claim that, because a Government has dissimulated one time, it would be obliged always to dissimulate: if it is a negligence, one can redress it; if it is a silence forced by circumstances or by policy, there would be little justice in making it the matter of a reproach. I do not claim to justify the works indicated in the Remonstrances; but in conscience is there parity between Books in which one finds some scattered and indiscreet barbs against Religion, and Books in which without detour, without consideration, it is attacked in its dogmas, in its morality, in its influence over civil Society? Let us compare these Works impartially, let us judge them by the impression they have made in

---

* There would be, upon the examination, much to reduce in the presumptive evidence that the Author of the Letters pretends to accumulate against me. He says, for example, that the Books submitted for judgment appeared under the same format as my other works. It is true that they were in duodecimo and in octavo; under what format are those of other Authors then? He adds that they were printed by the same Bookseller; that is not true. *Emile* was printed by Booksellers different from mine, and with characters that were not used in any of my other Writings. Thus the evidence that resulted from that confrontation was not against me, it was for my acquittal.

the world; some are printed and sold everywhere; one knows how the others have been received there." *

I believed I should first transcribe this paragraph in its entirety. Now I will take it up again in fragments. It deserves a little analysis.

What isn't printed at Geneva? What isn't tolerated there? Works one can hardly read without indignation are sold publicly there;[31] everyone reads them, everyone loves them, the Magistrates keep silent, the Ministers smile, the austere aspect is no longer in good form. I alone and my Books have deserved the animadversion of the Council, and what animadversion? One cannot even imagine it as any more violent or more terrible. My God! I would never have believed I was such a great scoundrel.

The comparison of Emile *and the* Social Contract *with other tolerated Works does not seem to me to have any foundation.* Ah I hope so. *It would not be reasoning well to claim that, because a Government has dissimulated one time, it would be obliged always to dissimulate.* So be it; but look at the times, the places, the persons; look at the writings about which they dissimulate, and those they choose in order not to dissimulate any longer; look at the Authors they celebrate at Geneva, and look at those whom they prosecute.

If it is a negligence one can redress it. One could, one should have, has one done so? My writings and their Author have been stigmatized without deserving to be so; and those that have deserved it are not less tolerated than before. The exception is for me alone.

If it is a silence forced by circumstances or by policy, there would be little justice in making it the matter of a reproach. If they force you to tolerate punishable Writings, then also tolerate those that are not. Decency at least requires that one hide from the people this shocking partiality, which punishes the weak innocent man for the faults of the powerful guilty one. What! Are these scandalous distinctions reasons then, and will they always make people into dupes? Wouldn't one say that the fate of some obscene satires interests the Potentates very much, and that your Town is going to be crushed if one does not tolerate there, if one does not print there, if one does not publicly sell there these same Works that are proscribed in their Authors' countries?[32] Peoples, how much does one delude you into believing by so often making the Powers intervene in order to authorize the harm that they are unaware of and that one wants to commit in their name!

When I arrived in this country it was as if the whole Kingdom of France was at my heels. They burn my Books at Geneva; it is done in order to please France. They issue a warrant for my arrest; France wanted it that way. They have me chased from the Canton of Berne; it is France that

---

* Pages 23 and 24.

demanded it. They pursue me as far as these Mountains; if they could have chased me from them, it would have been France again. Forced by a thousand insults, I write a letter in defense of myself.[33] This time, all was lost. I was surrounded, watched over; France was sending spies to lie in wait for me, soldiers to carry me off, brigands to murder me; it was even imprudent to leave my house. All dangers always came to me from France, from the Parlement, from the Clergy, from the Court itself; never in one's life did one see a poor scribbler on paper become, for his misfortune, such an important man. Bored with so many stupidities, I go into France;[34] I knew the French, and I was unhappy. They welcome me, they make much of me, I receive a thousand acts of decency, and it is only up to me to receive more of them. I return home tranquilly. They are thunderstruck; they can't get over it; they strongly blame my heedlessness, but they stop threatening me with France; they are right. If murderers ever deign to end my sufferings, that is certainly not the country they will come from.

I am not confusing the various causes of my disfavor; I know very well how to distinguish those that are the effect of circumstances, the work of sad necessity, from those that come to me solely from the hatred of my enemies. Ah! God willing that I did not have more of them at Geneva than in France, and that they were not more implacable there! Today everyone knows where the blows came from that were struck at me and to which I was most susceptible. Your people reproach me for my misfortunes as if they were not their work. What could be a more cruel calumny than to make a crime for me in Geneva out of the persecutions that they were instigating against me in Switzerland, and to accuse me of not being allowed anywhere, while having me chased from everywhere! Must I blame that friendship that called me to these regions for the vicinity of my country? I dare to call to witness all the Peoples of Europe; is there a single one of them, except Switzerland, where I might not have been received, even with honor? Nevertheless, should I complain of the choice of my retreat? No, in spite of so much animosity and so many insults, I have gained more than I lost; I found a man. Noble and great soul! Oh George Keith![35] My protector, my friend, my father! Wherever you might be, wherever I finish my sad days, and though I should not see you again in my life; no, I will not reproach Heaven for my miseries; I owe them your friendship.

In conscience is there parity between Books in which one finds some scattered and indiscreet barbs against Religion, and Books in which without detour, without consideration, it is attacked in its dogmas, in its morality, in its influence over society?[36]

In conscience! . . . It would not suit an impious man such as me to dare to speak about conscience . . . above all, over against these good Christians

... so I keep silent.... Nevertheless it is a peculiar conscience that has some Magistrates say; we willingly allow one to blaspheme, but we do not allow one to reason! Take away, Sir, the disparity between the subjects; it is with these same ways of thinking that the Athenians applauded the impieties of Aristophanes and had Socrates put to death.

One of the things that gives me the most confidence in my principles is to find their application always accurate in the cases I had least foreseen; such is the one that presents itself here. One of the maxims that flows from the analysis that I have made of Religion and of what is essential to it is that men ought not to meddle with that of anyone else except in what concerns them; from which it follows that they ought never to punish offenses* made solely to God, who will know very well how to punish them himself. *The Divinity must be honored and never avenged*, say the Remonstrators following Montesquieu; they are right.[37] Nevertheless offensive pieces of ridicule, coarse impieties, blasphemies against Religion are punishable, never arguments. Why so? Because in this first case one is not attacking only Religion, but those who profess it, one is insulting them, one is offending them in their form of worship, one is showing a revolting disdain for what they respect and consequently for them. Such offenses ought to be punished by the laws, because they fall on men, and because men have the right to feel them deeply. But where is the mortal on the earth that reasoning ought to offend? Where is the one who can get angry because one is treating him as a man and assumes him to be reasonable? If the reasoner is mistaken or deceives us, and you take an interest in him or in us, show him his error, disabuse us, beat him with his own weapons. If you do not want to take the trouble, don't say anything, don't listen to him, let him reason or misreason, and it is all over without any fuss, without any quarrel, without any insult whatsoever for anyone whomsoever. But on what can one found the opposite maxim of tolerating raillery, disdain, offense, and of punishing reason? My reason gets lost in this.

These Gentlemen see M. de Voltaire so often.[38] How has he not in-

---

* Note that I make use of this word *to offend God* in accordance with common practice, although I am very far from accepting it in its proper sense, and although I find it very badly applied; as if any being whatsoever, a man, an Angel, the Devil himself could ever offend God. The word that we render by *offenses* is translated as almost all the rest of the sacred text is; that says it all. Some men infatuated with their Theology have rendered and disfigured this admirable Book in accordance with their petty ideas, and that is what they feed the folly and the fanaticism of the people with. I find very wise the circumspection of the Roman Church about translations of the Scripture into the vulgar tongue, and since it is not necessary always to offer to the people the voluptuous meditations of the Song of Songs, nor David's continuous curses against his enemies, nor St. Paul's subtleties about grace, it is dangerous to offer it the sublime morality of the Gospel in terms that do not render the sense of the Author exactly; for however little one deviates from it, one goes very far by taking another route.

spired them with that spirit of toleration that he preaches ceaselessly, and that he sometimes needs? If they had consulted him a little in this affair, it appears to me that he might have spoken to them just about this way.

"Gentlemen, it is not the reasoners who do evil, it is the sanctimonious people. Philosophy can move along without risk; the people do not understand it or let it talk, and give it back all the disdain they receive from it. Of all the follies of men, to reason is the one that harms the human race the least, and one sees even wise people infatuated with that folly sometimes. I do not reason, myself, that is true, but others do reason; what harm comes from it? See such, such, and such work; are there anything but pleasantries in these Books? Myself in the end, if I do not reason, I do better; I make my readers reason. See my chapter on the Jews;[39] see the same chapter more developed in the *Oath of the Fifty*. There is reasoning or the equivalent there, I think. You will also agree that there is not much *indirection* there, and something more than *some scattered and indiscreet barbs*.

"We have arranged that my great influence at Court and my so-called omnipotence would serve you as a pretext for letting the playful games of my old age circulate in peace: that is good, but do not burn more serious writings because of that; for then that would be too shocking.

"I have preached tolerance so much! One must not always demand it from others without ever practicing it with them. This poor man believes in God? Let that pass in him, he will not make a sect. He is boring? All reasoners are. We will not make him part of our suppers; besides, what does it matter to us? If one burned all the boring Books, what would happen to the Bookstores? And if one burned all the boring people, it would be necessary to make the country into a bonfire. Believe me, let us allow those to reason who allow us to joke; let's not burn either people or Books; and remain in peace; that is my advice." There, according to me, is what M. de Voltaire could have said in a better style, and that would not have been, it seems to me, the worst council he would have given.

Let us compare these Works impartially, let us judge them by the impression they have made in the world. I consent to this with all my heart. *Some are printed and sold everywhere; one knows how the others have been received there.*

These words *some* and *others* are equivocal. I will not say under which the Author understands my books; but what I can say is that they print them in every country, they translate them into all languages, that they have even made two translations of *Emile* at London at the same time, an honor that no other Book except *Heloise* ever had, at least that I know of. I will say, moreover, that in France, in England, in Germany, even in Italy they pity me, they love me, they would like to welcome me, and that everywhere there is only a cry of indignation against the Council of

Geneva. That is what I know about the fate of my Writings; I do not know that of the others.

It is time to conclude. You see, Sir, that in this Letter and in the preceding one I assumed myself to be guilty; but in the first three I showed that I was not so. Now judge what an unjust proceeding against a guilty man must be when it is against an innocent one!

Nevertheless these Gentlemen, very determined to let this proceeding remain, have loudly declared that the good of Religion did not allow them to acknowledge their wrong nor did the honor of the Government allow them to set right their injustice. A whole work would be necessary to show the consequences of that maxim which consecrates and changes all the iniquities of the Ministers of the Laws into a decree of destiny. That is not what is still at issue here, and up to now I have only proposed to examine whether injustice had been committed, and not whether it ought to be set right. In the case of the affirmative, we will see below what resource your Laws have reserved for themselves in order to remedy their violation. While waiting, what must be thought about these inflexible judges, who proceed as lightly in their judgments as if they did not tend toward any consequence, and who maintain them with as much obstinacy as if they had brought the most mature examination to them?

However long these discussion have been, I believed that their object would give you the patience to follow them; I even dare to say that you ought to, since they are as much the defense of your laws as they are mine. In a free country and in a reasonable Religion, the Law that would make a Book similar to mine criminal would be a fatal Law, which it would be necessary to hasten to repeal for the honor and the good of the State. But thank Heaven none of this sort exists among you, as I have just proven, and it is preferable that the injustice of which I am the victim be the work of the Magistrate than of the Laws; for the errors of men are transitory, but those of the Laws endure as long as they do. Far from the ostracism that exiles me forever from my country being the result of my faults, I have never fulfilled my duty as a Citizen better than at the moment I cease to be one, and I would have deserved the title of one by the act that made me renounce it.

Recall what had just happened a few years ago on the subject of the Article *Geneva* by M. d'Alembert.[40] Far from calming the murmurs excited by that Article, the Writing published by the Pastors had increased them, and there was no one who didn't know that my work did them more good than their own. The Protestant party, dissatisfied with them, did not flare up, but it could have flared up at any moment, and unfortunately Governments get alarmed over the slightest thing in these matters, that the quarrels of Theologians, made to fall into oblivion by themselves, always take on importance from the importance one wants to attribute to them.

As for me, I regarded it as the glory and the happiness of the Fatherland to have a Clergy animated by a spirit so rare in its order, and that, without being attached to purely speculative doctrine, related everything to morality, and to the duties of man and of Citizen. I thought that, without directly making its defense, to justify the maxims that I assumed to be theirs and to prevent the censures that could be made of them was a service to render to the State. By showing that what they neglected was neither certain nor useful, I hoped to restrain those who would make it into a crime on their part: without naming it, without designating it, without compromising its orthodoxy, it was to offer it as an example to other Theologians.

The enterprise was bold, but it was not rash, and without circumstances that it was hard to foresee, it ought naturally to succeed. I was not alone in this sentiment; very enlightened people, even illustrious Magistrates thought as I did. Consider the religious condition of Europe at the moment I published my Book, and you will see that it was more than probable that it would be welcomed everywhere. Religion, discredited everywhere by philosophy, had lost its ascendancy even over the people. The Clergy, obstinate about propping it up on its weak side, had let all the rest be undermined, and, being out of plumb, the entire edifice was ready to collapse. Controversies had stopped because they no longer interested anyone, and peace reigned among the different parties, because none cared about his own anymore. In order to remove the bad branches they had cut down the tree; in order to replant it, it was necessary to leave nothing but the trunk.

What more fortunate moment for establishing universal peace solidly than the one in which the suspended animosity of the parties left everyone in a condition to listen to reason? Who could be displeased by a work in which without blaming, at least without excluding anyone, one caused it to be seen that at bottom all were in agreement; that so many dissensions had been raised, that so much blood had been spilled only out of misunderstandings; that each should remain at rest in his form of worship, without disturbing that of others; that everywhere one ought to serve God, love one's neighbor, obey the Laws, and that the essence of all good Religion consisted in that alone? To do this was to establish philosophic liberty and religious piety at the same time; it was to reconcile love of order and consideration for the prejudices of others; it was, without destroying the various parties, to lead them all back to the common term of humanity and reason; far from stirring up quarrels, it was to cut the root of those that were still sprouting up, and that will infallibly be reborn from one day to the next, when the zeal of fanaticism—which is only napping—wakes up: it was, in a word, in this century that is peaceful out of indifference, to give to each very strong reasons always to be what he is now without knowing why.

How many evils on the point of being reborn would not have been prevented if they had listened to me! What inconveniences were attached to that advantage? Not one, no, not one. I defy anyone to show me a single probable and even possible one, unless it is impunity for innocent errors and the impotence of persecutors. Ah, how can it be that after so many sad experiences and in such an enlightened century, Governments have not yet learned to throw down and break that terrible weapon, which one cannot handle with sufficient skill for it not to cut the hand that wants to make use of it? The Abbé de Saint Pierre wanted the schools of theology to be removed and Religion to be sustained. What choice must be made to succeed without ado in this double object, which, well considered, merges into one? The choice I had made.

By stopping the effect of my good plans, an unfortunate circumstance gathered upon my head all the evils from which I wanted to deliver the human race. Will another friend of the truth ever be born whom my fate will not frighten? I do not know. Let him be wiser, if he has the same zeal will he be more fortunate because of it? I doubt it. Since it was missed, the moment that I had seized will not come back again. I wish with all my heart that the Parlement of Paris itself does not repent one day for having put back into the hand of superstition the dagger that I caused to fall from it.

But let's leave distant places and times, and return to Geneva. It is there that I want to bring you back by means of a final observation that you are well within reach of making, and that certainly ought to strike you. Cast your eyes on what is happening around you. Who are the ones who are prosecuting me, who are the ones who are defending me? See among the Remonstrators the elite of your Citizens. Does Geneva have any more estimable ones? I do not want to talk about my persecutors; may it please God that I never sully my pen and my cause with strokes of Satire; I leave this weapon to my enemies without regret: But compare and judge yourself. On what side are morals, virtues, solid piety, the truest patriotism? What! I offend against the laws, and their most zealous defenders are mine! I attack the Government, and the best Citizens approve of me! I attack Religion, and I have for me those who have the most Religion! That observation alone says everything; it alone shows my true crime and the true subject of my disfavor. Those who hate me and insult me make my eulogy in spite of themselves. Their hatred explains itself. Can a Genevan be fooled in this?

Sixth Letter

One more letter, Sir, and you are rid of me. But in beginning it I find myself in a very bizarre situation; obliged to write it, and not knowing what to fill it with. Can you imagine that one had to justify oneself from a crime about which one is ignorant, and that one must defend oneself without knowing of what one is accused? Nevertheless that is what I have to do on the subject of Governments. I am, not accused, but judged, but stigmatized for having published two Works that are *reckless, scandalous, impious, tending to destroy the Christian religion and all Governments*. As to Religion we at least have some grip on finding what they wanted to say, and we have examined it. But as to Governments, nothing can furnish us the slightest indication. They have always avoided every sort of explanation on this point: they have never wanted to say in what place I undertook to destroy them this way, nor how, nor why, nor anything that can establish that the offense is not imaginary. It is as if one were judging someone for having killed a man without saying either where, or whom, or when; for an abstract murder. At the Inquisition indeed, they force the accused to guess what they are accusing him of, but they do not judge him without saying what.

With the same care the Author of the *Letters Written from the Country* avoids explaining himself on this pretended offense; he joins Religion and Governments equally in the same general accusation: then, entering into substance on Religion, he declares he wants to limit himself to it, and he keeps his word. How will we succeed in establishing the accusation that concerns Governments, if those who bring it refuse to state on what it bears?

Note even how this Author changes the state of the question with one stroke of the pen. The Council pronounces that my Books tend to destroy all Governments. The Author of the Letters says only that in them Governments are given over to the most audacious critique. That is very different. A critique, however audacious it might be, is not at all a conspiracy. To criticize or to blame some Laws is not to overturn all Laws. One might as well accuse someone of assassinating sick people when he shows the faults of Doctors.

Once again, how to respond to reasons they do not want to state: How to justify oneself against a judgment brought without grounds? That, without proof on one side or the other, these Gentlemen say that I want to overturn all Governments, and that I say, myself, that I do not want to overturn all Governments, in these assertions there is an exact parity, except that the prejudice is for me; for it is to be presumed that I know better than anyone what I want to do.

But where parity is lacking is in the effect of the assertion. Based on theirs my Book is burned, a warrant is issued for my person; and what I affirm restores nothing. Only, if I prove that the accusation is false and the judgment iniquitous, the affront they have given me turns back onto themselves. The warrant, the Executioner, everything ought to turn back onto them; since nothing destroys the Government so radically as the one who makes use of it directly contrary to the end for which it is instituted.

It is not enough for me to affirm, I must prove; and it is here that one sees how deplorable is the fate of a private individual subjected to unjust Magistrates, when they have nothing to fear from the Sovereign, and when they put themselves above the laws. Out of an affirmation without proof, they make a demonstration; behold the innocent person punished. Much more, they make another crime for him out of his very defense, and it depends only on them to punish him again for having proven that he was innocent.

How can I set about showing that they have not spoken truly; proving that I do not destroy Governments at all? Whatever place in my Writings I defend, they will say that it is not that one that they have condemned; although they have condemned everything, the good as well as the bad, without any distinction. In order not to leave them any way out, it would thus be necessary to take up everything, to follow everything from one end to the other, Book by Book, page by page, line by line, and finally almost word by word. It would be necessary further to examine all the Governments of the world, since they say that I destroy all of them. What an undertaking! How many years would have to be used for it? How many folio volumes would have to be written; and after that, who would read them?

Require what is feasible of me. Every sensible man ought to be satisfied with what I have to say to you: surely you do not want anything more.

Of my two Books burned at the same time under shared imputations, there is only one that treats political right and matters of Government. If the other does treat them, it is only in an abridgment of the former.[41] Thus I assume that it is upon this one alone that the accusation falls. If this accusation bore on any particular passage, they doubtless would have cited it; they would at least have extracted some maxim, faithful or unfaithful, as they did on the points concerning Religion.

Thus it is the System established in the body of the work that destroys Governments; thus it is only a question of exposing this System or of making an analysis of the Book; and if we do not obviously see in this the destructive principles at issue, we will at least know where to find them in the book, by following the method of the Author.

But, Sir, if during this analysis, which will be short, you find some consequence to draw, please do not rush. Wait until we reason about it together. After that you will return to it if you wish.

What makes it so that the State is one? It is the union of its members. And from what is the union of its members born? From the obligation that ties them together. Up to this point all are in agreement.

But what is the foundation of this obligation? That is what Authors are divided upon. According to some, it is force, according to others, paternal authority; according to others, the will of God. Each establishes his principle and attacks that of the others: I have not done otherwise myself, and following the soundest portion of those who have discussed these matters, I posited as foundation of the body politic the convention of its members, I refuted the principles different from my own.

Independently of the truth of this principle, it prevails over all the others by the solidity of the foundation it establishes, for what more certain foundation can obligation among men have than the free engagement of the one who obliges himself? One can dispute every other principle*; one cannot dispute that one.

But by this condition of liberty, which includes others, not all sorts of engagements are valid, even before human Tribunals. Thus in order to determine this one, one ought to explain its nature, one ought to find its use and end, one ought to prove that it is suitable to men, and that it has nothing contrary to natural Laws: for it is no more permitted to infringe natural Laws by the Social Contract than it is permitted to infringe positive Laws by the Contracts of private individuals, and it is only by these Laws themselves that the liberty that gives force to the engagement exists.

As a result of this examination, I have it that the establishment of the Social Contract is a pact of a particular sort, by which each engages himself toward all, from which follows the reciprocal engagement of all toward each, which is the immediate object of the union.

I say that this engagement is of a particular sort in that by being absolute, without condition, without reserve, it, nevertheless, cannot be unjust

---

* Even the one of the will of God, at least as to its application. For although it might be clear that man ought to want what God wants, it is not clear that God wants one to prefer such Government to such a different one, nor that one obey James rather than William. Now this is what is at issue.

or susceptible of abuse; since it is not possible that the body would want to hurt itself, as long as the whole wills only for all.

It is also of a particular sort in that it binds the contracting people together without subjecting them to anyone, and that by giving them their will alone as rule it leaves them as free as before.

The will of all is thus the order, the supreme rule, and that general and personified rule is what I call the Sovereign.

It follows from that that the Sovereign is indivisible, inalienable, and that it resides essentially in all the members of the body.

But how does this abstract and collective being act? It acts by means of Laws, and it cannot act otherwise.

And what is a Law? It is a public and solemn declaration of the general will, on an object of common interest.

I say, on an object of common interest; because the Law would lose its force and would cease to be legitimate if the object did not matter to all.

By its nature Law cannot have a particular and individual object: but the application of the Law falls on particular and individual objects.

The Legislative power that is the Sovereign thus needs another power that executes, that is to say, that reduces the Law into particular actions. This second power ought to be established in a manner so that it always executes the Law and it never executes anything but the Law. Here comes the institution of the Government.

What is the Government? It is an intermediate body established between the subjects and the Sovereign for their mutual communication and charged with the execution of the Laws and the maintenance of civil as well as political Liberty.[42]

As an integral part of the body politic the Government participates in the general will that constitutes it; as a body itself, it has its own will. These two will sometimes agree with and sometimes combat each other. From the combined effect of this agreement and of this conflict results the action of the whole machine.

The principle that constitutes the various forms of Government consists in the number of members that compose it. The smaller this number is, the more force the Government has; the larger the number is, the weaker the Government is; and since sovereignty always tends toward relaxation, the Government always tends to become stronger. Thus the executive Body ought in the long run to prevail over the legislative body, and when the Law is finally subjected to men, only slaves and masters remain; the State is destroyed.

Before this destruction, the Government ought by its natural progress to change form and pass by degrees from the greater number to the smaller.

Sixth Letter (Pl., III, 807–810)

The diverse forms of which the Government is susceptible are reduced to three principal ones. After having compared them by their advantages and their inconveniences, I give the preference to the one that is intermediate between the two extremes and that bears the name of Aristocracy. Here one ought to remember that the constitution of the State and that of the Government are two very distinct things, and that I have not mixed them up. The best of Governments is the aristocratic; the worst of sovereignties is the aristocratic.

These discussions lead to others on the manner by which the Government degenerates, and on the means of slowing down the destruction of the body politic.

Finally in the last Book I examine by means of comparison with the best Government that has existed, namely that of Rome, the public order most favorable to the good constitution of the State; then I conclude this Book and the entire Work with researches on the manner in which Religion can and ought to enter as a constitutive part into the composition of the body politic.

What do you think, Sir, upon reading this short and faithful analysis of my Book? I guess it. You are saying to yourself; there is the history of the Government of Geneva. That is what all those who are acquainted with your Constitution say upon reading the same Work.

And in fact, that primitive Contract, that essence of Sovereignty, that empire of the Laws, that institution of Government, that manner of confining it in various degrees in order to balance authority with force, that tendency to usurpation, those periodic assemblies, that skill in getting rid of them, finally that imminent destruction that menaces you and that I wished to prevent; isn't this stroke for stroke the image of your Republic, since its birth up to this day?

Thus I took your Constitution, which I found to be beautiful, as the model of political institutions, and proposing you as an example to Europe, far from seeking to destroy you I set out the means of preserving you. This Constitution, completely good as it is, is not faultless; one could have prevented the alterations it has suffered, protected it from the danger it is running today. I foresaw this danger, I caused it to be understood, I indicated preservatives. Was showing what had to be done to maintain it to want to destroy it? It was out of my attachment for it that I would have wanted nothing to be able to alter it. There is my whole crime; I was wrong, perhaps; but if love of the fatherland blinded me on this point, was it up to it to punish me for this?

How could I tend toward overthrowing all Governments, by positing as principles all of yours? This fact alone destroys the accusation. Since there was a Government existing upon my model, I thus did not tend toward destroying all those that existed. What! Sir; if I had only made a System, you can be sure that they would have said nothing. They would have been content to relegate the *Social Contract* along with the *Republic* of Plato, *Utopia*, and *Severambes*[43] into the land of the chimeras. But I depicted an existing object, and they wanted to change that object's face. My Book bore witness against the attack they were going to make. That is what they did not pardon me for.

But here is what will appear bizarre to you. My Book attacks all Governments, and it is not proscribed in any![44] It established a single one, it proposes it as an example, and that is the one it is burned in! Isn't it peculiar that the Governments attacked are silent, and the Government respected deals severely? What! The body of Magistrates of Geneva makes itself the protector of other Governments against its very own! It punishes its own Citizen for having preferred the Laws of his country to all others! Is that conceivable, and would you believe it if you had not seen it? In all the rest of Europe has anyone taken it into his head to stigmatize the work? No; not even the State in which it was printed.* Not even France where the Magistrates are so severe about it. Did they forbid the Book? Nothing like it; at first they did not allow the edition of Holland to enter, but it was counterfeited in France, and the work circulated there without difficulty. Thus it was an affair of commerce and not of public order: they preferred the profit of the Bookseller of France to that of the foreign Bookseller. That is all.

The *Social Contract* was not burned anywhere except at Geneva where it was not printed; only the Magistrate of Geneva found principles destructive of all Governments in it. In truth, this Magistrate did not say at all what these principles were; in that I believe he acted extremely prudently.

The effect of indiscreet prohibitions is not to be observed and to enervate the force of authority. My Book is in the hands of everyone at Geneva, and would that it were equally in everyone's heart! Read it, Sir, this Book that is so decried, but so necessary; throughout you will see the Law put above men; throughout you will see liberty laid claim to, but always under the authority of the laws, without which liberty cannot exist, and under which one is always free, in whatever manner one might be governed. From that I do not, they say, pay my court to the powers: so much the worse for them; for I know their true interests, if they knew how to see them and follow them. But passions blind men about their own good.

---

* At the height of the earliest clamors caused by the proceedings of Paris and Geneva, the surprised Magistrate forbade the two Books: but based on his own examination this wise Magistrate changed his sentiment, above all with regard to the *Social Contract*.

Those who subject Laws to human passions are the true destroyers of Governments: there are the people who should be punished.

The foundations of the State are the same in all Governments, and these foundations are better set down in my Book than in any other. When it is a question afterward of comparing the various forms of Government, one cannot avoid weighing separately the advantages and inconveniences of each: that is what I believe I did with impartiality. Everything weighed, I gave the preference to the Government of my country. That was natural and reasonable; they would have blamed me if I had not done so. But I did not exclude other Governments; on the contrary: I showed that each had its reason which could render it preferable to all others, in accordance with men, times, and places. Thus far from destroying all Governments, I have established all of them.

In speaking about Monarchic Government in particular, I insisted very much upon its advantage, and I did not disguise its defects either. That is, I think, within the right of a man who reasons; and if I had refused to permit it, which I assuredly did not do, would it follow that they ought to punish me in Geneva? Was a warrant issued for Hobbes's arrest in some Monarchy because his principles are destructive of every republican Government, and do Kings put on trial Authors who reject and belittle Republics? Isn't the right reciprocal, and aren't Republicans Sovereigns in their country as Kings are in theirs. As for me, I have rejected no Government, I have not scorned any of them. In examining them, in comparing them, I have held the scale and I have calculated the weight: I have done nothing more.

One ought not to punish reason anywhere, nor even reasoning; that punishment would prove too much against those who would impose it. The Remonstrators have very well established that my Book, in which I do not depart from the general thesis, not attacking the Government of Geneva at all and printed out of its territory, can only be considered to be among the number of those that treat of natural and political right, over which the Laws do not give the Council any power, and which are always sold publicly in the Town, whatever principle is advanced in them and whatever sentiment is supported in them. I am not the only one who, discussing questions of politics by abstraction, might have treated them with some boldness; not everyone has done it, but every man has the right to do it; several make use of this right, and I am the only one who is punished for having made use of it. The unfortunate Sydnei thought as I did, but he acted; it is for his deed and not for his Book that he had the honor of shedding his blood.[45] In Germany Althusius drew enemies down on him, but they did not take it into their heads to prosecute him criminally.[46] Locke,

Montesquieu, the Abbé de Saint Pierre[47] treated the same matters, and often with at least the same liberty. Locke in particular treated them exactly in the same principles as I did.[48] All three were born under Kings, lived tranquilly and died honored in their country. You know how I have been treated in mine.

Also rest assured that far from blushing at these stigmas I glorify myself for them, because they serve only to put into evidence the motive that drew them down on me, and that this motive is only to have deserved well from my country. The conduct of the Council toward me afflicts me, without a doubt, by breaking the bonds that were so dear to me; but can it debase me? No, it raises me up, it puts me in the rank of those who have suffered for liberty. My Books, whatever might be done, will always bear witness for themselves, and the treatment they have received will do nothing but save from opprobrium those that will have the honor of being burned after them.

END OF THE FIRST PART

SECOND PART

Seventh Letter

You will have found me diffuse, Sir; but I had to be so, and the subjects that I had to treat are not to be discussed by means of epigrams. Besides, these subjects took me less far away than it seems from the one that interests you. In speaking about myself I was thinking about you; and your question depends so much on mine that the one is already resolved along with the other, there is nothing left for me but to draw the consequence. Everywhere that innocence is not in safety, nothing can be: everywhere that the Laws are violated with impunity, there is no longer any liberty.

Nevertheless since one can separate the interest of a private individual from that of the public, your ideas on this point are still uncertain; you persist in wanting me to aid you in fixing them. You ask what the present state of your Republic is, and what its Citizens ought to do? It is easier to respond to the first question than to the other.

That first question surely perplexes you less by itself than by the contradictory solutions that are given to it around you. Some People of very good sense tell you: we are the most free of all peoples, and other People of very good sense tell you: we are living under the harshest slavery. Which are right, do you ask me? All, Sir; but in different regards: a very simple distinction reconciles them. Nothing is more free than your legitimate state; nothing is more servile than your actual state.

Your laws derive their authority only from you; you acknowledge only the ones that you make; you pay only the taxes that you impose; you elect the Leaders who govern you; they have the right to judge you only by means of prescribed forms. In the general Council you are Legislators, Sovereigns, independent of all human power; you ratify treaties, you decide peace and war; your Magistrates themselves refer to you as *Magnificent, very honored and sovereign Lords*.[49] There is your liberty: here is your servitude.

The body charged with the execution of your Laws is their interpreter and supreme arbiter; it makes them speak as it pleases; it can make them fall silent; it can even violate them without your being able to set them to rights; it is above the Laws.

The Leaders whom you elect have, independently of your choice, other powers that they do not derive from you, and that they extend at the expense of those they do so derive. Limited in your elections to a small number of men, all having the same principles and all animated by the same interest, with a great show you make a choice of little importance. What would matter to you in this business would be to be able to reject all of the ones from among whom they force you to choose. In an election free in appearance you are so obstructed from all sides that you cannot even elect a first Syndic nor a Syndic of the Guard: the Leader of the Republic and the Commandant of the Fortress are not of your choice.

If they do not have the right of imposing new taxes on you, you do not have that of rejecting the old ones. The finances of the State are on such a footing that without your cooperation they can suffice for everything. Thus they never need to show you consideration in that purpose, and your rights in that regard are reduced to being exempt in part and to being necessary never.

The procedures they ought to follow in judging you are prescribed; but when the Council does not want to follow them no one can constrain it to, nor oblige it to set right the irregularities it commits. On this I am qualified to constitute a proof, and you know whether I am the only one.

In the general Council your Sovereign power is enchained: you cannot act except when it pleases your Magistrates, nor speak except when they interrogate you. If they even want not to assemble the general Council at all, your authority, your existence is annihilated, without you being able to oppose them except with vain murmurs that they are in a condition to scorn.

In sum, if you are Sovereign Lords in the assembly, upon leaving there you are no longer anything. Four hours a year subordinate Sovereigns, you are subjects the rest of your life and abandoned without reserve to the discretion of someone else.

What happens to all Governments like yours, Gentlemen, has happened to you. At first the Legislative power and executive power that constitute sovereignty are not distinct. The Sovereign People wills by itself, and by itself it does what it wills. Soon the inconvenience of this cooperation of all in everything forces the Sovereign People to charge some of its members to execute its wills. These Officers, after having fulfilled their commission, account for it and return into the common equality. Little by little these commissions become frequent, finally permanent. Insensibly a body forms that always acts. A body that always acts cannot account for each act: it no longer accounts for any but the principal ones; soon it reaches the point of accounting for none of them. The more active the power that acts is, the more it enervates the power that wills. Yesterday's will is deemed to be today's also; whereas yesterday's action does not dispense from acting today. Finally the inaction of the power that wills subjects it to the power that executes; little by little the latter renders its actions independent, soon its wills; instead of acting for the power that wills, it acts upon it. Then there remains in the State only an acting power, that is the executive. The executive power is only force, and where force alone reigns the State is dissolved. There, Sir, is how all democratic States perish in the end.

Look through the annals of yours, since the time in which your Syndics, simple procurators established by the Community in order to attend to this or that piece of business, accounted to it for their Commission with hats off, and instantly returned into the order of private individuals, up to the one in which these same Syndics, disdaining the rights of Leaders and of Judges, which they hold from their election, prefer over them the arbitrary power of a body whose members are not elected by the Community, and that establishes itself above it contrary to the Laws: follow the progress that separates these two terms, you will know at which point you are and by what degrees you arrived there.

Two centuries ago a Political Thinker could have foreseen what has happened to you. He would have said; the Institution that you are forming is good for the present, and bad for the future; it is good for establishing public liberty, bad for preserving it, and what causes your safety now will be the substance of your chains in a little while. These three bodies,[50] which are so interdependent that the activity of the largest depends on the smallest, are in such an equilibrium that the action of the largest is necessary and that the Legislation cannot do without the Legislator. But once the establishment is done, the body that formed it, lacking power to maintain it, will have to fall into ruin, and it will be your Laws themselves that will cause your destruction. There precisely is what has happened to you. It is, aside from the disproportion, the fall of the Polish Government by the opposite extreme. The constitution of the Republic of Poland is good only for a Government in which there is no longer anything to do.[51] Yours, on the contrary, is good only as long as the legislative Body always acts.

Your Magistrates have labored at all times and without respite to make the supreme power of the general Council pass to the small Council through the gradation of the Two-Hundred; but their efforts have had different effects, in accordance with the manner in which they have gone about it. Almost all of their showy enterprises have failed, because then they have found some resistance, and because in a State such as yours, public resistance is always certain when it is founded upon the Laws.

The reason for this is obvious. In every State the Law speaks where the Sovereign speaks. Now in a Democracy where the People is Sovereign, when internal divisions suspend all forms and silence all authorities, only its authority remains, and then where the greater number stands, there resides Law and authority.

If the Citizens and Bourgeois united are not the Sovereign, the Councils without the Citizens and Bourgeois are still much less so, since they make up only the smallest part of it in quantity. As soon as it is a question of supreme authority, in Geneva everything returns to equality, in accordance with the terms of the Edict. *Let all be content with the rank of Citizens and Bourgeois, without wanting to be preferred and to attribute to himself some authority and Lordship above the others.* Outside of the general Council, there is no other Sovereign than the Law, but when the Law itself is being attacked by its Ministers, it is up to the Legislator to support it. That is why, everywhere a genuine liberty reigns, in clear-cut undertakings the People almost always has the advantage.

But it is not by means of clear-cut undertakings that your Magistrates have brought things to the point where they are; it is by means of moderate and continuous efforts, by means of almost intangible changes whose consequence you could not foresee, and which you could hardly even notice. It is not possible for the People to maintain itself ceaselessly on guard against everything that is done, and such vigilance would even turn into a reproach against it. They would accuse it of being restless and turbulent, always ready to become alarmed over nothings. But with time the Council knows how to make something out of these nothings about which one is silent. What is happening at present under your eyes is the proof of it.

All the authority of the Republic resides in the Syndics who are elected in the general Council. They take their oath there because it is their sole Superior, and they take it only in this Council, because it is to it alone that they owe an account of their conduct, of their fidelity in fulfilling the oath they have taken there. They swear to render good and upright justice; they are the only Magistrates who swear that in this assembly, because they are the only ones to whom this right is conferred by the Sovereign,* and who

---

* It is conferred to their Lieutenant only subordinately, and it is for that reason that he does not take an oath in general Council. *But,* says the Author of the Letters, *is the oath that the members of the Council take any less obligatory, and does the execution of engagements contracted with the divinity itself depend on the place in which one contracts them?* No, without a doubt, but does it follow that it is indifferent in what places and in whose hands the oath be taken, and doesn't this choice show either by whom the authority is conferred, or to whom one must account for the use one makes of it? With what sort of Statesmen are we dealing if we have to tell them these things? Are they ignorant of them, or are they pretending to be ignorant of them?

exercise it under its sole authority. In the public judgment of criminals they again swear only in front of the People, by standing up* and raising their staffs, that *they have passed upright judgment, without hatred or favor, praying God to punish them if they have acted to the contrary*; and formerly criminal sentences were rendered in their name alone, without any other Council than that of the Citizens being mentioned, as one sees from the sentence of Morelli transcribed above,[52] and from that of Valentin Gentil reported in the opuscula of Calvin.

Now you feel very well that this exclusive power, received this way immediately from the People, obstructs the pretensions of the Council a great deal. Thus it is natural that in order to free itself from this dependence it tries to weaken the authority of the Syndics little by little, to blend into the Council the jurisdiction they have received, and to transmit imperceptibly to this permanent body, whose members the People does not elect, the great but transitory power of the Magistrates it does elect. Far from opposing this change, the Syndics themselves ought to favor it also; because they are Syndics only every four years, and because they can even not be Syndics; instead of which, whatever happens, they are Councilors their whole life, the Grabeau no longer being anything but an empty ceremony.**

That having been gained, in the same way the election of the Syndics will become a ceremony entirely as vain as the holding of the general Councils already is, and the small Council will see very peacefully the exclusions or preferences for the Syndicate that the People can give to its members, when all that will no longer settle anything.

In order to succeed in that end, there is first a great means that the People cannot be acquainted with: that is the interior public order of the Council, the form of which—although it is regulated by the Edicts—it can

---

* The Council is also present, but its members do not swear and remain seated.

** In the first Institution, every year the four newly elected Syndics and the four former Syndics rejected eight members of the sixteen remaining on the small Council and proposed eight new ones, who afterward passed to the vote of the Two-Hundred, in order to be admitted or rejected. But imperceptibly they rejected only those of the old Councilors whose conduct had laid itself open to blame, and when they had committed some grave fault, they did not wait for the elections to punish them; but they first put them into prison, and they tried them like the lowest private individual. From this rule of anticipating the punishment and making it severe, the remaining Councilors, all being irreproachable, did not lay themselves open to exclusion: which changed this practice into the ceremonial and vain formality that today bears the name of *Grabeau*. Admirable effect of free Governments, where even usurpations can establish themselves only with the support of virtue!

Besides, the reciprocal right of the two Councils alone would prevent either of the two from daring to make use of it on the other except in concert with it, out of fear of exposing itself to reprisals. Properly speaking the Grabeau serves only to keep them well united against the bourgeoisie, and for one to use the other to throw out members who do not have corporate spirit.

direct at its will* having no supervisor who prevents it from doing so; for as to the Procurator general, one should count him for nothing in this.** But that is not yet enough, the People itself must be made accustomed to this transfer of jurisdiction. For that purpose one does not begin by setting up Tribunals composed only of Councilors for important cases, but first one sets up less noteworthy ones for rather uninteresting objects. One usually has these Tribunals presided over by a Syndic for whom one sometimes substitutes a former Syndic, then a Councilor, without anyone paying attention to it; one repeats this maneuver without commotion until it is an established practice; one transfers it to the criminal Tribunal. On a more important occasion one sets up a Tribunal for judging Citizens. Under favor of the Law of recusals one has this Tribunal presided over by a Councilor. Then the People opens its eyes and murmurs. One says to it, what are you complaining about? See the precedents; we are not innovating anything.

There, Sir, is the policy of your Magistrates. They make their innovations little by little, slowly without anyone seeing their consequence; and when one finally does notice it and one wants to remedy it, they cry out that one wants to innovate.

And see, in fact, without departing from this example, what they said on that occasion. They relied upon the Law of recusals: one replies to them; the fundamental Law of the State requires that Citizens be judged only by their Syndics. In the concurrence of these two Laws the latter ought to exclude the other; in order to observe both of them in such a case one ought rather to elect a Syndic *ad actum*. At this word, all is lost! A Syndic *ad actum*! Innovation! As for me, I do not see anything there that is as new as they say: if it is the word, it is made use of every year at the elections; and if it is the thing, it is still less new; since the first Syndics that the Town had were not Syndics except *ad actum*: When the Procurator general is recusable, isn't another one necessary *ad actum* in order to per-

---

* This is how since the year 1655 the small Council and the Two-Hundred established in their Bodies the ballot and the tickets contrary to the Edict.

** The Procurator general, established to be the man of the Law, is only the man of the Council. Two causes almost always make this charge exercised against the spirit of its institution. One is the vice of the institution itself, which makes this Magistracy into a step in rank toward arriving at the Council: instead of which a Procurator general ought to have seen nothing above his place and he ought to have been prohibited by Law from aspiring to any other. The second cause is the imprudence of the People who entrust this charge to men related to those in the Council, or who are from families in a position to enter it, without considering that they thus will not fail to use against the People the arms it gave them for its defense. I have heard Genevans distinguish the man of the people from the man of the Law, as if it were not the same thing. During their six years the Procurators general ought to be the Leaders of the Bourgeoisie, and to become its advisor after that: but don't you see it well protected and well advised, and shouldn't it congratulate itself very much on its choice?

form his functions; and what else are the adjuncts drawn from the Two-Hundred to fill the Tribunals but Councilors *ad actum*? When a new abuse is introduced, to propose a new remedy for it is not to innovate; on the contrary, it is to seek to re-establish things on their former footing. But these Gentlemen do not like one to forage thus into the antiquities of their Town: It is only in those of Carthage and of Rome that they permit one to look for the explanation of your Laws.

I will not undertake to draw a parallel between those of their undertakings that have failed and those that have succeeded: even if there were compensation in the number, there would be none at all in the total effect. In an executed undertaking they gain force; in a failed undertaking they lose only time. You, on the contrary, who do not seek and cannot seek anything but to maintain your constitution, when you lose, your losses are real, and when you gain, you gain nothing. In a progression of this sort how can one hope to remain at the same point?

Of all the epochs offered for meditation by the instructive history of your Government, the most noteworthy by its cause and the most important by its effect is the one that produced the settlement of the Mediation. What initially gave rise to this celebrated epoch was an indiscreet undertaking, made inopportunely by your Magistrates. They had stealthily usurped the right of levying taxes. Before having solidified their power enough, they wanted to abuse this right. Instead of holding this blow back for the last, greed made them strike it before the others, and precisely after a commotion that had not completely subsided. This mistake drew on greater ones, hard to set right. How were such subtle political thinkers unaware of such a simple maxim as the one they contradicted on that occasion? In every country the people do not notice that one is attacking its liberty until one attacks its purse; which therefore skilful usurpers take great care not to do until all the rest is completed. They wanted to reverse this order and found themselves badly off for it.* The consequences of this affair produced the movements of 1734 and the frightful plot that was their fruit.

This was a second fault worse than the first. All the advantages of time are for them; they deprive themselves of them in sudden undertakings, and put the machine in a position to wind itself back up all at once: that is what very nearly happened in that business. The events that preceded the

* The object of the taxes established in 1716 was the expense of the new fortifications: The plan for these new fortifications was immense and it was executed in part. Such vast fortifications rendered a large garrison necessary, and that large garrison had as its goal to keep the Citizens and Bourgeois under the yoke. By this means they succeeded in forming at their own expense the chains that they were preparing for them. The project was well tied together, but it proceeded in reverse order. Thus it could not succeed.

Mediation caused them to lose a century and produced another unfavorable effect for them. This was to teach Europe that that Bourgeoisie, which they had wanted to destroy and which they depicted as an ungovernable populace, knew how to maintain in its ascendancy the moderation that they had never known in theirs.

I shall not say whether this recourse to the Mediation ought to be counted as a third fault. This Mediation was or appeared offered; whether this offer was real or solicited is what I neither can nor want to penetrate: I know only that while you were running the greatest danger everything maintained silence, and that this silence was broken only when the danger passed over to the other party. Besides, I want all the less to impute it to your Magistrates that they implored the Mediation, since to dare even to speak about it is the greatest of crimes in their eyes.

A Citizen complaining about an illegal, unjust, and dishonorable imprisonment asked how one must go about having recourse to the guarantee. The Magistrate to whom he addressed himself dared to answer him that by itself this proposition deserved death. Now in regard to the Sovereign the crime would be as great and perhaps greater on the part of the Council than on the part of a simple private individual; and I do not see where one can find one of them worthy of death in a second recourse, rendered legitimate by the guarantee that was the effect of the first.

Once again, I do not undertake to discuss a question so delicate to treat and so difficult to resolve. I simply undertake to examine, concerning the object that occupies us, the state of your Government, formerly fixed by the settlement of the Plenipotentiaries, but now denatured by the new undertakings of your Magistrates. I am obliged to make a long circuit in order to reach my goal, but condescend to follow me, and we will find our bearings.

I do not at all have the temerity to wish to criticize this settlement; on the contrary, I admire its wisdom and I respect its impartiality. I believe I see the most upright intentions and the most judicious dispositions in it. When one knows how many things were against you in this critical moment, how many prejudices you had to vanquish, what influence to overcome, what false statements to destroy; when one recalls with what confidence your adversaries counted on crushing you by means of another's hands, one can only honor the zeal, the consistency, and the talents of your defenders, the equity of the mediating Powers, and the integrity of the Plenipotentiaries who completed this work of peace.

Whatever one could say about it, the Edict of the Mediation has been the salvation of the Republic, and, if it is not transgressed, it will be its preservation. If this Work is not perfect in itself, it is relatively so; it is so as to times, to places, to circumstances; it is the best that could have suited you. It ought to be inviolable and sacred to you out of prudence, even if it were not so by necessity, and you shouldn't remove a Line from it, even if you were the masters of annihilating it. Moreover, the very reason that renders it necessary, renders it necessary in its entirety. Since all the articles in a balance form equilibrium, a single article altered destroys it. The more useful the settlement is, the more harmful it would be mutilated this way. Nothing would be more dangerous than several articles taken separately and detached from the body they strengthen. It would be better that the edifice be razed than shaken. Let a single stone be removed from the vault, and you will be crushed under its ruins.

Nothing is easier to feel from the examination of the articles of which the Council avails itself and those it wants to evade. Remember, Sir, the spirit in which I am undertaking this examination. Far from advising you to tamper with the Edict of the Mediation, I wish to make you feel how important it is to you not to allow any attack to be made against it. If I appear to criticize some articles, it is to show what consequence there would be from removing those that rectify them. If I appear to propose expedients that are unrelated to it, it is to show the bad faith of those who find insurmountable difficulties where nothing is easier than to remove these difficulties. After this explanation I enter into the subject without scruple, well persuaded that I am speaking to a man too equitable to attribute to me a design entirely contrary to mine.

I feel very well that if I were addressing myself to foreigners in order to make myself understood it would be appropriate to begin with a tableau of your constitution; but this tableau is found already sketched sufficiently for them in the article Geneva of M. d'Alembert,[53] and a more detailed exposition would be superfluous for you who are better acquainted with your political Laws than I am myself, or who at least have seen their operation from closer. Thus I limit myself to surveying the articles of the settlement that pertain to the present question and that can best provide the solution to it.

From the first I see your Government composed of five subordinate but independent orders, that is to say existing necessarily, of which none can derogate from the rights and attributes of another, and in these five orders I see the general Council comprehended. From that I see in each of the five a particular portion of the Government; but I do not see at all the constitutive Power that establishes them, that ties them together, and upon which they all depend: I do not see the Sovereign at all there. Now in every political State there must be a supreme Power, a center in which everything is related, a principle from which everything derives, a Sovereign who could do everything.

Imagine, Sir, that someone giving you an account of the constitution of England speaks to you this way. "The Government of Great Britain is composed of four Orders none of which can attack the rights and attributions of the others; namely, the King, the upper House, the lower House, and Parliament." Wouldn't you immediately say; you are mistaken: there are only three Orders. Parliament which, when the King is sitting in it, comprehends all of them, is not a fourth one: it is the whole; it is the unique and supreme power from which each draws its existence and its rights. Vested with the legislative authority, it can change even the fundamental Law by virtue of which each of these orders exists; it can do so, and moreover, it has done so.

This answer is correct, its application is clear; and nevertheless there is still this difference that the Parliament of England is sovereign only in virtue of the Law and only by attribution and deputation. Whereas the general Council of Geneva is neither established nor deputed by anyone; it is sovereign by its own authority: it is the living and fundamental Law that gives life and force to all the rest, and that knows no other rights than its own. The general Council is not an order in the State, it is the State itself.

The second article states that the Syndics cannot be selected except in the Council of the Twenty-Five. Now the Syndics are annual Magistrates whom the people elect and choose, not only to be its judges, but to be its Protectors at need against the perpetual members of the Councils, whom it did not choose.*

The effect of this restriction depends on the difference there is between the authority of the members of the Council and that of the Syndics. For if the difference is not very great, and a Syndic does not esteem his annual authority as Syndic more than his perpetual authority as Councilor, this election will be almost indifferent to him; he will do little to obtain it and will do nothing to justify it. When all the members of the Council animated by the same spirit will follow the same maxims, the People, being unable to exclude anyone because of a conduct common to all, or to choose any Syndics who are not already Councilors, far from securing for itself Patrons against the attacks of the Council by means of this election, will do nothing but give to the Council new forces to oppress liberty.

* In attributing the nomination of the members of the small Council to the Two-Hundred, nothing was easier than to order this attribution in accordance with the fundamental Law. For that it was sufficient to add that one could not enter into the Council until after having been an Auditor. In this manner the gradation of offices was better observed, and the three Councils cooperated in the choice of the one who makes everything move; which was not only important but indispensable, in order to maintain the unity of the constitution. The Genevans may not feel the advantage of that clause, considering that the choice of the Auditors is of little consequence today; but it would have been considered very differently when that office had become the only door to the Council.

Seventh Letter (Pl., III, 824–826)

Although the same choice ordinarily took place at the origin of the institution, as long as it was free it did not have the same consequence. When the People named the Councilors itself, or when it named them indirectly by means of the Syndics whom it had named, it was indifferent to it and even advantageous to choose its Syndics among the Councilors already of its choice,* and it was wise then to prefer leaders already versed in business: but a more important consideration ought to have prevailed over that one today. So true it is that the same practice has different effects from the changes of practices that relate to it, and that in such a case not to innovate is to innovate!

Article III of the Settlement is the most substantial. It treats of the general Council legitimately assembled: it treats of it in order to fix the rights and attributions that are proper to it, and it returns to it several that the inferior Councils had usurped. In totality these rights are great and fine, without a doubt; but first they are specified, and by that alone, limited; what one sets down excludes what one does not set down, and even the word *limited* is in the Article. Now it is of the essence of the Sovereign Power not to be able to be limited: it can do everything or it is nothing. Since it eminently contains all the active powers of the State and the State only exists by means of it, it cannot recognize any other rights than its own and those it communicates. Otherwise the possessors of these rights would not make up a part of the body politic; they would be foreigners by means of these rights that would not be in it, and lacking unity the moral person would disappear.

This very limitation is positive in what concerns Taxes. The Sovereign Council itself does not have the right to abolish those that were established before 1714. Thus in this respect it is subject to a superior power. What is this Power?

The Legislative power consists in two inseparable things: to make the Laws and to maintain them; that is to say, to have inspection over the executive power. There is no State in the world in which the Sovereign does not have this inspection. Without that, all connection, all subordination lacking between these two powers, the latter would not depend on

---

* In its origin the small Council was only a choice made among the People, by the Syndics, of some Notables or Men of Probity in order to serve them as Assessors. Each Syndic chose four or five whose functions ended with his own: sometimes he even changed them during the course of his Syndicate. *Henry* called l'*Espagne* was the first Councilor for life in 1487, and he was established by the general Council. It was not even necessary to be a Citizen to fill this post. The Law for that was made only upon the occasion of a certain Michel Guillet de Thonon, who, having been admitted to the privy Council, was dismissed from it for having made use of a thousand ultramontane tricks which he brought from Rome where he had been brought up. The Magistrats of the Town, at that time true Genevans and Fathers of the People, were horrified at all these subtleties.

the other at all; execution would have no necessary relation to the Laws; the *Law* would only be a word, and this word would signify nothing. The general Council always had this right of protection over its own work, it has always exercised it: Nevertheless it is not spoken of in this article, and if it were not made up for in another, by this very silence your State would be overthrown. This point is important and I shall return to it below.

If your rights are limited on one side in this Article, they are extended on the other side in it by paragraphs 3 and 4: but does that compensate for it? From the principles established in the *Social Contract*, one sees that, in spite of common opinion, alliances of State to State, declarations of War, and treaties of peace are not acts of sovereignty but of Government, and this sentiment is in conformity with the practice of the Nations who have best known the true principles of political Right. The external exercise of Power does not suit the People at all; the great maxims of State are not within its reach; on these it ought to rely on its leaders who, always more enlightened than it on this point, have hardly any interest in making treaties outside that are disadvantageous to the fatherland; order wishes it to leave all external show to them and attach itself solely to the solid. What matters essentially to each Citizen is the observation of the Laws inside, the property of belongings, the safety of private individuals. As long as everything goes well on these three points, let the Councils negotiate and treat with foreign affairs; it is not from there that your dangers most to be feared will come. It is around individuals that the rights of the People must be gathered together, and when one can attack it separately one always subjugates it. I could cite the wisdom of the Romans who, leaving to the Senate a great power outside, in the Town forced it to respect the lowest Citizen; but let's not go so far to look for models. The Bourgeois of Neuchâtel have conducted themselves much more wisely under their Princes than you have under your Magistrates.* They make neither peace nor war, they do not ratify treaties; but they enjoy their franchises in safety; and, since the Law has not presumed that in a small Town a small number of honest Bourgeois would be scoundrels, inside their walls one does not reclaim,[54] one is not even acquainted with the odious right of imprisoning without formalities. Among you one always allowed oneself to be seduced by appearances, and one has neglected the essential. One was too occupied with the general Council, and not enough with its members: it was necessary to think less about authority, and more about liberty. Let us return to the general Councils.

Aside from the Limitations of Article III, Articles V and VI offer very

---

* This may be said setting aside the abuses, which assuredly I am very far from approving.

much stranger ones: a sovereign body that can neither form itself nor form any operation of itself, and absolutely subject, as to its activity and as to the matters it treats, to subordinate tribunals. Since these Tribunals will certainly not approve propositions that would be prejudicial to them in particular, if the interest of the State is found to be in conflict with theirs, the latter always has the preference, because the Legislator is not permitted to take cognizance of anything except what they approve.

As a result of subjecting everything to rule, one destroys the first of rules, which is justice and the public good. When will men feel that there is no disorder as fatal as the arbitrary power with which they think of remedying it? This power is itself the worst of all disorders: to use such a means to prevent them is to kill people so that they might not have a fever.

A large Host formed in tumult can do a lot of harm. In a numerous assembly, however regular it might be, if each person can say and propose what he wants, one loses much time in listening to foolishness and one can be in danger of acting foolishly. These are incontestable truths; but is it preventing the abuse in a reasonable manner to make this assembly depend solely on those who would like to destroy it, and to make it so that none can propose anything in it except those who have the greatest interest in harming it? For, Sir, isn't that exactly the state of things, and is there a single Genevan who can doubt that, if the existence of the general Council depended completely on the small Council, the general Council would be suppressed forever?

Nevertheless that is the Body that alone convokes these assemblies and that alone proposes what it pleases in them: for as for the Two-Hundred it does nothing but repeat the orders of the small Council, and when the latter is once freed from the general Council the Two-Hundred will hardly encumber it; it will only follow with it the path that it traced out with you.

Now what do I have to fear from an inconvenient superior that I never need, that can show itself only when I allow it to, nor respond except when I interrogate it? When I have reduced it to this point can't I regard myself as freed from it?

If one says that the Law of the State has prevented the abolition of the general Councils by making them necessary for the election of the Magistrates and for sanctioning new Edicts; I answer, as to the first point, that, all the force of the Government having passed from the hands of the Magistrates elected by the People into those of the small Council which it does not elect at all and from which are drawn the principal ones of these Magistrates, the election and assembly in which it occurs are nothing more than a vain formality without solidity; and that general Councils held for that sole object can be regarded as null. I also answer that from the turn things are taking it would even be easy to evade this Law without the course of business being stopped by it: for let us assume that, either by the rejection of all the subjects presented, or under other pretexts, the election of the Syndics does not take place, won't the Council, into which their jurisdiction imperceptibly merges, exercise it in default of them, as it exercises it independently of them even now? Don't they dare already to tell you that the small Council, even without the Syndics, is the Government? Thus without the Syndics the State will not be any less governed. And as to new Edicts, I answer that they will never be sufficiently necessary for this same Council not to find the means to take their place easily with the aid of the old ones and its usurpations. Anyone who sets himself above the old Laws can very well do without new ones.

All the measures have been taken so that your general Assemblies might never be necessary. Not only has the periodical Council, instituted or rather re-established* in the year 1707, only been held one time and only in order to abolish it,** but by paragraph 5 of the third Article of the settlement it has been provided for without you and forever at the expense of the administration. There is only the chimerical case of an unavoidable war in which the general Council absolutely must be convoked.

Thus the small Council would be able absolutely to suppress the general Councils without any other inconvenience than to draw upon itself some remonstrances that it is in a position to rebuff, or to stir up some vain murmuring that it can disdain without risk; for by articles VII, XXIII, XXIV, XXV, XLIII, every sort of resistance is forbidden in any case whatsoever, and the resources that are outside of the constitution do not make up a part of it and do not correct its defects.

It does not do this, however, because at bottom that is very indifferent to it, and because a simulacrum of liberty causes servitude to be endured more patiently. It amuses you at little cost, either by means of elections that are inconsequential as to the power they confer and as to the choice of subjects elected, or by means of Laws that appear important, but that it takes care to render vain, by observing them only as much as it pleases to.

Moreover one cannot propose anything in these assemblies, one can-

---

* These periodical Councils are as old as the Legislation, as one sees from the final Article of the ecclesiastical Ordinance. In that of 1576 printed in 1735 these Councils are fixed at every five years; but in the Ordinance of 1561 printed in 1562 they were fixed at every three years. It is not reasonable to say that these Councils had as their object only the reading of that Ordinance, since the printing that was made of it at the same time gave each person the ability to read it any time at his leisure, without the device of a general Council being needed only for that. Unfortunately they have taken great care to efface many old traditions that would now be very useful for the clarification of the Edicts.

** I shall examine this Edict of abolition below.

not discuss anything in them, one cannot deliberate over anything in them. The small Council presides in them, both by itself and by the Syndics who bring only the corporate spirit into them. Even there it is still Magistrate and master of its Sovereign. Isn't it contrary to all reason that the executive body rule the public order of the Legislative body, that it prescribe to it the matters it must take cognizance of, that it forbid it the right of giving an opinion, and that it exercise its absolute power even in the acts made to hold it within limits?

That such a numerous body* needs supervision[55] and order, I grant it: But do not let this supervision and this order overturn the goal of its institution. Is it then a more difficult thing to establish rule without servitude among some hundreds of naturally serious and cold men, than it was at Athens, about which they speak to us, in the assembly of several

---

* Formerly general Councils were very frequent at Geneva, and everything of any importance that was done was brought there. In 1707 M. the Syndic Chouet said in a harangue that has become famous that in days gone by the weakness and the misfortune of the State came from that frequency; we will soon see what must be believed about this. He also insists upon the extreme increase in the number of members, which would today make that frequency impossible, affirming that formerly that assembly did not surpass two to three hundred, and that it is at present between thirteen and fourteen hundred. There is much exaggeration on both sides.

The oldest general Councils were at least between five and six hundred members; one would perhaps be rather at a loss to cite a single one of them that had only two or three hundred. In 1420 they counted 720 stipulants there for all the others, and shortly afterward two hundred more Bourgeois were received.

Although the Town of Geneva has become more commercial and richer, it has not been able to become much more populated, the fortifications not having allowed the enclosure of its walls to be increased in size and having had its suburbs razed. Besides, almost without territory and at the mercy of its neighbors for its subsistence, it would not have been able to increase its size without weakening itself. In 1404 they counted thirteen hundred hearths there making up at least thirteen thousand souls. There are hardly more than twenty thousand of them today; a ratio very far from that of 3 to 14. Now from this number must further be deducted that of the natives, inhabitants, foreigners, who do not enter the general Council; a number very much increased relative to that of the Bourgeois since the refuge of the French and the progress of industry. Some general councils in our days have gone to fourteen and even to fifteen hundred; but usually they do not approach that number; if some of them even go to thirteen, this is only on critical occasions when all good Citizens would believe they were not keeping their oath to be absent, and when the Magistrates, on their side, have their clients come from outside in order to favor their maneuvers; now these maneuvers, unknown in the fifteenth century did not then demand such expedients. Generally the ordinary number fluctuates from eight to nine hundred; sometimes it remains beneath that of the year 1420, above all when the assembly is held in the summer and it is a question of rather unimportant things. I myself assisted in 1754 at a general Council that was certainly not seven hundred members.

From these various considerations it results that, all things weighed, the general Council is today, with regard to number, just about what it was two or three centuries ago, or at least that the difference is not very considerable. Nevertheless everyone spoke in them then; the public order and decency that are seen to reign in them today were not established. Sometimes they shouted; but the people was free, the Magistrate respected, and the Council was frequently assembled. Thus M. the Syndic Chouet accused falsely, and reasoned badly.

thousands of quick-tempered, ardent, and almost unrestrained Citizens; than it was in the Capital of the world, where the People in a body exercised in part the executive Power, and than it is even today in the great Council of Venice, as numerous as your general Council? They complain about the lack of public order[56] that reigns in the Parliament of England; and yet in that body composed of more than seven hundred members, in which such great affairs are treated, in which so many interests clash, in which so many cabals are fomented, in which so many heads become overheated, in which each member has the right to speak, everything is done, everything is expedited, that great Monarchy goes along as usual; and among you where the interests are so simple, so uncomplicated, where one has, so to speak, only the business of a family to regulate, they make you scared of storms as if everything was going to be overturned! Sir, the public order of your general Council is the easiest thing in the world; let them sincerely wish to establish it for the public good, then everything will be free there, and everything will take place there more tranquilly than today.

Let us assume that in the Settlement they had taken the opposite method from the one they did follow; that, instead of fixing the Rights of the general Council, they had fixed those of the other Councils, which by that very thing would have shown its rights; agree that one would have found in the small Council alone an assemblage of powers that are very strange for a free and democratic State, in leaders whom the People did not choose and who remain in office their whole life.

First the union of two things that are incompatible everywhere else; namely, the administration of affairs of State and the supreme exercise of justice over the goods, the life, and the honor of the Citizens.

An Order, the last of all from its rank and the first from its power.

An inferior Council without which everything is dead in the Republic; which alone proposes, which decides first, and whose voice alone, even in its own cause, permits its superiors to have one.

One Body that recognizes the authority of another one, and that alone has the nomination of the members of this body to which it is subordinated.

A supreme Tribunal from which one appeals; or rather on the contrary, an inferior Judge who presides in Tribunals superior to his own.

Who, after having sat as inferior Judge in the Tribunal from which one appeals, not only goes to sit as supreme Judge in the Tribunal to which appeal is made, but in this supreme Tribunal has only the colleagues whom he has chosen himself.

Finally, an Order that alone has its own activity, that gives theirs to all the others, that in all of them, supporting the resolutions it has taken, gives an opinion two times and votes three times.*

The appeal from the small Council to the Two-Hundred is genuine child's play. It is a farce in politics, if there ever was one. Hence this appeal is not properly called an appeal; it is a favor one implores in justice, a recourse to quashing of a warrant; one does not understand what it is. Does one believe that if the small Council did not feel very well that this final recourse was inconsequential, it would willingly have stripped itself of it as it did? This disinterestedness is not among its maxims.

If the judgments of the small Council are not always confirmed in the Two-Hundred, it is in particular and contradictory affairs in which it hardly matters to the Magistrate which of the two Parties loses or wins his trial. But in the affairs that are pursued *ex officio*, in every affair in which the Council itself takes an interest, does the Two-Hundred ever set right its injustices, does it ever protect the oppressed, does it dare not to confirm everything the Council has done, has it ever honorably made use of its right to pardon a single time? I recall with regret times whose memory is terrible and necessary. A Citizen whom the Council immolates to its vengeance has recourse to the Two-Hundred; the unfortunate man debases himself to the point of asking for pardon; his innocence is unknown to no one; all the rules had been violated in his trial: pardon is refused, and the innocent man perished.[57] Fatio felt the uselessness of recourse to the Two-Hundred so well that he did not even deign to make use of it.

I see clearly what the Two-Hundred is at Zurich, at Berne, at Fribourg, and in the other aristocratic States; but I cannot see what it is in your Constitution nor what place it holds there.[58] Is it a superior Tribunal? In that case, it is absurd that the inferior Tribunal sits on it. Is it a body that represents the Sovereign? In this case it is up to the Represented to name its Representative. The establishment of the Two-Hundred can have no other

---

* In a State that governs itself as a Republic and in which they speak the French tongue, a separate language would have to be made for the Government. For example, *To Deliberate, To Give an Opinion, To Vote*, are three very different things that the French do not distinguish enough. *To Deliberate* is to weigh the pro and the con; *To Give an Opinion* is to state one's advice and to give the reasons for it; *To Vote* is one's suffrage, when nothing is left to do but to collect the votes. First the matter is put into deliberation. On the first round one gives one's opinion; one votes on the last round. Everywhere Tribunals have just about the same forms, but since in Monarchies the public does not need to learn their terms, they remain consecrated to the Bar. It is out of another imprecision of the Language in these matters that M. de Montesquieu, who knew it so well, did not omit to say always *the executrix Power*, wounding analogy in doing so, and making the word, *executor*, which is a substantive, into an adjective. It is the same fault as if he had said: *the legislator Power*.

aim than to moderate the enormous power of the small Council; and on the contrary, it only gives more weight to that very power. Now every Body that constantly acts contrary to the spirit of its Institution is badly instituted.

What does it serve to dwell here on notorious things that are unknown to no Genevan? The Two-Hundred is nothing by itself; it is only the small Council which reappears under another form. A single time it wanted to try to throw off the yoke of its masters and to give itself an independent existence, and by this single effort the State was almost overturned. It is only from the general Council alone that the Two-Hundred still owe an appearance of authority. This was seen very clearly in the period about which I am speaking, and it will be seen even better in what follows, if the small Council succeeds in its goal: thus when the Two-Hundred works in concert with the latter to put down the general Council, it is working toward its own ruin, and if it believes it is following the lead of the Two-Hundred of Berne, it is being grossly led astray; but almost always little enlightenment and less courage has been seen in this Body, and that can hardly be otherwise from the manner in which it is filled.*

You see, Sir, how much more useful it would have been, instead of specifying the rights of the Sovereign Council, to specify the attributions of the bodies that are subordinate to it, and without going any farther, you see even more evidently that, by the force of certain articles taken separately, the small Council is the supreme arbiter of the Laws and by means of them of the fate of all the private individuals. When one considers the rights of the Citizens and Bourgeois assembled in general Council, nothing is more brilliant: But consider those same Citizens and Bourgeois outside of it as individuals; what are they, what are they becoming? Slaves to an arbitrary power, they are abandoned without defense to the mercy of twenty-five Despots; at least the Athenians had thirty of them.[59] What am I saying, twenty-five? Nine are enough for a civil judgment, thirteen for

---

* This is to be understood in general and only about the corporate spirit: for I know that there are very enlightened members who do not lack zeal in the Two-Hundred: but ceaselessly under the eyes of the small Council, given over to its mercy without support, without resource, and feeling very well that they would be abandoned by their Body, they abstain from attempting useless proceedings that would only compromise them and ruin them. The ignoble rabble buzzes and triumphs. The wise man keeps silent and moans under his breath.

Besides, the Two-Hundred has not always been in the discredit into which it has fallen. Formerly it enjoyed public consideration and the confidence of the Citizens: therefore without anxiety they let it exercise the rights of the general Council, which the small Council attempted from that time onward to draw to itself by that indirect method. A new proof of what will be said below, that the Bourgeoisie of Geneva is not very turbulent and hardly seeks to meddle in affairs of State.

a criminal judgment.* Seven or eight of this number in agreement are going to be as many Decemvirs for you; still the Decemvirs were elected by the people; instead of which none of these judges is of your choice; and that is called being free!

---

* Civil Edicts, Title I. Article XXXVI.

Eighth Letter

I have drawn, Sir, the examination of your present Government from the Settlement of the Mediation by which this Government is fixed; but far from imputing that the Mediators wanted to reduce you to servitude, I would easily prove on the contrary that in several respects they rendered your situation better than it was before the troubles that forced you to accept their good offices. They found a Town in arms; at their arrival everything was in a condition of crisis and confusion, which did not allow them to draw the rule for their work from that condition. They went back to peaceful times, they studied the primitive constitution of your Government; given the course of development it had followed, in order to set it back up it was necessary to refound it: reason, equity did not allow them to give you a different one, and you would not have accepted it. Thus, not being able to remove its defects, they limited their efforts to strengthening it as your fathers had left it; they even corrected it in various points, and of the abuses I just noted, there is not one that did not exist in the Republic long before the Mediators took cognizance of it. The only wrong they seem to have done you was to remove from the Legislator all exercise of the executive power and the use of force for the support of justice; but by giving you a resource that is as sure and more legitimate, they changed this apparent evil into a true benefit: By making themselves guarantor of your rights they have dispensed you from defending them yourselves. Ah! in the misery of human things what good is worth the trouble of being purchased with the blood of our brothers? Even liberty is too expensive at this price.

The Mediators might have deceived themselves, they were men; but they did not want to deceive you; they wanted to be just. That is seen, that is even proven; and everything shows, in effect, that what is equivocal or defective in their work often comes from necessity, sometimes from error, never from ill will. They had to reconcile almost incompatible things, the rights of the People and the pretensions of the Council, the empire of the Laws and the power of men, the independence of the State and the guarantee of the Settlement. All that could not be done without a little contradiction, and it is this contradiction that your Magistrates take advantage of, by turning everything in their favor, and making half of your Laws serve for violating the other half.

It is clear at first that the Settlement itself is not at all a Law that the Mediators wanted to impose on the Republic, but only an agreement they established among its members, and that they consequently did not make any attempt against its sovereignty. That is clear, I say, from Article XLIV,[60] which leaves to the General Council legitimately assembled the right to make whatever change it pleases to the articles of the Settlement. Thus the Mediators did not at all put their will above its own; they intervene only in case of division. That is the sense of Article XV.[61]

But from that results also the nullity of the reservations and limitations given in Article III[62] to the rights and attributions of the General Council: for if the General Council decides that these reservations and limitations will not limit its power any longer, they will not limit it any longer; and when all the members of a sovereign State regulate its power over themselves, who has the right to oppose it? The exclusions that one can infer from Article II thus do not signify anything other than that the General Council restricts itself within their limits until it finds it appropriate to exceed them.

Here is one of the contradictions I have spoken about, and the cause of which one will easily unravel. Moreover it was very difficult for the Plenipotentiaries, full of entirely different maxims of Government, to fathom the true principles of yours. Up to the present the democratic Constitution has been poorly examined. All those who have spoken about it either did not know it, or took too little interest in it, or had an interest in presenting it in a false light. None of them have sufficiently distinguished the Sovereign from the Government, the legislative Power from the executive. There is no State in which these two powers are so separate, and in which people have so affected to mix them up. Some imagine that a Democracy is a Government in which the whole People is Magistrate and Judge. Others do not see liberty except in the right to elect one's leaders, and (being subject only to Princes) believe that the one who commands is always the Sovereign. The democratic Constitution is certainly the Masterpiece of the political art: but the more admirable its artifice is, the less it belongs to all eyes to penetrate it. Isn't it true, Sir, that the first precaution of not admitting any legitimate general Council except under the convocation of the small Council, and the second precaution of not allowing any proposal except with the approval of the small Council, are enough by themselves to maintain the general Council in the most complete dependency? The third precaution of regulating the competence of matters there was, then, the most superfluous thing in the world; and what would have been the inconvenience of leaving the plenitude of the supreme rights to the general Council, since it cannot make any use of it except to the extent that the small Council allows it to? By not limiting the rights of the sovereign Power they did not render it any less dependent in fact and they avoided a contradiction: which proves that it is because they did not know your Constitution very well that they took precautions that were vain in themselves and contradictory in their object.

It will be said that the only end of these limitations was to mark out the cases in which the inferior Councils would be obliged to assemble the general Council. I understand that very well; but wasn't it more natural and simple to mark out by themselves the rights that were attributed to them, and which they could exercise without the cooperation of the general Council? Were the limits less fixed by what is on one side than by what is on the other, and when the inferior Councils wanted to exceed these limits, isn't it clear that they needed to be authorized to do so? From that, I admit it, one made more visible so many powers gathered together in the same hands, but one presented the objects in their genuine light, one drew from the nature of the thing the means of fixing the respective rights of various bodies, and one prevented every contradiction.

In truth the Author of the Letters claims that, since the small Council is the Government, by this title it even ought to exercise all the authority that is not attributed to other bodies of the State; but that assumes its own to be prior to the Edicts; that assumes that the small Council—primitive source of the power—this way keeps all the rights that it has not alienated. Do you recognize, Sir, the principle of your Constitution in this one? Such a curious proof deserves to stop us for a moment.

Note to begin with that there* it is a question of the power of the small Council, set into opposition with that of the Syndics, that is to say, of each of these two powers separated from the other. The Edict speaks about the power of the Syndics without the Council, it does not speak at all about the power of the Council without the Syndics. Why so? Because the Council without the Syndics is the Government. Thus, far from proving the nullity of this power, the very silence of the Edicts about the power of the Council proves its extent. There, doubtless, is a very new conclusion. Let us admit it, however, provided that the antecedent be proven.

If it is because the small Council is the Government that the Edicts do not speak at all about its power, at least they will say that the small Council is the Government; unless from proof to proof their silence always establishes the opposite of what they have said.

Now I ask to be shown in your Edicts where it is said that the small Council is the Government, and while waiting I myself am going to show

---

* *Letters Written from the Country*, page 66.

you where exactly the opposite is said. In the political Edict of 1568, I find the preamble worded in these terms. *Because the Government and the State of this Town consists in four Syndics, the Council of the twenty-five, the Council of the sixty, of the Two-Hundred, of the General, and a Lieutenant in ordinary justice with other Offices, in accordance with what good public order requires, both for the administration of the public good as for justice, we have recollected the order that has been observed until now . . . so that it might be kept in the future . . . as follows.*

From the first article of the Edict of 1738, I also see that *five Orders compose the Government of Geneva*. Now of these five Orders the four Syndics all by themselves make up one; the Council of the twenty-five, in which are certainly included the four Syndics, makes up another; and the Syndics also enter into the three following. The small Council without the Syndics, thus, is not the Government.

I open the Edict of 1707, and I see there at Article V in express terms, that *Messieurs the Syndics have the direction and the Government of the State*. Immediately I close the Book and I say: certainly according to the Edicts the small Council without the Syndics is not the Government, even though the Author of the Letters affirms that it is.

It will be said that I myself often attribute the Government to the small Council in these Letters. I agree; but it is to the small Council presided over by the Syndics; and then it is certain that the provisional Government does reside there in the meaning that I give to this word: but this meaning is not that of the Author of the Letters; since in mine the Government has only the powers that are given to it by the Law, and in his, on the contrary, the Government has all the powers that the Law does not take away from it.

Thus the objection of the Remonstrators that, when the Edict speaks about the Syndics, it is speaking about their power, and that, when it speaks about the Council, it is speaking only about its duty, remains in all its force. I say that this objection remains in all its force; for the Author of the Letters responds to it only with an assertion belied by all the Edicts. If I am mistaken, Sir, you will do me the pleasure of teaching me in what respect my reasoning sins.

Nevertheless this Author, very satisfied with his own reasoning, asks how, *if the Legislator had not considered the small Council in this way, one could conceive that in no place in the Edict does he regulate its authority; that he supposes it everywhere and that he defines it nowhere?* *

I will dare to attempt to clarify this profound mystery. The Legislator

---

* *Letters Written from the Country*, page 67.

does not regulate the power of the Council at all, because he does not give it any independent of the Syndics, and when he does assume it, it is while supposing it also presided over by them. He did define theirs, consequently it is superfluous to define its. The Syndics cannot do everything without the Council, but the Council cannot do anything without the Syndics; it is nothing without them, it is less than the Two-Hundred even when it was presided over by the Auditor Sarrizin.[63]

There, I believe, is the only reasonable manner of explaining the silence of the Edicts about the power of the Council; but it is not the one it suits the Magistrates to adopt. Their singular interpretations might have been prevented in the settlement if an opposite method had been taken, and if, instead of taking note of the right of the general Council, theirs had been defined. But for not having wanted to say what the Edicts did not say, they have caused to be understood what the Edicts never assumed.

How many things contrary to the public liberty and to the rights of the Citizens and Bourgeois are here, and how many more of them couldn't I add? Nevertheless all these disadvantages, which were given birth to or seemed to be given birth to by your Constitution and which could not have been destroyed without unsettling it, have been balanced and mended with the greatest wisdom by means of compensations that were also given birth to by it, and such was precisely the intention of the Mediators, which, according to their own declaration, was *to preserve to each his rights, his peculiar attributions deriving from the fundamental Law of the State*. M. Micheli Du Cret, embittered by misfortunes against that work in which he was forgotten, accuses it of subverting the fundamental institution of the Government, of despoiling the Citizens and Bourgeois of their rights; without wanting to see how much these rights, both public and private, have been preserved or re-established by that Edict, in Articles III, IV, X, XI, XII, XXII, XXX, XXXI, XXXII, XXXIV, XLII, and XLIV; without considering above all that the force of all these Articles depends on a single one, which has also been preserved for you. An essential Article, an Article equiponderant[64] to all those that are against you, and so necessary to the effect of those that are favorable to you that they would all be useless if someone succeeded in eluding that one, as they have attempted to. Here we have arrived at the important point; but in order to feel its importance well we must weigh everything that I have just shown.

Many attempts have been made to confuse independence and liberty. These two things are so different that they are even mutually exclusive. When each does what he pleases, he often does what displeases others, and that is not called a free state. Liberty consists less in doing one's will than in not being subject to someone else's; it also consists in not subjecting someone else's will to ours. Whoever is master cannot be free, and to rule is to obey. Your Magistrates know that better than anyone, those who like Otho[65] omit nothing servile in order to command.* I know no truly free will other than the one to which no one has the right to oppose resistance; in common freedom no one has the right to what the liberty of another forbids him, and true liberty is never self-destructive. Thus liberty without justice is a genuine contradiction; for however one sets about it, everything hinders the execution of an ill-regulated will.

Thus there is no liberty without Laws, nor where someone is above the Laws: in the very state of nature man is free only under cover of the natural Law that commands everyone. A free people obeys, but it does not serve; it has leaders and not masters; it obeys the Laws, but it obeys only the Laws and it is from the force of the Laws that it does not obey men. All the barriers that are given in Republics to the power of the Magistrates are established only to protect the sacred precinct of the Laws from their attacks: they are their Ministers not their arbiters, they ought to protect them, not break them. A People is free, whatever form its Government has, when in the one who governs it one does not see the man, but the organ of the Law. In a word, liberty always follows the fate of the Laws, it reigns or perishes with them; I do not know anything more certain.

You have good and wise Laws, either in themselves, or by the sole fact that they are Laws. Every condition imposed on each by all cannot be onerous to anyone, and the worst of Laws is worth even more than the best master; for every master has preferences, and the Law never has any.

Since the Constitution of your State took on a fixed and stable form, your functions of Legislator have ended. At present the safety of the edifice requires that one find as many obstacles to touching it as at first were needed opportunities for constructing it. Taken in this sense, the negative right of the Councils is the support of the Republic: Article VI of the Settlement is clear and precise; on this point I accept the arguments of the Author of the Letters, I find them to be unanswerable, and when this right so justly claimed by your Magistrates is contrary to your interests, you

---

* *In general*, says the Author of the Letters, *men fear to obey more than they love to command*. Tacitus judged differently about it and knew the human heart. If the maxim were true, the Valets of the Great would be less insolent with the Bourgeois, and one would see fewer good-for-nothings groveling in the Courts of Princes. Few men have healthy enough hearts to be able to love liberty: All wish to command, and at that price none fear to obey. A little upstart gives himself a hundred masters in order to acquire ten valets. One has only to see the pride of the nobles in Monarchies; with what emphasis they pronounce those words of *service* and *serve*; how great and respectable they esteem themselves when they can have the honor of saying, *the King my master*; how much they despise Republicans who are only free, and who are certainly more noble than they are.

have to suffer and remain silent. Upright men ought never to close their eyes to the evidence, nor dispute against the truth.

The work has been consummated, it is no longer a question of anything but making it unchangeable. Now the work of the Legislator is never changed and destroyed except in one manner; that is when the depositaries of this work abuse what has been entrusted to them, and make themselves obeyed in the name of the Laws while disobeying them themselves.* Then the worst thing is born from the best, and the Law that serves as the safeguard of Tyranny is more fatal than Tyranny itself. This is precisely what is anticipated by the right of Remonstrance, stipulated in your Edicts and restrained but confirmed by the Mediation. This right gives you inspection, no longer over Legislation as previously, but over administration; and your Magistrates, all powerful in the name of the Laws, sole masters of proposing new ones to the Legislator, are subject to its judgments if they deviate from the ones that are established. By this Article alone your Government, otherwise subject to several considerable defects, becomes the best that has ever existed: for what better Government is there than the one whose parties are all balanced in a perfect equilibrium, in which private individuals cannot transgress the Laws because they are subject to Judges, and in which the Judges cannot transgress them either, because they are watched over by the People?

It is true that in order to find some reality in this advantage it must not be founded upon a vain right: but whoever says a right does not say something vain. To tell the one who has transgressed the Law that he has transgressed the Law is to make a very ridiculous effort; it is to teach him a thing that he knows as well as you do.

According to Puffendorf, right is a moral quality by which something is due to us.[66] Thus the simple liberty to complain is not a right, or at least it is a right that nature grants to everyone, and that the Law of no country deprives anyone of. Did anyone take it into his head to stipulate in the Laws that the one who loses a proceeding would have the liberty of complaining? Did anyone ever take it into his head to punish anyone for having done so? Where is the Government, however absolute it might be, in which every Citizen does not have the right to give memoranda to the

---

* Never has the People rebelled against the Laws when the Leaders did not begin by breaking them in some respect. It is upon this certain principle that, when there is some revolt in a Province in China, they always begin by punishing the Governor. In Europe Kings constantly follow the opposite maxim, therefore see how their States prosper! Everywhere the population diminishes by a tenth every thirty years; it does not diminish at all in China. Oriental Despotism maintains itself because it is more severe over the Great than over the People: thus it draws from itself its own remedy. I have heard it said that they have begun to adopt the Christian maxim at the Porte. If that is true, what will result from it will be seen in a short time.

Prince or to his Minister about what he believes to be useful to the State, and what jeering wouldn't be stirred up by a public Edict by which one explicitly granted to the subjects the right to give such memoranda? Nevertheless this is not in a despotic State, it is in a Republic, it is in a Democracy, that one gives authentically to the Citizens, to the members of the Sovereign, permission to use with their body of Magistrates the same right that no Despot ever dared to take away from the least of his slaves.

What! This right of Remonstrance would consist solely in delivering a paper that they are even dispensed from reading, by the means of a curtly negative response?* This right so solemnly stipulated in compensation for so many sacrifices would be limited to the rare prerogative of asking and obtaining nothing? To dare to advance such a proposition is to accuse the Mediators of having employed with the Bourgeoisie of Geneva the most unworthy fraud, it is to insult the probity of the Plenipotentiaries, the equity of the mediating Powers; it is to wound all decorum, it is even to outrage good sense.

But in the end what is this right? How far does it extend? How can it be exercised? Why isn't any of that specified in Article VII? Those are reasonable questions; they offer difficulties that deserve examination.

The solution of a single one will give us that of all the others, and we will unveil the genuine spirit of this institution.

In a State such as yours, where the sovereignty is in the hands of the People, the Legislator always exists, although it does not always show itself. It is assembled and speaks authentically only in the general Council; but outside of the general Council it is not annihilated; its members are scattered, but they are not dead; they cannot speak by means of Laws, but they can always keep watch over the administration of the Laws; this is a right, this is even a duty attached to their persons, and which cannot be taken away from them at any time. From that the right of Remonstrance. Thus the Remonstrance of a Citizen, of a Bourgeois, or of several is nothing but the declaration of their opinion on a matter within their competence. This is the clear and necessary sense of the Edict of 1707, in Article V which concerns Remonstrances.

In this Article the proceeding by signatures is reasonably proscribed, because this proceeding is a manner of giving one's suffrage, of voting by head as if one were already in General Council, and because the form of the general Council ought to be followed only when it is legitimately assembled. The proceeding of Remonstrances has the same advantage without the same inconvenience. This is not to vote in general Council,

* Such, for example, as the one the Council made August 10, 1763, to the Remonstrances delivered on the 8th to M. the first Syndic by a great number of Citizens and Bourgeois.

it is to state an opinion about matters that ought to be brought there; since one does not count the votes this is not to give one's suffrage, it is only to state one's opinion. This opinion is, in truth, only that of a private individual or of several; but since these private individuals are members of the Sovereign and can represent it sometimes by their multitude, reason wants one to pay respect to their opinion then, not as a decision, but as a proposition that demands a decision, and that sometimes makes one necessary.

These Remonstrances can turn on two principal objects, and the difference between these objects decides the several manners in which the Council ought to accede to these same Remonstrances. Of these two objects, one is to make some change in the Law, the other is to correct some transgression of the Law. This division is complete and comprehends the whole matter on which Remonstrances can turn. It is founded on the Edict itself when, distinguishing the terms in accordance with which these objects require the Procurer General to make *instances* or *remonstrances* depending on whether the Citizens have made *complaints* or *requisitions* to him.*

Once this distinction has been established, the Council to which these Remonstrances are addressed ought to envisage them very differently in accordance with the one of these two objects to which they relate. In States where the Government and the Laws are already established, one ought to avoid touching them as much as possible, and above all in small Republics, where the slightest disturbance sets everything at variance. Aversion for innovations is thus generally well founded; it is above all well founded for you who can only lose from them, and the Government cannot provide too great an obstacle to their establishment; for however useful new Laws might be, their advantages are almost always less certain than their dangers are great. In this regard when the Citizen, when the Bourgeois has proposed his opinion he has done his duty, he ought moreover to have enough confidence in his Magistrate to judge him capable of weighing the advantage of what he proposes to him and inclined to approve it if he believes it useful to the public good. Thus the Law has very wisely provided that the establishment and even the proposing of such innovations would not pass without the approval of the Councils, and

---

* *To Require* is not only to demand, but to demand in virtue of a right one has to obtain. This meaning is established by all the judicial formulas in which this term of Lawcourts is used. One says *to require justice*; one never says *to require grace*. Thus in the two cases equally the Citizens have the right to demand that their *requisitions* or their *complaints*, rejected by the inferior Councils, be brought into the general Council. But by the word added in Article VI of the Edict of 1738, this right is limited only to the case of complaint, as will be said in the text.

that is what the negative right they lay claim to consists of, which, according to me, incontestably belongs to them.

But the second object, having a completely opposite principle, ought to be envisaged very differently. It is not a question here of innovating; on the contrary it is a question of preventing anyone from innovating; it is not a question of establishing new Laws, but of maintaining the old ones. When things are tending to change by their bent, new efforts are ceaselessly necessary to stop them. That is what the Citizens and Bourgeois, who have such a great interest in preventing all change, propose in the complaints about which the Edict speaks. The Legislator, existing always, sees the effect or the abuse of its laws: it sees whether they are followed or transgressed, interpreted in good or in bad faith; it watches over it; it ought to watch over it; that is its right, its duty, even its sworn oath. It is this duty it fulfills in Remonstrances, it is this right, then, that it exercises; and it would be against all reason, it would even be indecent, to wish to extend the negative right of the Council to that object.

That would be against all reason, as to the Legislator; because then all the solemnity of the Laws would be vain and ridiculous, and because the State would not really have any other Law at all than the will of the small Council, absolute master of neglecting, despising, violating, turning in its fashion the rules that would be prescribed to it, and to pronounce *black* where the Law would say *white*, without answering to anyone for it. What good would it do to assemble solemnly in the Temple of Saint Peter, in order to give to the Edicts a sanction without effect; in order to say to the small Council: *Gentlemen, behold the Body of Laws that we establish in the State, and of which we make you the depositories, in order for you to conform to it when you judge it appropriate, and in order to transgress it when you please.*

That would be against all reason as to Remonstrances. Because then the right stipulated by an express Article of the Edict of 1707 and confirmed by an express Article of the Edict of 1738 would be an illusory and fallacious right that would signify only the liberty of complaining uselessly when one is vexed; a liberty that, never having been disputed by anyone, is ridiculous to establish by Law.

Finally that would be indecent in that by such a supposition the probity of the Mediators would be insulted, in that this would be to take your Magistrates for cheats and your Bourgeois for dupes for having negotiated, treated, compounded with so much display in order to put one of the Parties at the entire discretion of the other, and for having compensated the concessions of the stronger by securities that would signify nothing.

But, say these Gentlemen, the terms of the Edict are explicit: *Nothing will be brought to the general Council that has not been treated and approved, first in the Council of the Twenty-Five, then in that of the Two-Hundred.*

First, what does that prove that is relevant to the present question, other than that this is a regulated proceeding in conformity with Order, and the obligation in the inferior Councils of treating and approving preliminarily what is to be brought to the general Council? Aren't the Councils bound to approve what is prescribed by Law? What! If the Councils did not approve proceeding to the election of the Syndics, should one no longer proceed to it, and if the subjects they do propose are rejected, aren't they constrained to approve whichever ones might be proposed by others?

Moreover, who does not see that this right of approving and of rejecting, taken in its absolute sense, is applied only to propositions that contain innovations, and not to those that have as their object only the maintenance of what is established? Do you find any good sense in assuming that a new approval is necessary to correct transgressions of an old Law? In the approval given to that Law when it was promulgated are contained all those that relate to its execution: When the Councils approved that that Law would be established, they approved that it would be observed, consequently that its transgressors would be punished; and when the Bourgeois in their complaints limit themselves to demanding reparation without punishment, is it expected that such a proposal needs to be approved anew? Sir, if that is not to make a mockery of people, tell me how one can make a mockery of them?

All the difficulty here, then, consists in the question of fact alone. Has the Law been transgressed, or hasn't it? The Citizens and Bourgeois say that it has been; the Magistrates deny it. Now see, I beg you, if one can conceive anything less reasonable in such a case than this negative right that they are appropriating for themselves? One says to them, "You have transgressed the Law." They answer, "We have not transgressed it"; and having in this way become supreme judges in their own case, behold them justified against the evidence by their affirmation alone.

You will ask me whether I claim that the contrary affirmation is always evidence? I do not say that; I say that when it is, your Magistrates would not stick any less to their claimed negative right against the evidence. The case is under your eyes at present; and for whom ought the most legitimate prejudice be here? Is it believable, is it natural that private individuals without power, without authority might come to say to their Magistrates who can be their Judges tomorrow: *you have committed an injustice*, when that isn't true? What can these private citizens hope from such a foolish step, even if they were sure of impunity? Can they think that Magistrates, who are so haughty even in their wrongs, will stupidly even acknowledge wrongs they would not have committed? On the contrary, is there anything more natural than to deny the faults one has committed? Doesn't one have an interest in supporting them, and isn't one always tempted to do it when one can do so with impunity and one is in a position of strength? When the weak and the strong have some dispute together, which hardly happens except to the detriment of the former, the most probable sentiment from that fact alone is that it is the stronger who is in the wrong.

Probabilities, I know it, are not proofs: But in acknowledged facts in comparison to the Laws, when a number of Citizens affirm that there is injustice, and when the Magistrate accused of that injustice affirms that there isn't, who can be judge, if it is not the informed public, and where can this informed public be found at Geneva, if it is not in the general Council composed of the two parties?

There is no State in the world in which the subject wronged by an unjust magistrate cannot bring his complaint to the Sovereign by some route, and the fear that this resource inspires is a brake that holds back many iniquities. Even in France, where the attachment of the Parlements to the Laws is extreme, the judicial route is open against them in numerous cases by means of requests for quashing Decrees. The Genevans are deprived of a similar advantage; the Party condemned by the Councils can no longer, in any case whatsoever, have any recourse to the Sovereign: but what a private individual cannot do for his private interest, all can do for the common interest: for, since every transgression of the Laws is an attack made upon liberty, it becomes a public affair, and when the public voice is raised, the complaint ought to be brought to the Sovereign. If this were not the case, there would be neither Parlement, nor Senate, nor Tribunal on the earth that would be armed with the deadly power that your Magistrate dares to usurp; there would not be a fate in any State as harsh as yours. You will admit to me that this would be a strange liberty.

The right of Remonstrance is intimately linked to your constitution: it is the only possible means of uniting liberty to subordination, and of maintaining the body of Magistrates in dependency on the Laws without altering its authority over the people. If the complaints are clearly founded, if the reasons are palpable, one ought to presume the Council to be equitable enough to defer to them. If it isn't, or the grievances do not have that degree of evidence that puts them beyond doubt, the case would change, and it would then be up to the general will to decide; for in your State that will is the supreme Judge and the unique Sovereign. Now since from the beginning of the Republic this will always had the means of making itself understood and these means pertained to your Constitution, it follows that the Edict of 1707, founded moreover on an immemorial right and on the constant exercise of this right, did not need any greater explanation.

Having as their fundamental maxim to set aside the old Edicts as little as was possible, the Mediators left this Article as it was before, and even referred to it. Thus by the Settlement of the Mediation your right on this point has remained perfectly the same, since the Article that posited it is entirely recalled.

But the Mediators did not see that the changes they were forced to make to other Articles obliged them to be consistent, to clarify this one, and to add to it new explanations that their labor made necessary. The effect of the neglect of Remonstrances of private individuals is that these Remonstrances finally become the voice of the public and thus provide against the denial of justice. This transformation, then, was legitimate and in conformity with the fundamental Law, which, in every country in the last resort arms the Sovereign with the public force for the execution of what it wills.

The Mediators did not provide for this denial of justice. The event proves that they should have done so. In order to secure public tranquillity, they judged it appropriate to separate power from the Right and suppress even peaceful assemblies and deputations of the bourgeoisie; but since they otherwise confirmed its right, in the form of the institution, they should have provided the bourgeoisie with other means of enforcing its right in place of the ones they took away from it: they did not do this. In this regard, thus, their work has remained defective; for the right, having remained the same, ought still to have the same effects.

Also see with what art your Magistrates took advantage of the oversight of the Mediators! However numerous you might be, they no longer see in you anything but private individuals, and since you have been forbidden to show yourselves in a body, they regard this body as annihilated: it is not, however, since it preserves all its rights, all its privileges, and since it still makes up the principal part of the State and of the Legislator. They depart from this false assumption in order to make a thousand chimerical difficulties for you over the authority that can oblige them to assemble the general Council. There is no authority that can do it aside from that of the Laws, when they observe them: but the authority of the Law, which they are transgressing, returns to the Legislator; and not daring to deny completely that in such a case this authority resides in the greater number, they gather together their objections over the means of verifying it. These means will always be easy as soon as they are permitted, and they will be without inconvenience, since it is easy to prevent their abuse.

Eighth Letter (Pl., III, 850–852)

There was no question there of tumults or of violence: there was no question of those resources sometimes necessary but always terrible, that have been very wisely forbidden to you. Not that you have ever abused them, since on the contrary you never used them except in the final extremity, only for your defense, and always with a moderation that perhaps ought to have preserved the right of arms for you, if any people could have it without danger. Whatever happens, I will always bless Heaven that one will no longer see that horrible display in your midst. *Everything is permitted in extreme evils*, the Author of the Letters says several times. Even if that were true, not everything would be expedient. When the excess of Tyranny puts the one who suffers it above the Laws, it is still necessary that what he attempts in order to destroy it leave him some hope of succeeding. Would you want to be reduced to that extremity? I cannot believe it, and if you were, I think even less that any violent assault could extract you from it. In your position every false step is fatal, everything that might lead you to take it is a trap, and if you were the masters for an instant, in less than fifteen days you would be crushed forever. Whatever your Magistrates might do, whatever the Author of the Letters might say, violent means do not suit the just cause: without believing that they want to force you to take them, I do believe that they would see you take them with pleasure; and I believe they ought not to make you envisage as a resource the one that could deprive you of all others. Justice and the Laws are for you; these supports, I know it, are very weak against influence and intrigue; but they are the only ones left to you: stick with them up to the end.

Eh! How would I approve someone wanting to disturb civil peace for any interest whatsoever, I who have sacrificed to it the dearest of all of mine? You know it, Sir, I was desired, solicited; I had only to appear; my rights would have been upheld; perhaps compensation given for my injuries. My presence would have at least perplexed my persecutors, and I was in one of those enviable positions, of which anyone who loves to play a role always avidly avails himself. I preferred perpetual exile from my fatherland; I renounced everything, even hope, rather than risk public tranquillity: I deserve to be believed to be sincere when I speak in favor of it.

But why suppress peaceful and purely civil assemblies, which can only have a legitimate object, since they always remain in the subordination due to the Magistrate? Why, leaving to the Bourgeoisie the right of making Remonstrances, not let it make them with seemly order and authenticity? Why deprive it of the means of deliberating within itself, in order to avoid excessively numerous assemblies, at least through its deputies? Can one imagine anything better regulated, more decent, and more seemly than the assemblies by companies[67] and the mode of behavior adapted by the Bourgeoisie when it was mistress of the State? Isn't the ascent of thirty deputies to the City Hall in the name of their Fellow Citizens a better version of public order than the ascent of an entire Bourgeoisie in a crowd, each having his own declaration to make, and none being able to speak except in his own behalf? You have seen, Sir, the Remonstrators in great number,[68] forced to divide themselves by packs in order not to cause tumult and crush, to come separately by groups of thirty or forty, and to put into their proceeding even more decorum and modesty than was prescribed to them by the Law. But such is the spirit of the Bourgeoisie of Geneva; always within rather than beyond its rights, it is sometimes firm, it is never seditious. Always the Law in its heart, always respect for the Magistrate under its eyes, at the very time in which the most lively indignation ought to enliven its anger, and in which nothing prevented it from satisfying it, it never abandoned itself to it. It was just when it was the stronger; it even knew how to pardon. Can as much be said of its oppressors? The fate they caused the Bourgeoisie to suffer previously is known; the one they are preparing for it is also known.

Such are the men truly worthy of liberty because they never abuse it, who are nevertheless burdened with bonds and shackles like the most base populace. Such are the Citizens, the members of the Sovereign, who are treated as subjects, and worse even than subjects; since in the most absolute Governments assemblies of communities that are not presided over by any Magistrate are permitted.

Contradictory regulations will never be able to be observed at the same time, as they go about it. They permit, they authorize the right of Remonstrance, and they reproach the Remonstrators for lacking consistency while preventing them from having any. That is not just, and when they make it impossible for you to take your steps as a body, they must not object to you that you are only private individuals. How do they not see that if the weight of the Remonstrances depends on the number of Remonstrators, it is impossible to make them one by one when they are general; and wouldn't the Magistrate be in a quandary if he had to read the Memoranda one after another or to listen to the speeches of a thousand men, as he is obliged to by the Law?

Here, then, is the easy solution of this great difficulty that the Author of the Letters insists is insoluble.* That when the Magistrate has paid no regard to the complaints of private individuals brought in Remonstrances, he permit the assembly of the bourgeois Companies; that he permit it

---

* Page 88.

separately in different places and times; that, by the plurality of votes, those Companies who want to support the Remonstrances do so by means of their Deputies. That the number of Deputies remonstrating then be counted; their total number be established; it will soon be seen whether their votes are or are not those of the State.

This does not signify, note well, that these partial assemblies can have any authority, except to make their sentiment about the matter of the Remonstrances be heard. As assemblies authorized for this case alone, they will not have any other right than that of private individuals; their object is not to change the Law but to judge whether it is being followed, nor to redress grievances but to show the need to provide for them. Even if it is unanimous their opinion will never be anything but a Remonstrance. It will be known only from that whether this Remonstrance deserves to be deferred to, either to assemble the general Council if the Magistrates approve it, or to dispense with it if they prefer, while by themselves acceding to the just complaints of the Citizens and Bourgeois.

This route is simple, natural, safe. It has no inconveniences. There is no new Law to make, there is only one Article to revoke for this case alone. Nevertheless if it still frightens your Magistrates too much, there remains another one no less easy, and which is not any newer: it is to re-establish the periodic general Councils, and to limit their object to complaints put into Remonstrances during the Interval elapsed from one to the other, without it being permitted to bring any other question there. These assemblies, which by a very important distinction[69]* will not have the authority of the Sovereign but of the supreme Magistrate, far from being able to innovate anything, will only be able to prevent all innovation on the part of the Councils, and to put all things back into the order of Legislation, which the Body that is the depository of the public force now can set aside as much as it pleases without any hindrance. So that to make these assemblies fall by themselves, the Magistrates will have nothing to do but to follow the Laws exactly: for the convocation of a general Council would be useless and ridiculous when there is nothing to bring to it; and it very much appears that this is how the practice of periodic general Councils was lost in the sixteenth century, as has been said above.

It was with the aim I just set forth that they were re-established in 1707, and this old question reopened today was settled at that time by the very fact of three consecutive general Councils, in the last of which the Article concerning the right of Remonstrance passed. This right was not contested but evaded. When they refused to satisfy the complaints of the

---

* See the *Social Contract*. L. III. Chap. 17.

Bourgeoisie, the Magistrates did not dare to deny that the question should be brought into the general Council; but since it belonged to them alone to convoke it, under this pretext they claimed to be able to put off the session at their will, and counted on tiring out the constancy of the Bourgeoisie by dint of delays. Nevertheless, its right was finally so well acknowledged that as early as April 9 it had the general assembly convoked for the 5th[70] of May, *in order*, the Placard said, *to remove by this means the insinuations that have been widespread that its convocation could be evaded and postponed until even later.*

And let it not be said that this convocation was forced by some act of violence or by some tumult tending toward sedition, since everything was then treated by means of deputation, as the Council had desired, and since the Citizens and Bourgeois were never more peaceful in their assemblies, avoiding making them too numerous and giving them an imposing air. They even pushed decency and, I dare to say, dignity so far, that those among them who habitually wore a sword always laid it aside in order to attend them.* It was only after everything had been done, that is to say, at the end of the third general Council, that there was a call to arms caused through the fault of the Council, which had the imprudence to send three Companies from the garrison, bayonet at the end of their rifles, to use force against two or three hundred Citizens still assembled at Saint Peter.

Re-established in 1707, these periodic Councils were revoked five years afterward; but by what means and in what circumstances? A short examination of that Edict of 1712 will allow us to judge its validity.

First the people, frightened by the recent executions and proscriptions, had neither liberty nor security; they could no longer count on anything after the fraudulent amnesty that had been used to take them by surprise.[71] At every moment it believed it saw again at its gates the Swiss who served as archers in those bloody executions. Poorly recovered from a fright that the commencement of the Edict was very suited to reawakening, it granted everything out of fear alone; it felt very well that it was not being assembled in order to give the Law but to receive it.

The motives for this revocation, founded on the dangers of periodic general Councils, are of a palpable absurdity to anyone with the slightest knowledge of the spirit of your Constitution and that of your Bourgeoisie. The times of plague, of famine, and of war are alleged, as if famine or war were an obstacle to the holding of a Council, and as to plague, you

---

* They had the same thoughtfulness in 1734 in their Remonstrances of March 4, supported by a thousand or twelve hundred Citizens or Bourgeois in person, not a single one of whom had his sword at his side. This carefulness, which would appear punctilious in any other State, is not so in a Democracy, and perhaps shows the character of a people better than more striking features.

will admit to me that that is taking very distant precautions. They were afraid of the enemy, of ill-intentioned people, of cabals; never were such timid people seen; the experience of the past should have reassured them: in the most unsettled times frequent general Councils were the salvation of the Republic, as will be shown below, and nothing but wise and courageous resolutions were ever taken in them. They maintain that these assemblies are contrary to the Constitution, whose firmest support they are; they say they are contrary to the Edicts, and they are established by the Edicts; they accuse them of innovation, and they are as old as the Legislation. There is not a line in this preamble that is not a falsehood or a piece of foolishness, and the revocation passes based on this fine exposition, without prior proclamation that instructed the members of the assembly about the proposition they wished to make to them, without giving them the leisure to deliberate among themselves, even to think about it, and at a time in which the Bourgeoisie, poorly instructed about the history of its Government, let itself be easily imposed upon by the body of Magistrates.

But a still more serious means of invalidity is the violation of the Edict in its most important part in this regard, namely the manner of deciphering the tickets or of counting the votes; for in Article 4 of the Edict of 1707 it is said that four Secretaries *ad actum* will be established to collect the votes, two from the Two-Hundred and two from the People, which will be chosen on the spot by M. the first Syndic and will take an oath in the Temple. And nevertheless in the general Council of 1712, without any regard for the preceding Edict, they had the votes collected by the two Secretaries of State. What, then, was the reason for this change, and why this illegal maneuver in such a capital point, as if they wanted to transgress at pleasure the Law that had just been made? One begins by violating in one article the Edict one wants to annul in another! Was this a regular proceeding? If, as this Edict of Revocation states, the advice of the Council was approved *almost unanimously*,* why then the surprise and the con-

---

* From the manner in which it is reported to me that they set about it, this unanimity was not hard to obtain, and it was only up to these Gentlemen to make it complete.

Before the assembly, the Secretary of State Mestrezat said: *Let them come; I have them.* He employed, they say, for this end the two words *Approbation, and Rejection*, which since have remained in use in the tickets: so that whatever choice one makes it all comes back to the same. For if one chose *Approbation* one approved the advice of the Councils, who rejected the periodic assembly; and if one chose *Rejection* one rejected the periodic assembly. I am not inventing this fact, and I beg the reader to believe that I am not reporting it without authority; but I owe it to the truth to say that it does not come to me from Geneva, and to justice to add that I do not believe it to be true: I know only that the equivocation of these two words deceived the voters very much about which one they should choose to express their intention, and I also admit that I cannot imagine any honest motive nor any legitimate excuse for the transgression of the law in this collecting of the votes. Nothing proves better the terror with which the People were seized than the silence with which they let this irregularity pass.

sternation shown by the Citizens upon leaving the Council, when an air of triumph and satisfaction was seen on the faces of the Magistrates?* Are these different countenances natural to people who have just been unanimously of the same opinion?

Thus, then, in order to extract this Edict of revocation they made use of terror, of surprise, very likely of fraud, and at the least they certainly violated the Law. Judge whether these characteristics are compatible with those of a sacred Law, as they affect to call it?

But let us assume that this revocation were legitimate and that they did not infringe its conditions,** what other effect can one give it than to put things back on the footing they were on before the establishment of the revoked Law, and consequently the Bourgeoisie having the right it was in possession of? When one quashes a transaction, don't the Parties remain as they were before it took place?

Let us agree that these periodic general Councils would have had only a single inconvenience, but a terrible one; that would have been to force the Magistrates and all the orders to restrain themselves within the limits of their duties and of their rights. From that alone I know that these so shocking assemblies will never be re-established, no more than those of the Bourgeoisie by companies; but also that is not what is at issue; I am not at all examining here what ought or ought not to be done; what will be done or what will not be done. The expedients that I am indicating simply as possible and easy, as drawn from your constitution, no longer being in conformity with the new Edicts, can pass only with the consent of the Councils, and my advice is certainly not to propose them to them: but adopting for a moment the assumption of the Author of the Letters, I am resolving frivolous objections; I am making it clear that he is looking in the nature of things for obstacles that are not there at all, that none of them exists except in the ill will of the Council, and that, if they wanted to, there would be a hundred ways of removing these so-called obstacles, without altering the Constitution, without disturbing order, and without ever risking public repose.

But to return to the question let us keep exactly to the last Edict, and you will not see in it a single real difficulty against the necessary effect of the right of Remonstrance.

---

* They said among themselves while leaving, and many others heard it: *we have just done a good day's work*. The next day a number of Citizens complained that they had been deceived, and that they had not at all meant to reject the general assemblies, but the advice of the Councils. They were laughed at.

** These conditions state that *any change to the Edict will not have force unless it has been approved in this sovereign Council*. It remains, then, to know whether the infractions of the Edict are not changes to the Edict.

Eighth Letter (Pl., III, 857–860)

1. First the difficulty of fixing the number of Remonstrators is vain by the Edict itself, which does not make any distinction in the number, and does not give any less force to the Remonstrance of a single person than to that of a hundred.

2. The difficulty of giving to private individuals the right of bringing about the assembly of the general Council is also vain; since this right, dangerous or not, does not result from the necessary effect of Remonstrances. Since there are two general Councils every year for elections, there is no need for an extraordinary assembly for that effect. It suffices that the Remonstrance, after having been examined in the Councils, be brought to the closest general Council when it is of a nature to be so.* The session will not even be prolonged for an hour, as is manifest to anyone who is acquainted with the order observed in these assemblies. It is only necessary to take the precaution that the proposition pass to a vote before the elections: for if one waited until the election was done, the Syndics would not fail to dissolve the assembly as soon as possible, as they did in 1735.

3. The difficulty of multiplying the general Councils is removed with the preceding one and if it were not, where would the dangers be that are found in it? That is what I am unable to see.

One shudders upon reading the enumeration of these dangers in the *Letters Written from the Country*, in the Edict of 1712, in the Harangue of M. Chouet; but let us confirm. This last says that the Republic was not tranquil except when these assemblies became more rare. In this there is a little inversion to be set straight. It must be said that these assemblies became more rare when the Republic was tranquil. Read, Sir, the annals of your Town during the sixteenth century. How did it shake off the double yoke that was crushing it? How did it stifle the factions that were tearing it apart? How did it resist its greedy neighbors, who assisted it only to enslave it? How was evangelical and political liberty established in its bosom? How did its constitution take on any consistency? How was the system of its Government formed? The history of these memorable times is a sequence of prodigies. Tyrants, Neighbors, enemies, friends, subjects, Citizens, war, plague, famine, all seemed to co-operate in the ruin of this unhappy Town. One hardly conceives how a State already formed could escape all these perils. Not only did Geneva escape from them, but it is during these terrible crises that the great Work of its Legislation was consummated. It was by means of its frequent general Councils,** it was by

---

* I have distinguished above the cases in which the Councils are bound to bring it there, and those in which they are not.

** Since they were assembled at that time in all *arduous* cases in accordance with the Edicts, and since these arduous cases recurred very often in those stormy times, the general Council was more frequently convoked at that time than the Two-Hundred is today. Let it be

means of the prudence and the firmness that its Citizens brought to them that they finally overcame all obstacles, and made their Town free and tranquil, having previously been subjected and torn apart; it was after having put everything in order inside that it saw itself in a condition to make war with glory outside. Then the Sovereign Council had completed its functions, it was up to the Government to do its: nothing was left for the Genevans other than to defend the liberty they had just established, and to show themselves to be as brave soldiers in the field as they had shown themselves worthy Citizens in the Council: that is what they did. Your annals attest throughout to the utility of the general Councils; your Gentlemen see in them only frightening evils. They make the objection, but history resolves it.

4. The difficulty of being exposed to the sallies of the People when one is close to great Powers is resolved the same way. In this I do not know any better response to sophisms than constant facts. At all times all the resolutions of the general Councils have been as full of wisdom as of courage; they have never been insolent or cowardly; Sometimes in them they swore to die for the fatherland; but I challenge anyone to cite me a single one, even from those that the People influenced the most, in which the neighboring powers were antagonized out of stupidity, or a single one in which the People groveled before them. I would not make a similar challenge for all the decisions of the small Council: but let that pass. When it is a question of making new resolutions, it is up to the inferior Councils to propose them, to the general Council to reject them or to accept them; it can do nothing more; that is not disputed: Thus that objection is inapposite.

5. The difficulty of casting doubt and obscurity over all the Laws is no more solid, because it is not a question here of an interpretation that is vague, general, and susceptible of subtleties; but of a clear and precise application of a fact to the Law. The body of Magistrates can have reasons for finding a clear thing obscure, but that does not destroy its clarity. These Gentlemen denature the question. To show by the letter of a Law that it has been violated is not to propose doubts about that Law. If there is among the terms of the Law a single meaning in accordance with which the fact might be justified, the Council will not fail to establish this meaning in its response. Then the Remonstrance loses its force, and if it is persisted in, it falls infallibly into the general Council: For the interest of all is too great, too present, too tangible, above all in a commercial Town, for the generality ever to want to shake authority, Government, Legislation,

---

judged by a single period. During the first eight months of the year 1540 eighteen general Councils were held, and that year had nothing more extraordinary than those that had preceded it and than those that followed.

by pronouncing that a Law has been transgressed, when it is possible that it has not been.

It is up to the Legislator, it is up to the drafter of the Laws not to leave equivocal terms in them. When they are there, it is up to the equity of the Magistrate to fix their meaning in practice; when the Law has several meanings, he uses his right by preferring the one that he pleases: but this right does not at all go to the point of changing the literal sense of the laws and of giving them one they do not have; otherwise there would no longer be any Law. Posed this way, the question is so clear that it is easy for good sense to pronounce, and this good sense that pronounces is then found in the general Council. Far from interminable discussions being born from that, on the contrary they are prevented by it; one is sure from it that, by raising the Edicts above arbitrary and peculiar interpretations that interest or passion can suggest, they always say what they say, and that private individuals are no longer in doubt in each affair about the meaning the Magistrate will be pleased to give to the Law. Isn't it clear that the difficulties that are at issue now would no longer exist if one had taken this means of resolving them from the beginning?

6. The difficulty of subjecting the Councils to the orders of the Citizens is ridiculous. It is certain that Remonstrances are not orders, any more than the petition of a man who demands justice is an order; but the Magistrate is not less obliged from this to render to the supplicant the justice he is demanding, and the Council to act rightly upon the Remonstrances of the Citizens and Bourgeois. Although the Magistrates are the superiors of private individuals, this superiority does not dispense them from granting to their inferiors what they owe to them, and the respectful terms the latter employ in order to demand it take nothing away from the right they have to obtain it. A Remonstrance is, if you wish it, an order given to the Council, as it is an order given to the first Syndic to whom one presents it to communicate it to the Council; for that is what he is always obliged to do, whether he approves the Remonstrance, or he does not approve it.

Moreover when the Council takes advantage of the word *Représentation*,[72] which shows inferiority by saying a thing that no one disputes, it nevertheless forgets that this word employed in the Settlement is not in the Edict to which it refers. The edict contains the very word *Remontrances*, which has a completely different sense. To which one can add that there is a difference between the Remonstrances that a body of Magistracy makes to its Sovereign, and those that the members of the Sovereign make to a body of Magistracy. You will say that I am wrong to answer such an objection, but it is worth as much as the majority of the others.

7. Finally, the difficulty of an influential man contesting the meaning

or the application of a Law that condemns him, and seducing the public in his favor, is such that I believe I ought to abstain from characterizing it. What! Who then has known the Bourgeoisie of Geneva as a servile, ardent, imitative, stupid people, an enemy of the laws, and so prompt to flare up on behalf of someone else's interest? It is necessary for each one to have seen his own interest very much compromised in public affairs before he can resolve to take a hand in these affairs.

Often injustice and fraud find protectors; they never have the public on their side; it is in this that the voice of the People is the voice of God; but unfortunately that sacred voice is always weak in affairs against the outcry of power, and the complaint of oppressed innocence is uttered in murmurs despised by tyranny. Everything that is done by intrigue and seduction tends to be done for the profit of those who govern; that could not be otherwise. Ruse, prejudice, interest, fear, hope, vanity, specious appearances, an air of order and of subordination, everything favors skilful men vested with authority and versed in the art of deceiving the people. When it is a question of opposing skill to skill, or influence to influence, what immense opportunity is there in a small Town for the leading families, always united, to dominate their friends, their clients, their creatures, all this joined to all the power of the Councils; to crush—with sophisms as their only weapons—the private individuals who would dare to frown at them? Look around you at this very moment. The support of the laws, equity, truth, evidence, the common interest, the concern for private safety, everything that should incite the crowd is hardly enough to protect the respected Citizens who clamor against the most manifest iniquity; and they claim that among an enlightened People the interest of a troublemaker forms more partisans than the interest of the State can? Either I know your Bourgeoisie and your Leaders poorly, or if a single ill-founded Remonstrance is ever made—which has not yet happened that I know of—the Author, if he is not contemptible, is a ruined man.

Is there a need to refute objections of this sort when one is speaking to Genevans? Is there a single man in your Town who does not feel its bad faith, and can one seriously compare the use of a sacred, fundamental, confirmed, necessary right with chimerical inconveniences that the very ones who raise them in objection know better than anyone cannot exist? Whereas on the contrary, the infringement of this right opens the door to the excesses of the most odious Oligarchy, to the point that one already sees it without pretext, making an attempt against the liberty of the Citizens, haughtily arrogating to itself the power of imprisoning them without restriction or condition, without any sort of formality, against the purport of the most precise Laws, and in spite of all protests.

The explanation they dare to give of these Laws is even more insulting than the tyranny they exercise in their name. With what arguments do they pay you? It is not enough to treat you as slaves without treating you as children too. My God! How can they have put such clear questions into doubt, how can they have confused them to this point? See, Sir, whether merely to pose them isn't to resolve them? By finishing this Letter with that, I hope not to stretch it out much.

A man can be made a prisoner in three ways. One at the instance of another man who is Party to a formal suit against him; the second being surprised in *flagrante delicto* and seized on the spot, or, what amounts to the same thing, for a notorious crime of which the public is witness; and the third, *ex officio*, by the simple authority of the Magistrate, based on secret information, based on indications, or on other reasons that he finds sufficient.

In the first case, it is ordered by the Laws of Geneva that the accuser be taken into custody, along with the accused; and moreover, if the accuser is not solvent, that he give security for the legal expenses and the judgment. Thus in this way, one has a reasonable security in the interest of the accuser that the accused has not been unjustly arrested.

In the second case the proof is in the very fact, and the accused is in a way convicted by his own detention.

But in the third case one has neither the same security as in the first, nor the same evidence as in the second, and it is for this last case that the Law, assuming the Magistrate to be equitable, takes measures only so that he might not be deceived.

These are the principles upon which the Legislator directs himself in the three cases; here now is their application.

In the case of the formal Law Suit, from the beginning one has a regular trial that must be conducted in all its judicial formalities: that is why the matter is treated as pending. Imprisonment cannot be imposed, *if, the parties having been heard, it has not been permitted by the justice.** You know that what is called the Justice is the Tribunal of the Lieutenant and of his assistants called *Auditors*. Thus it is to these Magistrates and not to others, not even to the Syndics, that the complaint in cases like this one ought to be brought, and it is up to them to order the imprisonment of the two parties; aside from the case of recourse of one of the two to the Syndics, *if,* in accordance with the terms of the Edict, *he feels himself burdened by what has been ordered.*** The first three Articles of title XII, on criminal matters, obviously relate to that case.

* Civil Edicts. Tit. XII. Art. I.
** Ibid. Art. 2.

In the case of *flagrante delicto*, either for a crime, or for excesses that public order ought to punish, every person is permitted to arrest the guilty one; but only the Magistrates charged with some part of the executive power, such as the Syndics, the Council, the Lieutenant, an Auditor, can lock him up; neither a Councilor nor several of them would be able to; and the prisoner must be interrogated within twenty-four hours. The five following Articles of the same Edict are related solely to this second case, as is clear as much from the order of the material as from the name of *criminal* given to the accused, since it is only in the single case of *flagrante delicto* or of notorious crime that one can call an accused man *criminal* before his trial has taken place. If one persists in wanting *accused* and *criminal* to be synonyms, it will be necessary, from this very language, that *innocent* and *criminal* also be so.

In the remainder of Title XII it is no longer a question of imprisonment, and from Article 9 on inclusively everything pertains to procedure and the form of judgment in every sort of criminal trial. Imprisonments made *ex officio* are not spoken of at all there.

But they are spoken of in the political Edict on the Office of the four Syndics. Why so? Because that Article pertains immediately to civil liberty, because the power exercised on this point by the body of Magistrates is an act of Government rather than of Magistracy, and because a simple Tribunal of justice ought not to be vested with such a power. Also the Edict grants it to the Syndics alone, not to the Lieutenant nor to any other Magistrate.

Now to protect the Syndics from being deceived, as I mentioned, the Edict prescribes that they *summon* first *those it concerns to examine, to interrogate*, and finally, *to have imprisoned if it is necessary*. I believe that in a free country the Law could not do less to put a restraint on this terrible power. The Citizens must have all reasonable securities that while doing their duty they will be able to sleep in their bed.

The following Article of the same Title returns, as is manifest, to the case of notorious crime and of *flagrante delicto*, in the same way as the first Article of the Title on criminal matters, in the same political Edict. All that might appear to be a repetition: but in the civil Edict the matter is considered in regard to the practice of justice, and in the political Edict in regard to the safety of the Citizens. Moreover, the Laws, having been made at different times, and these Laws being the work of men, one should not look for an order that is never inconsistent and a perfection without defect. It is enough that upon meditating upon the whole and upon comparing the Articles, one discovers the spirit of the Legislator in them and the reasons for the ordering of his work.

Eighth Letter (Pl., III, 865–867)

Add a reflection. These rights so judiciously combined; these rights laid claim to by the Remonstrators by virtue of the Edicts, you enjoyed them under the sovereignty of the Bishops, Neuchâtel enjoyed them under its Princes, and they want to take them away from you Republicans! See Articles 10, 11, and several others on the franchises of Geneva in the act of Ademarus Fabri. This monument is no less respectable to Genevans than the even older Magna Carta is to the English, and I doubt one would be very welcome among these latter in speaking about their Magna Carta with as much disdain as the Author of the Letters dares to show for yours.

He claims that it was repealed by the Constitutions of the Republic.* But on the contrary I very often see in your Edicts this phrase, *as from antiquity*, which refers to ancient practices, consequently to the rights upon which they were founded; and as if the Bishop had foreseen that those who ought to protect the franchises would attack them, I see that he declares in the Act itself that they will be perpetual, without either non-use or any prescription being able to abolish them. Here, you will agree to it, is a very peculiar opposition. The learned Syndic Chouet says in his Memorandum to Lord Towsend that the People of Geneva entered, by means of the Reformation, into the rights of the Bishop, who was temporal and spiritual Prince of this Town. The Author of the Letters assures us on the contrary that on that occasion this same People lost the franchises that the Bishop had accorded to it. Which of the two will you believe?

What! Being free you will lose the rights you enjoyed as subjects! Your Magistrates despoil you of those that your Princes granted you! If such is the liberty that your fathers acquired for you, you have reason to lament the blood they spilled for it. This peculiar act, which deprived you of your franchises in making you Sovereigns, is worth the trouble, it seems to me, of being stated, and, at least in order to make it believable, it cannot be too solemnized. Where then is this act of repeal? Assuredly the least one can do to avail oneself of such a bizarre piece is to begin by demonstrating it.

From all this I believe I can conclude with certainty that in no possible case does the Law in Geneva grant to the Syndics, nor to anyone, the absolute right of imprisoning private individuals without restriction or condition. But it doesn't matter: in response to the Remonstrances the Council establishes this incontestable right. It has only to wish, and it immediately possesses. Such is the convenience of the negative right.

In this Letter I proposed to show that the right of Remonstrance, inti-

---

* It was by a completely similar Logic that in 1742 they had no regard for the Treaty of Soleure of 1579, maintaining that it was superannuated; even though it was declared to be perpetual in the Act itself, even though it was never repealed by any other, and even though it has been recalled several times, notably in the act of Mediation.

mately linked to the form of your Constitution, was not an illusory and vain right; but that, having been formally established by the Edict of 1707 and confirmed by that of 1738, it must necessarily have a real effect: that this effect was not stipulated in the Act of Mediation because it was not in the Edict, and that it was not in the Edict, both because at that time it resulted by itself from the nature of your Constitution and because the same Edict established its security in another manner: That this right and its necessary effect, along with giving consistency to all the others, was the sole and genuine equivalent of those that had been taken away from the Bourgeoisie; that this equivalent, sufficing to establish a solid equilibrium among all the parts of the State, showed the wisdom of the Settlement, which without that would be the most iniquitous work that could be imagined: finally that the difficulties they raise against the exercise of this right were frivolous difficulties, which existed only in the ill will of those who proposed them, and which did not balance in any manner the dangers of the absolute negative right. That, Sir, is what I wanted to do; it is up to you to see whether I have succeeded.

Ninth Letter

I believed, Sir, that it was better to establish what I had to say directly, rather than to stick to long refutations. To undertake a sustained examination of the *Letters Written from the Country* would be to launch out onto a sea of sophisms. In my opinion, to seize, to expose them would be to refute them; but they swim in such a flux of doctrine, they are so swamped by it, that one drowns while attempting to get them on dry land.

Nevertheless, in completing my labor I cannot dispense myself from casting a glance on that of this Author. Without analyzing the political subtleties with which he lures you, I will content myself with examining their principles, and with showing you the vice of his reasonings in several examples.

You have seen their inconsistency in relation to me above: in relation to your Republic they are sometimes more captious, and are never any more solid. The sole and genuine object of these Letters is to establish the so-called negative right in the fullness given to it by the usurpations of the Council. Everything is in relation to this goal; either directly, by a necessary sequence; or indirectly by sleight of hand, leading the public astray about the basis of the question.

The imputations that concern me are of the first sort. The Council has judged me contrary to the Law: Remonstrances are raised. To establish the negative right it is necessary to send the Remonstrators packing; to send them packing it is necessary to prove that they are wrong; to prove that they are wrong it is necessary to maintain that I am guilty, but guilty to such a point that it was necessary to deviate from the Law in order to punish my crime.

How men would shudder at the first evil they do, if they saw that they put themselves under the sad necessity of always doing it, of being wicked for their whole life as a result of having been so for one moment so as to hound to death the wretch whom they persecuted one time.

The question of the presidency of the Syndics in criminal Tribunals relates to the second sort. Do you believe that at bottom the Council troubles itself very much whether it is Syndics or Councilors who preside, since they have founded the rights of the former in the whole body? The

Syndics, formerly chosen from among the whole People,* no longer being chosen except from among the Council, rather than being the chiefs of the other Magistrates as they used to be, have remained their colleagues, and you were able to see clearly in this business that your Syndics—hardly attached to a temporary authority—are no longer anything other than Councilors. But they pretend to treat this question as important, in order to distract you from the one that genuinely is important, in order to let you still believe that your foremost Magistrates are still elected by you, and that their power is still the same.

Let us, then, leave here these subordinate questions, which, from the manner they are treated by the Author, one sees that he hardly takes to heart. Let us limit ourselves to weighing the reasons he alleges in favor of the negative right to which he applies himself more carefully, and from which alone, accepted or rejected, you are slaves or free.

The art he employs most skillfully for this is to reduce into general propositions a system whose weakness would be seen too easily if he always applied it. In order to divert you from the particular object, he flatters your amour-propre by extending your view to great questions, and while he puts these questions out of the grasp of those he wishes to seduce, he cajoles them and wins them over by appearing to treat them as Statesmen. He dazzles the people this way in order to blind them, and changes questions that require only good sense into theses of philosophy, so that one cannot contradict him, and so that—not understanding him—one does not dare to disavow him.

To wish to follow him in his abstract sophisms would be to fall into the error for which I reproach him. Moreover, on questions treated this way one takes the side one wants without ever being wrong: for so many elements enter into these propositions, one can envisage them from so many angles, that there is always some side susceptible to the appearance one wants to give them. When one writes a Book of politics for the whole public in general, one can philosophize at one's ease in it: Not wanting to be read and judged except by the educated men of all Nations who are well versed in the matter he treats, the Author abstracts and generalizes without fear; he does not dwell on elementary points. If I were speaking to you alone, I could use this method; but the subject of these Letters interests an entire people, composed in its greatest number by men who have more sense and judgment than reading and study, and who, for not having the scientific jargon, are all the more fit for grasping what is true in all its

* They were so attentive to there being neither exclusivity nor preference other than that of merit in this choice that, by an Edict that was rescinded, two Syndics were always supposed to be taken from the low part of the Town and two from the high.

simplicity. In such a case one must choose between the interest of the Author and that of the Readers, and anyone who wants to make himself more useful must resolve to be less dazzling.

Another source of errors and false applications is from having left the ideas of this negative right too vague, too inexact; which is useful for citing with an air of proof examples that are least related to it, turning your Fellow Citizens away from their object by means of the pomp of those presented to them, rousing their pride against their reason, and sweetly consoling them for not being any more free than the masters of the world. They eruditely ransack the obscurity of the ages, they ostentatiously take you for a walk among the Peoples of antiquity. They successively display Athens, Sparta, Rome, and Carthage for you; they throw the sand of Libya into your eyes in order to keep you from seeing what is happening in front of you.

Let them fix, as I have attempted to do, this negative right precisely, such as the Council claims to exercise it; and I maintain that there was never a single Government on the earth in which the Legislator—enchained in every way by the executive body—after having delivered the Laws to its mercy without reserve, was reduced to seeing them explained to it, eluded, transgressed at will, without ever being able to bring to bear on this abuse any other opposition, any other right, any other resistance than a useless murmur and impotent outcries.

See in effect to what point your Anonymous man is forced to denature the question, in order to relate his examples to it less inappropriately.

The negative right, not being, he says on page 110, *the power of making Laws, but of preventing everyone indiscriminately from being able to set into motion the power that makes the Laws, and not conferring means for innovating, but the power of opposing innovations, proceeds directly to the great aim that a political society proposes for itself, which is to preserve itself while preserving its constitution.*

Here is a very reasonable negative right, and in the sense set forth this right is in fact such an essential part of the democratic constitution that it would be generally impossible for it to maintain itself if the Legislative Power could always be set into motion by each of those who compose it. You conceive that it is not difficult to bring to bear examples in confirmation of such a certain principle.

But if this concept is not at all that of the negative right in question, if there is not a single word in this passage that is not erroneous by the application the Author wants to make of it, you will admit to me that the proofs to the advantage of an entirely different negative right are not greatly conclusive in favor of the one he does want to establish.

The negative right is not that of making Laws. No, but it is that of dispensing with Laws. Making a particular Law out of each act of one's will is much more convenient than following general Laws, even if one is their Author oneself. *But of preventing everyone indiscriminately from being able to set into motion the power that makes the Laws.* Instead of this it should have been said: *but to prevent anyone at all from being able to protect the Laws against the power that subjugates them.*

Which not conferring ease at innovating.... Why not? Who can prevent from innovating the one who has the force in his hands, and who is not obliged to be responsible for his conduct to anyone: *But the power to prevent innovations.*[73] Let us state more accurately, *the power to prevent anyone from opposing innovations.*

Here, Sir, is the most subtle sophism, which recurs the most often in the writing I am examining. The one who has the executive Power never needs to innovate by brilliant feats of arms. He never needs to establish this innovation by solemn acts. It is enough for him, in the continuous exercise of his power, to bend each thing to his will little by little, and that never causes a very strong sensation.

On the contrary, those who have an attentive enough eye and penetrating enough mind to notice this progress and to foresee its outcome have only one of these two courses to take to prevent it; either at the beginning to oppose the first innovation, which is never more than a bagatelle, and then they are treated as restless, troublemaking, touchy people, always ready to look for a fight; or finally to make a stand against an abuse that is growing stronger, and then they complain loudly about innovation. Whatever your Magistrates undertake, I defy you to be able to avoid both of these two reproaches at the same time in opposing them. But by choice, prefer the first. Every time the Council alters some practice, it has its goal that no one sees, and that it takes good care not to show. When in doubt, always stop every innovation, small or large. If the Syndics were in the custom of entering the Council with their right foot, and they wanted to enter with the left foot, I say that they should be prevented from doing so.

Here we have the very tangible proof of the ease of concluding the pro and the con by the method followed by our Author: for apply to the right of Remonstrance of the Citizens what he applies to the negative right of the Councils, and you will find that his general proposition suits your application even better than his. *The right of Remonstrance,* you will say, *not being the power of making Laws, but of preventing the power that ought to administer them from transgressing them, and not giving the power of innovating but of opposing innovations, proceeds directly to the great aim that a political society proposes for itself, which is to preserve itself while preserving its constitution.*

Isn't that exactly what the Remonstrators should have said, and doesn't it seem that the Author reasoned for them? Words must not lead us astray about ideas. The alleged negative right of the Council is really a positive right, and even the most positive that one can imagine, since it makes the small Council alone direct and absolute master of the State and of all the Laws, and the right of Remonstrance taken in its true sense is itself only a negative right. It consists solely in preventing the executive power from executing anything against the Laws.

Let us follow the Author's admissions concerning the propositions he presents; with three words added, nobody could have set down your present state better.

As there would not be any liberty at all in a State in which the body charged with the execution of the Laws had the right to make them speak at its fancy,[74] *since it could have the most tyrannical of its wills executed as Laws.*

There, I think, is a tableau drawn from nature; you are going to see a tableau drawn from fancy set into opposition with it.

There also would not be any Government at all in a State in which the People exercised the Legislative power without a rule. Agreed; but who proposed that the people exercise the legislative power without a rule?

After having thus posited a different negative right than the one at issue, the Author troubles himself very much to know where one should place this negative right that is not at all at issue, and on that head he established a principle that I certainly will not contest. It is, *if that negative force can reside in the Government without inconvenience, it will be of the nature and for the good of the thing that it be placed there.* Then come the examples, which I will not apply myself to following; because they are too distant from us and in every respect alien to the question.

Only that of England, which is under our eyes and which he reasonably cites as a model of the just balance of the respective powers, deserves a moment of examination, and only following him do I here allow myself the comparison of the smaller to the larger.

In spite of the Royal power, which is very great, the Nation did not fear also to give the negative voice to the King. But since he cannot do without the legislative power for very long, and there would be no security for him in irritating it, this negative force is in fact only a means of stopping the undertakings of the legislative power, and the Prince, tranquil in the possession of the extended power that the Constitution fixes on him, will be interested in protecting it.[75]*

Based on this reasoning and on the application they want to make of it, you would believe that the executive power of the King of England is

---

* Page 117.

greater than that of the Council of Geneva, that the negative right this Prince has is similar to the one your Magistrates are usurping, that your Government cannot do without the legislative power anymore than that of England can, and in sum that both one and the other have the same interest in protecting the constitution. If the Author did not wish to say that, what did he wish to say then, and what does this example have to do with his subject?

Nevertheless it is completely the opposite in every respect. The King of England, invested with such a great power by the Laws in order to protect them, has none to transgress them: in such a case no one would want to obey him, each would fear for his head; the Ministers themselves can lose it if they irritate Parliament: his own conduct is examined there. Sheltered by the Laws, every Englishman can defy the Royal power; the lowest of the people can demand and obtain the most authentic reparation if he is offended to the slightest degree; assuming that the Prince dared to transgress the Law in the smallest thing, the infraction would instantly be set straight; he is without right and would be without power to maintain it.

Among you the Power of the small Council is absolute in every respect; it is the Minister and the Prince, the party and the Judge all at the same time: it orders and it executes; it cites, it seizes, it imprisons, it judges, it punishes by itself: it has the force at hand to do everything; all those it employs are unaccountable; it does not give an account of its conduct or of theirs to anyone; it has nothing to fear from the Legislator, whose mouth it alone has the right to open, and before which it will not go to accuse itself. It is never constrained to make reparations for its acts of injustice, and the most fortunate outcome that can be hoped for by the innocent person it oppresses is in the end to escape safe and sound, but without either satisfaction or compensation.

Judge this difference from the most recent facts. A violently satirical work is printed at London against the Ministers, the Government, the King himself. The Printers are arrested. The Law does not authorize this arrest, a public outcry is raised, they must be released. The business does not end there: the Workers sue the Magistrate in their turn, and they obtain immense damages and interest.[76] Put that case into parallel with that of Master Bardin bookseller at Geneva; I will speak of it below.[77] Another case, there is a robbery in the Town; without evidence and based on idle suspicions, a Citizen is imprisoned against the laws; his house is searched, he is spared none of the affronts made for malefactors. Finally his innocence is acknowledged, he is released, he complains, he is ignored, and everything is finished.[78]

Let us suppose that at London I had the misfortune of displeasing the

Court, that without justice and without reason it seized the pretext of one of my Books in order to have it burned and to have a warrant issued for my arrest. I would have submitted a petition to Parliament claiming that I had been judged contrary to the Laws; I would have proven it; I would have obtained the most authentic satisfaction, and the judge would have been punished, perhaps discharged from office.

Let us now transport Mr. Wilkes to Geneva, saying, writing, printing, publishing against the small Council a quarter of what he did say, write, print, publish openly at London against the Government, the Court, the Prince. I will not absolutely affirm that he would have been put to death, although I think so; but surely he would have been seized at the very moment, and very grievously punished in a short time.*

It will be said that Mr. Wilkes was a member of the legislative body in his country; and I, was I not also one in mine? It is true that the Author of the Letters does not want anyone to have any consideration for the status of Citizen. *The rules*, he says, *of procedure are and ought to be equal for all men; they do not derive from the right of the City; they emanate from the right of humanity.***

Fortunately for you the fact is not true***; and as for the maxim, it is to hide a very cruel sophism under very decent words. The interest of the Magistrate, which in your State often renders him a party against the Citizen, but never against the foreigner, demands in the first case that the Law take much greater precautions in order for the accused not to be condemned unjustly. This distinction is only too well confirmed by the facts. There is perhaps not, since the establishment of the Republic, a single example of an unjust judgment against a foreigner, and who will count how

---

* Since the law shelters Mr. Wilkes on this side, another trick was necessary in order to harrass him, and Religion was made to intervene in this business also.

** Page 54.

*** By the Edict the right of recourse to pardon belonged only to Citizens and Bourgeois; but from their good offices this and other rights were imparted to the natives and inhabitants, who, having made common cause with them, needed the same precautions for their safety; foreigners have remained excluded from it. It is also felt that the selection of four relatives or friends to assist the accused in a criminal procedure is not extremely useful to foreigners; it is so only to those whom the Magistrate can have an interest in ruining, and to whom the Law gives their natural enemy as Judge. It is even surprising that, after so many frightening examples, the Citizens and Bourgeois did not take more measures for the safety of their persons, and that the whole criminal matter rests, without Edicts and without Laws, almost abandoned to the discretion of the Council. A service for which alone the Genevans and all just men ought to bless the Mediators forever is the abolition of the preparatory question. I always have a bitter laugh on my lips when I see so many fine Books, in which the Europeans admire themselves and pay themselves a compliment upon their humanity, coming from the same countries in which they amuse themselves at dislocating and breaking men's members, while waiting to learn whether they are guilty or not. I define torture as an almost infallible means used by the stronger to charge the weak with the crimes for which he wishes to punish him.

many unjust and even atrocious ones there are against Citizens in your annals? Moreover, it is very true that the precautions it is important to take for the safety of the latter can be extended to all accused without inconvenience, because they have as their goal, not saving the guilty, but protecting the innocent. It is for this reason that no exception is made in article XXX of the settlement, which one sees clearly enough is useful only to Genevans. Let us return to the comparison of the negative right in the two States.

That of the King of England consists in two things; to be able alone to convoke and dissolve the legislative body, and to be able to reject the Laws that are proposed to him; but it never consisted in preventing the legislative power from taking cognizance of the infractions he can make of the Law.

Besides, this negative force is very tempered; first by the triennial Law,* which obliges him to convoke a new Parliament at the end of a definite time; more, by his own necessity, which obliges him to leave it almost always assembled**; finally by the negative right of the house of commons, which has, toward him, one no less powerful than his own.

It is further tempered by the complete authority that each of the two Houses has over itself once it is assembled; either to propose, to deal with, to discuss, to examine Laws and all matters of Government; or from the portion of the executive power they exercise both conjointly and separately; both in the House of Commons, which takes cognizance of public grievances and attacks made upon the Laws, and in the House of Lords, supreme Judges in criminal matters, and above all in those that relate to crimes against the State.

That, Sir, is what the negative right of the King of England is. If your Magistrates lay claim only to such a one, I advise you not to contest it with them. But I do not see what need, in your present situation, they can ever have for the legislative power, or what can constrain them to convoke it in order to act in fact, whatever the case might be; since new Laws are never necessary for people who are above Laws, since a Government that subsists within its revenues and does not have a war has no need for new taxes, and since, by investing the entire body with the power of leaders that are drawn from it, one renders the selection of these leaders almost indifferent.

I do not even see in what they could be constrained by the Legislator, which, when it exists, exists only for a moment and can never decide anything except the unique point about which they are interrogating it.

---

* Having become septennial by a mistake for which the English have not yet reached the point of repenting.

** Granting subsidies for only one year, Parliament thus forces the King to ask it for them again every year.

It is true that the King of England can make war and peace; but aside from the fact that that power is more apparent than real, at least as to war, I have already shown above[79] and in the *Social Contract*[80] that that is not the issue for you, and one must renounce honorific rights when one wants to enjoy liberty. I admit in addition that this Prince can grant and remove from positions just as he sees fit, and corrupt the Legislator piecemeal. This is precisely what puts all the advantage on the side of the Council, for which such means are hardly necessary and which enchains you at less expense. Corruption is an abuse of liberty; but it is a proof that liberty exists, and one does not need to corrupt people whom one holds in one's power: as for positions, without speaking of those that the Council disposes of either by itself or by the Two-Hundred, it does better for the most important ones; it fills them with its own members, which is even more advantageous for it; for one is always more sure of what one does with one's own hands than of what one does by someone else's. The history of England is full of proofs of the resistance that royal Officers have made to their Princes when they wanted to transgress the Laws. See whether you will find among you many features of a similar resistance made to the Council by the Officers of the State, even in the most odious cases? At Geneva whoever is a hired hand of the Republic at the very instant ceases to be a Citizen; he is nothing more than the slave and the satellite of the twenty-five, ready to crush under foot the Fatherland and the Laws as soon as they order it. Finally the Law, which in England does not leave any power to the King to do ill, gives him a very great one to do good; it does not appear that it is on this side that the Council is jealous of extending its power.

Assured of their advantages, the Kings of England are interested in protecting the present constitution, because they have little hope of changing it. Your Magistrates, on the contrary, sure of making use of the forms of yours in order to change its basis completely, are interested in preserving these forms as the instrument of their usurpations. The last dangerous step that remains for them to take is the one they are taking today. Once this step is taken, they will be able to call themselves even more interested than the King of England in preserving the established constitution, but from a very different motive. There is all the parity I find between the political state of England and yours. I leave you to judge in which one liberty is.

After this comparison, the Author, who is pleased to present you with great examples, offers you that of ancient Rome. He disdainfully reproaches it for its troublemaking and seditious Tribunes: He bitterly deplores the sad fate of that unfortunate City under that stormy administration, a city that nevertheless—not yet being anything at the time of the erection of that Magistracy—had five hundred years of glory and prosperity under it, and became the capital of the world.[81] It finally ended because everything must end; it ended from the usurpations of its Great, of its Consuls, of its Generals who invaded it: it perished from the excess of its power; but it had acquired it only from the goodness of its Government. In this sense one can say that its Tribunes destroyed it.*

Moreover I do not excuse the faults of the Roman People, I have stated them in the *Social Contract*[82]; I blamed it for having usurped the executive power that it should have only held in check.** I have shown upon what principles the Tribunate should be instituted, the limits one ought to give it, and how all that can be done. These rules were poorly followed at Rome; they could have been better followed. Nevertheless see what the Tribunate did along with its abuses, what might it not have done if well directed? I hardly see what the Author of the Letters wants here: in order to conclude against him I would have taken the very example he has chosen.

Let us not seek from so far away these illustrious examples, so ostentatious by themselves, and so deceitful by their application. Do not let your chains be forged by amour-propre. Too small to compare yourselves to anything, stay within yourselves, and do not blind yourselves about your position. Ancient Peoples are no longer a model for modern ones; they are too alien to them in every respect. You above all, Genevans, keep your place, and do not go for the lofty objects that are presented to you in order to hide the abyss that is being dug in front of you. You are neither Romans, nor Spartans; you are not even Athenians. Leave aside these great

---

* The Tribunes did not leave the Town at all; they did not have any authority outside its walls; hence, in order to hide themselves from their inspection, the Consuls sometimes held the Comitia in the country. Now the chains of the Romans were not at all forged in Rome, but in its armies, and it was from their conquests that they lost their liberty. This loss did not, then, come from the Tribunes.

It is true that Caesar made use of them as Sylla had made use of the Senate; each took the means he judged most prompt or most sure to succeed; but someone was necessarily going to succeed, and what difference did it make who out of Marius or Sylla, Caesar or Pompey, Octavius or Antony was the usurper? Whichever party triumphed, its usurpation was not any less inevitable; leaders were needed for distant Armies, and it was certain that one of these leaders would become master of the State: The Tribunate did not contribute to that to the slightest extent.

Moreover, this very attack made here by the Author of the *Letters Written from the Country* on the Tribunes of the People, had already been made in 1715 by M. de Chapeaurouge Councilor of State in a Memorandum against the Office of Procurator General. M. Louis Le Fort, who was then fulfilling that responsibility brilliantly, showed him in a very fine letter in answer to this Memorandum, that the credit and authority of the Tribunes had been the salvation of the Republic, and that its destruction did not at all come from them, but from the Consuls. Surely Procurator General Le Fort hardly foresaw by whom the sentiment he refuted so well would be renewed in our time.

** See the *Social Contract* Book IV. Chap. V. I believe that one will find in this Chapter, which is very short, some good maxims on this matter.

names that do not suit you. You are Merchants, Artisans, Bourgeois, always occupied with their private interests, with their work, with their trafficking, with their gain; people for whom even liberty is only a means for acquiring without obstacle and for possessing in safety.

This situation demands maxims particular to you. Not being idle as the ancient Peoples were, you cannot ceaselessly occupy yourselves with the Government as they did: but by that very fact that you can less constantly keep watch over it, it should be instituted in such a way that it might be easier for you to see its intrigues and provide for abuses. Every public effort that your interest demands ought to be made all the easier for you to fulfill since it is an effort that costs you and that you do not make willingly. For to wish to unburden yourselves of them completely is to wish to cease being free. "It is necessary to choose," says the beneficent Philosopher,[83] "and those who cannot bear work have only to seek rest in servitude."

A restless, unoccupied, turbulent people always ready, for lack of private business, to get mixed up in that of the State, needs to be held within bounds, I know it; but once again, is the Bourgeoisie of Geneva that People? Nothing resembles it less; it is its polar opposite. Your Citizens, completely absorbed in their domestic occupations and always cool about the rest, consider the public interest only when their own is being attacked. Not careful enough about casting light on the conduct of their leaders, they see the chains that are being prepared for them only when they feel their weight. Always distracted, always deceived, always fixed on other objects, they let themselves be led astray about the most important one of all, and always go looking for the remedy for lack of having known how to prevent the ill. As a result of measuring out their steps they never take them until too late. Their sluggishness would already have ruined them a hundred times if the impatience of the Magistracy had not saved them and if, in a hurry to exercise this supreme power to which it aspires, it had not warned them of the danger itself.

Follow the historic account of your Government, you will always see the Council, ardent in its undertakings, most often failing in them out of too much eagerness to accomplish them, and you will always see the Bourgeoisie finally reconsidering what it had allowed to be done without opposing it.

In 1570 the State was encumbered with debts and afflicted with numerous scourges. Since it was difficult to assemble the general Council often in the circumstances, it is proposed in it to authorize the Councils to provide for present needs: the proposition passes. They started from there to arrogate to themselves the perpetual right of establishing taxes, and for more than a century they were allowed to do so without the slightest opposition.

In 1714 out of secret designs*[84] the immense and ridiculous undertaking of the fortifications was made, without deigning to consult the general Council, and against the tenor of the Edicts. In consequence of this fine project, they establish for ten years taxes about which they do not consult it anymore. Some complaints are raised; they are disdained; and all is silent.

In 1725 the term of the taxes expires; it is a question of prolonging them. For the Bourgeoisie this was the tardy but necessary moment to assert its right, which had been neglected for so long. But with the plague at Marseille and with the royal Bank having disturbed commerce, each, occupied with the dangers to his fortune, forgets those to his liberty. The Council, which does not forget its intentions, renews the taxes in the Two-Hundred, without its being a question of the general Council.

At the expiration of the second term the Citizens wake up, and after one hundred sixty years of indolence, they finally claim back their right in real earnest. Then, instead of ceding or temporizing, the Council weaves a conspiracy.** The plot is discovered; the Bourgeois are forced to take up arms, and by that violent undertaking the Council loses a century of usurpation in a moment.

Everything hardly seems pacified when, not being able to put up with this sort of defeat, they form a new plot. Once again it is necessary to have recourse to arms; the neighboring Powers intervene, and mutual rights are finally set into order.

In 1650 the inferior Councils introduce into their body a manner of collecting the votes, better than the one that is established, but which is not in agreement with the Edicts. In the general Council they continue to follow the old one, into which many abuses slip, and that lasts for fifty years and more before the Citizens consider complaining about the contravention or demanding the introduction of a similar practice in the

---

* This was discussed above.

** It was a question of forming, by means of a barricaded enclosure, a sort of Citadel around the heights on which the City Hall is, in order to subjugate the whole People from there. The lumber already prepared for this enclosure, a plan of disposition for garrisoning it, the orders given in consequence to the Captains of the garrison, transports of munitions and arms from the Arsenal to the City Hall, the spiking of twenty-two cannons in a distant boulevard, the clandestine removal of numerous others. In a word all the preparations for the most violent undertaking made without the acknowledgment of the Councils by the Syndic of the guard and by other Magistrates could not suffice, when all that was discovered, to obtain that proceedings be instituted against the guilty, nor even that their project be clearly blamed. Nevertheless, the Bourgeoisie, at that time master of the Place, let them leave peacefully without troubling their retreat, without giving them the slightest insult, without entering into their houses, without bothering their families, without touching anything that belonged to them. In any other country the People would have begun by massacring these conspirators, and pillaging their houses.

Council of which they are members. They finally demand it, and what is unbelievable is that the same Edict that has been violated for a half-century is calmly cited in opposition to them.

In 1707, contrary to the Laws, a Citizen is judged clandestinely, condemned, shot in prison, another is hanged based on the deposition of a single false witness known as such, another is found dead. All that passes, and it is not spoken of any more until 1734, when someone takes it into his head to ask the Magistrate for news of the Citizen shot thirty years before.

In 1736 criminal Tribunals without Syndics are erected. In the midst of the disturbances that reigned then, the Citizens, being occupied with so much other business, cannot consider everything. In 1758, the same maneuver is repeated, the one concerned with this wants to complain, he is silenced, and all is silent. In 1762 it is renewed again*[85]: the Citizens finally complain the following year. The Council answers: you come too late; the practice is established.

In June 1762 a Citizen for whom the Council had conceived a strong aversion is denounced in his Books, and has a warrant issued against him personally contrary to the most express Edict.[86] His astonished relatives ask for communication of the warrant by petition; it is refused to them, and all is silent. At the end of a year of waiting, seeing that no one is protesting, the denounced Citizen renounces his right of Citizenship. Finally the Bourgeoisie opens its eyes and protests against the violation of the Law: it was too late.

A fact that is more memorable from its type, although it was only a matter of a bagatelle, is that of Master Bardin. A Bookseller entrusts to his correspondent some copies of a new Book; the Book is forbidden before the copies arrive. The Bookseller goes to declare his commission to the Magistrate, and to ask what he should do. He is ordered to give notice when the copies arrive; they arrive, he declares them, they are seized; he waits for

---

* And on what an occasion! Here is a State inquisition to make one shudder. Is it conceivable that in a free country a Citizen would be punished criminally for having, in a letter to another Citizen that was not printed, reasoned in decent and measured terms about the conduct of the Magistrate toward a third citizen? Do you find similar examples of violence in the most absolute Governments? At the time of M. Silhouette's retirement I wrote him a letter that circulated through Paris. This Letter was so bold that I do not find myself exempt from blame; this is perhaps the only reprehensible thing I have written in my life. Nevertheless, did anyone say the slightest thing to me on this subject? They did not even dream of doing so. In France they punish libelous writings; they do very well; but they leave private people a decent liberty to reason among themselves about public affairs, and it is unheard of for anyone to have picked a fight with someone for having stated his opinion, in letters that remain in manuscript, without satire and without invective, about what is done in Tribunals. After having loved republican Government so much, will it be necessary to change my sentiment in my old age, and finally find that there is more genuine liberty in Monarchies than in our Republics?

them to be returned to him or to be paid for them; neither the one nor the other is done; he asks for them back, they are kept. He presents a petition for them to be sent back, returned, or paid for: everything is refused. He loses his Books, and it is public men charged with punishing theft who kept them.[87]

Let all the circumstances of this fact be weighed well, and I doubt that one will find any other example like it in any Parliament, in any Senate, in any Council, in any Divan, in any Tribunal whatsoever. If one wanted to attack the right of property without reason, without pretext and down to its root, it would be impossible to set about it more openly. Nevertheless the affair blows over, everyone remains silent, and, without more serious grievances, that one might never have been at issue. How many others have remained in obscurity for lack of occasions to enter them into evidence?

If the preceding example is hardly important in itself, here is one of a very different sort. Pay a little attention again, Sir, to this affair, and I will suppress all the ones I could add.

November 20, 1763, at the general Council assembled for the election of the Lieutenant and of the Treasurer, the Citizens notice a difference between the printed Edict they have and the manuscript Edict from which a Secretary of State is reading, in that the election of the Treasurer ought from the former to be done with that of the Syndics, and from the second with that of the Lieutenant. They notice, in addition, that the election of the Treasurer, which ought to be done every three years according to the Edict, is done only every six years according to custom, and that at the end of three years they were satisfied to propose the confirmation of the one who is in office.

These differences of the text of the Law between the Manuscript of the Council and the printed Edict, which had not yet been observed, cause others to be noticed which cause anxiety about the rest. In spite of experience that teaches the Citizens the uselessness of their best founded Remonstrances, they make new ones on this subject, asking that the original text of the Edicts be deposited in the Chancellery or in some other public place of the Council's choosing, where one could compare this text with the printed one.

Now you will recall, Sir, that by Article XLII of the Edict of 1738 it is said that *as soon as possible* a general Code of the Laws of the State will be printed that will contain all the Edicts and Settlements. This Code hasn't been spoken about for twenty-six years, and the Citizens have maintained silence.*

---

* With what excuse, with what pretext can one cover the non-compliance with such an express and such an important Article? That cannot be conceived. When one speaks about it

Ninth Letter (Pl., III, 884–887)

You will also recall that, in a Memorandum printed in 1745, an exiled member of the Two-Hundred cast strong suspicion on the faithfulness of the Edicts printed in 1713 and reprinted in 1735, two equally suspicious periods. He said he had compared the manuscript Edicts with these printed ones, in which he affirms he found a quantity of errors that he took note of, and he reports the particular terms of an Edict from 1556, entirely omitted in the printed version. The Council gave no answer to such grave imputations, and the Citizens have maintained silence.

Let us grant, if you wish, that the dignity of the Council did not allow it to respond at that time to the imputations of an exile. This same dignity, compromised honor, suspect faithfulness now demanded a verification which so many indicators rendered necessary, and which those who asked for it had the right to obtain.

Not at all. The small Council justifies the change made to the Edict by an ancient practice that, since the general Council did not oppose it in its origin, it no longer has a right to oppose today.

It gives as the reason for the difference that exists between the Manuscript of the Council and the printed version, that this Manuscript is a collection of Edicts with changes put into practice and consented to by the silence of the general Council; while the printed version is only the collection of the same Edicts, as they passed in the general Council.

It justifies the confirmation of the Treasurer in contradiction to the Edict that requires that another be elected, also by an ancient practice. The Citizens notice no contravention to the Edicts that it does not authorize by prior contraventions: they make no complaint that it does not rebut by reproaching them for not having complained earlier.

And as for the communication of the original text of the Laws, it is flatly refused;*[88] either *as being contrary to the rules*; or because the Citizens

---

by chance to some Magistrates in conversation, they answer coldly, *Each particular Edict is printed, bring them together*. As if one was sure that all were printed, and as if the collection of these scraps formed a complete body of Laws, a general code invested with the required authenticity, and of the sort announced by Article XLII! Is this the way that these Gentlemen fulfill such an express engagement? What sinister consequences could one not draw from omissions like this one?

* These refusals, so harsh and so definite, of all the most reasonable and most just Remonstrances hardly appear natural. Is it conceivable that the Council of Geneva, composed in its greater part of enlightened and judicious men, were not conscious of the odious and even frightening scandal of refusing the communication of the authentic text of the Laws to free men, to members of the Legislator, and of thus wantonly fomenting suspicions produced by the air of mystery and darkness with which it surrounds itself ceaselessly in their eyes? As for me, I incline to believe that these refusals grieve it, but that it has prescribed itself as a rule to bring down the use of Remonstrances by means of constantly negative responses. In fact, is it to be presumed that the most patient men will not lose heart at asking only to receive nothing? Add the proposition already made in the Two-Hundred to inform against the Authors of the latest Remonstrances, for having made use of a right that the Law gives

and Bourgeois *ought to recognize no other text of the Laws than the printed text*, even though the small Council follows a different one and causes this to be followed in the general Council.*

Thus it is against the rules for the one who has passed an act to have the original of that act communicated to him, when the variations in the copies make him suspect them of falsification or incorrectness, and it is according to the rule to have two different texts of the same Laws, one for private individuals and the other for the Government! Have you ever heard anything like it? And nevertheless concerning all these late discoveries, concerning all these outrageous refusals, the Citizens, sent packing in their most legitimate demands, keep quiet, wait, and remain at rest.

There, Sir, are facts notorious in your Town, and all known better by you than by me; I could add a hundred others, without counting those that have escaped me. These will be enough to judge whether the Bourgeoisie of Geneva is or ever was, I do not say turbulent and seditious, but vigilant, attentive, easily stirred up to defend its best established and most openly attacked rights?

We are told that *a Nation that is lively, ingenious, and very much taken up with its political rights would have an extreme need to give its government a negative force.*** In commenting upon this negative force one can agree on the principle; but is it to you they want to apply it? Has it been forgotten then that elsewhere more coolness is attributed to you than to other Peoples?*** And how can it be said that the people of Geneva greatly attends to its political rights, when it is seen that it never attends to them except tardily, with repugnance, and only when the most urgent peril constrains it to? So that by not attacking the rights of the bourgeoisie so abruptly, the Council is able to keep the bourgeoisie from ever attending to them.

Let us draw a parallel between the two parties for a moment in order to judge which one's activity is more to be feared, and where the negative right ought to be placed in order to moderate that activity.

On the one side I see a not very numerous people, peaceful and cold, composed of laborious men, lovers of gain, having submitted to Laws and to their Ministers for their own interest; completely busy with their trade or their professions. All, equal by their rights and hardly distinguished by fortune, have among them neither leaders nor clients. All, kept in a great

---

them. Henceforward who will want to expose himself to prosecution for measures one knows in advance to be unsuccessful? If that is the plan that the small Council has made for itself, it must be admitted that it is following it very well.

* Extract from the Registers of the Council from December 7, 1763, in response to the verbal Remonstrances made November 21 by six Citizens or Bourgeois.
** Page 170.
*** Page 154.

dependence on the body of Magistrates by their commerce, by their condition, by their goods, have to treat it considerately. All are afraid of displeasing it. If they want to meddle with public affairs it is always at the prejudice of their own. On the one side, distracted by objects that interest their families more; on the other, stopped by considerations of prudence, by the experience of all times, which teaches them how dangerous it is to offend the Council in a State as small as yours in which every private individual is ceaselessly under its eyes, they are induced by the strongest reasons to sacrifice everything to peace; for they can prosper through it alone; and in this state of things each—deceived by his private interest—prefers even more to be protected than to be free, and pays his court in order to make his profit.

On the other side I see in a small Town, whose business amounts to very little at bottom, a body of independent and perpetual Magistrates, almost idle by station, making its principal occupation out of a very great and very natural interest, on the part of those who command, to increase its empire ceaselessly; for, like avarice, ambition nourishes itself with its advantages, and the more one extends his power, the more one is devoured by the desire to be able to do everything. Ceaselessly attentive to marking out distances too imperceptible in its equals by birth, it sees in them only its inferiors, and burns to see in them its subjects. Armed with all the public force, depositary of all authority, interpreter and dispenser of the Laws that hinder it, it makes an offensive and defensive arm out of them for itself, which makes it formidable, respectable, sacred to all those it wants to outrage. It is in the very name of the Law that it can transgress it with impunity. It can attack the constitution while pretending to defend it; it can punish as a rebel anyone who dares to defend it in fact. All the enterprises of this body become easy for it; it leaves to no one the right of stopping or being acquainted with them; it can act, defer, suspend; it can seduce, frighten, punish those who resist it, and if it deigns to employ pretexts for this, it is more out of decorum than out of necessity. Thus it has the will to extend its power, and the means to succeed at everything it wills. Such is the relative condition of the small Council and the Bourgeoisie of Geneva. Which of these two bodies ought to have the negative power to stop the undertakings of the other? The Author of the Letters assures that it is the former.

In the majority of States internal troubles come from a brutalized and stupid populace, at first inflamed by unbearable vexations, then stirred up in secret by skillful troublemakers, invested with some authority that they want to extend. But is there anything more false than an idea like this one applied to the Bourgeoisie of Geneva, at least to the part of it that is opposing power in order to support the Laws? At all times this part has always been the middle order between the rich and the poor, between the leaders of the State and the populace. This order, composed of men just about equal in fortune, in station, in enlightenment, is neither elevated enough to have pretensions, nor low enough to have nothing to lose. Their great interest, their common interest is that the Laws be observed, the Magistrates respected, that the constitution maintain itself, and that the State be tranquil. No one in this order enjoys any sort of superiority over the others that allows him to set them into motion for his private interest. It is the healthiest part of the Republic, the only part that one is assured cannot propose any object for itself in its conduct other than the good of all. Therefore one always sees in their common proceedings a decency, a modesty, a respectful firmness, a certain gravity of men who feel themselves to be within their right and who keep themselves within their duty. See, on the contrary, what the other party props itself up with; people who swim in opulence and the most abject people. Is it in these two extremes, the one made to buy, the other to sell itself, that one should look for love of justice and the laws? It is by means of them that the State always degenerates: the rich man holds the Law in his purse, and the poor prefers bread to liberty. It is enough to compare these two parties to judge which should make the first attack on the Laws; and look in fact in your history to see whether all the plots haven't always come from the side of the Magistracy, and whether the Citizens have ever had recourse to force except when it was necessary to protect themselves against it?

No doubt, they are mocking when, concerning the consequences of the right that your Fellow Citizens claim, they represent to you the State prey to intrigue, to seduction, to the first comer. This negative right that the Council wants to have was unknown until now; what ills have happened because of it? Frightful ones would have happened if the Council had insisted on it when the Bourgeoisie asserted its own. Turn the argument that is drawn from two hundred years of prosperity against them; what can be answered? Isn't this Government, you will say, established by time, sustained by so many titles, authorized by such a long practice, consecrated by its successes, and in which the negative right of the Councils was always unknown, worth as much as this other arbitrary Government, whose properties or connection to our happiness we do not yet know, and in which reason can show us only the depth of our misery?

To assume all the abuses in the party one is attacking and to assume none of them in one's own, is a very coarse and very ordinary sophism, from which every sensible man must protect himself. One must assume abuses on both sides, because some creep in everywhere; but that is not to say that their consequences are equal. Every abuse is an evil, often inevitable, for the sake of which one should not proscribe what is good in itself. But compare, and you will find on one side certain evils, terrible evils without limit and without end; on the other, even the difficult abuse, though it is great, will pass, and is such that when it takes place it always brings its remedy along with it. For once again, no liberty is possible except in the observation of the Laws or the general will, and it is no more in the general will to hurt everyone than in the particular will to hurt oneself. But let us assume this abuse of liberty to be as natural as the abuse of power. There will always be this difference between the one and the other, that the abuse of liberty turns against the people who abuse it and, punishing them for their own wrong, forces them to look for its remedy; thus on this side the evil is never anything but a crisis, it cannot constitute a permanent state. Instead of which, since the abuse of power does not turn against the powerful but the weak, it is by its nature without measure, without brake, without limits: it ends only by destroying the only one who feels the evil. Let us say then that the Government must belong to the small number, the oversight of the Government to the generality, and if abuse is necessary from both parts, it would be better for a people to be unhappy through its own fault than oppressed under someone else's hand.

The first and greatest public interest is always justice. All wish the conditions to be equal for all, and justice is nothing but this equality. The Citizen wants only the Laws and the observation of the Laws. Each private individual in the people knows well that, if there are exceptions, they will not be in his favor. Thus all fear the exceptions, and the one who fears exceptions loves the Law. Among the Leaders it is a completely different thing: their very station is a station of preference, and they seek preferences everywhere.* If they want Laws, it is not in order to obey them, it is in order to be their arbiters. They want Laws in order to put themselves in the place and to make themselves feared in the name of the Laws. Everything favors them in this project. They make use of the rights they have in order to usurp without risk those they do not have. Since they always speak in the name of the Law, even while violating it, whoever dares to defend it against them is a seditious person, a rebel: he ought to perish; and as for them, always certain of impunity in their undertakings, the

---

* Justice in the people is a virtue of station; and violence and Tyranny in the Leaders is a vice of station in the same way. If we other private individuals were in their places, we would become violent, usurpers, iniquitous as they are. Thus when some Magistrates come to preach their integrity, their moderation, their justice to us, they are deceiving us, if they want to obtain the confidence that we do not owe them this way: not that they cannot personally have these virtues of which they boast; but then they form an exception; and the Law must not consider exceptions.

worst that happens to them is not to succeed. If they need support, they find some everywhere. The league of the stronger is a natural one, and what constitutes the weakness of the weak is not to be able to league together this way. Such is the destiny of the people always to have its opponents as judges inside and out. The people are fortunate when they can find judges equitable enough to protect them against the judges' own maxims, against this sentiment so graven in the human heart: to love and favor interests similar to our own. You had that advantage one time, and this was contrary to all expectation. When the Mediation was accepted, one would have believed you were crushed: but you had enlightened and firm defenders, upright and generous Mediators; justice and truth triumphed. May you be fortunate twice! You will have enjoyed a very rare happiness, and your oppressors hardly appear alarmed about the likelihood.

After having laid out before you all the imaginary evils of a right as old as your Constitution and which never produced any evil, they palliate, they deny those of the new Right they are usurping and that are making themselves felt even now. Forced to admit that the Government can abuse the negative right to the point of the most intolerable tyranny, they affirm that what is happening will not happen, and they change what is happening under your eyes today into a possibility without likelihood. No one, they dare to say, will say that the Government is not equitable and gentle; and notice that that is said in answer to Remonstrances in which the injustices and acts of violence of the Government are complained about. That is truly what one can call fine style: it is the eloquence of Pericles, who, overcome by Thucydides in wrestling, proved to the spectators that he was the one who had thrown him.[89]

In this way, then, while seizing someone else's property without pretext, while imprisoning innocent people without reason, while denouncing a Citizen without hearing him, while judging another illegally, while protecting obscene Books, while burning those that breathe virtue, while persecuting their authors, while hiding the true text of the Laws, while refusing the most just reparations, while exercising the harshest despotism, while destroying the liberty they should defend, while oppressing the Fatherland whose fathers they should be, these Gentlemen compliment themselves over the great equity of their judgments, they go into raptures over the gentleness of their administration, they affirm with confidence that the whole world is of their opinion on this point. I doubt very much, nevertheless, that this opinion is yours, and I am sure at least that it is not that of the Remonstrators.

Let not private interest make me unjust. Of all our inclinations, that is the one against which I guard myself the most and which I hope I have best resisted. Your Magistrate is equitable in indifferent things, I even believe him to be prone to be so always; his positions are hardly lucrative; he renders justice and does not sell it; he is personally upright, disinterested, and I know that in this Council that is so despotic uprightness and virtues still reign. By showing you the consequences of the negative right I have told you less what they will do after having become Sovereigns than what they will continue to do in order to be so. Once recognized as such, their interest will be always to be just, and even now it is their interest to be just most often: but woe to anyone who will dare to have recourse to the Laws again, and to demand liberty! It is against these unfortunate people that everything becomes permitted, legitimate. Equity, virtue, even interest do not hold fast before love of domination, and the one who will be just when he is master spares no injustice to become it.

The true road of Tyranny is not at all to attack the public good directly; that would be to wake up the whole world to defend it; but it is to attack all its defenders successively, and to frighten anyone who would still dare to aspire to be one. Persuade everyone that the public interest is not that of anyone, and by that alone servitude is established; for when each will be under the yoke, where will common liberty be? If whoever dares to speak is crushed at the very instant, where will those be who would want to imitate him, and what will be the organ of the generality when each individual will keep silent? Then the Government will deal severely with the zealous and will be just with the others, until it can be unjust with everyone with impunity. Then its justice will no longer be anything but an economy in order not to dissipate its own belongings without reason.

Thus there is a sense in which the Council is just and ought to be so out of interest: but there is one in which it belongs to the system it has made for itself to be sovereignly unjust, and a thousand examples should have taught you how insufficient the protection of the Laws is against the hatred of the Magistrate. How will this be sufficient when, having become sole, absolute master by means of his negative right, he will no longer be hindered by anything in his conduct, and will no longer find any obstacle to his passions? In such a little State in which none can hide himself in the crowd, who will not live then in eternal fear, and will not feel at every instant of his life the misfortune of having his equals as masters? In large States private individuals are too far from the Prince and the leaders to be seen by them, their smallness saves them, and provided that the people pay, they are left in peace. But you will not be able to take a step without feeling the weight of your irons. The relatives, the friends, the protégés, the spies of your masters will be more your masters than they will; you will dare neither to defend your rights nor to claim your belongings, for fear of making enemies for yourself; the most obscure recesses will not be able to hide you from Tyranny, one will necessarily have to be its satellite or its victim: You will feel political and civil slavery at the same time, you will hardly dare to breathe in liberty. There, Sir, is where the practice of the negative right as the Council is arrogating it for itself ought naturally to lead you. I believe that it will not want to make such a fatal practice of it, but it certainly will be able to, and the certitude alone that it can be unjust with impunity will make you feel the same evils as if it was so in fact.

I have shown you, Sir, the condition of your Constitution as it presents itself to my eyes. It results from this exposition that this Constitution, taken in its totality, is good and healthy, and that by giving liberty its genuine limits, at the same time gives it all the solidity it ought to have. For the Government having a negative right against the innovations of the Legislator, and the People a negative right against the usurpations of the Council, the Laws alone reign and reign over all; the first person of the State is no less subject to them than the last, no one can break them, no private interest can change them, and the Constitution remains unshakable.

But if on the contrary the Ministers of the Laws become their sole arbiters, and can make them speak or keep silent at will: if the right of Remonstrance, the sole guarantee of the Laws and of liberty, is only an illusory and vain right that does not have any necessary effect in any case; I do not see any servitude comparable to yours, and the image of liberty is no longer anything among you but a contemptuous and puerile lure, which it is even indecent to offer to sensible men. What use is it then to assemble the Legislator, since the will of the Council is the unique Law? What use is it solemnly to elect Magistrates who were already your Judges in advance, and who from that election hold only a power they exercised previously? Submit with good grace, and renounce those children's games, which, having become frivolous, are only an additional debasement for you.

Since this condition is the worst into which one could fall, it has only one advantage; that is that it cannot change except for the better. That is the unique advantage of extreme evils; but this advantage is always great, when men of sense and of heart feel it and know how to avail themselves of it. How firm the certainty of not being able to fall lower than you are ought to render you in your proceedings! But be sure that you will not leave the abyss as long as you are divided, as long as some want to act and the others to stay tranquil.

Here I am, Sir, at the conclusion of these Letters. After having shown you the condition in which you are, I will not undertake to trace out for

Ninth Letter (Pl., III, 894–897) 305

you the road that you must follow in order to leave it. If there is one, being on the very spot, you and your Fellow Citizens must see it better than I can; when one knows where one is and where one ought to go, one can direct oneself without effort.

The Author of the Letters says that *if one remarked an inclination toward violence in a Government, one would not have to wait until Tyranny has fortified itself there in order to redress it.** He says further, in assuming a case that he treats in truth as a chimera, that *there would remain a sad but legal remedy, which in this extreme case could be employed as one employs the hand of a Surgeon when gangrene breaks out.*** Whether or not you are in this supposedly chimerical case is what I just examined. My counsel is thus no longer necessary here; the Author of the Letters has given it to you for me. All means of protesting against injustice are permitted when they are peaceful, with greater reason those authorized by the laws are permitted.

When they are transgressed in particular cases you have the right of Remonstrance to provide for it. But when this very right is contested, it is a matter for the guarantee.[90] I did not number it among the means that can render a Remonstrance efficacious, the Mediators themselves did not intend to put it there, since they have declared they did not wish to make any attempt upon the independence of the State, and because then, nevertheless, they would have put, so to speak, the Key of the Government into their pocket.*** Thus in the particular case the effect of rejected Remonstrances is to produce a general Council; but the effect of the rejection of the very right of Remonstrance appears to be recourse to the guarantee. The machine must have in itself all the springs that ought to make it go: when it stops, one must call in the Workman in order to wind it up.

I see too well where that recourse goes, and I still feel my patriot heart groan at it. Therefore, I repeat it, I propose nothing to you; what would I dare to say? Deliberate with your Fellow Citizens and do not count the votes until after having weighed them. Be on your guard against turbulent youth, against insolent opulence, and venal indigence; no healthy advice can come from those directions. Consult those whom a decent mediocrity protects against the seductions of ambition and of misery; those whose honorable old age crowns a life without reproach; those whom a long

---

* Page 172.
** Page 101.
*** The consequence of such a system would have been to establish a Tribunal of the Mediation in residence at Geneva, in order to take cognizance of the transgressions of the Laws. By this Tribunal the sovereignty of the Republic would soon have been destroyed, but the liberty of the Citizens would have been much better assured than it can be if one removes the right of Remonstrance. Now to be Sovereign only in name does not mean much, but to be free in fact means a lot.

experience has versed in public business; those who, without ambition in the State, do not wish any other rank there than that of Citizens; finally those who, having never had as an object in their proceedings anything but the good of the fatherland and the maintenance of the Laws, have deserved by their virtues the esteem of the public and the confidence of their equals.

But above all come together. You are ruined without resource if you remain divided. And why would you be divided when such great common interests unite you? How do base jealousy and petty passions dare to make themselves heard in such danger? Are they worth being satisfied at such a high price, and will it be necessary for your children to say someday while weeping over their chains: here is the fruit of our fathers' dissentions? In a word, it is less a question of deliberation here than of concord; the choice of which course you will take is not the greatest question: Were it bad in itself, take it all together; by that alone it will become the best, and you will always do what needs to be done provided that you do so in concert. There is my advice, Sir, and I end where I began. By obeying you I have fulfilled my final duty toward the Fatherland. Now I take leave of those who live there; they have no evil left to do to me, and I can no longer do them any good.

THE VISION OF PIERRE OF THE MOUNTAIN, CALLED THE SEER

Here are written the three Chapters of the vision of Pierre of the mountain called the Seer, *concerning the disobedience and damnable rebellion of Pierre of the Valley called* Pierrot of the Ladies.

Chapter I

1. And I was in my meadow mowing my second crop, and it was hot, and I was weary, and a plum tree with green plums to me was nigh.

2. And lying down under the plum tree, I slumbered.

3. And during my sleep I had a vision, and I heard a voice sharp and ringing like the sound of a posthorn.

4. And that voice was sometimes weak and sometimes strong, sometimes booming and sometimes clear, passing alternately and rapidly from the deepest to the sharpest sounds, like the mewing of a cat on a gutter, or like the declamation of Reverend Imer, Deacon of Val de Travers.[1]

5. And the voice addressing itself to me spoke to me thus: Pierre the Seer, my son, listen to my words; and I kept quiet while slumbering, and the voice continued.

6. Listen to the word that I address to thee on behalf of the Spirit, and hold it in thine heart. Broadcast it throughout the earth and throughout Val-de-Travers, so that it might edify all the faithful;

7. And so that, taught about the punishment of the rebel Pierre of the Valley called Pierrot of the Ladies, they learn no longer to despise the nocturnal inspirations of the voice.

8. For I had chosen him in the abjectness of his mind and in the stupidity of his heart to be my interpreter.

9. I had made him the honorable successor of my Servant la *Batizarde*,* so that, like her, he might carry the light of my inspirations to all the Church.

10. I had charged him with being, like her, the organ of my word so

---

* An old gossip, from the dregs of the People, who formerly prided herself for having visions.

that my glory might be manifested, and so that it might be seen that when I please I can draw gold from mud, and pearls from manure.

11. I had said to him: go speak to thine errant brother Jean-Jacques who is going astray, and lead him back to the good path.

12. For at bottom thy brother Jean-Jacques is a good man who does wrong to no one, who fears God and who loves the truth.

13. But in order to lead him back from an aberration this people falls into one itself, and for wishing to bring him back to the faith, this people renounces the Law.

14. For the law forbids avenging the offenses one has received and they ceaselessly revile a man who has not offended them at all.

15. The law commands returning good for evil, and they return him evil for good.

16. The Law commands loving those who hate us, and they hate the one who loves them.

17. The Law commands employing mercy, and they do not even employ justice.

18. The Law forbids lying, and there is no sort of lie that they do not invent against him.

19. The Law forbids slander, and they ceaselessly calumniate him.

20. They accuse him of having said that women did not have any soul, and he says on the contrary that all lovable women have at least two of them.[2]

21. They accuse him of not believing in God, and no one has so strongly proven the existence of God.

22. They say that he is the Antichrist, and no one has honored Christ in such a worthy manner.

23. They say that he wishes to unsettle their consciences, and never has he spoken to them about Religion.

24. If they read Books written for his defense in other countries, is it His fault and has he entreated them to read them? But on the contrary, it is because they have not read them that they believe that there are bad things in these Books that are not there, and they do not believe that the good things that are in them are in fact in them.

25. For those who have read them think completely otherwise about them, and say so if they are of good faith.

26. Yet this People is naturally good, but they are deceived; and they do not see that they are made to defend the cause of Good with the arms of Satan.

27. Let us draw them from the bad way where they are being led, and let us remove this stumbling block from in front of their feet.

Chapter II

1. Go then and speak to thine errant brother Jean-Jacques, and address these words to him in my name: thus has spoken the voice on behalf of the spirit.

2. My son Jean-Jacques, thou losest thy way in thine ideas. Come back to thyself, be docile, and receive my words of correction.

3. Thou believest in the powerful, intelligent, good, just and rewarding God; and in that thou doest well.

4. Thou believest in his son Jesus his Christ and in his word; and in that thou doest well.

5. Thou followest with all thy power the precepts of the Holy Gospel; and in that thou doest well.

6. Thou lovest men as thy neighbor and Christians as thy brothers. Thou doest good when thou canst, and never doest evil to anyone except for thy defense and that of justice.

7. Based on experience thou awaitest little equity on the part of men; but thou puttest thine hope in the other life which will compensate thee for the miseries of this one; and in all that thou doest well.

8. I know thy works; I love the good ones, thine heart and my clemency will efface the bad ones. But one thing displeases me in thee.

9. Thou persisteth in rejecting miracles; and what do miracles matter to thee? Since moreover thou believest in the Law without them, speaketh not about them, and no longer cause scandal to the weak.

10. And when thou, Pierre of the Valley, called Pierrot of the Ladies, will have said these words to thine errant brother Jean-Jacques, he will be seized with astonishment.

11. And seeing that thou, who art a coarse and a stupid man, speakest to him reasonably and decently, he will be struck by this prodigy, and he will recognize the finger of God.

12. And prostrating himself on the earth he will say. Behold my brother Pierrot of the Ladies who utters sensible and decent speeches. My disbelief gives way to this obvious sign. I believe in miracles, for none is greater than this one.

13. And all of Val de Travers witness of this double prodigy will intone canticles of joy; and it will be proclaimed from all sides in the six communities. Jean-Jacques believes in miracles, and sensible speeches come out of the mouth of Pierrot of the Ladies. The Almighty shows himself in his works: let his holy name be blessed.

14. Then, ashamed at having insulted a peaceful and gentle man, they will hasten to make him forget their outrages, and they will love him as

their neighbor, and he will love them as his brothers. Seditious cries will no longer stir them up, hypocrisy will exhale its gall in vain murmurs to which even women will not listen at all. The peace of Christ will reign among Christians and scandal will be removed from their midst.

15. It is thus that I had spoken to Pierre of the Valley, called Pierrot of the Ladies, when I deigned to choose him to carry my word to his errant brother.

16. But instead of submitting to the mission that I had given him, and going to find Jean-Jacques as I had commanded him, he did not have faith in my promise, and was not able to believe in the miracle of which he was to be the instrument. Wild like the Onager of the desert and stubborn as Edom's Mule, he could not believe that persuasive speeches could be put in his mouth and has persisted in his rebellion.

17. This is why, having rejected him, I order thee Pierre of the mountain, called the Seer, to write this anathema and to address it to him either directly or through the public, so that he cannot claim ignorance of it, and so that everyone may learn from the accomplishment of the punishment that I predict for him, not to disobey holy visions any longer.

Chapter III

1. Here are the words dictated by the voice under the plum tree with green plums to me, Pierre of the Mountain, called the Seer; to be the sentence conveyed in the same duly signified and pronounced to the said Pierre of the Valley, called Pierrot of the Ladies, so that he might prepare himself for its execution, and all the People being witness to it might become wise by this example, and learn not to disobey holy visions any longer.

2. Stiff-necked man, didst thou fear that he who caused fleshly nourishment to be given to the prophet through crows could not give spiritual nourishment to thy brother through thee? Fearest thou that he who made an ass speak cannot make a Horse speak?

3. Instead of proceeding uprightly and confidently to fulfill the mission I had given thee, thou hast lost thyself in the aberration of thy bad heart. Out of fear of leading thy brother to repentence thou hast not wished to bring him my word. Instead of that, abandoning thyself to the spirit of cabal and lying, thou hast divulged the order that I had given thee in secret, and malignantly suppressing the good that I had charged thee to say, thou hast falsely substituted for it the evil about which I had not spoken to thee.

4. This is why I have brought against thee this irrevocable judgment of

which nothing can stay or change the effect. Thou then, Pierre of the Valley called Pierrot of the Ladies, listen and tremble; for behold thine hour draweth nigh; its speed will be ruled by thy thirst.

5. I know all thy secret machinations; thy plots have been formed while drinking; it is while drinking that they will be punished. Since the memorable night of thy vision until this day the thirteenth of the Month of Elul* at the ninth hour,** one hundred and sixteen hours have passed.

6. In my clemency to give thee time to know thyself and to mend thy ways, I grant thee the power to drink one hundred and fifteen more bumpers of pure wine, or their value, measured in the same cup in which thou hast drunk thy last draught, on the eve of thy vision.

7. But as soon as thy lips will have touched the one hundred and sixteenth bumper, thou must die; and before it has been emptied, thou wilt die suddenly.

8. And do thou not think to deceive me about the count by drinking furtively or in cups of varying measure. For I follow thee everywhere with my eye, and my measure is as sure as that of thy servant's bread, and as the balance in which thou weighest thy coins.

9. In whatever time and in whatever place thou drinkest the one hundred and sixteenth bumper, thou wilt die suddenly.

10. If thou drinkest it in the depths of thy cellar hidden alone among thy barrels of bad wine, thou wilt die suddenly.

11. If thou drinkest it at table in the midst of thy family at the end of thy meager dinner, thou wilt die suddenly.

12. If thou drinkest it at Joseph Clerc's[3] seeking some lie in the wine along with him, thou wilt die suddenly.

13. If thou drinkest it at Mayor Baillod's[4] house listening to one of his old sermons, thou wilt fall asleep for ever, even if he does not continue to read.

14. If thou drinkest it while chatting with the Professor[5] in secret, even while scheming some new vision, thou wilt die suddenly.

15. Happy mortal, until thy final moment and beyond, thou wilt put more spirit[6] into thy stomach while dying than thy brain will yield of it, and the most pompous funeral oration in which thy visions will be celebrated will yield thee more honor after thy death than thou hadst in thy life.

16. Boy,[7] too happy Pierre Boy,[8] hasten thee to drink. Thou canst not hurry too much to go to win the laurels that await thee in the country of visions. Thou wilt die, but thanks to this one thy name will live among

---

* The month of Elul corresponds just about to our month of August.
** At this season the ninth hour comes around two hours after noon.

men. Boy, Pierre Boy: go promptly to the immortality that is owed thee. So be it; Amen, Amen.

17. And when I heard these words, I, Pierre of the Mountain called the Seer, I was seized by a great fear, and I said to the voice.

18. God forbid that I should herald these things without being assured of them by a sign. I know my brother Pierrot of the Ladies: he wants to have visions all to himself. He will not wish to believe in mine, even though I have been named *the Seer*. But if it must come to pass as thou sayest, giveth me a sign under whose authority I can speak.

19. And as I was finishing these words, behold I was awakened by a terrible blow, and putting my hand onto my head, I felt my face completely bloodied: for my nose was bleeding very much and the blood streamed down my face. Nevertheless after having stanched it as much as I could, I arose without any other wound, except that my nose was bruised and extremely swollen.

20. Then, looking around me from whence this blow could come, at last I saw that a plum had fallen from the tree and had struck me.

21. Seeing the plum near me, I took it up; and after having considered it well, I recognized that it was extremely healthy, extremely big, extremely green, and extremely hard, as the condition of my nose attested.

22. Then, my understanding having been opened, I saw that the plum in this condition could not naturally have fallen by itself. I saw in addition that the direct hit on the end of my nose was another miracle not less manifest, which confirmed the first one and showed clearly the work of the Spirit.

23. And, giving thanks to the voice for such an evident sign, I resolved to publish the vision as it was commanded me, and to keep the plum as evidence for my words, as I have done up to this day.

Notes

Bloom   Jean-Jacques Rousseau. *Emile*. Edited by Allan Bloom. New York: Basic Books, 1979.
Collected Writings   Jean-Jacques Rousseau. *Collected Writings of Rousseau*, Volumes I–VIII, Edited by Roger D. Masters and Christopher Kelly. Hanover, N.H.: University Press of New England, 1991– .
Launay   Jean-Jacques Rousseau, *Oeuvres complètes*, Vols. 1–3. Paris: Editions du Seuil [Collection L'Intrégale], 1967ff.
Pléiade (or Pl.)   Jean-Jacques Rousseau, *Oeuvres complètes*, Vols. 1–5. Paris: NRF-Editions de la Pléiade, 1959ff.

EDITORS' INTRODUCTION

1. See *Confessions*, *Collected Writings*, V, 508 and 521.
2. Ibid., 430.
3. Ibid., 473.
4. Ibid., 503.
5. Ibid., 522.
6. The most complete account of these events, along with the best edition of the *Vision*, can be found in Fréderic S. Eigeldinger, *"Des Pierres dans mon jardin": Les années neuchâteloises de J.J. Rousseau et la crise de 1765* (Paris-Genève: Champion-Slatkine, 1992). We have followed Eigeldinger's numbering of the verses.
7. These responses and the attacks to which they respond can be found in *Collected Writings*, II.
8. See *Collected Writings*, II, 84–85 and 110–129.
9. See pp. 21 and 133 below.
10. See p. 227 below.
11. See p. 16 below.
12. See p. 14 below.
13. See pp. 55 and 66 below.
14. See p. 26 below.
15. See pp. 46–47 below.
16. Certain objectors have complained that "this frankness is misplaced with the public" and that "not every truth is good to state." (See p. 51 below.) In his last work, Rousseau agrees with this last objection; the "sacred" truth which he claims he has always tried to tell is that which is useful for the "moral order." *Reveries*, *Collected Writings*, VIII, 28–34.
17. *Emile*, Bloom, 40.
18. *Reveries*, *Collected Writings*, VIII, 23.

19. *Emile*, Bloom, 313–314.
20. Cf. p. 54 below. The version of this statement cited here is from the first draft of the *Letter*.
21. *Confessions, Collected Writings*, V, 342.
22. See p. 59 below.
23. See p. 61 below.
24. See p. 57 below.
25. See p. 57 below.
26. Rousseau attacks the French policy of civil tolerance combined with theological tolerance in the *Social Contract* (*Collected Writings*, IV, 223), arguing that it is impossible to live with people whom one believes to be damned.
27. *Second Discourse, Collected Writings*, III, 19.
28. See p. 77 below. Throughout the *Letter* Rousseau seems to take the side of the "reasoner" in the *Profession*, whom the Archbishop qualifies as an "unbeliever": "And who are you to dare tell me that God contradicts Himself, and whom would I prefer to believe—Him who teaches me eternal truths by reason, or you who proclaim an absurdity on His behalf?" (*Emile*, Bloom, 300).
29. See p. 5 below.
30. *Emile*, Bloom, 280.
31. See p. 68 below.
32. See p. 68 below.
33. See p. 70 below.
34. See p. 77 below.
35. See p. 74 below.
36. See p. 45 below.
37. See pp. 43–44 below.
38. See pp. 44–45 below.
39. See p. 44 below.
40. See p. 42 below.
41. See p. 43 below.
42. See p. 75 below. The second time Rousseau discusses only the sublimity of the Gospel's "author."
43. *Emile*, Bloom, 282.
44. See p. 46 below.
45. *Emile*, Bloom, 282–283.
46. This is also one of the themes of the *Letter to Voltaire, Collected Writings*, III, 108–121.
47. See p. 46 below.
48. See p. 75 below.
49. *Reveries, Collected Writings*, VIII, 24.
50. See p. 4 below; *Second Discourse, Collected Writings*, III, 27, 86.
51. *Emile*, Bloom, 81–82.
52. See p. 5 below.
53. See p. 4 below.
54. See p. 4 below. The argument that the simultaneous misery and greatness of the human soul is unintelligible to philosophy, but explained by Christianity, is

made most powerfully by Pascal. This part of the *Letter* can be taken as Rousseau's most direct response to Pascal.

55. See p. 32 below.
56. See p. 46 below.
57. See p. 154 below.
58. See p. 155 below.
59. See p. 311 below.
60. See p. 174 below.
61. See p. 178 below.
62. See p. 166 below.
63. Rousseau does concede that "other passages present a meaning contrary" to the ones he cites (p. 172 below).
64. See p. 167 below.
65. See p. 232 below.
66. A very useful treatment of Rousseau's thought with particular emphasis on the *Letters Written from the Mountain* is James Miller, *Rousseau: Dreamer of Democracy* (New Haven and London: Yale University Press, 1984).
67. See p. 237 below.
68. See p. 257 below.
69. See p. 103 below.
70. See pp. 257–258 below.
71. See p. 242 below.
72. *Collected Writings*, IV, 196–197.
73. See p. 263 below.
74. See p. 271 below.
75. See p. 305 below.

PASTORAL LETTER OF HIS GRACE THE ARCHBISHOP

1. 2 Timothy 3: 1–4 and 8.
2. Wisdom 4: 12. Wisdom is a part of the apocrypha.
3. This is a reference to Rousseau's *Discourse on the Sciences and the Arts*.
4. This is a reference to the *Discourse on the Origin of Inequality*.
5. This is a reference to *Julie*.
6. 1 Peter 2: 2.
7. *Emile*, Bloom, 92.
8. *Emile*, Bloom, 260. Beaumont abridges and alters the passage slightly.
9. Epistle to the Romans, 12: 1.
10. Psalms 92: 5.
11. This is a paraphrase of *Emile*, Bloom, 256.
12. Saint Augustine, *Confessions*, I.9.
13. *Emile*, Bloom, 257.
14. *Emile*, Bloom, 178–179.
15. *Emile*, Bloom, 94.
16. *Emile*, Bloom, 258.

17. Epistle to the Romans 1: 19–22.
18. *Emile*, Bloom, 276–277.
19. Tertullian, *Adversus Marcionem*, I.
20. *Emile*, Bloom, 295.
21. *Emile*, Bloom, 297.
22. *Emile*, Bloom, 298–299.
23. *Emile*, Bloom, 299. Beaumont abridges the paragraph.
24. *Emile*, Bloom, 307–308. As Rousseau points out (72 below), Beaumont both misquotes and abridges the passage.
25. *Emile*, Bloom, 308. Beaumont abridges slightly.
26. Psalms, 26: 12.
27. *Emile*, Bloom, 212.
28. *Emile*, Bloom, 266.
29. *Emile*, Bloom, 300.
30. *Emile*, Bloom, 303.
31. *Emile*, Bloom, 236.
32. Proverbs 8: 15.
33. First Epistle of Peter 2: 17.
34. Epistle to the Romans 13: 1, 2.
35. Saint Augustine, *Enarrat, in psal.*, 124.
36. Epistle to Titus 2: 12, 13.
37. 2 Timothy 4: 1, 2.
38. Tobias 14: 11.
39. Tobias 14: 17.
40. Proverbs 22: 6.
41. Jean Damascene, t. II, 462–463.

LETTER TO BEAUMONT

1. "Pardon me if I speak freely, not to insult you, but to defend myself. I presume upon your seriousness and prudence, because you can consider the necessity of responding that you have imposed on me."
2. Rousseau wrote the *First Discourse* in response to the question, "Has the restoration of the sciences and arts tended to purify morals?" posed by the Academy of Dijon in 1749 when he was thirty-seven years old. The *Discourse*, some of the attacks on it referred to below, and Rousseau's responses can be found in *Collected Writings*, II. An account of the effect of his new fame can be found in *Confessions*, VIII, in *Collected Writings*, V.
3. After attacking French opera in the "Letter on French Music" (*Collected Writings*, VII, 141–174) in 1753, one year after his great triumph with his opera, *The Village Soothsayer*, Rousseau was burned in effigy. There was in fact a *lettre de cachet* issued against him. See *Confessions, Collected Writings*, V, 322–323. For an excellent account of these events that supports much of what Rousseau says about them, see Robert Wokler, "Rousseau on Rameau and Revolution," *Studies in the Eighteenth Century* 44 (1978), 251–283.
4. This was a commonplace of the attacks on the *First Discourse*; see *Collected Writings*, II, 28–32, 66, 70, 95, and 132.

5. After sending the manuscript to the publisher Rousseau changed the original "opinions" to prejudices. The reason for this change was to use a masculine word to make it clear that the "my own" later in the sentence (which is a feminine) would be read as referring back to "wills" and not to "opinions."

6. A warrant for Rousseau's arrest was issued by the Parlement of Paris on June 9, 1762, not long after the publication of *Emile*. Upon being informed of the warrant, Rousseau fled France and began a period of wandering through Europe. The events around the condemnation of *Emile* can be found in Book XI of the *Confessions*.

7. *Emile* was published with legal permission of the government of Holland, which was indicated on the title page.

8. Rousseau uses the expression *droit des gens*, which refers to standards of justice between peoples of different communities, not merely to treaties and other formally recognized agreements.

9. In the manuscript opposite this passage Rousseau wrote fragment 1, p. 84 below.

10. For Rousseau's account of his flight from France, see *Confessions*, XII. Ham is cursed by his father, Noah, for having seen him naked without covering him (Genesis, IX: 20–25).

11. Spinoza (1632–1677) had his *Theological-Political Treatise* published anonymously in 1671. It was greeted by intense criticism and circulated only with false title pages. He was, however, offered pensions and professorships, which he declined.

12. The "illustrious protector" is Lord Marshal George Keith who was governor of Neuchâtel for the "enlightened Prince," Frederick the Great. Rousseau found refuge at Môtiers in the territory of Neuchâtel from 1762 to 1765.

13. In the manuscript opposite this paragraph Rousseau wrote fragment 2, p. 84 below.

14. The word translated "prig" is "*cuistre*." Rousseau first wrote *Grimaud*, which is a term for a bad writer or artist.

15. The Pléiade editors suggest that the two anecdotes could be the ones reported in the *Confessions*, 477 and 484–485, which concern Rousseau's suspicions of machinations against him while *Emile* was in press and shortly after its publication.

16. The Jesuits were banished from France in 1762.

17. *Collected Writings*, VI, 562–563. The note is to the term "pietists" and says: "A kind of madmen who took it into their heads to be Christians, and to follow the Gospel to the letter: more or less like the Methodists in England, the Moravians in Germany, the Jansenists in France; except that these latter have only to become the masters to be harsher and more intolerant than their enemies."

18. On Rousseau's suspicions of his neighbors at Montmorency, see *Confessions*, XI, *Collected Writings*, V, 477–478.

19. In the manuscript opposite this paragraph Rousseau wrote fragment 3, pp. 84–85 below.

20. The Profession of Faith of the Savoyard Vicar contains a dialogue between a "reasoner" and an "inspired man" (*Emile*, Bloom, 300–301).

21. Fragment 5, pp. 85–87 below, originally took the place of this paragraph.

22. In the Profession of Faith, Rousseau identifies himself as its editor, not its author.

23. The published edition reads *amour-propre* here rather than *amour de soi*. Editors have generally followed the draft, which says *amour de soi*, and changed the reading. This is consistent with Rousseau's normal distinction between the two terms.

24. The word *politique*, translated here and elsewhere as "political thinker," covers a range of meanings from politician to statesman and from advisor to rulers to political philosopher.

25. St. Augustine was a teacher of rhetoric by profession.

26. Thomas Burnet (1635–1715) was a theologian at Cambridge.

27. Some of the terms of this passage occur at pp. 85–90 below.

28. The French word translated "Grace" here is *Grandeur*, an ecclesiastical title that is not identical to *Monseigneur*, which is also translated as "Grace." Rousseau thus makes a slight distinction between this hypothetical interlocutor and Beaumont.

29. See p. 5 above.

30. Rousseau alters Beaumont's formulation.

31. Rousseau is referring to Henri IV (1553–1610).

32. Rousseau changes Beaumont's statement slightly.

33. Opposite this paragraph in the manuscript Rousseau wrote fragment 6, p. 90 below.

34. See p. 6 above.

35. In the manuscript Rousseau wrote fragment 7, pp. 90–91 below, opposite this paragraph.

36. Rousseau abridges slightly.

37. The text of fragment 8, p. 91 below, occurs here in the first draft.

38. Romans, I: 19–22; see p. 8 above.

39. *Emile*, Bloom, 258.

40. The Vicar actually begins by saying "I believe" rather than "I know." The missing sentence reads, "As soon as this knowledge has something to do with my interests, I shall make an effort to acquire it. Until then," (*Emile*, Bloom, 276–277).

41. The remainder of this paragraph is a revision that Rousseau made after sending the manuscript to the publisher. The omitted passage reads, "The first manner is greater, simpler, more sublime, but it is less proportionate to the human mind above all when the ideas of the heterogeneous substances are mutually exclusive and when one of them must owe its existence to the other without anyone being able to imagine how this can be.

"The second manner is clearer and more conceivable to the understanding, but it satisfies reason less in that it assumes that two principles are known, the existence of which is absolute and independent, and nevertheless one of which acts on the other as if this latter depended on it."

42. In the manuscript sent to the publisher this note concluded, "It is not at all a question of entering into debate with Plato." Rousseau had the publisher delete this conclusion.

43. In an edition of the letter printed in London in 1782 the passage beginning

with the next sentence and ending, "have this same meaning, since," reads, "Nothing is less rare than words whose meaning changes with the passage of time, and that cause one to attribute to ancient Authors who used them ideas they did not have at all. The Hebrew word that has been translated by 'create, to make something out of nothing,' signifies instead, 'to make, to produce something with magnificence.' Rivet even claims that neither this Hebrew word, *Bara*, nor the Greek word that corresponds to it, nor even the Latin word *creare* can be restricted to this particular signification of 'to produce something out of nothing.' It is so certain, at least, that the Latin word is taken in another sense that Lucretius, formally denies the possibility of all creation." See *Pléiade*, IV, 1739.

44. Isaac de Beausobre published *Histoire de Manichée et Manichéism* in several volumes from 1734 to 1739.

45. The word *torts*, translated "errors" here, also has the sense of "wrongs." Thus Rousseau is pointing out Beaumont's mistakes that have wronged Rousseau by distorting his position. In the first sentence of each of the next three paragraphs *tort* is translated "wrong."

46. Rousseau is referring to Frédéric-Guillaume de Montmollin, who was his pastor at Môtiers. Montmollin originally welcomed Rousseau, but after the publication of the *Letter to Beaumont* and the *Letters Written from the Mountain* stirred up the public against Rousseau by comparing him to the Antichrist in a number of sermons.

47. The term translated "nominal Christians" would be literally "Christians in effigy."

48. Rousseau's translation is rather free.

49. There were two Joly de Fleury brothers who successively held the post of *avocate général*. One of them was responsible for demanding the warrant for Rousseau's arrest issued by the Parlement of Paris.

50. Rousseau's statement about marriage here should be compared with the letter to Mme. de Francueil of 1751, which he appended to the *Confessions* (*Collected Writings*, V, 551–552). Although Rousseau lived with Thérèse Le Vasseur (a Catholic) from 1745, he did not marry her until 1768, when he did so in a sort of civil ceremony. Legally Protestants and Catholics were not allowed to marry.

51. As always the term translated as "morality" is *la morale*, which means moral doctrine or system of ethics. It is distinguished from "morals," or *moeurs*, which occurs in the following sentence. Rousseau's point is that moral doctrine does not correspond to actual practices.

52. The argument developed in this and subsequent paragraphs is a working out of the implications of the discussion of civil religion in the *Social Contract*, *Collected Writings*, IV, 216–224.

53. The issue of hypostasis concerns the question of the Trinity, whether there can be three persons in only one God without saying that there are three substances, and the question of how Jesus can be one person with two natures (divine and human). These issues were debated in the Christianity of the third and fourth centuries in the disputes with the Arians.

54. The "Constitution" was the papal bull *Unigenitus*, September 8, 1713, which attacked Jansenism.

55. Rousseau discusses civil and theological intolerance in the *Social Contract* (*Collected Writings*, IV, 223).

56. In 1762 Jean Calas, a Protestant, was accused of murdering his son for wishing to convert to Catholicism. Calas the elder was tortured to death. After a campaign of protest led by Voltaire he was posthumously exonerated.

57. Rousseau is referring to *Apologie de Louis XIV et de son Conseil, sur la révocation de l'édit de Nantes, pour servir de réponse à la "Lettre d'un patriote sur la tolérance civile des protestants de France"* avec une dissertation sur la journée de Saint-Barthélemi published in 1758 by the abbé Jean Novi de Caveirac.

58. Rousseau translates the Latin passage.

59. Anne du Bourg was hanged in 1559 and the inhabitants of the villages referred to by Rousseau were accused of heresy and killed in 1545.

60. Rousseau abridges the passage.

61. The so-called St. John of Paris (1690–1727) was revered in Jansenist circles. His tomb in Saint-Médard Cemetery was the location of many supposed miracles. The cemetery was closed in 1732 by order of the king.

62. Rousseau uses the technical term *diallelus* for circular reasoning here.

63. *Emile*, Bloom, 308.

64. The Chevalier de Mauléon de Causans claimed to have discovered how to square the circle.

65. Antoine de Malvin de Montazet was archbishop of Lyon and sympathized with the Jansenists. He had opposed Beaumont and written a public letter attacking him in 1758. Beaumont did not respond to the attack.

66. *Emile*, Bloom, 303.

67. The word translated as "stupid" is *bête*, the plural of which is translated as "beasts" immediately above. The same ambiguity is contained in Voltaire's remark on the *Second Discourse*, "Never has so much intelligence been used in seeking to make us stupid" (*Collected Writings*, III, 102).

68. Rousseau refers to the notoriously obscene book *Aloisiae Sigaeae Toletanae satyra sotadica de arcanis amoris et Venris, Aloisia hispanice scripsit, altinitate donavit Joannes Meursius* by Nicholas Chorier (1612–1692).

FRAGMENTS OF THE LETTER TO CHRISTOPHE DE BEAUMONT

1. The term *libelles* refers to a genre of writing involving defamatory personal attacks.

2. The idea that Rousseau's enemies have used personal attacks to give his books a bad reputation is at the foundation of the argument of *Rousseau Judge of Jean-Jacques*.

3. Rousseau is referring to *Republic*, Books II–III.

4. Rousseau is referring to Voltaire, who had entered the Académie française in 1746.

5. Rousseau first wrote, "What! Is error always a crime."

6. Here Rousseau first wrote, "and you man."

7. At this point Rousseau wrote and then crossed out, "It is for that that aban-

doning all these writings and their cowardly authors to the disdain and to the indignation they deserve," after which he wrote and also crossed out, "I separate you, Your Grace, from the crowd, you and your pastoral letter."

8. Rousseau first wrote, "Fire, water."

9. Rousseau discusses the Abbé de St. Pierre's boldness in the *Confessions* (*Collected Writings*, V, 356).

10. The term *Monseigneur* does, in fact, occur in the final version of the *Letter*. Literally it would be "My lord."

11. Rousseau first wrote and then crossed out, "more sincerely."

12. In the manuscript this note (probably written earlier) occurs with the remainder of the text: "Perform your profession, Your Grace, I will continue to perform mine, your arms will be (like those of the inspired man) epithets and insults, mine will be proofs and reasons."

13. At the end of this paragraph Rousseau first wrote and then crossed out, "Let us now enter."

14. This sentence is unfinished in the manuscript. It would appear that Rousseau intended to quote or paraphrase the beginning of the Pastoral Letter. See p. 3 above.

15. Rousseau first wrote and then crossed out "could God have inflicted."

16. In the manuscript Rousseau wrote the following opposite this paragraph: "their little heads are filled with such narrow prejudices and their hearts with passions so base.

"all the ministers of Kings can persecute me at their ease, they will never hate me as much as I despise [them] and will never do me as much evil as I have received for the good of the human race."

17. Rousseau first wrote and then crossed out, "soldiers."

18. Rousseau first wrote and then crossed out, "subjects."

19. Opposite these lines Rousseau wrote, "May I see this day of glory born and have contributed to it."

20. Rousseau first wrote, "upon which opinion has no hold at all."

21. After this Rousseau wrote and crossed out, "Is the one who occupies himself with them by that very fact an abominable scoundrel who ought to be forbidden fire and water everywhere?"

22. After this Rousseau wrote and then crossed out, "The true Christian leaves obscure what is obscure in scripture and does not at all meddle in being."

23. After this Rousseau wrote, "it says too much about it to be believed."

24. Rousseau first wrote and then crossed out, "orthodox enough."

25. Rousseau first wrote and then crossed out, "transgressed."

26. The Profession of Faith of the Savoyard Vicar is part of a story within the story of *Emile*. It is presented as a separate work by an unidentified author.

27. Rousseau first wrote and then crossed out, "See in effect what absurdity would follow."

28. Rousseau first wrote and then crossed out, "the propositions of his book that he advances as from himself, or as those from someone else."

29. Following "impute" Rousseau first wrote and then crossed out, "at the same time."

30. Following "con" Rousseau first wrote and then crossed out, "at will."

31. *Julie* contains a lengthy debate about suicide (*Collected Writings*, VI, 310–323).

32. In place of "these opinions" Rousseau successively wrote and crossed out, "the sentiment that is claimed to be mine," "that is judged appropriate to attribute to me," and "that they take pleasure in attributing to me."

33. Following this sentence Rousseau wrote and then crossed out, "I am certainly careful to find it bad that my enemies talk nonsense and I am not seen to be very excited by rare arguments."

34. The term translated "at law" is *en justice*. Rousseau first wrote and then crossed out, "before the tribunals, that could be because everything becomes feasible and just as soon as it is a question of oppressing me, but you will agree very much." In this version, instead of "feasible" Rousseau first wrote "possible" and instead of "you will agree very much," he first wrote "at least I think that."

35. In 1703 Baron de Lahontan published a book entitled *New Voyages of the Baron de Lahontan in South America* . . . The objections to the clergy and religion in this book are expressed by the Indians met by the Baron.

36. The fragment ends here.

HISTORY OF THE GOVERNMENT OF GENEVA

1. This and the four following paragraphs are on a separate sheet and have been added to the manuscript.

2. This refers to Aristotle's account of climate in forming the character of nations (*Politics*, VII.1327b19–1328a15.

3. Rousseau's term, *metropolitain*, applies to an archbishop having authority over a city.

4. The term *droits regaliens* applies to kingly and hence sovereign rights.

5. Vidomne is the Genevan equivalent of vidame. A viscount is the lieutenant or representative of a count, while a vidame is the temporal representative of a bishop.

6. A native was the child of a resident foreigner. Natives had more legal rights than their parents, but not as many as citizens.

7. Rousseau and his source both leave the date blank.

8. On this formulation see *Social Contract*, I, 1 (*Collected Writings*, IV, 131).

9. Equestrian colony.

10. In other words, it would have been absorbed by France.

LETTERS WRITTEN FROM THE MOUNTAIN

1. This motto from Juvenal (*Satires*, 4.91) means "to consecrate one's life to the truth." Rousseau used it as his motto from the time he wrote the *Letter to d'Alembert*.

2. This is the way we will translate the term *représentants*, which indicates the people who made official remonstrations (*représentations*) to the government on Rousseau's behalf.

3. The book to which Rousseau refers in this note is *De l'esprit* by Helvétius, which appeared in 1758 and was promptly condemned by the Parlement of Paris.

4. D'Alembert argues this most notably in his "Justification of the Article, 'Geneva,' in the Encyclopedia."

5. On the Minister Montmollin, see pp. 47–48 above.

6. Rousseau praised the Genevan clergy in both the *Letter to d'Alembert* and the Dedicatory Letter to the *Second Discourse*.

7. The expression Rousseau uses is a colloquial one, the literal meaning of which would be, "they do not know which saint to dedicate themselves to."

8. These speeches occur in Chapters XI and XII of *Pantagruel*.

9. The "Constitution" was the papal bull *Unigenitus* issued against the Jansenists in 1713.

10. *Emile*, Bloom, 310.

11. The temple of Fortune at Praenestum was famous in antiquity for its oracle.

12. Guillaume-François Rouelle was a famous chemist with whom Rousseau had studied in the 1740s.

13. Jean-Antoine Nollet was a famous physicist.

14. Brioché and the peasant of North Holland were prominent attractions at the Paris fairs.

15. Albert the Great (thirteenth century) was said to have constructed a mechanical man who could answer questions.

16. In the middle of the eighteenth century numerous miracles were alleged to have occurred at the cemetery of Saint Médard.

17. Jacques-Jean Brouhier wrote a two-volume study of premature burials and embalmings.

18. The word translated as magic trick is *prestige*, which can mean "illusion," but Rousseau questions the assumption that such tricks are different from miracles.

19. Acts, VIII: 9–24.

20. The translation has been altered to reflect a change Rousseau made in his quotation of the passage.

21. The declaration Rousseau refers to is his proclaimed decision to stop responding to his critics after he had written answers to several attacks on his *First Discourse*.

22. *Emile*, Bloom, 298.

23. *Emile*, Bloom, 374.

24. Joseph-Isaac Beruyer was a Jesuit priest who wrote fashionable versions of biblical episodes.

25. Rousseau had officially reconverted to Calvinism and been restored to his citizenship during a visit to Geneva in 1754.

26. This story, which can be found in numerous sources, is not from Brantome.

27. The word is *pratiquer*.

28. The condemnation of *Emile* took place about two weeks after its appearance in Paris.

29. *Reflections and Maxims*, CLXIII, by Luc Clapiers, marquis de Vauvenargue (1715–1747).

30. See *Emile* (Bloom ed.), 33, and *Confessions, Collected Writings*, V, 300–302 and 344, on Louise-Alexandrine-Julie de Chenonceaux and her request that Rousseau write a treatise on education.

31. Rousseau is referring in particular to anonymous works by Voltaire.

32. All of Voltaire's works were printed in Geneva and most of them were prohibited in France.

33. Rousseau is referring to the *Letter to Beaumont*.

34. See *Confessions*, XII, *Collected Writings*, V, 516–517.

35. For Rousseau's relations with George Keith, see *Confessions*, XII.

36. There are a few alterations in this quotation.

37. *Spirit of the Laws*, XII, 4.

38. Voltaire had taken up residence outside of Geneva and was in frequent contact with its leading citizens. The speech Rousseau puts into Voltaire's mouth immediately below enraged the latter because it made him admit that he was the author of works he had published anonymously. Voltaire considered Rousseau to be a police informer because of this and urged the government of Geneva to issue a death sentence against him.

39. In the *Essai sur les moeurs*.

40. This article was published in the *Encyclopédie* in 1758. Rousseau's *Letter to d'Alembert* was a response to it, and the Genevan clergy also responded as a body.

41. Book V of *Emile* contains a summary of much of the argument of the *Social Contract*. See *Emile*, Bloom, 458–467.

42. This is a direct quotation from *Social Contract*, III, 1 (*Collected Writings*, IV, 166).

43. Rousseau ordered copies of both Thomas More's *Utopia* and Denis Vairasse's *Histoire de Sévérambes* (originally published in 1677) from a bookseller around the time the *Letters Written from the Mountain* was published.

44. While *Emile* was banned throughout Europe, the *Social Contract* was not generally banned.

45. Algernon Sidney was arrested and executed in 1682. His *Discourses Concerning Government* were published in 1698.

46. Johannes Althusius was the author of *Politica*, which was published in 1603.

47. Charles Castel de Saint-Pierre (1658–1743). Rousseau abridged and commented on the Abbé de Saint-Pierre's *Polysynody* and *Perpetual Peace*. In the *Confessions* Rousseau indicates that he became aware of the dangers of being involved in the publication of the Abbé's works (*Collected Writings*, V, 354–356).

48. This statement is sometimes taken as a claim that Rousseau agreed with Locke's conclusions about the principles of political right, but, in context, it seems more obviously to be a claim that the two of them wrote bold general treatments of political right without making explicit applications to particular governments.

49. Rousseau uses this formula in his dedication of the *Second Discourse*, thereby indicating that he is dedicating it to the people of Geneva rather than its government, the members of which he refers to as "Magnificent and most honored lords." See *Collected Writings*, III,

50. The three bodies are the general Council, the Two-Hundred, and the small Council.

51. This is a common remark about the government of Poland in the eighteenth century. Rousseau proposes a remedy for it in his *Considerations on the Government of Poland*.

52. See the Fourth Letter, pp. 192–193 above.

53. This article appeared in volume seven of the *Encyclopédie*.

54. To reclaim is to demand that someone be captured and brought to a particular jurisdiction. In this context it is the equivalent of a request for extradition.

55. The word translated as "supervision" is *police*, otherwise translated as "public order."

56. "Lack of public order" is the translation of Rousseau's neologism *impolice*, which he uses occasionally elsewhere, but it is otherwise not common in French.

57. The case took place in 1707 and involved Nicolas Lemaître, an ally of Pierre Fatio in defending popular rights.

58. In these states the Two-Hundred is the sovereign council, equivalent to the Genevan general Council.

59. The so-called Thirty Tyrants ruled in Athens for a short time near the end of the fifth century B.C.

60. Article XLIV reads, "All the Articles contained in the present Settlement will have the force of Laws in the future, and will not be capable of being susceptible to any change, whatever it might be, except with the consent of the General Council legitimately assembled by the Small and Great Council."

61. Article XV stipulates that the garrison of the town cannot be increased except with the consent of the General Council.

62. Article III says, "The Rights and Attributions of the General Council, legitimately assembled, will remain invariably fixed and limited to the following Articles.

63. Sarrazin was auditor in 1667.

64. Rousseau invents the word *équipondérant*, which clearly means "is equal to in weight." It can be compared to the word *pondérant*, which Rousseau also invented and used in the "Letter to Franquières." See *Collected Writings*, VIII, 336–337, n. 30.

65. Otho's career is described in Tacitus, *History*, I.36.

66. *Du Droit de la nature et des gens*, I, 1, 20.

67. The companies were the divisions of the militia.

68. The estimates of the number of Remonstrators at the height of their assemblies range from 480 to over 700.

69. See *Collected Writings*, IV, 196–197.

70. The assembly was actually convoked for the 15th of May.

71. Three leaders of the Bourgeoisie were arrested less than three months after the declaration of an amnesty.

72. The word translated as "remonstrance" throughout this text is *réprésentation*, except for the case immediately below in which Rousseau, in fact, uses *remontrances*.

73. In order to sharpen his own interpretation of the significance of this

passage, immediately below Rousseau changes the formulation from the *Letters Written from the Country* given here, substituting "prevent" for "oppose."

74. The words "speak at his fancy" are not in the *Letters Written from the Country*.

75. This is a summary of the passage in the *Letters Written from the Country*, rather than a quotation.

76. Rousseau is referring to an affair involving John Wilkes and the periodical *The North Britain* in 1763. Wilkes was granted one thousand pounds in damages because of the violation of *habeus corpus* in his case.

77. See pp. 295–296 below.

78. On the case of Abraham-Gédéon Binet, see the Seventh Letter, p. 244 above.

79. See the Seventh Letter, p. 248 above.

80. On the right of declaring war and making peace, see *Social Contract*, II, 2, *Collected Writings*, IV, 146.

81. For Rousseau's treatment of the Tribunes, see *Social Contract*, IV, 5, *Collected Writings*, IV, 211–212.

82. Book IV, Chapters 4–7, of the *Social Contract* are concerned with Roman institutions.

83. The "beneficent philosopher" is the title taken by Stanislas Leszczynski, the former King of Poland with whom Rousseau had had an exchange after the publication of the *First Discourse*. See *Collected Writings*, II, 28–54. The remark quoted here by Rousseau occurs in Stanislas's *Observations on the Government of Poland*.

84. See p. 243 above.

85. For a copy of Rousseau's letter to Silhouette and an account of the circumstances in which he wrote it, see *Confessions*, *Collected Writings*, V, 445.

86. This is the case of Rousseau himself.

87. The book in question was Rousseau's *Emile*, and Bardin was ultimately paid for the books.

88. We read *sait* rather than *fait*, following the first edition of the *Letters* rather than Pléiade.

89. This story can be found in Plutarch's *Life of Pericles*.

90. See letter 8, p. 256 above.

THE VISION OF PIERRE OF THE MOUNTAIN, CALLED THE SEER

1. Jean Jacques Imer (1740–1804) was named Deacon in 1763.

2. In fact, a rumor did circulate in Val-de-Travers that Rousseau had claimed in *Emile* that women had no souls.

3. Apparently a local innkeeper.

4. A neighbor of Rousseau, Henri Baillods (1700–1791) had been mayor of Travers from 1731 to 1742.

5. On Montmollin, see note 46 above to the *Letter to Beaumont*.

6. Esprit has the sense of wit or intelligence as well as of spirit. The last is used here to preserve Rousseau's play on words.

7. This verse puns on Boy's name, which could be taken as a form of the verb "boire" or drink.

8. Rousseau originally wrote and then crossed out the following footnote to be placed at this point: "His real name is Pierre Boy, and the nickname *Pierrot of the Ladies* has really been given to him by the People."

Index

Aaron, 179
Acts, 147, 325n19
Adam, 30–31, 89
Albert the Great, 176, 325n13
Albigensians, 66
Alembert, Jean le Rond d', 141, 198, 226, 245, 325n4
Allobrogians, 103
Aloisia, 146, 322n68
Althusius, Johannes, 235, 326n46
Amadeus VIII, 107
Amé V, 114
Amé VIII, 119
Amedée of Savoy, 119
amour-propre, 9, 25, 29, 42, 55, 284, 292
Amsterdam, 16
Antichrist, xiv, 81, 163, 310, 321n46
Antioch, 144
Antoine, Nicholas, 216–217
Antonin, 66
Archimedes, 133
Aristides, 72
Aristophanes, 224
Aristotle, 108, 324n2
Asia, 64
atheism, atheists, xvi, xxi, 6, 12, 26, 49–50, 75–76, 87
Athens, Athenians, 10, 172, 224, 254, 285, 292
Augustine, Saint, 7, 14, 19, 29, 53, 78, 90, 317n12, 318n35, 320n25
Aymon, 110

Baal, 175
Baillods, Henri, 313, 328n4
Balard, Jean, 127
Bantu, 40
Bardin, Isaac, 288, 295
Basel, 108
Baume, Pierre de la, 113, 119, 121, 125
Beausobre, Isaac de, 44, 321n44
Belial, 3
Berne, 127, 253
Berruyer, Father, 186, 325n24
Binet, Abraham-Gédéon, 328n78
Bourg, Anne du, 66, 322n59
Boyle Society, 173

Brantôme [Brantome], Pierre de Bourdeilles, seigneur de, 190, 325n26
Brioché, 175, 325n14
Bruhier, Jacques-Jean d'Ablaincourt, 176, 325n17
Burgundy, 102, 105, 107, 108
Burnet, Thomas, 30, 320n26

Cabrières, 67
Caesar, 103, 292
Caiaphas, 164
Calas, Jean, 6, 167, 322n36
Calvin, Jean, 156, 159, 165, 241
Camisards, 62
Cana, 168–169
Carlos, Don, 190
Carthage, 243, 285
Causens, Chevalier de Mauléon de, 78, 322n64
Charlemagne, 103, 107, 109
Charles III, Duke, 123
Charles IV, 119, 121
Charles V, 119, 121, 123
Charles the Bold, 123
Chenelat, P., 193
China, 262
Chorier, Nicholas, 322n68
Chouet, Jean-Louis, 275, 281
Cicero, 68, 166
Clement of Alexandria, 44
Clerc, Joseph, 313
Confignon, Pierre de, 114
Conflans, Bishop Guillaume, 114
conscience, xxii, 28–29, 49, 51, 53, 75, 126, 145, 148, 160, 163, 221, 223
Corinthians, 47, 58, 97
creator, creation, xv, xvii, 7, 40, 42, 59

David, 224
De Deo uno et trino, 91
De Trinitate, 78, 90
Decemvirs, 255
Deuteronomy, 57, 70
Dominick, 66
Domitian, 14
Ducals, 127

331

Edict of Nantes, 61
Edom, 312
Eigeldinger, Fréderic S., 315n6
Eignots, 127
Elijah, 175
Elul, 313
England, 62, 176, 225, 246, 252, 287–291
Epictetus, 92
Eskimos, 40
Espagne, Henri, l', 116
Euclid, 137
Exodus, 180

Fabri, Bishop Ademarus, 112, 114, 281
Farel, Guillaume, 164
Fleury, Cardinal de, 162
Four, Borough of, 111
François I, 123
Francueil, Mme. de, 321n50
Frawstat, 170
Frederick the Great, xiii, 170
Fribourg, 107, 113, 124, 127, 253
Froment, Antoine, 164

Gaillard, Castellan of, 116
Galatians, 47, 95
Galilee, 169
general will, 232, 267, 301
Genesis, 31, 44
genius, 60, 156, 212
Gentil, Valentin, 241
Gentilis, Albéric, 216
Germany, 108, 225, 235
Girardin de la Rive, 127
Goths, 108
Grabeau, 241
Grammont, Bishop Humbert de, 114
Greece, Greeks, 72, 108
Gregory XII, Pope, 121
Grotius, Hugo, 173
Guinea, 175
Gustave, 170

Ham, 24, 319n10
Harcourt, College of, 175
Hardouin, Jean, 173
Hebrew, 44, 95, 173
Henri IV, 320n31
Heraclitus, 44
History of Manicheanism, 44
History of the Severambes, 234, 326n43
Hobbes, Thomas, 235
Hypotiposes, 44

Imer, Jean-Jacques, 309, 328n1
Ishmael, 64

Israel, 50, 216
Italy, 123, 225

James, Saint 146
James II, 231
Jansenism, Jansenists, 26, 54, 69, 186, 319n17, 321n54
Jesuits, 25, 34, 158, 319n16
Jesus, xvi, xx, 3, 11–13, 15, 47–48, 58, 72–73, 78, 81, 89, 97, 142–146, 151, 170–180, 186, 321n53
Jews, 169–171, 225
John, 168, 169, 170, 172
John, Saint, 176
John Damascene, Saint, 15, 318n41
Joli de Fleuri, 54, 321n49
Jonah, 169
Joseph, 168
Joshua, 175
Judea, 169
Justin Martyr, 44
Juvenal, 324n1

Keith, George, 223, 319n12, 326n35
Koran, 149

La Bruyère, Jean de, 150
La Mare, Henri de, 186
La Rochefoucauld [La Rochefoucault], François, duc de, 150
Lahontan, Baron de, 101, 324n35
Lapland, Lapps, 40
Lausanne, 108
law of nature, xiv, 62, 174
Lazarus, 176
Le Fort, Louis, 292
Le Vasseur, Thérèse, 321n50
Leipzig, 170
Leon X, Pope, 119
Leonidas, 72
Leszczynski, Stanislas, 328n83
Leti, Gregorio, 115
Libya, 285
Livy, 68
Locke, John, 235
Lombards, 108
Louis XIV, 126
love of oneself, 28–30
Lucretius, 44
Luke, 151, 168, 169
Lullin, P. E., 135
Lutherans, 137
Lutzen, 170

Magna Carta, 281
Manicheans, 44

Index

Marius, 292
Mark, 151, 169, 171, 172, 180
Marseille, 294
Martin V, Pope, 113
Mary, 72
Matthew, 47, 151, 168, 169, 170, 172, 180
Maximillian, Emperor, 119
Mercurey of Neufchâtel, 162
Merindol, 67
Messiah, 85, 169, 171
Mestrezat, Philippe, 273
Methodists, 186
Micheli du Crest, Jacques-Bartélemy, 260
Milan, Milanese, 124
Miller, James 317n66
misanthrope, 22
Mishnah, 57
Mohammed, 63, 64
monster, 26, 50, 65, 94
Montazet, Antoine de Malvin de, 78, 322n65
Montelli, Canon, 115
Montesquieu, Charles-Louis de Secondat, baron de, 224, 236, 253, 325n5, 328n5
Montmollin, Frédéric-Guillaume de, xiv, 321n46, 325n5, 328n5
More, Thomas, 326n43
Morelli, Jean, 136, 192, 200, 214–216, 241,
Moses, xix, 45, 68, 70, 170, 180

Narva, 170
natural law, xvi, 16, 54, 108
natural right, 62, 136
Nero, 14
Neufchâtel, 112, 248
Newton, Isaac, 174
Ninevites, 169
Nollet, Jean-Antoine, abbé, 175, 325n13

Octavius, 292
Odo de Villars, 119
Origen, 44
Otho, 261, 327n65

Pâris, Jean de, 68–69, 322n61
Parsi, 63
Pascal, Blaise, 316–317n54
Paul, Saint, 3, 8, 15, 38, 41, 47, 58, 81, 89, 144, 146, 172, 186–187, 224
Pericles, 302
Perrin, François, 192
Peter, 317n6, 318n33
Peter, Saint, 89
Pharisees, 47
Philibert, Duke, 122
Philip, 180

philosopher, xvi, 3, 6, 39, 41, 81, 142, 166, 293, 328n83
philosophy, xv, xxii, 3, 5, 15, 24, 31–32, 39, 44, 81, 153, 208, 212, 225, 227, 267, 284
Photius, 44
Plato, 44, 72, 84, 160, 234, 320n42
Plutarch, 328n89
Poland, 198, 239, 327n51, 328n83
political thinker, 29, 149, 239, 243, 320n24
Pompey, 292
Praenestum, 175, 325n11
Proverbs, 318nn32, 40
providence, xxi, 46, 59, 85, 140
Puffendorf, Samuel, 262

Rabelais, François, 158
Richardet, Claude, 127
right of nature, 61
Rivet, Dom Antoine, 321n43
Romans, 317n9, 318nn17, 34
Rome, Roman Empire, Romans, xxvi, 10, 68, 103, 108, 109, 112, 116, 125, 154, 233, 243, 285, 291, 292
Rouelle, Guillaume-Francois, 175, 325n12

Saint Pierre, Charles Castel, Abbé de, 236, 323n9
Salleneuve de, 121
Sarrisin, Jean, 260, 327n13
Satan, 163, 165, 310
Savoy, Jean de, 119
Savoy, Jean Louis de, 124
Savoye, Claude, 127
Servet, Michel, 165, 216
Sesson, Bishop Pierre de, 114
Sidney, Algernon, 235, 326n45
Sigismund, Emperor, 119, 121
Silhouette, Etienne de, 295, 328n85
Simon, 180
Sion, 108
Sixtus IV, Pope, 121
Socinians, 158
Socrates, 72–73, 126–127, 224
Sophroniscus, 72
Sorlin, 121
Sparta, Spartans, 10, 68, 72, 285, 292
Spinoza, 24, 87, 319n11
Spon, 121
State of nature, xvii
Stephen, Saint, 144
Strasbourg, 126,
Stromates, 44
Surat, 63
Sylla, 292
Syracuse, 133
Syria, 175

Tacitus, 261, 327n65
Talmud, 57
Tertullian, 9, 42, 45, 318n19
Thomas, Saint, 58
Thonon, Michel Guillet de, 247
Thucydides, 302
Timothy, 74, 317n1, 318n37
Titus, 318n36
Tobias, 15, 318nn38–39.
Toulouse, 66
Townsend, Lord, 281
Treaty of Soleure, 281
Trinity, 78, 97, 148
Tronchin, Louis, 204
Turks, 59

Ulpian, 83
Utopia, 234, 326n43

Vairasse, Denis, 326n43
Vauvenargues, Marquis de, 208, 326n29
Venice, 175, 252
Verneau, Vidomne, 127
Vernes, Jacob, 173
Vernet, Jacob, 173
Vienna, 116, 125
Voltaire, xxiv, 224, 322n4, 326nn31, 32, 38

Wido, Bishop, 110, 114
Wilkes, John, 289, 328n76
William of Orange, 231
Wisdom, 317n2
wise man, the wise, sage, 11, 15, 41, 69, 73, 167, 174, 178, 179, 211

Zeringhen, Duke of, 119
Zoroaster, 63
Zurich, 253

www.ingramcontent.com/pod-product-compliance
Lightning Source LLC
Chambersburg PA
CBHW030301080526
44584CB00012B/402